The International Crimes Tribunal in Bangladesh

Miriam Beringmeier

The International Crimes Tribunal in Bangladesh

Critical Appraisal of Legal Framework
and Jurisprudence

BWV | BERLINER WISSENSCHAFTS-VERLAG

Bibliografische Information der Deutschen Nationalbibliothek:
Die Deutsche Nationalbibliothek verzeichnet diese Publikation in der Deutschen National-
bibliografie; detaillierte bibliografische Daten sind im Internet über http://dnb.d-nb.de abrufbar.

Dieses Werk einschließlich aller seiner Teile ist urheberrechtlich geschützt. Jede Verwertung
außerhalb der engen Grenzen des Urheberrechtes ist unzulässig und strafbar.

Hinweis: Sämtliche Angaben in diesem Fachbuch/wissenschaftlichen Werk erfolgen trotz sorgfältiger
Bearbeitung und Kontrolle ohne Gewähr. Eine Haftung der Autoren oder des Verlags aus dem Inhalt
dieses Werkes ist ausgeschlossen.

© 2018 BWV | BERLINER WISSENSCHAFTS-VERLAG GmbH,
Markgrafenstraße 12–14, 10969 Berlin,
E-Mail: bwv@bwv-verlag.de, Internet: http://www.bwv-verlag.de

Druck: docupoint, Magdeburg
Gedruckt auf holzfreiem, chlor- und säurefreiem, alterungsbeständigem Papier.
Printed in Germany.

ISBN Print: 978-3-8305-3860-8
ISBN E-Book: 978-3-8305-4030-4

Acknowledgments

This study was accepted as a doctoral dissertation by the faculty of law of the University of Hamburg in the summer semester 2017. All views expressed in this dissertation remain solely my own and do not necessarily reflect the views of the United Nations.

Judgments from the International Crimes Tribunal that were published after April 2015 and related appeal judgments from the Supreme Court of Bangladesh published after October 2015 could not be taken into consideration for the study.

The realisation of this dissertation would not have been possible without the collaboration and support of innumerable people.

In particular, I thank my doctoral supervisor Prof. Dr. Rainer Keller for his guidance and constructive advice throughout the writing process as well as Prof. Dr. Florian Jessberger for his second opinion on my dissertation and valuable comments.

I thank Ms. Penelope Van Tuyl from the WSD Handa Center for Human Rights and International Justice, University of Stanford, for her indispensable assistance in the preparation of my research stay at the International Crimes Tribunal in Bangladesh.

I also thank Mr. Mofidul Hoque from the Liberation War Museum in Dhaka for his extensive and valuable support in facilitating my research stay at the Tribunal. Moreover, I wish to thank all the other Bangladeshis who have extensively assisted me in gaining access to relevant sources, provided input and contributed to my research.

I am also grateful to the German Academic Exchange Service (DAAD) for generously funding my research stay at the International Crimes Tribunal in Bangladesh.

Finally, special thanks are due to my family and friends for their indispensable moral support and interesting discussions related to my research during the entire writing process of the dissertation.

Miriam Beringmeier

Table of contents

Acknowledgments	5
List of abbreviations	13
Part I: Introduction and outline of the investigation	17
1 Introduction and statement of the problem	17
2 Objectives of the study and considered jurisprudence	19
3 Outline of the investigation	20
Part II: Towards an International Crimes Tribunal	21
1 Historical background	21
1.1 The province of Bengal	21
1.2 The Partition of British India	22
1.3 The Liberation War	23
1.3.1 The dimensions of the Liberation War	30
1.3.2 Compensation and rehabilitation	35
1.3.3 Genocide debates	37
2 First attempts to deal with the war crimes	39
2.1 The Bangladesh Collaborators (Special Tribunal) Order, 1972	40
2.2 The Bangladesh National Liberation Struggle (Indemnity) Order, 1973	44
2.3 The International Crimes (Tribunals) Act, 1973	44
2.4 Constitutional amendments	45
2.5 International agreements	47
2.6 Political environment in post-war Bangladesh	48
3 Ending impunity	49
3.1 Politics after 1991	49
3.2 Emerging call for trials of war criminals	50
3.3 Establishment of the ICT	52
3.4 Controversies surrounding the ICT	53

Table of contents

Part III: The ICT in comparison to other accountability mechanisms 59

1 The different accountability mechanisms and their applicability in the context of Bangladesh 59
   1.1 The International Criminal Court 59
       1.1.1 Jurisdiction *ratione temporis* 60
       1.1.2 Principle of complementarity 60
   1.2 Ad hoc international criminal tribunals 64
   1.3 Mixed tribunals 65
   1.4 Domestic trials 65
   1.5 Truth and reconciliation commissions 66
   1.6 Trials in third states 67
   1.7 Decision-making process in Bangladesh 68

2 The domestic character of the International Crimes Tribunal in Bangladesh 69
   2.1 Structure of the ICT 70
   2.2 Jurisdiction of the ICT 71
       2.2.1 Jurisdiction *ratione temporis* 72
       2.2.2 Jurisdiction *ratione personae* 72
       2.2.3 Jurisdiction *ratione loci* 74
       2.2.4 Jurisdiction *ratione materiae* 74
   2.3 Applicable law and jurisprudence 74
       2.3.1 Domestic sources 75
           2.3.1.1 Applicability of the ICT Act and its amendments 75
               2.3.1.1.1 The ICT Act, 1973 in the light of the principle of legality 75
               2.3.1.1.2 Statutory limitations 81
               2.3.1.1.3 The ICT Act as amended in 2009 83
               2.3.1.1.4 The amendments of 2012 and 2013 85
           2.3.1.2 Constitutional restrictions 88
           2.3.1.3 General domestic law 92
           2.3.1.4 Rules of Procedure 93
           2.3.1.5 Domestic jurisprudence 95
       2.3.2 International and foreign sources 95
           2.3.2.1 Applicability of international law 95
           2.3.2.2 International criminal law jurisprudence 100
           2.3.2.3 Foreign jurisprudence 101
   2.4 Amnesties 101
   2.5 Ne bis in idem 107
   2.6 Funding 109
   2.7 Interim findings 110

Part IV: Compliance of the ICT Act, the Rules of Procedure and the ICT's jurisprudence with international standards 111

1 Criteria of investigation 111
   1.1 International treaties 113
   1.2 Customary international law 116
   1.3 Jurisprudence of international criminal law 116
2 The crimes within the ICT's jurisdiction 117
   2.1 Genocide 117
      2.1.1 Genocide under the ICT Act and customary international law 117
      2.1.2 The definition in the ICT jurisprudence 120
          2.1.2.1 Acts of genocide 122
          2.1.2.2 A national, ethnic, racial, religious or political group 122
          2.1.2.3 The specific intent 127
      2.1.3 Conclusion 132
   2.2 Crimes against humanity 132
      2.2.1 Crimes against humanity under the ICT Act and customary international law 133
      2.2.2 The ICT's jurisprudence on crimes against humanity 137
          2.2.2.1 Chapeau requirements 138
          2.2.2.2 Murder 144
          2.2.2.3 Extermination 145
          2.2.2.4 Deportation 147
          2.2.2.5 Abduction 149
          2.2.2.6 Confinement 152
          2.2.2.7 Torture 153
          2.2.2.8 Rape 155
          2.2.2.9 Other inhumane acts 159
          2.2.2.10 Persecution 162
      2.2.3 Conclusion 165
   2.3 War crimes 166
   2.4 Crimes against peace 169
   2.5 Violation of any humanitarian rules applicable in armed conflicts laid down in the Geneva Conventions of 1949 169
   2.6 Any other crimes under international law 170
      2.6.1 Other crimes under international law in 1971 170
      2.6.2 Application of the clause in the jurisprudence of the ICT 170
          2.6.2.1 Incitement 170
          2.6.2.2 Planning 175
          2.6.2.3 Conclusion 177

Table of contents

- 2.7 Inchoate crimes 178
  - 2.7.1 Conspiracy and attempt under customary international law 178
  - 2.7.2 Conspiracy and attempt in the jurisprudence of the ICT 179
  - 2.7.3 Conclusion 184
- 2.8 Interim findings 184

3 The modes of liability of the ICT Act 184
- 3.1 The modes of liability of the ICT Act and customary international law 185
- 3.2 The modes of liability in the jurisprudence of the ICT 188
  - 3.2.1 Abetment 190
  - 3.2.2 Complicity 196
  - 3.2.3 Joint criminal enterprise 201
  - 3.2.4 Superior liability 207
  - 3.2.5 The modes of liability and sentence 217
- 3.3 Interim findings 219

4 Procedural rights 219
- 4.1 Right to legal assistance and to an interpreter 221
- 4.2 Right not to be subjected to arbitrary arrest or detention and to be informed of the reasons for arrest 222
- 4.3 Right not to be compelled to incriminate oneself or to confess guilt and to remain silent 228
- 4.4 Presumption of innocence 231
- 4.5 Right to be tried by an independent and impartial tribunal 237
- 4.6 Right to be tried without undue delay 242
- 4.7 Right to a fair and public hearing 244
- 4.8 Right to adequate time and facilities for preparation 246
- 4.9 The right to be present and trials in absentia 248
- 4.10 Legal remedies 252
- 4.11 Penalties 255
- 4.12 Witnesses and victims 258
- 4.13 Interim findings 263

Part V: The ICT in the context of transitional justice in Bangladesh 265

1 The role of criminal trials in the process of transitional justice 265
   1.1   Measures and aims of transitional justice 265
   1.2   Objectives and limitations of criminal trials in transitional
        justice processes 267

2 The ICT's contribution to the process of transitional justice 269
   2.1   Factors that determine and limit transitional justice in Bangladesh 270
   2.2   The ICT as a transitional justice mechanism 272
        2.2.1 Contribution to justice 272
        2.2.2 Contribution to establishment of truth 276
        2.2.3 Contribution to reparations 277
   2.3   Interim findings 277

Part VI: Conclusion and outlook 279

References 283

Appendix 301

The International Crimes Tribunals Act 301

The Rules of Procedure of Tribunal 2 313

List of abbreviations

AD	Appellate Division
Additional Protocol I	Protocol Additional to Geneva Conventions of 12 August 1949, and Relating to the Protection of Victims of International Armed Conflicts of 8 June 1977
Additional Protocol II	Protocol Additional to the Geneva Conventions of 12 August 1949, and Relating to the Protection of Victims of Non-International Armed Conflicts of 8 June 1977
AC	Appeals Chamber
BNP	Bangladesh Nationalist Party
CCL	Control Council Law No. 10 of 20 December 1945
Collaborators Order	Bangladesh Collaborators (Special Tribunal) Order, 1972
Declaration on Torture	Declaration on the Protection of All Persons from Being Subjected to Torture and Other Cruel, Inhumane or Degrading Treatment or Punishment of 9 December 1975
ECCC	Extraordinary Chambers in the Courts of Cambodia
ECCC Law	Law on the Establishment of the Extraordinary Chambers in the Courts of Cambodia
ECHR	European Court for Human Rights
ed./eds.	editor(s)
edn.	edition
e.g.	for example (*exempli gratia*)
et al.	and others (*et alii*)
ff.	and the following pages
General Assembly	United Nations General Assembly
Genocide Convention	Convention on the Prevention and Punishment of the Crime of Genocide of 9 December 1948
HCD	High Court Division
ICC	International Criminal Court
ICCPR	International Covenant on Civil and Political Rights
ICJ	International Court of Justice
ICLR	International Criminal Law Review
ICT	International Crimes Tribunal
ICT Act	International Crimes (Tribunals) Act, 1973
ICTR	International Criminal Tribunal for Rwanda
ICTR Statute	Statute of the International Criminal Tribunal for Rwanda
ICTY	International Criminal Tribunal for the former Yugoslavia
ICTY Statute	Statute of the International Criminal Tribunal for the former Yugoslavia

List of abbreviations

i.e.	that is (*id est*)
IMT	International Military Tribunal at Nuremberg
IMT Charter	Charter of the International Military Tribunal at Nuremberg
Indemnity Order	Bangladesh National Liberation Struggle (Indemnity) Order, 1973
JCE	Joint Criminal Enterprise
marginal no.	marginal number
n. pag.	no pages
no.	number
OTP	The Office of the Prosecutor at the ICC
PTC	Pre-Trial Chamber
PP	Patterns of Prejudice
PPP	Pakistan People's Party
p./pp.	page(s)
para./paras.	paragraph(s)
RAB	Rapid Action Battalion
Repeal Ordinance	Bangladesh Collaborators (Special Tribunals) (Repeal) Ordinance, 1975
Rome Statute	Rome Statute of the International Criminal Court
RoP	Rules of Procedure
Rome Statute	Rome Statute of the International Criminal Court
SC	Supreme Court
SCSL	Special Court Sierra Leone
SCC	Supreme Court Chamber
Security Council	United Nations Security Council
STL	Special Tribunal for the Lebanon
STL Statute	Statute of the Special Tribunal for the Lebanon
TC	Trial Chamber
Tribunal 1	Tribunal 1 of the International Crimes Tribunal
Tribunal 2	Tribunal 2 of the International Crimes Tribunal
Tripartite Agreement	Agreement on the Repatriation of Prisoners of War and Civilian Internees, 1974
UDHR	Universal Declaration of Human Rights, 10 December 1948
UNCAT	United Nations Convention against Torture and Other Cruel, Inhuman, or Degrading Treatment or Punishment of 10 December 1984
UN	United Nations
UN Doc.	Documents of the United Nations

UNHRC	United Nations Human Rights Committee
Vienna Convention	Vienna Convention on the Law of Treaties of 23 May 1969
v.	versus
vol.	volume

Part I: Introduction and outline of the investigation

1 Introduction and statement of the problem

Bangladesh is situated in South Asia and shares borders with Myanmar and India. The country ranks among the 10 most densely populated countries in the world: 159.1 million people[1] live within 144.000 km². The population in rural areas constitutes 66.5% of the total.[2] Approximately 89.1% of Bangladeshis are Muslims but there are several other religious minorities in the country, of which Hindus constitute the biggest group at approximately 10%.[3]

The country came into existence after the Liberation War in 1971 when Bangladesh, at that time East Pakistan, seceded from West Pakistan. After independence, the perpetrators of the atrocities committed during the nine-month Liberation War were subjected to few if any legal procedures. International politics tolerated the impunity of the main perpetrators, whereas the domestic political situation after 1974 impeded any process of transitional justice. It was not until 2010, with the establishment of the International Crimes Tribunal (ICT), that the process of ending the impunity started.

International criminal tribunals have gained importance over the last few decades. Various tribunals and the underlying conflicts that they address have been discussed around the world and have attracted public attention. The case of Bangladesh has been absent from most of these discussions. The Tribunal in Bangladesh has hit the headlines primarily because of the violent protests in answer to the verdicts and the criticism from several human rights organisations. Unfortunately, detailed information on the Tribunal's work is poorly disseminated outside of the country.

The decision to set up the ICT was taken in 2009 after the Awami League came to power. The establishment of the Tribunal was part of the Awami League's election manifesto and was of great interest to the party since it was one of the main targets of Pakistani repression in the war of 1971. During the process of establishment, Bangladesh explicitly decided against the involvement of international stakeholders and so rejected the trials being conducted through an internationalised tribunal.

The legal framework of the ICT, the International Crimes (Tribunals) Act, 1973 (ICT Act), was drafted and enacted as domestic law in 1973 and was extensively amended in 2009, 2012 and 2013. In 2010, the ICT passed the International Crimes

---

1　*The World Bank*, data from 2014, http://data.worldbank.org/country/bangladesh, accessed 20 March 2016.
2　*The World Bank*, data from 2014, http://data.un.org/CountryProfile.aspx?crName=Bangladesh#Social, accessed 20 March 2016.
3　The World Fact Book of the Central Intelligence Agency of the USA, data from 2013, https://www.cia.gov/library/publications/the-world-factbook/geos/bg.html, accessed 22 December 2016.

Part I: Introduction and outline of the investigation

Tribunal Rules of Procedure (RoP), as provided for in Section 22 of the Act. Hence, the ICT is a domestic court that applies domestic law for the prosecution of perpetrators of international crimes. At the same time, the general domestic criminal procedure regulations, the Criminal Procedure Code and the Evidence Act are declared inapplicable under the Act.

The Tribunal finally took up its work in 2011. To date, numerous judgments have been delivered, among them several death and life imprisonment sentences. The accused are Bangladeshi nationals who cooperated with the Pakistani military during the Liberation War. The ICT Act enjoys a special status under the Constitution of Bangladesh, which was amended for this purpose in 1973. The amendment repeals certain constitutional safeguards for those accused of international crimes. Article 47(3) of the Constitution determines that those charged with genocide, crimes against humanity or war crimes as well as other crimes under international law cannot challenge the relevant laws as being void or unlawful on the grounds that they are inconsistent with the Constitution. Beyond that, Article 47A denies those accused of international crimes several fundamental rights as guaranteed under the Constitution. Those rights include the right to a speedy and public trial by an independent and impartial court, the right to the protection of the law and the ability to enforce fundamental rights safeguarded under the Constitution.

Yet, at the same time, Bangladesh has acceded to several international treaties which stipulate important rights of the accused during criminal trials and also define international crimes. Although, under the domestic law of Bangladesh, international treaties cannot be applied directly but require implementation at the national level, this cannot be utilised as an excuse for non-compliance with international law.

As a domestic accountability mechanism, the ICT is also fraught with practical country-specific challenges. The judges appointed to the Tribunal are not experienced in dealing with cases of international criminal law, an area of law with significant challenges because of the complexity of the cases. Beyond that, the lack of financial resources engenders a poor infrastructure that certainly influences many aspects of the trials. Undoubtedly, the long lapse of time between the Liberation War and the initiation of the trials constitutes one of the major hurdles and has had a huge impact on the evidence. Many victims, witnesses and perpetrators have passed away since the war or are very old, and the journey from the rural areas to Dhaka to give testimony is a heavy burden.

The politically-tense environment in the country and the divided society also encumber the Tribunal's work. The trials led to mass protests in 2013, provoked by the verdict against Abdul Quader Molla who was sentenced to life imprisonment.[4] The

---

[4] ICT 2, *The Chief Prosecutor v. Molla*, case no. 02/2012, Judgment, 5 February 2013.

participants of the so-called Shahbag protests demanded capital punishment for the convict. The protests escalated when protesters were confronted by a countermovement led by Islamic groups. Several other verdicts have led to countrywide *'hartals'* (general strikes), called out by opposition parties in protest against the convictions of their party leaders.

The political situation and the fact that the Liberation War as well as the trials before the ICT continue to be a very sensitive and politically-loaded issue also have a strong impact on the research environment. While one of the essential difficulties consists in accessing documents, and the Tribunal, challenges also arise from the restrictions on freedom of speech imposed on any criticism of the Tribunal's work. This has inevitably created a tense research environment that has impeded an open exchange of ideas on the issue. Since the ICT has been criticised strongly by foreign organisations, foreigners encounter particular distrust from within the Tribunal. Despite these difficulties, it must be highlighted that Bangladeshis are extremely friendly, open and extraordinarily hospitable, especially towards foreigners. None of the tensions surrounding the professional environment have influenced the incredible personal warmth with which I was received in all quarters during my stay at the Tribunal. Many Bangladeshis were also rather pleased by the idea of foreigners showing an interest in their ICT.

2 Objectives of the study and considered jurisprudence

The overall objective of the study is to examine the compliance of the ICT with rule of law standards. To this end, the applicable legal sources as well as jurisprudence are scrutinised by means of standards stipulated by international treaties in order to show the extent to which the Tribunal is able to deliver justice in compliance with these recognised human rights standards. Beyond that, the study aims to examine the interpretation of the internationally-recognised crimes by this domestic accountability mechanism despite restrictions in the applicability of international law. The study also evaluates the Tribunal's contribution to the process of transitional justice in Bangladesh.

For the analysis of jurisprudence, all cases that were completed with the delivery of a judgment[5] in April 2015 have been considered. In total, 17 judgments were available at that point. Appeal judgments have been taken into account in those cases in which they were published until end of October 2015.[6]

---

5 With exception of the case ICT 2, *The Chief Prosecutor v. A. K. M. Yusuf*, case no. 02/2013, in which the accused died before the delivery of the judgment. This case was considered insofar as orders were available and relevant.
6 It has to be noted that in some cases the time span between the announcement of the verdict by the Appellate Division and the publication of the appeal judgment is extremely

Part I: Introduction and outline of the investigation

Although judgments and charge framing orders are now publicly available, this is not the case with interlocutory appeals and orders. The latter are thus not available through official channels and could only be considered in some cases. The orders in contempt proceedings have been examined in cases of specific interest.

3 Outline of the investigation

The study is divided into six parts. Part I introduces the subject as well as the objectives of the study and outlines the framework of the investigation. Part II illustrates the historical background and provides an understanding of the circumstances that led to the Liberation War in 1971. Beyond that, the first attempts to deal with the war crimes are outlined, and the circumstances that finally favoured the establishment of the Tribunal more than 40 years after the war are highlighted.

Part III scrutinises the different accountability mechanisms applied in post-conflict situations from the angle of their possible implementation in Bangladesh. The decision-making process and the considerations that finally led to the choice of a domestic tribunal are outlined. The focus lies on the consequences for the structure and the applicable legal sources that arise from the domestic character of the ICT.

Part IV analyses the legal framework of the ICT as well as its jurisprudence and the findings of the Appellate Division by means of international standards. In order to determine the criteria of examination, the international obligations assumed by Bangladesh are outlined. This part provides a detailed analysis of the application of the material and procedural law by the Tribunal and identifies discrepancies between the domestic law and its interpretation on the one hand and the standards set by international criminal law on the other. The scrutiny focuses on the application of the elements of crimes as well as the modes of liability. With regard to procedural law, the study emphasises the procedural rights of the accused. At the same time, the application of the law in practice also sheds light on the extent to which the country complies with the obligations it assumed under several international instruments.

Part V and Part VI conclude the study. Part V locates the ICT in the context of transitional justice and examines the extent to which this accountability mechanism is able to contribute to the process of transitional justice in Bangladesh. It also sets out whether, and the extent to which, the Tribunal contributes to the reconciliation process. Part VI of the dissertation summarises the research results and discusses prospects for the future of the ICT.

long. For that reason, the appeal judgment in the case of *Sayeedi* could not be considered for this study. While the Appellate Division announced the verdict in September 2014, the judgment was only published in December 2015.

Part II: Towards an International Crimes Tribunal

The ICT was established in 2010, almost 40 years after Bangladesh's Liberation War. The Awami League coming to power through the elections in 2008 was a crucial event in its formation. However, the idea to set up a tribunal to try war criminals dates back to 1973 when the statutory source, the ICT Act, 1973, was drafted. Yet, the national and international political situation impeded its implementation and led to a policy of oblivion and forgiveness for many years. The issue returned to the political agenda in the 1990s when different civil society organisations began to advocate for the trial of war criminals.

1 Historical background

The ICT tries perpetrators of crimes committed during the Liberation War with Pakistan in 1971, through which Bangladesh, at that time East Pakistan, seceded and emerged as a state. In order to understand the underlying conflict of the war, the historical background must be viewed from the Partition of British India, which played a major role in the foundation of contemporary Bangladesh.[7]

1.1 The province of Bengal

The territories of Bangladesh and Pakistan were part of British India until the country's partition in 1947 when British colonial rule ended. Within British India, the territory of modern-day Bangladesh belonged to the province of Bengal. The province experienced its first partition in 1905 when the plan by Lord George Curzon of Keddleston to divide the region to improve its administration and better develop the district of Assam was implemented.[8] While the new province of Eastern Bengal and Assam (comprising the territory of today's Bangladesh) was ruled by a governor based in Dhaka, the province's western region was governed from Calcutta.[9] Many perceived the division as a strategy to weaken the strong anti-colonial movement in the province.[10]

The Bengali Muslim community, which constituted the majority in East Bengal and Assam, welcomed the division, expecting to find good career opportunities in the new administrative capital of Dhaka[11] without the unfair competition with Hindus

---

7   *Van Schendel*, History of Bangladesh, p. 96.
8   *Ali*, Understanding Bangladesh, p. 4; *Baxter*, Bangladesh, p. 39.
9   *Ali*, Understanding Bangladesh, p. 5; *Baxter*, Bangladesh, p. 39.
10 *Al-Masum*, JPHS, 2003, LI(4), p. 95, at 96.
11 *Murshid*, Sacred and Secular, p. 27; *Van Schendel*, History of Bangladesh, p. 81.

they had previously experienced[12]. This was due to the community's economic, educational and political disadvantages in the united state of Bengal.[13] The anti-division movement, instead, was led mainly by high-caste Hindus from Kolkata.[14] Hindus and Muslims increasingly became political categories.[15] Although parts of the Muslim community initially opposed the division as well, the Hindu community later dominated the protests when they started to utilise religion for their political aims.[16] The Muslim community began to organise itself and founded the All-India Muslim League in Dhaka in 1906 as a countermovement to the protests against the partition by the Indian National Congress.[17] Political mobilisation began to be based on religious affiliation, a phenomenon known as communalism.[18] Revolutionary groups were formed and the protests and violent riots led to the annulment of the partition in 1911.[19] The state of Bengal then remained united until 1947.

1.2 The Partition of British India

In the 1945 election in Great Britain, the Labour Party, which advocated India's independence, came to power.[20] From then on, the preparation for the implementation of the transfer of power began.[21]

The idea of dividing India into two different countries to separate Muslims and Hindus was based on the 'two-nations theory': Muslims were considered not just a community in the Indian nation but rather a separate nation from Hindus with the need for self-determination.[22] This theory was concretised in the late 1930s and was first announced officially in 1940 in the Lahore Resolution by the Muslim League.[23] The concrete implementation of this idea was, however, not yet determined and it was still not clear whether there should be one or several states.[24]

---

12 *Mclane*, in: *Islam* (ed.), History of Bangladesh, Vol. 1, p. 126, at 130.
13 *Mclane*, in: *Islam* (ed.), History of Bangladesh, Vol. 1, p. 126, at 129.
14 *Van Schendel*, History of Bangladesh, p. 81.
15 *Van Schendel*, History of Bangladesh, p. 80.
16 *Van Schendel*, History of Bangladesh, p. 81.
17 *Mclane*, in: *Islam* (ed.), History of Bangladesh, Vol. 1, p. 126, at 127; *Van Schendel*, History of Bangladesh, p. 83.
18 *Van Schendel*, History of Bangladesh, p. 83.
19 *Baxter*, Bangladesh, p. 40; *Dil/Dil*, Bengali Language Movement, p. 44.
20 *Baxter*, Bangladesh, p. 55.
21 *Baxter*, Bangladesh, p. 55; *Talbot/Singh*, Partition of India, p. 7.
22 *Van Schendel*, History of Bangladesh, p. 89.
23 *Pandey*, Remembering Partition, p. 21; *Van Schendel*, History of Bangladesh, p. 88.
24 *Van Schendel*, History of Bangladesh, p. 89.

1 Historical background

A plan designed by Lord Mountbatten in May 1947 concretised the division of the Indian territory.[25] In the beginning, no clear decision was made on how to proceed with the province of Bengal, a state with a strong presence of both religious groups. In the discussions about the country's partition, even demands for a separate united and independent state of Bengal arose.[26] However, this idea was vehemently opposed by the Hindu majority who feared the loss of their economic and intellectual advantages in an independent state of Bengal.[27]

The Mountbatten Plan provided for a division of the Bengal Legislative Assembly into the representatives of the Muslim-majority districts and the representatives of the Hindu-majority districts so that each of the two assemblies could decide on the partition of the region.[28] Whereas most of the representatives of Hindu-majority districts voted in favour of the partition, the Muslim-majority districts mainly opposed it.[29] Yet, the overall majority voted in favour of the partition of Bengal. In answer to this result, the Bengal Boundary Commission was founded to determine the precise partition borders in the province of Bengal, which became known as the Radcliffe Line.[30]

Based on the Mountbatten Plan, the British Parliament passed the Indian Independence Act that set 15 August 1947 as the date of independence and the foundation of the dominions of India and Pakistan. Partition caused the largest uprooting of people in the twentieth century and hundreds of thousands died during the riots preceding it.[31] Approximately four million Muslims remained in West Bengal and almost 11.5 million Hindus in East Pakistan.[32]

After Independence on 15 August 1947, Pakistan was a country consisting of two territories separated by 1,600 kilometres: West Pakistan (today's Pakistan) and East Pakistan (today's Bangladesh).

1.3 The Liberation War

Though East Pakistan had become independent from India, the majority of East Pakistanis still felt as though they were under colonial rule, this time headed by West Pakistan.[33] The nine-month Liberation War from March to December 1971 led to the

---

25 *Pandey*, Remembering Partition, p. 39.
26 *Baxter*, Bangladesh, p. 56.
27 *Baxter*, Bangladesh, p. 56.
28 *Chatterji*, in; *Talbot/Singh* (eds), Region and Partition, p. 168, at 170.
29 *Chatterji*, in; *Talbot/Singh* (eds), Region and Partition, p. 168, at 170–171.
30 *Baxter*, Bangladesh, 57; *Chatterji*, in; *Talbot/Singh* (eds), Region and Partition, p. 168, at 171.
31 *Talbot/Singh*, Partition of India, pp. 62, 90.
32 *Talbot/Singh*, Partition of India, p. 100.
33 *Baxter*, Bangladesh, p. 61.

secession of East from West Pakistan and to the foundation of Bangladesh. Different circumstances played a significant role in the breaking-up of Pakistan. Cultural, economic, territorial and political factors can be highlighted as the main ones that contributed to the national independence movement.[34]

From the beginning of Pakistan's emergence, it was difficult to create a united Pakistani nation. The different languages spoken in the two parts made the development of a lingua franca impossible because none of the languages had a general acceptance in both parts of the country.[35] This created a major conflict when Urdu was introduced as the official language of Pakistan in 1948.[36] Though the language was spoken by only 3.5% of the Pakistani population, the Urdu-speaking minority held 21% of the civil service jobs.[37] On the other hand, the East Pakistani population, 54% of Pakistan's total population,[38] spoke predominantly Bengali and demanded the use of their language in the Assembly alongside Urdu[39]. The idea of imposing Urdu as the only national language was part of the government's intended Islamisation of Pakistan.[40] Urdu was the first South Asian language in which interpretations of the Quran were made in the late eighteenth century.[41] In a speech made on a visit to Dhaka in 1948, Governor-General Muhammad Ali Jinnah stated that Urdu embodied Islamic culture and Muslim tradition and was nearest to the languages in other Islamic countries and, therefore, had to be the national language of Pakistan.[42] The Bengali language as well as numerous practices of Bengali Muslim culture were considered 'un-Islamic' by many Muslims of West Pakistan.[43] Like Hindi, the Bengali language derives from Sanskrit and was therefore regarded as the language of the Hindus, who were the main target group of the 'Islamisation' programme.[44] For that reason, the population of East Pakistan was frequently associated with the Hindu culture.[45] In 1952, a language movement, headed mostly by students, started in East Pakistan and led to violent riots in which many students were killed.[46] The protests were, nevertheless, successful with regard to their aim and the Constituent Assembly decided in 1954

---

34 *D'Costa*, Nationbuilding, p. 83.
35 *Jahan*, Pakistan, p. 13.
36 *D'Costa*, Nationbuilding, p. 86; *Saikia*, Making of Bangladesh, p. 35.
37 *Saikia*, Making of Bangladesh, p. 251, n. 4.
38 *Jahan*, in: Totten/Parsons (eds), Centuries of Genocide, 4. edn, p. 249, at 251.
39 *Van Schendel*, History of Bangladesh, p. 110.
40 *Van Schendel*, History of Bangladesh, p. 110.
41 *Uddin*, Constructing Bangladesh, p. 77.
42 *Ahmad*, Speeches and Writings of Jinnah, Vol. 2, pp. 496–497.
43 *Uddin*, Constructing Bangladesh, p. 119.
44 *Saikia*, Making of Bangladesh, p. 38.
45 *Saikia*, Making of Bangladesh, p. 38.
46 *Jahan*, Pakistan, p. 44.

1 Historical background

that Urdu and Bengali would be the official languages of Pakistan.[47] Language, however, was not the only conflict. The populations in the two parts of the country were also culturally different. Many traditions, dressing habits and their admiration for Rabindranath Tagore in East Pakistan were close to Hindu culture and thus not accepted by West Pakistan.[48]

While the language issue was the core of the conflict during the 1950s, economic problems came to the fore afterwards.[49] East Pakistan was the main supplier of raw materials and thereby financed the industrial accumulation in the western part.[50] It earned approximately 60 % of the country's foreign currency but obtained less than 30 % of Pakistan's imports.[51] These circumstances led to economic exploitation as occurred under colonial rule.[52]

The territorial conditions likewise hampered the building of a common Pakistani nation. The absence of any direct land communication between East and West Pakistan prevented social mobilisation and hindered the process of nation-building.[53] The territorial isolation also nurtured the economic disparity between the two regions.[54] Any socio-economic investment in one part of the country had no effect on the other part so that a dual economic and administrative apparatus was required.[55]

At the beginning of the conflicts between East and West Pakistan, a new political party was created. The Awami League[56] was founded in 1949 and at that time mainly opposed the government's decision to declare Urdu the national language.[57] The party was formed by several factions and was the first Muslim opposition party.[58] With the growing discontent in East Pakistan, the party's request for autonomy arose in 1966 when it presented its Six-Point-Programme. This included the demand for a confederation of East and West Pakistan in which only defence and foreign affairs would remain issues of the central government.[59] The Six-Point-Programme proposed solu-

---

47 *Baxter*, Bangladesh, p. 63.
48 *Uddin*, Constructing Bangladesh, p. 120.
49 *Gerlach*, Societies, p. 125.
50 *D'Costa*, Nationbuilding, p. 83; *Gerlach*, Societies, p. 126.
51 *D'Costa*, Nationbuilding, p. 83.
52 *Gerlach*, Societies, p. 126; *Jahan*, in: Totten/Parsons (eds), Centuries of Genocide, 4. edn, p. 249, at 252.
53 *D'Costa*, Nationbuilding, p. 83; Jahan, Pakistan, p. 10.
54 *D'Costa*, Nationbuilding, p. 83.
55 *Jahan*, Pakistan, p. 10.
56 The party was founded with the name 'East Pakistan Awami Muslim League' and renamed to 'East Pakistan Awami League' in 1955, *Nair*, Politics, p. 49.
57 *Uddin*, Constructing Bangladesh, p. 121; *Van Schendel*, History of Bangladesh, p. 111.
58 *Jahan*, Pakistan, p. 38.
59 *Umar*, Emergence of Bangladesh, p. 110; *Van Schendel*, History of Bangladesh, p. 121.

tions for the main conflicts between the East and West regions. To improve East Pakistan's economic situation, the Programme demanded separate accounts of the foreign exchange earnings of each of the federating units.[60]

The situation escalated with the growth of the Bengali independence movement after the election in 1970. This was the first free national election held in Pakistan, and the Awami League, under its Bengali leader Sheikh Mujibur Rahman, won the majority of the parliamentary seats. While the Awami League obtained 160 of the 300 national seats (162 seats for East Pakistan and 138 for West Pakistan), the Pakistan People's Party (PPP), under the leadership of Zulfiqar Ali Bhutto, won only 81 seats.[61] Both parties achieved their results due only to their success in their respective parts of the country; neither party won any seats in the other part.[62]

Soon after the elections, the Awami League announced its intention to create a constitution based on the Six-Point-Programme.[63] Although the party claimed to represent a national majority, its programme fulfilled only the demands of the eastern part and did not include a political programme for the rest of the country.[64] Bhutto's reaction was aggressive and confrontational.[65] The crisis came to a head in December 1970 when Bhutto publicly announced that no government could be formed and no constitution drafted without the participation of the PPP.[66] President Yahya Khan postponed the scheduled parliamentary session in March 1971.[67] In answer to this postponement, Sheikh Mujibur Rahman declared a five-day general strike in the eastern part lasting every day from six in the morning until two in the afternoon.[68] Although he called for non-violent, non-cooperation protests, violent riots soon ensued between demonstrators and the armed forces.[69]

The Pakistani government decided to sanction a military intervention during the night of 25/26 March 1971. The government considered military intervention the only solution to stop the political crisis and the increasing loss of control over the East Pakistan military units.[70] So-called 'Operation Searchlight' was aimed at the elimination of the political power of the Awami League and the reestablishment of public

---

60 In *Sisson/Rose*, War and Secession, p. 20 the full text of the Six-Point-Programme is provided.
61 *Bose*, Dead Reckoning, p. 21.
62 *Bose*, Dead Reckoning, p. 21.
63 *Rahman*, My Bangladesh, p. 21.
64 *Sisson/Rose*, War and Secession, p. 61.
65 *Sisson/Rose*, War and Secession, p. 59.
66 *Sisson/Rose*, War and Secession, p. 60.
67 *Jahan*, in: Totten/Parsons (eds), Centuries of Genocide, 4. edn, p. 249, at 253.
68 *Ali*, Understanding Bangladesh, p. 51.
69 *Ali*, Understanding Bangladesh, p. 51.
70 *Sisson/Rose*, War and Secession, p. 157.

order.[71] Targets were Dhaka University, which was the centre of the liberation activists' activities; the old part of Dhaka, which was mostly inhabited by Hindus; the police; the Bengali armed forces; and Awami League leaders.[72] West Pakistani propaganda had declared Hindus the enemy of an Islamic Pakistan and the Pakistani army became convinced that Hindus played a significant role in the independence movement.[73] On 26 March 1971, Rahman was arrested at his home and brought to West Pakistan where he was imprisoned and accused of treason.[74] Most of the Awami League leaders fled to India where they formed a government-in-exile.[75] From India, they also proclaimed Bangladesh's independence under the presidency of Rahman on 10 April 1971.[76]

Despite the strong support for the independence struggle in East Pakistan, some sections of the population also backed the idea of a united Islamic Pakistan: members of the Muslim League and the Jamaat-e-Islami party, as well as many Biharis residing in East Pakistan, opposed independence.[77] The term 'Bihari' is frequently used to refer to a group of non-Bengali Urdu-speaking Muslims who migrated to Bangladesh after 1947 although many were not originally from Bihar.[78] Most of them supported the idea of a united Pakistan and many also assisted the Pakistani army in its military interventions in East Pakistan.[79]

The Pakistani military replaced the local councils, traditionally led by local leaders, with so-called Peace Committees under the leadership of orthodox Muslims.[80] As a consequence, tensions between Muslims and Hindus increased drastically at the communal level.[81] To implement its military operations, the Pakistani army needed assistance from East Pakistan and created paramilitary groups. Local volunteers, so-called Razakars, were recruited to serve as an auxiliary force to fight the freedom

---

71 *Sisson/Rose*, War and Secession, p. 157.
72 *Ali*, Understanding Bangladesh, pp. 56–57; *Gerlach*, Societies, p. 128; *International Commission of Jurists*, Events in Pakistan, pp. 27–30; *Sisson/Rose*, War and Secession, pp. 157–158.
73 *International Commission of Jurists*, Events in Pakistan, p. 29.
74 *Van Schendel*, History of Bangladesh, p. 162.
75 *Baxter*, Bangladesh, p. 86; *International Commission of Jurists*, Events in East Pakistan, p. 30.
76 For the full text of the proclamation, see: International Legal Materials, 1972, 11(1), pp. 119–120.
77 *International Commission of Jurists*, Events in East Pakistan, p. 31.
78 *Paulsen*, RSQ, 2006, 25(3) p. 54, at 68, n. 1. Also, the ICT applies the term 'Bihari' to refer to Urdu-speaking people. See, for instance, ICT 2, *The Chief Prosecutor v. Azad*, case no. 05/2012, Judgment, 21 January 2013, para. 174.
79 *Paulsen*, RSQ, 2006, 25(3), p. 54, at 54; *Van Schendel*, History of Bangladesh, p. 173.
80 *Ali*, Understanding Bangladesh, pp. 74–75.
81 *Ali*, Understanding Bangladesh, p. 75.

fighters in the inner areas of the country.[82] With this support, the Pakistani army gained manpower and local knowledge in East Pakistan[83] but, in practice, the Razakars also acted as the death squads of the Pakistani army[84].

The legal basis for the establishment of the Razakar force, the East Pakistan Razakars Ordinance, was promulgated on 2 August 1971. The Razakars replaced many former auxiliary police (so-called Ansars).[85] Two different wings of Razakars were established: the Al-Badr (Arabic: the full moon) and the Al-Shams (Arabic: the sun).[86] The former consisted of well-educated students from schools and madrasas (Islamic schools), and these were employed for the implementation of special operations.[87] The latter were mainly used to secure strategically important points such as bridges.[88] Many Biharis also joined the Razakars.[89] By September 1971, 50,000 Razakars had been recruited.[90]

Rape and other forms of sexual violence were extensively employed by the Pakistani army and the Razakars to intimidate civilians, to destroy the enemy's community honour and for retaliation.[91] Sexual violence was also committed by the other side and many Bihari women were raped[92] in the course of the war, although their experiences remained mostly undocumented[93].

Initially, the government believed that it would be able to re-establish public order after a short military intervention but the resistance in East Pakistan was a lot stronger than expected.[94] The Pakistani army targeted Awami League supporters, intellectuals, students and Hindus with their attacks.[95] The resistance against the Pakistani army became more organised after the first few months of aggression and more people joined the *'mukti bahini'* (freedom fighters).[96] By November 1971, the number of freedom fighters was 100,000.[97]

---

82 *International Commission of Jurists*, Events in East Pakistan, pp. 41–42.
83 *Gerlach*, Societies, p. 130.
84 *Van Schendel*, History of Bangladesh, p. 167.
85 *Gerlach*, Societies, p. 130.
86 *Niazi*, East Pakistan, p. 78; *Sisson/Rose*, War and Secession, p. 165.
87 *Niazi*, East Pakistan, p. 78; *Sisson/Rose*, War and Secession, p. 165.
88 *Niazi*, East Pakistan, p. 78; *Sisson/Rose*, War and Secession, p. 165.
89 *International Commission of Jurists*, Events in East Pakistan, p. 41.
90 *Haqqani*, Pakistan, p. 79.
91 *D'Costa/Hossain*, CLF, 2010, 21(3), p. 331, at 334.
92 *Brownmiller*, Against Our Will, p. 81.
93 *D'Costa*, Nationbuilding, p. 103.
94 *International Commission of Jurists*, Events in East Pakistan, p. 31; *Sisson/Rose*, War and Secession, pp. 158, 160.
95 *International Commission of Jurists*, Events in East Pakistan, p. 31.
96 *Van Schendel*, History of Bangladesh, p. 164.
97 *Van Schendel*, History of Bangladesh, p. 167.

1 Historical background

The struggle for independence also received international assistance. India very soon became involved in the war and, backing Bangladesh's right to self-determination, provided military training and arms to the freedom fighters.[98] This was crucial because the freedom fighters were ill-equipped and lacked proper training.[99] There were several reasons that disposed India to support East Pakistan in its independence struggle: the refugees rushing to Indian territory, the fear of the influence of the East Pakistani conflict on the insurgent state of West Bengal and also the expectation that an independent Bangladesh would weaken Pakistan's position in the region.[100] India increased its assistance gradually and by October 1971 direct support from the Indian military for rebel operations in East Pakistan became more frequent.[101] However, in October, it also became clear that the Pakistani army had failed to gain control over East Pakistan although at the same time the freedom fighters had also been unable to gain victory.[102] India expanded its direct military interventions in East Pakistan in November and the third Indo-Pakistani War started on 3 December 1971 with West Pakistani air force attacks in north-western India.[103] Assisted by the Indian armed forces, the freedom fighters enjoyed several advantages: they had direct access to East Pakistani territory from every direction, they were better armed than the Pakistani army and they had control of air and sea.[104]

The Liberation War ended with the unconditional surrender of the Pakistani army to the Indian military on 16 December 1971. With the secession from Pakistan, Bangladesh suffered no territorial changes but continued to exist with the same borders as East Pakistan.[105]

Before the establishment of a government in post-war Bangladesh, Razakars and West Pakistanis were attacked and killed by freedom fighters as acts of reprisal.[106] Many Biharis also became targets of mob violence and tens of thousands were killed.[107]

---

98 *Van Schendel*, History of Bangladesh, p. 169.
99 *Sisson/Rose*, War and Secession, p. 182.
100 *Sisson/Rose*, War and Secession, pp. 206–207.
101 *Sisson/Rose*, War and Secession, p. 212.
102 *Van Schendel*, History of Bangladesh, p. 169.
103 *Sisson/Rose*, War and Secession, p. 214.
104 *Van Schendel*, History of Bangladesh, p. 170.
105 *Van Schendel*, History of Bangladesh, p. 96.
106 *International Commission of Jurists*, Events in East Pakistan, p. 44.
107 *International Commission of Jurists*, Events in East Pakistan, p. 44; *Van Schendel*, History of Bangladesh, p. 173.

1.3.1 The dimensions of the Liberation War

Even today, it is difficult to determine the dimensions of the Liberation War. The actual death toll remains unknown. In Bangladesh it is claimed that 'a genocide of three million' took place but there is no official proof to confirm this number; rather, it has gained strength through unchallenged repetition.[108] This number is also rarely questioned in Bangladesh. Likewise, the ICT treats it as fact and presumes that '[...] some three million people were killed, nearly [a] quarter million [sic] women were raped and over 10 million people were forced to flee [to] India',[109] but the Tribunal neither cites any proof for this conclusion nor mentions that the number is unproven. In *Ali*,[110] the ICT cited a source for the three million but the quoted author[111] herself does not mention where the number comes from. Further, in the latest version of the book from 2013, the author revised her text and now points out that three million is the number claimed by the Bangladeshi authorities.[112] In *Chowdhury*, the defence raised the issue of the death toll and the Tribunal dealt with it in more detail.[113] The Tribunal acknowledged that it was impossible to collect the actual numbers of deaths during the Liberation War because the surveys that were conducted in the aftermath of the war led to different numbers.[114] However, the Tribunal invoked newspaper articles published in *Pravda*, the *Daily Observer* and the *Daily Azad* in support of its assumption of a death toll of three million.[115] The Tribunal further referred to a statement President Yahya Khan is recorded to have said at a meeting on 22 February 1971: 'kill three million of them and the rest will eat out [of] our hands'.[116] It also referred to a book by Muhammad Zafar Iqbal[117] in which the author says that the exact number may never be known but that in Bangladesh the number is said to be

---

108 *Bose*, JGR, 2011, 13(4), p. 393, at 394, 399.
109 For instance, ICT 2, *The Chief Prosecutor v. Azad*, case no. 5/2012, Judgment, 21 January 2013, para. 3. This introduction is given in every judgment.
110 ICT 2, *The Chief Prosecutor v. Ali*, case no. 03/2013, Judgment, 2 November 2014, para. 7.
111 *Jahan*, in: Totten/Parsons/Charny (eds), Century of Genocide, 1997, p. 291, at 291. The first edition of the book has been revised thrice.
112 *Jahan*, in: Totten/Parsons (eds), Centuries of Genocide, 4. edn, p. 249, at 250.
113 ICT 1, *The Chief Prosecutor v. Chowdhury*, case no. 02/2011, Judgment, 1 October 2013, paras. 261–268.
114 ICT 1, *The Chief Prosecutor v. Chowdhury*, case no. 02/2011, Judgment, 1 October 2013, para. 262.
115 ICT 1, *The Chief Prosecutor v. Chowdhury*, case no. 02/2011, Judgment, 1 October 2013, paras. 264–265.
116 ICT 1, *The Chief Prosecutor v. Chowdhury* case no. 02/2011, Judgment, 1 October 2013, para. 266.
117 *Iqbal*, History of the Liberation War.

1 Historical background

three million.[118] Based on these sources, the Tribunal came to the conclusion that during the Liberation War 'at least three million people were killed by the Pakistan occupation forces and their Collaborators'.[119] It further argued that the number has been accepted in Bangladesh because it is based on the mentioned documents and, for this reason, the death toll of three million has become a part of world history and can be considered a fact of common knowledge.[120] Nevertheless, the sources do not corroborate the Tribunal's findings and the line of reasoning therefore remains questionable. While Yahya Khan's speech does not shed light on how many people actually died, the other cited sources merely repeat the number but do not confirm its accuracy.

It is unclear from where the number of three million deaths originally derived but it was first reported in the Soviet newspaper *Pravda* on 3 January 1972.[121] Subsequently, it became official when, on 10 January 1972, Sheikh Mujibur Rahman, after his release from prison in West Pakistan and his return to Bangladesh, announced publicly that three million people had been killed and 200,000 women raped.[122] The number was the highest that was reported and it is said that Rahman simply adopted this number from the *Pravda* article.[123] Sisson and Rose state that the number of three million was calculated by India and its reliability has to be questioned due to India's interest in influencing the view of the conflict in the West.[124]

Different attempts to examine the dimensions of the war were made. Sheikh Mujibur Rahman established an Inquiry Committee in 1972.[125] The results of the Committee, however, were based mainly on oral evidence and therefore do not constitute reliable numbers.[126] An incomplete résumé of the Committee's work estimates the approximate number of 1,247,000 deaths.[127] However, the official outcome of the Committee's work was never publicly announced.[128]

---

118 ICT 1, *The Chief Prosecutor v. Chowdhury*, case no. 02/2011, Judgment, 1 October 2013, para. 267.
119 ICT 1, *The Chief Prosecutor v. Chowdhury,* case no. 02/2011, Judgment, 1 October 2013, para. 268.
120 ICT 1, *The Chief Prosecutor v. Chowdhury*, case no. 02/2011, Judgment, 1 October 2013, para. 268.
121 Chaudhuri, Genocide in Bangladesh, p. 22.
122 Chaudhuri, Genocide in Bangladesh, p. 22; *Karim*, Sheikh Mujib, p. 340, n. 1.
123 Chaudhuri, Genocide in Bangladesh, p. 22; *Karim*, Sheikh Mujib, p. 340, n. 1.
124 *Sisson/Rose*, War and Secession, pp. 217, 306, n. 24.
125 *Gerlach*, Societies, p. 132.
126 *Gerlach*, Societies, p. 132.
127 *Chaudhuri*, Genocide in Bangladesh, pp. 199–202.
128 *Chowdhury*, Myth of Three Million, p. 28 claims that it was not published because the Committee could not confirm the number announced by Sheikh Mujibur Rahman.

Part II: Towards an International Crimes Tribunal

The Pakistani side also initiated an inquiry. Immediately after the war, Bhutto appointed an inquiry commission, the Hamoodur Rahman Commission. The Commission examined 213 witnesses and submitted its report in July 1972.[129] It concluded that a maximum of 26,000 people were killed by the Pakistani army and argued that even this number might constitute an exaggeration.[130] The Commission stated that the numbers claimed by Bangladesh (three million deaths and 200,000 rapes) were highly overstated because 'so much damage could not have been caused by the entire strength of the Pakistan Army then stationed in East Pakistan even if it had nothing else to do'.[131] It further questioned the number of rapes, elaborating that a British abortion team employed by Rahman had reported abortions of merely one hundred pregnancies.[132] However, this source clearly lacks objectivity.

In academic sources, different numbers ranging from 500,000[133] to 1.7 million[134] to 3 million deaths circulate. However, very often scholarly sources do not name the sources of their respective estimates.[135] Exaggerated numbers in this area of research are common and often derive from the tendency of scholars to exaggerate victim numbers in order to underline the significance of their topic.[136] Nevertheless, in the context of Bangladesh, it is probable that these figures merely cite the most frequently repeated number in the absence of reliable figures. In Bangladesh, inflated numbers are employed to show the seriousness of the violence and to justify the breaking apart of Pakistan.[137]

---

129 *Hamoodur Rahman Commission*, Report, p. 2.
130 *Hamoodur Rahman Commission*, Report, pp. 33–34.
131 *Hamoodur Rahman Commission*, Report, p. 33.
132 *Hamboodur Rahman Commission*, Report, p. 34.
133 *Gerlach*, Societies, p. 256 considers a death toll of 500,000 likely, including victims of famine. He doubts that the number exceeded one million.
134 *Rummel*, Democide, pp. 153–163 estimates a death toll between 1.7 and 3.6 million. However, his result is not based on empirical research but on an estimated average of different secondary sources regarding the and can thus not be considered reliable.
135 *Beachler*, PP, 2007, 41(5), p. 467, at 467 contends that 'according to most estimates', the Liberation War led to at least 1.5 million deaths; *Jahan*, in: *Totten/Parsons* (eds), Centuries of Genocide, 4. edn, p. 249, at 255 states that 'nearly 10 million people […] took refuge in neighbouring India'; *Jahan*, Pakistan, p. 204 states that 'between one and three million people were reportedly killed'; *Ziauddin*, in: *Jongman* (ed.), Contemporary Genocides, p. 95, at 95, 109, n. 3 states that the number of three million is widely accepted even though he acknowledges the absence of systematic research.
136 *Gerlach*, Societies, p. 257.
137 *D'Costa*, Nationbuilding, p. 77; *Gerlach*, Societies, p. 256.

The same uncertainty exists regarding other victim numbers as well. The estimated number of rape cases varies from 200,000 to 400,000,[138] leading to approximately 25,000 pregnancies[139]. Indian authorities reported that 10 million refugees from Bangladesh were registered under the Indian Foreigners Act, 1946 during the war but this figure also lacks proof.[140]

On the other hand, those who were killed in the post-war period are often disregarded. When the war was over, the Biharis retained the stigma of collaborators and were persecuted and killed, with more than one million displaced from their homes and forced to live in settlements.[141] Most of them were waiting for repatriation to Pakistan, but the problem has not been solved to date. The majority of the community today consider themselves Bangladeshi and demand citizenship.[142] It is estimated that between 240,000 and 500,000 Biharis still live as stateless persons in Bangladesh.[143] However, a comprehensive analysis of the perpetrated crimes during 1971 has not been realised and the actual numbers are not likely to be discovered.[144]

Yet, even today, the death toll is a very sensitive issue in Bangladesh. Questioning the three million figure is very often considered to be a denial of the atrocities committed during the war. In December 2015, Khaleda Zia, leader of the Bangladesh Nationalist Party (BNP), publicly expressed her doubts about the figure.[145] The statement not only provoked strong reactions and a call for a law that criminalises the questioning of this number[146] but also led to a sedition case being filed against Khaleda Zia[147]. In fact, at the beginning of 2016, the Bangladesh Law Commission produced a draft for a new 'Liberation War (Denial, Distortion, Opposition) Crime Law' to criminalise divergences from the official Liberation War narrative.[148]

---

138 *Brownmiller*, Against Our Will, p. 80 states that '200,000, 300,000 or possibly 400,000 women [...] were raped'. The Liberation War Museum estimates 278, 000 rape cases, see http://www.liberationwarmuseumbd.org/mission-statement-2/, accessed 27 September 2015.
139 *Brownmiller*, Against Our will, p. 80.
140 *Van Schendel*, History of Bangladesh, p. 164.
141 *Paulsen*, RSQ, 2006, 25(3), p. 54, at 55.
142 *Paulsen*, RSQ, 2006, 25(3), p. 54, at 55.
143 *Paulsen*, RSQ, 2006, 25(3), p. 54, at 54. Those born after 1971 were granted Bangladeshi citizenship some years back, see *Saikia*, Making of Bangladesh, p. 253, n. 17.
144 *Linton*, CLF, 2010, 21(2), p. 191, at 194; *Van Schendel*, History of Bangladesh, p. 173.
145 *The Daily Star*, Khaleda draws flak for martyrs remark, 23 December 2015.
146 *The Daily Star*, Khaleda draws flak for martyrs remark, 23 December 2015.
147 *The Daily Star*, Khaleda draws flak for martyrs remark, 23 December 2015
148 For an unofficial translation of the key sections of the law, see http://bangladeshpolitico.blogspot.de/2016/04/crime-of-distortion-of-history-of.html, accessed 17 April 2016. For further details on the law, see p. 258.

Even though the overall death toll is not of direct importance for the trials before the ICT and the determination of the responsibility of individuals, the issue has become highly relevant in the context of contempt proceedings. The ICT clarified that the number of three million is a historical fact and considers public criticism regarding the Tribunal's adoption of this number to be contempt of court.[149]

In February 2014, an application to initiate contempt proceedings against David Bergman, a British journalist based in Dhaka, was filed on the basis of three articles published on his blog. Whereas two of these articles dealt with the judgment of the ICT delivered in the case of *Azad*, the third was titled 'Sayeedi Indictment – 1971 deaths'.[150] In this article, Bergman criticised the Tribunal's acceptance of the death toll of three million as if it was a proven number without mentioning the reasonable controversy.[151] The author further cited various sources that estimated different numbers, thereby showing the difficulties in determining the correct number.

Section 11(4) of the ICT Act allows the Tribunal to punish any person for an action that constitutes contempt of the ICT with simple imprisonment of up to one year, with a fine of up to five thousand taka, or with both. In its order, the Tribunal acknowledged that Bergman was not giving his own opinion on the death toll but that he was merely citing other sources.[152] Nevertheless, according to the Tribunal, by doing so the journalist created severe confusion about a matter sub judice, which generally leads to contempt of court.[153] The Tribunal further insisted that 'despite all those [sic] differing information it is now settled to [sic] the nation that 3 millions [sic] of [sic] people laid their lives for the cause of our independence'.[154]

At the same time, the ICT recognised that there is no bar to initiate a discussion on a matter in the 'public interest' even if the matter becomes a matter sub judice.[155] However, according to the Tribunal the criticism made in the relevant article was not in the public interest, especially because of the specific point in time when it was

---

149 ICT 2, *Azam v. Bergman*, misc. case no. 01/2014, Order, 2 December 2014. For the examination of this particular blog article, see paras. 35–47.
150 For the revised version of the article, see *Bergman*, Sayeedi Indictment – 1971 deaths, 11 November 2011. However, the passages that were relevant for the Tribunal were deleted but they are quoted in the contempt order.
151 He wrote: 'The Tribunal could have dealt with the issue of the number of deaths in a more judicial manner rather than referring to it like repeating a 'mantra' that has little or no factual basis.' Quoted in: ICT 2, *Azam v. Bergman*, misc. case no. 01/2014, Order, 2 December 2014, para. 11.
152 ICT 2, *Azam v. Bergman*, misc. case no. 01/2014, Order, 2 December 2014, para. 35.
153 ICT 2, *Azam v. Bergman*, misc. case no. 01/2014, Order, 2 December 2014, paras. 35, 36.
154 ICT 2, *Azam v. Bergman*, misc. case no. 01/2014, Order, 2 December 2014, para. 35.
155 ICT 2, *Azam v. Bergman*, misc. case no. 01/2014, Order, 2 December 2014, para. 37.

published.[156] The Tribunal held that the article severely hurt the emotions of the nation and that the author questioned the authority of the Tribunal in making its observations in this regard.[157] The last point was crucial for the Tribunal's decision. It perceived that its authority was being questioned because of Bergman's conclusion that '[...] it may well have been preferable for it [the Tribunal] not to have mentioned these particular figures'.[158] The Tribunal considered this to be a demeaning comment that crossed the line of professional ethics and showed malicious intent.[159] Bergman was punished with imprisonment 'till the rising of the court' and a fine of 5,000 taka (approximately €55 at the time the order was passed).[160]

This case shows that the historical events of 1971 are still a very sensitive issue in the public discourse. The ICT considers itself empowered to define general historical facts and to repress critical public discourse in this regard. Though the general portrayal of the war does not directly influence the legal assessment of the crimes in a particular case, it is questionable whether a criminal tribunal is the right forum in which to determine facts that are not subject to proof.

1.3.2 Compensation and rehabilitation

Compensation and rehabilitation have been patchy and many of the victims have not been compensated to date. After the war, Sheikh Mujibur Rahman enacted a compensation scheme that allowed for reparation payments to families whose members had lost their lives during the Liberation War.[161] Under this scheme, every victim's family was awarded compensation of 2,000 taka.[162]

Rahman also introduced the term '*birangona*', which is generally translated as 'war heroine'. With this term, he originally intended to honour all the women for their contribution to the freedom struggle.[163] The term was given to those who took care of the families while their husbands were fighting in the war, those who themselves became freedom fighters or provided support for the freedom fighters with food and medical care, and also to the numerous rape victims.[164] Contrary to its original meaning, the term came to be used exclusively for rape victims, and women identifying

---

156 ICT 2, *Azam v. Bergman*, misc. case no. 01/2014, Order, 2 December 2014, para. 37.
157 ICT 2, *Azam v. Bergman*, misc. case no. 01/2014, Order, 2 December 2014, para. 47.
158 Quoted in: ICT 2, *Azam v. Bergman*, misc. case no. 01/2014, Order, 2 December 2014, para. 46.
159 ICT 2, *Azam v. Bergman*, misc. case no. 01/2014, Order, 2 December 2014, para. 47.
160 ICT 2, *Azam v. Bergman*, misc. case no. 01/2014, Order, 2 December 2014, para. 135.
161 Chowdhury, Myth of Three Million, p. 25.
162 Chowdhury, Myth of Three Million, p. 25.
163 D'Costa, Nationbuilding, p. 120
164 D'Costa/Hossain, CLF, 2010, 21(2), p. 331, at 340.

Part II: Towards an International Crimes Tribunal

themselves as *birangona* were stigmatised.[165] As a consequence, most of the women did not want to be associated with the concept.[166] However, the *birangona* label endures today. The ICT also utilises the term exclusively for rape victims as established in society. It promotes the term and requests the nation to recognise rape survivors as war heroines, to appreciate their sacrifice for the liberation of the country[167] and to honour them[168].

In 1972, the government of Bangladesh established the Women's Rehabilitation Organisation to implement three different programmes for the rehabilitation of women.[169] The primary rescue and rehabilitation programme included medical assistance and the possibility of abortion for pregnant rape victims.[170] Rape victims were regarded as dishonoured and expelled from society.[171] The programme also tried to reintegrate these women into society and to this end encouraged men to marry *birangonas* by providing them with jobs and land when they agreed to do so.[172] However, this campaign never became successful and the very few who agreed to marry a rape victim demanded considerable dowries from the government.[173] Beyond that, the programme also created social awareness aimed at encouraging families to take the *birangonas* back.[174]

Rehabilitation was also provided through an income-generating programme that included training programmes for women so that they could develop economic independence.[175] A third programme dealt with the rehabilitation of children resulting from rape through international adoption.[176] The so-called 'war babies' were mostly adopted by families from the Netherlands, Canada and other European countries with the help of the Mother Teresa Foundation.[177]

---

165 *D'Costa*, Nationbuilding, p. 120.
166 *Saikia*, Making of Bangladesh, p. 56.
167 ICT 2, *The Chief Prosecutor v. Qaiser*, case no. 04/2013, Judgment, 23 December 2014, para. 986.
168 ICT 1, *The Chief Prosecutor v. Islam*, case no. 05/2013, Judgment, 30 December 2014, para. 331.
169 *D'Costa*, Nationbuilding, p. 129.
170 *D'Costa*, Nationbuilding, p. 129.
171 For testimonies of rape victims on their post-war experiences, see *Saikia*, Making of Bangladesh, pp. 109–212.
172 *Brownmiller*, Against Our Will, p. 83; *Saikia*, Making of Bangladesh, p. 56.
173 *Brownmiller*, Against Our Will, p. 83.
174 *D'Costa/Hossain*, CLF, 2010, 21(2), p. 331, at 341.
175 *D'Costa*, Nationbuilding, p. 129.
176 *D'Costa/Hossain*, CLF, 2010, 21(2), p. 331, at 341–342; *Saikia*, Making of Bangladesh, p. 59.
177 *Saikia*, Making of Bangladesh, p. 59.

The struggle for compensation continues today. While freedom fighters receive monthly compensation, medical services and quotas in the public sector and in educational institutions for their children and grandchildren, the same benefits were awarded to rape victims for the first time only in 2015 when the government recognised some of them officially as freedom fighters.[178]

1.3.3 Genocide debates

A few scholars have discussed the controversial topic of whether and against whom genocide was committed during Bangladesh's Liberation War.[179] However, there is no extensive research in the field of genocide studies on the events of 1971.[180]

In Bangladesh, it is very common for people to refer to the atrocities of 1971 as genocide.[181] However, with the use of this term, many people do not intend to make a legal classification but to express the great extent or the gravity of the crimes committed. In fact, there is a general tendency of laymen to use the term 'genocide' to describe mass killings of civilians without considering the genocidal intent as required in the legal definition.[182]

The International Commission of Jurists analysed the question of whether genocide was committed in 1971 based on the definition in Article 2 of the Convention on the Prevention and Punishment of the Crime of Genocide (Genocide Convention), 1948.[183] According to this definition, a perpetrator of genocide needs to act with the intent to destroy, in whole or in part, a national, ethnic, racial or religious group.[184] The Commission questioned the claim that the operations of the Pakistani army were conducted with the intent to destroy, in whole or in part, the Bengali nation because

---

178 *Basher Anik*, Birangonas Get Freedom Fighter Status, Dhaka Tribune, 13 October 2015.
179 See, for instance, *Akmam*, JGR, 2002, 4(4), pp. 543–559; *Beachler*, PP, 2007, 41(5), pp. 467–492; *Bose*, JGR, 2011, 13(4), pp. 393–419; *Gerlach*, Societies, pp. 132 ff.
180 *Beachler*, PP, 2007, 41(5), p. 467, at 489; *Moses*, JGR, 2011, 13(4), p. 392, at 392.
181 *Bergsmo/Novic*, JGR, 2011, 13(4), p. 503, at 506; *Linton*, CLF, 2010, 21(2), p. 191, at 243; *Moses*, JGR, 2011, 13(4), p. 392, at 392. An example that reflects this widespread label is *National Coordinating Committee for the Realisation of Bangladesh Liberation War Ideals and Trials of Bangladesh War Criminals of 1971*, Report, p. 3.
182 *Bose*, JGR, 2011, 13(4), p. 393, at 393; *International Commission of Jurists*, Events in East Pakistan, p. 55.
183 *International Commission of Jurists*, Events in East Pakistan, pp. 55 ff.
184 The definition of genocide under Section 3(2)(c) of the ICT Act differs in two respects from the one in the Genocide Convention: (1) it also includes political groups as targeted groups; and (2) after the listing of the groups, it contains the words 'such as' whereas the definition of the Genocide Convention reads 'as such' referring to the groups. For further details on the definition of genocide under the ICT Act, see pp. 105 ff.

the main intention was to prevent political autonomy.[185] Yet, it asserted that there is a prima facie case that, in some cases, genocide with intent to destroy part of the Bengalis might have been committed.[186] In this regard, Bose points out that there were also many Bengalis who fought for the Pakistani army so that, with Bengalis acting on both sides, it would be difficult to establish the intent to destroy the Bengalis in whole or in part.[187]

Jahan holds that genocide was committed but argues that the reason behind the atrocities was to terrorise the population and to achieve submission.[188] This aim does not amount to genocidal intent. Invoking the memoirs of General Ayub Khan from 1967, in which he outlines the characteristics of Bengalis and describes them as inferior,[189] the author concludes that 'there were also[190] elements of racism in this act of genocide'[191]. It remains unclear how the author considers genocide to have been committed even without the elements of racism, and it rather shows that she refers to genocide as large-scale killing. It must be noted also that Ayub Khan was not Pakistan's president in 1971. Beyond that, Jahan also holds that the Pakistani army acted 'on the assumption of racial superiority and a desire to cleanse the Bengali Muslims of Hindu cultural linguistic influence'.[192]

The International Commission of Jurists further analysed the perpetration of genocide with regard to the different target groups of the Pakistani army. Throughout the war, the Pakistani army had three main target groups: members of the Awami League, students and Hindus.[193] However, genocide was not committed with respect to students or Awami League members because political groups are not included in the definition of genocide in the Genocide Convention.[194] On the other hand, the Commission concluded that there was 'a strong prima facie case' that genocide was committed against the Hindu population in East Pakistan because evidence has shown that Hindus were killed purely because of their religious affiliation.[195]

The Commission also examined whether the killing of non-Bengalis (Biharis) by Bengalis could fall under the definition of genocide but concluded that it would be

---

185 *International Commission of Jurists*, Events in East Pakistan, p. 56.
186 *International Commission of Jurists*, Events in East Pakistan, pp. 56–57.
187 *Bose*, JGR, 2011, 13(4), p. 393, at 398.
188 *Jahan*, in: *Jones* (ed.), Genocide, Vol. 2, p. 282, at 286.
189 *Ayub Khan*, Friends Not Masters, p. 187.
190 My emphasis.
191 *Jahan*, in: *Jones* (ed.), Genocide, Vol. 2, p. 282, at 286.
192 *Jahan*, in: *Jones* (ed.), Genocide, Vol. 2, p. 282, at 286.
193 *International Commission of Jurists*, Events in East Pakistan, p. 56.
194 *International Commission of Jurists*, Events in East Pakistan, p. 57.
195 *International Commission of Jurists*, Events in East Pakistan, p. 57.

difficult to establish the genocidal intent from spontaneous mob violence against a particular group from which the perpetrators sensed danger.[196]

In Bangladesh, the legal qualification has not been subject to public discourse for two main reasons. First, in Bangladeshi society, the debate about the 'genocide of three million' is constrained due to the fact that Bangladeshis questioning this number risk being labelled collaborators.[197] Secondly, there is a fear that, if the crimes committed during the Liberation War are not labelled genocide, no attention will be paid to them or they will be perceived as less severe.[198] The latter thought is, however, a very common phenomenon.[199] Nevertheless, considering the power the term 'genocide' bears, it should be used cautiously otherwise it loses its ability to classify a unique form of crime.[200]

The ICT asserted in its first judgment that 'the extermination of individuals because of their membership in a distinct national, ethnic, racial, religious or political group has been perpetrated throughout the period of [the] War of Liberation in 1971 within the territory of Bangladesh. It is the history of common knowledge and need not be proved'.[201] It thus considers the commission of genocide a fact of common knowledge but does not clarify how it comes to the conclusion that members of all five groups were targeted. However, the question of whether an accused committed the offence of genocide remains an issue to be dealt with in the context of individual cases.[202]

2 First attempts to deal with the war crimes

After the war, Sheikh Mujibur Rahman returned to Dhaka from West Pakistan where he had been detained since his arrest on 25 March 1971.[203] At a very early stage, he advocated the trial of war criminals through an international tribunal.[204] The United Nations High Commissioner for Human Rights promoted this idea but there was not

---

196 *International Commission of Jurists*, Events in East Pakistan, p. 57.
197 *Bose*, JGR, 2011, 13(4), p. 393, at 394.
198 *Bose*, JGR, 2011, 13(4), p. 393, at 396.
199 *Cryer et al.*, International Criminal Law, 3. edn, p. 206.
200 *Cryer et al.*, International Criminal Law, 3. edn, p. 206.
201 ICT 1, *The Chief Prosecutor v. Azad*, case no. 5/2012, Judgment, 15 July 2012, para. 154. The ICT applies the definition of genocide under Section 3(2) of the ICT Act, which protects also political groups.
202 For details on the definition of genocide under the ICT Act and its interpretation by the ICT, see pp. 104 ff.
203 *Baxter*, Bangladesh, p. 86.
204 *MacDermot*, IL, 1973, 7(2), p. 476, at 483.

enough support to implement such a project.[205] The International Commission of Jurists also expressed concerns regarding the establishment of a national tribunal and instead recommended trials by an international tribunal under the authority of the United Nations.[206] The Commission suggested the appointment of judges from neutral countries due to the experience with the International Military Tribunal at Nuremberg (IMT) which was criticised for having judges exclusively from the victorious countries.[207] Another argument in favour of an international tribunal was the possibility of trying the perpetrators without having to pass a retroactive law.[208]

The Pakistani side saw a need for action as well. The Hamoodur Rahman Commission recommended trials to call war criminals to account. In its report, it demanded the establishment of a court or an inquiry commission to investigate and prosecute the crimes committed by senior army commanders.[209] However, no serious initiative was ever taken in this regard and, to date, no trials have been held in Pakistan.

Despite the recommendations from international stakeholders, the problem was approached at the domestic level. Two different legal sources for the trial of war criminals were created: an order to try those who collaborated with the Pakistani army in East Pakistan, and a law for the trial of high-level perpetrators. At the same time, the government passed another order to guarantee exemption from punishment for those who had participated in the liberation struggle.

2.1 The Bangladesh Collaborators (Special Tribunal) Order, 1972

The Bangladesh Collaborators (Special Tribunal) Order (Collaborators Order)[210] was enacted on 24 January 1972 for the purpose of bringing collaborators of the Pakistani armed forces to trial. It was passed with retroactive effect from 26 March 1971.[211] A Special Tribunal was set up with exclusive jurisdiction to try the collaborators as defined in the Order. It was enacted as a presidential order and was amended three times.

The Order defined the term 'collaborator' but did not contain any special offences. In fact, a schedule, which referred to offences defined under the Penal Code and increased the penalties, was attached to it. For instance, under the Bangladesh Penal Code[212] an attempt to commit culpable homicide under Section 308 can be punishable

---

205 *MacDermot*, IL, 1973, 7(2), p. 476, at 483.
206 *International Commission of Jurists*, Events East Pakistan, p. 63.
207 *International Commission of Jurists*, Events in East Pakistan, p. 63.
208 *International Commission of Jurists*, Events in East Pakistan, p. 64.
209 *Hamoodur Rahman Commission*, Report, p. 37.
210 The text of the Order can be found in: *Kritz*, Transitional Justice, Vol. 3, pp. 540–545.
211 Section 1(3) of the Collaborators Order.
212 For the full text of the Bangladesh Penal Code, 1860, see http://bdlaws.minlaw.gov.bd/print_sections_all.php?id=11, accessed 20 September 2015.

by imprisonment of up to seven years or a fine, or both. The same offence committed as a collaborator with the Pakistan army under the Collaborators Order could be punished with rigorous imprisonment of up to ten years.[213]

The definition of 'collaborator' given in Section 2 was very extensive and included nearly any kind of behaviour that abetted the Pakistani army:

Section 2 of the Bangladesh Collaborators (Special Tribunal) Order
In this Order, –
- (b) 'collaborator' means a person who has –
  - (i) participated with or aided, or abetted the occupation army in maintaining, sustaining, strengthening, supporting or furthering the illegal occupation in Bangladesh by such army;
  - (ii) rendered material assistance in any way whatsoever to the occupation army by any act, whether by words, signs or conduct;
  - (iii) waged war or abetted in waging war against the People's Republic of Bangladesh;
  - (iv) actively resisted or sabotaged the efforts of the people and the liberation forces of Bangladesh in their liberation struggle against the occupation army;
  - (v) by a public statement or by voluntary participation in propagandas within and outside Bangladesh or by association in any delegation or committee or by participation in purported bye-elections attempted to aid or aided the occupation army in furthering its design of perpetrating its forcible occupation in Bangladesh.

Explanation – A person who has performed in good faith functions, which he was required by any purported law in force at the material time to do, shall not be deemed to be a collaborator: Provided that a person who has performed functions the direct object or result of which was the killing of any member of the civil population of the liberation forces of Bangladesh or the destruction of their property or the rape of or criminal assault on their women-folk, even if done under any purported law passed by the occupation army, shall be deemed to be a collaborator.

The International Commission of Jurists strongly criticised this wide definition and the retroactive enactment of the Order.[214]

The tribunals set up under the Order were to apply the Code of Criminal Procedure, 1898 as long as it was not inconsistent with the provisions of the Collaborators Order.[215] The Collaborators Order, however, had several procedural shortcomings which impeded due process. For instance, a person suspected of being a collaborator could be arrested by the police without a warrant on mere suspicion.[216] The magistrate could then order his or her detention for six months, and the government was empowered to extend the period of detention indefinitely if further time was required for the police inquiry.[217]

---

213 Section 9(b) of the Collaborators (Special Tribunal) Order, 1972 in conjunction with Part II of the Schedule of the Collaborators Order.
214 *International Commission of Jurists*, Review, 1972, 9, p. 8, at 8.
215 Section 8(1) of the Collaborators Order.
216 Section 3(1) of the Collaborators Order.
217 Section 3(4) of the Collaborators Order.

Also, the right to be released on bail was excluded without exception.[218] Further, the government could seize any property belonging to a suspect or his family if the person was absconding or otherwise concealing himself to avoid an appearance.[219]

The Bangladesh Bar Council objected to the Collaborators Order because of these shortcomings and named it 'the most unethical and unjust law contrary to all established principles of jurisprudence and fundamental rights as recognised throughout the civilised world'.[220] The Council demanded the replacement of the special procedural regulations under the Order by the general provisions contained in the Code of Criminal Procedure.[221]

Criticism was further expressed with regard to the selection of cases. Bengali politicians who had cooperated with the Pakistani army were brought to trial whereas the entire civilian administration of East Pakistan remained intact and was installed as the new administration of Bangladesh.[222]

Proceedings under the Order were also confronted with practical challenges: due to the severe shortage of experienced police personnel in the post-war period, proper investigations and collection of evidence were difficult to realise satisfactorily.[223]

Besides the penalty, a conviction also had ramifications for the right to vote and parliamentary activities. The Constitution of Bangladesh was adopted on 4 November 1972 and referred to the Collaborators Order in two Articles: Article 122(2)(e) denied convicts under the Collaborators Order the right to vote, and Article 66(2)(e) barred them from being elected as members of parliament.[224] These regulations were repealed with the fourth Constitutional Amendment but later reinserted by the Constitution (Fifteenth Amendment) Act in 2011.[225] The Collaborators Order was also protected by the Constitution and could not be challenged on the ground of inconsistency with any constitutional provision.[226]

---

218 Section 14 of the Collaborators Order.
219 Section 17(1)(b) of the Collaborators Order.
220 *International Commission of Jurists*, Review, 1973, 11, p. 9, at 9.
221 *International Commission of Jurists*, Review, 1973, 11, p. 9, at 9.
222 *Mascarenhas*, Legacy of Blood, p. 24.
223 *International Commission of Jurists*, Review, 1972, 9, p. 8, at 9.
224 See Article 122(2)(e) and Article 66(2)(e) of the Constitution. For the full text of the current version of the Constitution of Bangladesh, see http://bdlaws.minlaw.gov.bd/print_sections_all.php?id=367, accessed 18 June 2015.
225 Article 24(ii) and Article 26 of the Constitution (Fifteenth Amendment) Act, Act XIV of 2011.
226 The reason for that was Article 47 of the Constitution which is still in force in a slightly amended version. The Collaborators Order is listed in the First Schedule alongside several other laws.

2 First attempts to deal with the war crimes

On 3 October 1972, the Home Ministry announced that 41,800 persons had been arrested under the Order[227] and that the trials against some 2,000 people had started[228]. In total, 2,848 were brought to trial[229] and 752 of those were sentenced[230].

As little as one year after this announcement, the government took a new direction. On 30 November 1973, it took the decision to release most of the detainees and convicts through a presidential order, the General Amnesty Order.[231] The amnesty applied to all perpetrators except those who were charged with murder, rape, or arson.[232] It is said, however, that many perpetrators belonging to these categories were also released.[233] The International Commission of Jurists welcomed the decision and estimated that approximately 35,000 people would benefit from this clemency.[234]

Ziauddin argues that the amnesty was unconstitutional.[235] While amnesties are generally granted before a prosecution, a pardon is awarded after conviction. Pursuant to Article 49 of the Constitution, the president has the power 'to grant pardons, reprieves and respites, and to remit, suspend or commute any sentence passed by any court, tribunal or other authority'. The expression 'any sentence passed by' suggests that a conviction is required in order for the president to intervene.[236] Nevertheless, this argument is weakened by the fact that the term 'pardon' is not used merely for post-conviction situations in the Bangladeshi legal system. As will be outlined below, the ICT Act allows for conditional amnesties but refers to them as pardons.[237]

---

227 *International Commission of Jurists*, Review, 1972, 9, p. 8, at 9; *Mascarenhas*, Legacy of Blood, p. 25. Other authors mention different numbers: according to *Husain*, in: *Hoque* (ed.), Genocide Conference Papers, 2009, p. 43, at 47 and *Reza*, War Crimes, in: *Liberation War Museum* (ed.), Genocide Conference Papers, 2008, p. 55 at 56, 37,413 people were arrested under the Collaborators Order. There is no official document which proves these numbers.
228 *International Commission of Jurists*, Review, 1972, 9, p. 8, at 9.
229 *Hossain*, in: *Liberation War Museum* (ed.), Genocide Conference papers 2008, p. 51, at 53; *Husain*, in: *Hoque* (ed.), Genocide Conference Papers, 2009, p. 43, at 47; *Reza*, in: *Liberation War Museum* (ed.), Genocide Conference Papers, 2008, p. 55, at 56.
230 *Hossain*, in: *Liberation War Museum* (ed.), Genocide Conference Papers, 2008, p. 51, at 53.
231 *International Commission of Jurists*, Review, 1973, 11, p. 6, at 10; *Oette/Ferstman*, Torture in Bangladesh, p. 27. The text of the General Amnesty Order is not available but parts of the Order are cited in: *Matas*, in: *Hoque* (ed.), Genocide Conference Papers, 2009, p. 33, at 40–41.
232 *International Commission of Jurists*, Review, 1973, 11, p. 6, at 10; *Reza*, War Crimes, in: *Liberation War Museum* (ed.), Genocide Conference Papers, 2008, p. 55, at 57.
233 *Ziauddin*, in: *Jongman* (ed.), Contemporary Genocides, p. 95, at 103.
234 *International Commission of Jurists*, Review, 1973, 11, p. 6, at 10.
235 *Ziauddin*, in: *Jongman* (ed.), Contemporary Genocides, p. 95, at 103.
236 *Islam*, Constitutional Law, 3. edn, p. 437; *Ziauddin*, in: *Jongman* (ed.), Contemporary Genocides, p. 95, at 103.
237 On the admissibility of amnesties, see pp. 88 ff.

The Collaborators Order was a very short-lived legislation. It was repealed through the Bangladesh Collaborators (Special Tribunals) (Repeal) Ordinance, 1975 (Repeal Ordinance) on 31 December 1975.[238] As set out in Section 2(2), the Ordinance provided for the immediate termination of ongoing trials and investigations:

> *Section 2(2) of The Bangladesh Collaborators (Special Tribunals) (Repeal) Ordinance, 1975*
> Upon the repeal of the said Order under sub-section (1), all trials or other proceedings thereunder pending immediately before such repeal before any Tribunal, Magistrate or Court, and all investigations or other proceedings by or before any Police Officer or other authority under that Order, shall abate and shall not be proceeded with.

Pending appeals against any conviction or sentence, on the other hand, were not affected by this regulation.[239] The Ordinance did not differentiate between specific offences, and even the proceedings against those who did not benefit from the General Amnesty Order because they were charged with murder, arson and rape were withdrawn.[240]

2.2 The Bangladesh National Liberation Struggle (Indemnity) Order, 1973

A few months before the enactment of the ICT Act, 1973, the government passed the Bangladesh National Liberation Struggle (Indemnity) Order, 1973 (Indemnity Order) to ensure impunity for those who committed crimes 'in connection with the struggle for national liberation or for maintenance or restoration of order'[241]. In accordance with the Order, any case brought to a court in this context had to be withdrawn.[242] Crimes committed by those fighting for independence are thus barred from prosecution. The Indemnity Order continues to be in force.

2.3 The International Crimes (Tribunals) Act, 1973

In 1973, national and international experts drafted the ICT Act. This was enacted on 20 July 1973. The Act included contributions from Professor Hans-Heinrich Jescheck (at that time, Director of the Max Planck Institute for Foreign and International Criminal Law, Freiburg, Germany), Professor Otto Triffterer and international lawyers

---

238 For the full text of the Repeal Ordinance, see http://bdlaws.minlaw.gov.bd/print_sections_all.php?id=510, accessed 17 June 2015.
239 Section 2(3a) of the Repeal Ordinance.
240 *Matas*, in: *Hoque* (ed.), Genocide Conference Papers, 2009, p. 33, at 41.
241 Section 3 of the Bangladesh National Liberation Struggle (Indemnity) Order, 1973. For the full text of the Order, see http://bdlaws.minlaw.gov.bd/print_sections_all.php?id=450, accessed 4 August 2014.
242 Section 3 of the Bangladesh National Struggle (Indemnity) Order, 1973.

2 First attempts to deal with the war crimes

from the International Commission of Jurists.[243] In Bangladesh, even today, the ICT Act is often highlighted as a very progressive law.[244] At the time the Act was drafted, Blaustein and Paust came to the conclusion that it guaranteed better rights for the accused than the minimum standard required in international law.[245] Unlike the Collaborators Order, it was aimed at bringing the main perpetrators to trial. 'Any person irrespective of his nationality who, being a member of any armed, defence or auxiliary forces'[246] could be tried under the ICT Act.

The Tribunal was given jurisdiction over crimes against humanity, crimes against peace, genocide, war crimes, violations of any humanitarian rules applicable in armed conflicts laid down in the Geneva Conventions of 1949, and any other crimes under international law.[247] Yet, the Act was never implemented and international as well as national political decisions led to decades of impunity until the establishment of the ICT in 2010. In its amended version, the Act constitutes the legal framework for the current trials before the ICT.

2.4 Constitutional amendments

In the same year as the enactment of the ICT Act, the Constitution was amended through the Constitution (First Amendment) Act, 1973 (Act XV of 1973). The amendment inserted a new sub-section (3) into Article 47 and precluded the possibility to declare any law for the trial of war criminals as unconstitutional. The intention behind this amendment was to overcome conflicts that arose with regard to the retroactivity of the law, which were discussed broadly during the drafting process.[248] Yet, Article 47(3) refers not only to retroactivity but also excludes challenges based on any constitutional ground. It states the following:

Art. 47(3) of the Constitution
(3) Notwithstanding anything contained in this Constitution, no law nor any provision thereof providing for detention, prosecution or punishment of any person, who is a member of any armed or defence or auxiliary forces (or any individual, group of individuals or

---

243 *Linton*, CLF, 2010, 21(2), p. 191, at 207–208; *Rahman*, Brief History, pp. 38–39. There is no written documentation on the drafting process and the contributions from Prof. Triffterer and Prof. Jescheck, see also *Triffterer*, in: *Bergsmo/Wui Ling* (eds), Old Evidence, p. 257, at 259.
244 *Linton*, CLF, 2010, 21(2), p. 191, at 208.
245 *Blaustein/Paust*, in: *Paust* (ed.), International Criminal Law, 4. edn, p. 510, at 513.
246 Section 3(1) of the ICT Act, 1973.
247 Section 3(2) of the ICT Act, 1973.
248 *Islam*, in: *Hoque* (ed.), Genocide Conference Papers, 2009, p. 125, at 128.

organisation)[249] or who is a prisoner of war, for genocide, crimes against humanity or war crimes and other crimes under international law shall be deemed void or unlawful, or ever to have become void or unlawful, on the ground that such law or provision of any such law is inconsistent with, or repugnant to any of the provisions of this Constitution.

The amendment also inserted Article 47A into the Constitution, which denies the accused under the ICT Act several fundamental rights, among them the right to move the Supreme Court, the right to protection of the law and the right to an impartial and speedy trial:

Art. 47A of the Constitution
(1) The rights guaranteed under article 31, clauses (1) and (3) of article 35 and article 44 shall not apply to any person to whom a law specified in clause (3) of article 47 applies.
(2) Notwithstanding anything contained in this Constitution, no person to whom a law specified in clause (3) of article 47 applies shall have the right to move the Supreme Court for any of the remedies under this Constitution.

Article 31 of the Constitution
To enjoy the protection of the law, and to be treated in accordance with law, and only in accordance with law, is the inalienable right of every citizen, wherever he may be, and of every other person for the time being within Bangladesh, and in particular no action detrimental to the life, liberty, body, reputation or property of any person shall be taken except in accordance with law.

Article 35(1) and (3) of the Constitution
(1) No person shall be convicted of any offence except for violation of a law in force at the time of the commission of the act charged as an offence, nor be subjected to a penalty greater than, or different from, that which might have been inflicted under the law in force at the time of the commission of the offence.
(3) Every person accused of a criminal offence shall have the right to a speedy and public trial by an independent and impartial court or tribunal established by law.

Article 44 of the Constitution[250]
(1) The right to move the High Court Division, in accordance with clause (1) of article 102, for the enforcement of the rights conferred by this Part, is guaranteed.
(2) Without prejudice to the powers of the High Court Division under article 102, Parliament may by law empower any other court, within the local limits of its jurisdiction, to exercise all or any of those powers.

To date, these constitutional amendments continue to be in force and have a strong impact on the trials and the ICT's legal framework.

---

249 These words have been inserted by Section 19(ii) of the Constitution (Fifteenth Amendment) Act, 2011 (Act XIV of 2011), in accordance with the amendment of the ICT Act which inserted the same words into Section 3(1) of the ICT Act.
250 Article 44 of the Constitution has been amended by Section 18 of the Constitution (Fifteenth Amendment) Act, 2011 (Act XIV of 2011) through which the words 'the Supreme Court' have been replaced by the words 'the High Court Division'.

2.5 International agreements

International politics played a vital role in Bangladesh agreeing to abstain from legal action against high-level perpetrators in the post-war period. In addition, in third countries, no trials ever took place.

After the Liberation War, India held approximately 92,000 Pakistani prisoners of war.[251] Among them were 195 alleged war criminals who were supposed to be sent to Bangladesh in order to be brought to trial.[252] Pakistan filed a case against India on 11 May 1973 at the International Court of Justice (ICJ) seeking the repatriation of prisoners of war to Pakistan, including the 195 alleged war criminals.[253] India's real intention in the prolonged detention was to compel Pakistan to recognise Bangladesh as an independent state.[254] However, the case before the ICJ was never decided because the conflict was solved through several agreements between the two countries in the meantime. Pakistan finally requested that the case be removed from the list, which was done through an order on 15 December 1973.[255]

Due to international pressure and in return for its recognition as an independent state, Bangladesh finally agreed to the repatriation of the 195 prisoners from India, although Pakistan decided not to prosecute them.[256] Pakistan's refusal to recognise Bangladesh and 400,000 Bengalis held in Pakistan were crucial factors that contributed to this result.[257]

Several agreements paved the way for this outcome. Pakistan and India concluded a first agreement on the peaceful settlement of the conflict on 2 July 1972, the Simla Agreement.[258] General provisions were made and it was decided that further modalities for the establishment of a durable peace, including the repatriation of the prisoners of war, would be discussed in the future.[259] This rather general agreement was fol-

---

251 ICJ, *Pakistan v. India*, Case Concerning Trial of Pakistani Prisoners of War, Application, 11 May 1973, p. 3.
252 ICJ, *Pakistan v. India*, Case Concerning Trial of Pakistani Prisoners of War, Application, 11 May 1973, p. 3.
253 ICJ, *Pakistan v. India*, Case Concerning Trial of Pakistani Prisoners of War, Application, 11 May 1973.
254 *Levie*, AJIL, 1973, 67(3), p. 512, at 514.
255 ICJ, *Pakistan v. India*, Case Concerning Trial of Pakistani Prisoners of War, Order, 15 December 1973.
256 *Linton*, CLF, 2010, 21(2), p. 191, at 203.
257 *Blaustein/Paust*, Vanderbilt JTL, 1978, 11(1), p. 1, at 35; *Burke*, AS, 1973, 13(11), p. 1036, at 1037.
258 For the full text of the Simla Agreement can be found, see International Legal Materials, 1972, 11(5), pp. 954–957.
259 Simla Agreement, para. 6.

lowed by a second agreement. The Delhi Agreement[260] was reached on 28 August 1973 and concretised the actions to be taken. Although Bangladesh was not a party to this agreement, it concurred with it.[261] Pakistan still refused to recognise Bangladesh as an independent state but recognition was a condition set by Bangladesh for any further negotiations.[262] Through the Delhi Agreement the repatriation of all Bengalis held in Pakistan and all Pakistanis held in Bangladesh was decided, and Bangladesh agreed not to initiate any trials against the 195 prisoners held in India during the process of repatriation.[263] The recognition of Bangladesh in the meantime led to a third and final agreement to settle the issue of the prisoners of war. The Agreement on the Repatriation of Prisoners of War and Civilian Internees[264] on 9 April 1974 between Bangladesh, India and Pakistan, also called the Tripartite Agreement, became the legal foundation for the repatriation of the 195 alleged war criminals from India to Pakistan without any trials. A policy of forgiveness and oblivion was pursued. Sheikh Mujibur Rahman as the Prime Minister of Bangladesh requested people to forget the past and to make a new start, also affirming that the people of Bangladesh knew how to forgive.[265] The Foreign Minister of Bangladesh acknowledged that '[…] the Government of Bangladesh had decided not to proceed with the trials as an act of clemency'.[266] Many people considered this result a betrayal.[267] Nevertheless, no public protests arose against this decision for clemency.[268] Bangladesh also finally joined the United Nations on 17 September 1974 after its first application for membership from 9 August 1972 was rejected through the Chinese veto.

2.6 Political environment in post-war Bangladesh

The first elections were held in March 1973. The opposition parties were all leftist. Islamic right-wing parties, among them the Jamaat-e-Islami party, were banned after the Liberation War because of their support for the Pakistani army.[269] The prohibition of religion-based parties resulted from the Preamble, Article 12 and Article 38 of the

---

260 The text of the Delhi Agreement can be found in: International Legal Materials, 1973, 12(5), pp. 1080–1084.
261 Delhi Agreement, para. 10.
262 Delhi Agreement, para. 5.
263 Delhi Agreement, para. 5.
264 For the full text of the Agreement on the Repatriation of Prisoners of War and Civilian Internees, see International Legal Materials, 1974, 13(3), pp. 501–505.
265 Agreement on the Repatriation of Prisoners of War and Civilian Internees, para. 14.
266 Agreement on the Repatriation of Prisoners of War and Civilian Internees, para. 15.
267 *Ziauddin*, in: *Jongman*, (ed.), Contemporary Genocides, p. 95, at 105.
268 *Ahmed*, Historicizing 1971 Genocide, p. 15.
269 *Van Schendel*, History of Bangladesh, p. 207.

Bangladesh Constitution, 1972. Article 12 and the Preamble declared Bangladesh to be a secular state whereas Article 38 impeded the formation of parties with objectives that were inconsistent with the Constitution. The Awami League announced its election victory with a majority of 97% but the elections were dominated by vote-rigging in order to ensure the absolute majority.[270]

However, the party did not remain in power for long. Sheikh Mujibur Rahman and his family, except his two daughters, were murdered on 15 August 1975.[271] From then until 1990, the country was governed by military rule and parties of the religious right, and the process of transitional justice was blighted.[272] The fundamental constitutional principle of secularism was soon excluded from the Preamble based on a martial law proclamation, which was afterwards ratified through the Fifth Constitutional Amendment in 1979.[273] Thereafter, with the Eighth Constitutional Amendment in 1988,[274] Article 2A was introduced which declared Islam the state religion of the country.[275]

3 Ending impunity

The increasing demand in society to end impunity and the election of the Awami League in 2008 were crucial factors for the establishment of the ICT in 2010. The trial of war criminals was part of the Awami League's election manifesto and of great interest for the party since it was one of the main targets of the Pakistani military operations during the War of 1971.

3.1 Politics after 1991

The re-establishment of electoral democracy took place in 1991. Since then, and until 2008, the Awami League and the BNP have been elected alternately. The BNP, a nationalist conservative party, was founded in 1978 by President Ziaur Rahman. There continues to be a strong distrust between the two parties, and with every election the losing opposition raises concerns regarding the fairness and freedom of the elections.[276] In 2001, the BNP entered into a coalition with three Islamist parties, among

---

270 *Van Schendel,* History of Bangladesh, p. 179.
271 *Baxter,* Bangladesh, p. 92.
272 *D'Costa/Hossain,* CLF, 2010, 21(2), p. 331, at 337.
273 *Islam,* Constitutional Law, 3. edn, p. 68.
274 Section 4 of the Constitution Eighth (Amendment) Act, 1988 (Act XXX of 1988).
275 *Islam,* Constitutional Law, 3. edn, p. 68.
276 *Jahan,* Political Parties, pp. 7–8.

them the Jamaat-e-Islami party.[277] This four-party alliance won the election in 2001 and two Jamaat-e-Islami members became cabinet ministers.[278]

In 2008, the Awami League was elected and governed with Sheikh Hasina Wajed, Sheikh Mujibur Rahman's eldest daughter, as prime minister. Dynastic succession and familial politics are very common in Bangladesh's political parties even today.[279] For example, Khaleda Zia, the current chairperson of the BNP, is the widow of the party's founder, who was murdered in 1981.

Secularism was only reintroduced into the Constitution in 2010 when the Bangladesh High Court ruled that the Fifth Amendment was illegal. As a consequence, the Preamble in its original version was restored and Article 2A was amended in 2011 to overcome the inconsistency with the Preamble.[280] Nevertheless, the inconsistency was not removed entirely. Article 2A of the Bangladesh Constitution in its current version still declares Islam the state religion of Bangladesh and merely compels the state to ensure the equal status of other religions and an equal right to practise them.

The percentage of votes for parties from the religious right is relatively insignificant. The Jamaat-e-Islami party retained less than five per cent of the votes during the last two elections in which it participated.[281] However, the party was not allowed to run at the last election in 2014 due to not fulfilling the registration criteria. The cancellation was confirmed by the Bangladesh High Court on 1 August 2013, based on the party's discrimination on the grounds of religion and gender, among other reasons.[282]

The BNP boycotted the 2014 elections and, therefore, did not participate at all. Hence, the Awami League was re-elected and remains in power with Sheikh Hasina Wazed as prime minister today.

3.2 Emerging call for trials of war criminals

The idea of trying war criminals had disappeared for many years and only started to re-emerge publicly in the 1990s. The re-appointment of Ghulam Azam as the leader of the Jamaat-e-Islami party on 29 December 1991 provoked a strong movement demanding the trial of perpetrators of crimes committed during the Liberation War.[283]

---

277 *Jahan*, Political Parties, p. 48.
278 *Jahan*, Political Parties, p. 49.
279 *Jahan*, Political Parties, pp. 116–117.
280 *Islam*, Constitutional Law, 3. edn, p. 68.
281 For overview of the election results in Bangladesh since 1991, see *Jahan*, Political Parties, pp. 40 ff.
282 *Maulana Syed Rezaul Haque Chadpuri & others v. Bangladesh Jamaat-e-Islami & others*, 66 DLR (HCD) (2014), pp. 14 ff.
283 *Ziauddin*, in: *Jongman* (ed.), Contemporary Genocides, p. 95, at 106.

3 Ending impunity

Azam was the Ameer[284] of East Pakistan's Jamaat-e-Islami from 1969 until 1971. Prior to the end of the war, he left East Pakistan and went to West Pakistan where he resided until 1973, setting up an organisation called the 'Purbo Pakistan Punoruddhar Committee' (East Pakistan Restoration Committee).[285] In 1973, he emigrated to London where he continued to work for his organisation propagating the restoration of East Pakistan.[286] The government of Bangladesh cancelled his citizenship in 1973 but he came back to reside in Bangladesh with a Pakistani passport in 1978 and finally obtained Bangladeshi citizenship through a court order.[287]

An organisation called the 'Ekattorer Ghatak Dalal Nirmul Committee' (Committee for the Uprooting of Traitors and Collaborators of 1971[288]), under the leadership of the activist Jahanara Imam who lost her son during the war, was formed in 1992.[289] The Committee set up a People's Court to try Ghulam Azam through a symbolic public trial in which people from different professional backgrounds participated, and some 200,000 spectators attended the event.[290] He was found guilty of 12 counts of war crimes and crimes against humanity, and he was 'sentenced' to death.[291] Of course, this 'verdict' had no legal effect. With these mock trials, the Committee rather intended to gain public attention and to bring the prosecution of war criminals back on the political agenda.[292] The government largely ignored the Committee's activities and later 24 of the organisers were charged with treason.[293] On 15 July 2013, more than 20 years later, the ICT sentenced Ghulam Azam to 90 years of imprisonment for the perpetration of crimes against humanity, among others.[294] The verdict abstained from capital punishment due to the age and fragile health condition of the accused.

---

284 The Ameer is the executive head of the party. For an overview of the party's structure, see *Jahan*, Political Parties, p. 103.
285 ICT 1, *The Chief Prosecutor v. Azam*, case no. 6/2011, Judgment, 15 July 2013, paras. 14–15.
286 ICT 1, *The Chief Prosecutor v. Azam*, case no. 6/2011, Judgment, 15 July 2013, para. 15.
287 ICT 1, *The Chief Prosecutor v. Azam*, case no. 6/2011, Judgment, 15 July 2013, para. 15.
288 Different translations circulate. This translation is used by *Van Schendel*, History of Bangladesh, p. 21. Instead, *Ziauddin*, in: *Jongman* (ed.), Contemporary Genocides, p. 95, at 106 translates the Committee's name as 'Committee for the Elimination of the Killers and Collaborators of '71'.
289 *Van Schendel*, History of Bangladesh, p. 217; *Ziauddin*, in: *Jongman* (ed.), Contemporary Genocides, p. 95, at 106.
290 *Ziauddin*, in: *Jongman* (ed.), Contemporary Genocides, p. 95, at 106–107.
291 *National Coordinating Committee for the Realisation of Bangladesh Liberation War Ideals and Trials of Bangladesh War Criminals of 1971*, Report, p. 6.
292 *Van Schendel*, History of Bangladesh, p. 217.
293 *D'Costa/Hossain*, CLF, 2010, 21(2), p. 331, at 347; *Van Schendel*, History of Bangladesh, p. 217; *Ziauddin*, in: *Jongman* (ed.), Contemporary Genocides, p. 95, at 107.
294 ICT 1, *The Chief Prosecutor v. Azam*, case no. 6/2011, Judgment, 15 July 2013, para. 242.

Another organisation, the National Coordinating Committee for Realisation of Bangladesh Liberation War Ideals and Trials of Bangladesh War Criminals of 1971, emerged from this movement and, in 1993, the Committee formed the National People's Enquiry Commission to investigate other alleged war criminals.[295] This Commission collected evidence against eight alleged war criminals: Abbas Ali Khan, Maulana Matiur Rahman Nizami, Mohammad Kamaruzzaman, Abdul Alim, Maulana Delwar Hossain Sayeedi, Maulana Abdul Mannan, Anwar Zahid and Abdul Quader Molla.[296] It considered documents, books, newspaper articles and written witness statements to prepare the ground for the initiation of trials.[297] The Commission consisted of 11 members from different backgrounds, including two former judges of the Bangladesh Supreme Court.[298] It concluded its work with the recommendation to try the alleged war criminals under the ICT Act and to re-enact all relevant laws that had been repealed in the past.[299] Several of these alleged war criminals were later tried and sentenced by the ICT. The former chairperson of Tribunal 1, Nizamul Huq Nasim, was also a member of the Committee's secretariat.[300]

3.3 Establishment of the ICT

The ICT was finally established on 25 March 2010,[301] shortly after the Awami League's election victory. The date was the anniversary of Operation Searchlight and was certainly not selected at random.[302] It consisted initially of one tribunal but a second tribunal (Tribunal 2) was established two years later, on 22 March 2012, to reduce the workload and to speed up the proceedings.[303] Nevertheless, in August 2015, it was decided to

---

295 *National Coordinating Committee for the Realisation of Bangladesh Liberation War Ideals and Trials of Bangladesh War Criminals of 1971*, Report, p. 6; *Ziauddin*, in: *Jongman* (ed.), Contemporary Genocides, p. 95, at 107–108.
296 *National Coordinating Committee for the Realisation of Bangladesh Liberation War Ideals and Trials of Bangladesh War Criminals of 1971*, Report, p. 9.
297 *National Coordinating Committee for the Realisation of Bangladesh Liberation War Ideals and Trials of Bangladesh War Criminals of 1971*, Report, pp. 9, 11.
298 *National Coordinating Committee for the Realisation of Bangladesh Liberation War Ideals and Trials of Bangladesh War Criminals of 1971*, Report, p. 9.
299 *National Coordinating Committee for the Realisation of Bangladesh Liberation War Ideals and Trials of Bangladesh War Criminals of 1971*, Report, p. 35.
300 *National Coordinating Committee for the Realisation of Bangladesh Liberation War Ideals and Trials of Bangladesh War Criminals of 1971*, Report, Appendix B, no. 25, p. 36. On the defence's application for recusal of the chairperson based on his membership in the Committee's secretariat, see pp. 225 ff.
301 http://ict-bd.org/ict1/, accessed 3 July 2015.
302 *Robertson*, Report on the International Crimes Tribunal of Bangladesh, p. 60.
303 http://ict-bd.org/ict2/, accessed 3 July 2015.

merge both tribunals, allegedly due to a decrease of cases.[304] Tribunal 2 was therefore deactivated on 15 September 2015 and only one tribunal continues to function.

The over 40-year-old ICT Act was broadly amended through the International Crimes (Tribunals) (Amendment) Acts, 2009, 2012, 2013 and the International Crimes (Tribunals) (Amendment) Ordinance, 2012. Another amendment is currently being discussed with the aim of allowing the trial of political parties.[305] Though the trial of organisations is foreseen already under the current version of the ICT Act, the Act does not determine the punishment for organisations. The rationale behind this amendment is the banning of Jamaat-e-Islami as a party.[306]

The RoP were enacted in 2010, followed by amendments in 2010, 2011 and 2015. Section 22 of the ICT Act empowers the tribunals to frame their own procedural rules, that is, each tribunal can draft its own rules and decide on the procedural provisions upon which it needs to act. Nevertheless, in practice, the RoP of both tribunals coincided.

The accused and convicts are Bangladeshi nationals who allegedly cooperated with the Pakistani army as Razakars during the Liberation War. Although the ICT Act provides for the trial and punishment of 'any individual or group of individuals, or organisation, or any member of any armed, defence or auxiliary forces, irrespective of his nationality',[307] no intention to try Pakistani nationals has been expressed. The trial of Pakistani nationals would, however, also depend on extradition because a voluntary surrender is very unlikely.

The Tribunal passed its first charge framing order on 3 November 2011 and the first judgment approximately three years after its establishment on 28 February 2013.

3.4 Controversies surrounding the ICT

The ICT has evoked strong controversy. Bangladeshi political parties, lawyers and journalists, as well as human rights organisations, have expressed concerns regarding the trials before the ICT. Nevertheless, the ICT also finds approval.

The Jamaat-e-Islami party has accused the Awami League of taking political revenge through the trials before the ICT because most of the accused and convicts are high-ranking party leaders.[308] The party denies the involvement of its members in crimes committed during the Liberation War and argues that its leaders were not

---

304 *Bdnews24*, Bangladesh Keeps One 1971 War Crimes Tribunal in Operation, 15 September 2015.
305 *The Daily Star*, Amend War Crimes Act to Try Jamaat, 16 November 2014.
306 *The Daily Star*, Amend War Crimes Act to Try Jamaat, 16 November 2014.
307 Section 3(1) ICT Act.
308 *Jamaat-e-Islami*, War Crimes Law and the Constitution.

Part II: Towards an International Crimes Tribunal

among the 195 prisoners of war and that they were also not tried under the Collaborators Order.[309]

The BNP has not publicly opposed the trials in a general manner although one of its members, Salauddin Quader Chowdhury, was sentenced to death. The silence can be explained by the fact that the trials are extremely popular in society.[310] Yet, the party has criticised the fairness of the proceedings before the ICT and demanded an immediate suspension of the trials as well as amendments of the ICT Act in accordance with international standards.[311]

Concerns were also expressed by the Bangladeshi intelligentsia about the contempt proceedings against the journalist David Bergman. In a written communication, 52 people of different professions, including professors, journalists, human rights activists and lawyers, criticised the ICT for using contempt proceedings against Bergman to restrict freedom of expression.[312] In answer to this, the ICT initiated contempt proceedings against the signees of the statement and an order was passed against 23 of them who did not deliver an unconditional apology to the Tribunal.[313] One contemnor was punished with one hour of imprisonment and a fine of 5,000 taka; the others were exonerated.[314] The ICT's very strong reactions to public criticism repress an open and critical discourse on the topic, and it is therefore difficult to assess the extent to which the ICT enjoys approval in the country.

Nevertheless, the Shahbag movement has clearly shown that there is considerable support for the ICT in society although, at the same time, it has revealed its polarising effect. The movement began in reaction to the trial of Abdul Quader Molla, who was sentenced to life imprisonment in February 2013. Hundreds of thousands of protesters demanded the death penalty for the accused and generally for all war criminals as well as a ban on the Jamaat-e-Islami party. The atheist blogger, Ahmed Rajib Haider, who was also an initiator of the movement, was brutally murdered on 15 February 2013.[315]

---

309 See the official statement by Jamaat-e-Islami on the trials of party leaders: *Jamaat-e-Islami*, Allegations of War Crimes against the Leaders of Jamaat, p. 4.
310 *The Economist*, Final Sentence, 17 September 2013.
311 *The Daily Star*, Stop War Crimes Trial, 4 December 2011.
312 The full text of the statement is cited in ICT 2, *The State v. The Editor, the Daily Prothom Alo and others*, misc. case no. 04/2014, Order, 10 June 2015, para. 74.
313 ICT 2, *The State v. The Editor, the Daily Prothom Alo and others*, misc. case no. 04/2014, Order, 10 June 2015.
314 ICT 2, *The State v. The Editor, the Daily Prothom Alo and others*, misc. case no. 04/2014, Order, 10 June 2015, paras. 121, 131.
315 *The Daily Star*, Blogger Brutally Killed, 16 February 2013. The trial against 8 accused started in May 2015 and is still going on. The accused are leaders and followers of the banned Islamic extremist organisation Ansarulla Bangla Team, see *The Daily Star*, Trial Begins with Father's Deposition, 29 May 2015.

On the other hand, the announcement of the death verdict against Maulana Delwar Hossain Sayeedi triggered demonstrations by opponents of the verdict, among them many supporters of Jamaat-e-Islami.[316] The situation began to escalate. In April and May 2013, the organisation Hefazat-e-Islam (Protectorate of Islam) began protests to promote the implementation of their agenda. The organisation defines itself as a non-political Islamic organisation promoting Islam in Bangladesh. However, some of its members are linked with political parties.[317] The BNP as well requested its followers to support Hefazat-e-Islam.[318] The movement was a backlash against the Shahbag movement, which Hefazat-e-Islami accused of being atheistic and anti-Islamic.[319] Hefazat-e-Islami's 13-point agenda included the prosecution of atheist bloggers and the enactment of a blasphemy law imposing the death penalty.[320] During the period between February and May 2013, there was mass street violence which resulted in 150 dead and 2,000 injured.[321]

Opinion polls conducted by AC Nielsen in 2012 show that the ICT had considerable support but that this was not the case with the Shahbag movement.[322] Of the interviewees who knew of the ICT, 62 % considered the trials unfair or very unfair.[323] Interestingly, this did not influence opinion on the continuation of the trials: 86 % declared that they wanted the Tribunal to continue,[324] but only 31 % of those who knew of the Shahbag movement said that their family and friends supported or highly supported it.[325] The poll also revealed the correlation between party affiliation and the Shahbag movement: most Awami League supporters were in favour of the movement, whereas most BNP supporters opposed it.[326]

In 2011, Amnesty International addressed several issues in a letter sent to Justice Nizamul Huq, chairman of Tribunal 1 until 2012. The organisation accused the ICT of implementing a victors' justice due to the fact that trials had been initiated only against BNP and Jamaat-e-Islami leaders whereas those who supported the country's independence were not being investigated.[327] It also criticised the imposition of the death

---

316 *Human Rights Watch*, Blood on the Streets, p. 2.
317 *Human Rights Watch*, Blood on the Streets, p. 21.
318 *Human Rights Watch*, Blood on the Streets, p. 21, n. 36.
319 *Khalidi*, Behind the Rise of Bangladesh's Hifazat, Al Jazeera, 9 May 2013.
320 *Human Rights Watch*, Blood on the Streets, p. 3.
321 *Human Rights Watch*, Blood on the Streets, p. 1.
322 The original article, published in New Age on 11 September 2013, is no longer available but the article is cited in: *Bergman*, Nielsen/Democracy International Polls.
323 *Bergman*, Nielsen/Democracy International Polls.
324 *Bergman*, Nielsen/Democracy International Polls.
325 *Bergman*, Nielsen/Democracy International Polls.
326 *Bergman*, Nielsen/Democracy International Polls.
327 *Amnesty International*, Letter to the Chairman of the ICT, 21 June 2011.

penalty, the lack of witness protection and the absence of a legal provision guaranteeing the presumption of innocence.[328] The lack of fair trial standards in the proceedings before the ICT and the imposition of the death penalty was also criticised by Human Rights Watch.[329]

Several foreign experts have provided an opinion as to whether the ICT Act is consistent with international criminal law standards. British barrister Michael Beloff examined the 1973 version of the ICT Act and concluded that several provisions are inconsistent with international standards and with the Constitution of Bangladesh.[330] The War Crimes Committee of the International Bar Association gave specific recommendations to amend the ICT Act, as amended 2009, so that the rights of the accused at the investigation stage as well as during the trial are assured in accordance with international standards.[331]

In 2015, Geoffrey Robertson raised concerns regarding the impartiality of the trials, the imposition of the death penalty and several procedural flaws.[332] He also argued that, in order to overcome the deficiencies of the trials, the establishment of an ad hoc international criminal tribunal or a similar international justice mechanism would be elementary.[333]

The Tribunal hit the headlines in December 2012 when *The Economist* published insights on the Tribunal's work based on the content of more than 17 hours of telephone conversations and 230 emails exchanged between Nizamul Huq, former chairman of Tribunal 1, and Ahmed Ziauddin, a lawyer of Bangladeshi origin based in Brussels.[334] In these conversations, Huq explained that the government pressured him to deliver the verdict against Sayeedi on 'Victory Day' (16 December).[335] He further confided to Ziauddin that the chairman of the Appellate Division held out the prospect of a promotion if he would deliver fast verdicts.[336] The conversations also indicate that Ziauddin's role exceeded that of an ordinary advisor to the Tribunal and suggest

---

328 *Amnesty International*, Letter to the Chairman of the ICT, 21 June 2011.
329 *Human Rights Watch*, Bangladesh: Halt Execution of War Crimes Accused.
330 *Beloff*, International Crimes (Tribunals) Act, 1973, p. 2. It has to be observed though that these findings result from a request for advice from the legal department of Jamaat-e-Islami Bangladesh.
331 *War Crimes Committee of the International Bar Association*, Consistency of the ICT Act 1973 with International Standards, pp. 2–3.
332 *Robertson,* Report on the ICT Bangladesh.
333 *Robertson*, Report on the ICT Bangladesh, p. 123.
334 *The Economist*, The Trial of the Birth of a Nation, 15 December 2012. The conversations can be found here: http://tribunalleaks.blogspot.de, accessed 7 March 2016.
335 *The Economist*, The Trial of the Birth of a Nation, 15 December 2012.
336 http://tribunalleaks.blogspot.de, accessed 7 March 2016.

that the lawyer directly contributed to the drafting of indictments and orders.[337] At the same time, Ziauddin also advised the prosecution team and, apparently, there were regular exchanges between Ziauddin, the prosecution and Huq.[338] Such collaboration clearly leads to conflicts of interest. Journalists from the newspaper contacted Huq and Ziauddin after receiving the material and both confirmed that they had communicated frequently.[339]

In answer to the reporting of these materials, Tribunal 1, with Huq as chairman, initiated contempt proceedings against Adam Roberts, South Asia Bureau Chief of *The Economist* and Rob Gifford, Chief Editor of *The Economist* on 6 December 2012.[340] There was, however, no proof that Huq's computer was hacked by any employee of *The Economist*, and the case was therefore dismissed. Nevertheless, the Tribunal noted that the contemnors, after receiving the relevant material, had unlawfully called Huq for a statement.[341] For that reason, the Tribunal established general rules for the media and determined that no journalist or person is allowed to contact a judge by telephone or in person and that a journalist may obtain information about a specific case only with the help of a lawyer.[342] It further emphasised that the press should not circulate 'ordinary news as a big sensational news about the court proceedings'.[343] The conversations between Huq and Ziauddin create severe doubts regarding the independence of the Tribunal and, despite Huq's resignation, the ICT has certainly suffered a loss of credibility.

The ICT and the Liberation War in general continue to be very sensitive issues that polarise society. Approval or criticism of the Tribunal is very often linked to political orientation. But even if there is no association with any political party, critical comments are usually perceived as support for the opposition. The political environment puts the Tribunal under pressure and poses a risk to its independence.

---

337 *The Economist*, The Trial of the Birth of a Nation, 15 December 2012.
338 *The Economist*, The Trial of the Birth of a Nation, 15 December 2012.
339 *The Economist*, The Trial of the Birth of a Nation, 15 December 2012.
340 ICT 1, *The State v. Robert Adams and another*, misc. case no. 17/2012, Order, 29 December 2013.
341 ICT 1, *The State v. Robert Adams and another*, misc. case no. 17/2012, Order, 29 December 2013, p. 5.
342 ICT 1, *The State v. Robert Adams and another*, misc. case no. 17/2012, Order, 29 December 2013, p. 5.
343 ICT 1, *The State v. Robert Adams and another*, misc. case no. 17/2012, Order, 29 December 2013, p. 6.

Part III: The ICT in comparison to other accountability mechanisms

Unlike the name 'International Crimes Tribunal' would suggest, the ICT has been established as a domestic tribunal. This means that it is part of the Bangladeshi judicial system and its basis is domestic law. The decision to hold perpetrators of international crimes[344] accountable through the domestic judicial system is not self-evident. Different means of international involvement in the trials could have been considered. However, Bangladesh's decision to implement a domestic solution has a considerable impact on the applicable legal sources, the Tribunal's jurisdiction, the participating stakeholders and also the financial situation.

1 The different accountability mechanisms and their applicability in the context of Bangladesh

Different accountability mechanisms for the trial of perpetrators of international crimes can be employed. Generally, four types of tribunals can be taken into consideration: the International Criminal Court (ICC), a hybrid tribunal, an ad hoc tribunal and a domestic tribunal. Under certain conditions, perpetrators of international crimes can also be held accountable through domestic courts of third states. Beyond that, truth and reconciliation commissions can be employed as an accountability mechanism although they are not aimed at punishment. The choice between these mechanisms depends on several factors and determines the nature of the respective tribunal. Nevertheless, not all of them would have been a realistic option for the trials of perpetrators of crimes committed during Bangladesh's Liberation War.

1.1 The International Criminal Court

The ICC is the first permanent court to try perpetrators of international crimes and it was set up as an independent international organisation. On 17 July 1998, 120 states adopted the legal basis for the establishment of the International Criminal Court, the Rome Statute. It came into force after its ratification by 60 states on 1 July 2002. To date, 122 countries are states parties to the Rome Statute. Bangladesh signed the

---

344 There is no static definition of the term 'international crime', see *Cryer et al.*, International Criminal Law, 3. edn, p. 4. However, throughout this thesis the term is used to refer to the four core crimes: genocide, crimes against humanity, war crimes and the crime of aggression (called crimes against peace in the ICT Act).

Rome Statute on 16 September 1999 and ratified it on 23 March 2010 as the first South Asian state party.[345]

1.1.1 Jurisdiction *ratione temporis*

With regard to the crimes committed in 1971, the ICC lacks temporal jurisdiction. The Rome Statute restricts the ICC's jurisdiction *ratione temporis* to those crimes committed after the Court's establishment.[346] It therefore incorporates the principle of non-retroactivity into the Statute. As a consequence, when a state party signs the Rome Statute after its entry into force in 2002, the Court's jurisdiction over those new member states is restricted to crimes committed after the date of accession.[347] An exception to this rule is the declaration under Article 12(3) of the Rome Statute. By this declaration, a state can accept the exercise of the Court's jurisdiction with respect to crimes committed prior to its accession. However, even by this declaration, the jurisdiction of the ICC cannot be extended to crimes committed before the entry into force of the Rome Statute.[348] The ICC, therefore, has jurisdiction exclusively over crimes committed in Bangladesh since its accession to the Rome Statute in 2010.

1.1.2 Principle of complementarity

The ICC was established as a court of last resort. Thus, primarily, each state is responsible for the prosecution of international crimes committed on its territory. This decision is based mainly on the fact that domestic trials tend to be more efficient, less expensive and faster in their implementation.[349]

Whenever a state avails itself of its obligation to prosecute, the ICC is precluded from intervention. On the other hand, a case may nevertheless be admissible before the ICC if the investigating or prosecuting state is unwilling or unable genuinely to carry out the investigation or prosecution.[350] In the context of Bangladesh, admissibility based on unwillingness or inability could become relevant for future trials. If the trials before the ICT lack basic fair trial standards and if perpetrators of crimes com-

---

345 http://www.icc-cpi.int/en_menus/asp/states%20parties/asian%20states/Pages/bangladesh.aspx, accessed 12 August 2014.
346 Article 11(1) of the Rome Statute.
347 Article 11(2) of the Rome Statute.
348 *Cryer et al.*, International Criminal Law, 3. edn, p. 169; *Triffterer/Williams*, Commentary Rome Statute, 2. edn, Article 11, marginal no. 2.
349 *Werle/Jessberger*, International Criminal Law, 3. edn, marginal no. 264, *Cryer et al.*, International Criminal Law, 3. edn, p. 154.
350 Articles 17(1)(a) and 17(1)(b) of the Rome Statute.

mitted after accession to the Rome Statute are tried under the same conditions in the future, the cases could remain admissible to the ICC based on inability.

There is, however, disagreement regarding the question of whether a violation of fair trial standards in a domestic trial renders a case admissible before the ICC due to inability or unwillingness and, if it does, which standard must be applied to assess domestic trials. The prevailing opinion is that domestic proceedings that do not respect a certain level of fair trial standards render a case admissible before the ICC under Article 17 of the Rome Statute.[351] Nevertheless, the ICC does not have the function of a human rights court and assesses domestic proceedings only in cases of gross due process violations.[352] This position is supported by the drafters of the informal expert paper on the principle of complementarity commissioned by the Office of the Prosecutor (OTP).[353] The authors deduce from the word 'genuinely' that proceedings need to be conducted with 'a basic level of objective quality'.[354] Although human rights standards are considered for the assessment of the criterion 'genuinely', full compliance with all standards is not required.[355] Consequently, only a lack of the most basic due process rights leads to admissibility of a case before the ICC.[356] Beyond that, the mere lack of resources does not allow the conclusion that trials are not conducted genuinely.[357] Already during the drafting process of the Rome Statute, the admissibility provision was criticised for working in favour of developed countries and rendering the admissibility challenge difficult for poor countries because the claim of an ineffective legal system could be made more easily for reasons of poverty.[358] This moderate interpretation of the 'due process thesis'[359] helps to balance the demand for compliance with fair trial standards and the concerns of countries with fragile judicial systems.

In contrast, others see the competence of the ICC in this regard as more restricted and argue that it must consider human rights standards only when they manifest the

---

351 *Ellis*, Fla. JIL, 2002, 15(2), p. 215, at 237–238; *Fry*, CLF, 2012, 23(1), p. 35, at 45; *Kleffner*, JICJ, 2003, 1(1), p. 86, at 112; *Stahn*, CLF, 2008, 19(1), p. 87, at 99; *Triffterer/Williams/Schabas*, Commentary Rome Statute, 2. edn, Article 17, marginal no. 29; *Office of the Prosecutor*, Informal Expert Paper.
352 *Office of the Prosecutor*, Informal Expert Paper, para. 23.
353 *Office of the Prosecutor*, Informal Expert Paper, paras. 21 ff.
354 *Office of the Prosecutor*, Informal Expert Paper, para. 23.
355 *Office of the Prosecutor*, Informal Expert Paper, para. 23; *Stigen*, ICC and National Jurisdictions, p. 229.
356 *Fry*, CLF, 2012, 23(1), p. 35, at 42.
357 *Office of the Prosecutor*, Informal Expert Paper, para. 23.
358 *Schabas*, International Criminal Court, 4. edn, p. 196.
359 This notion was introduced by *Heller*, CLF, 2006, 17(3), p. 255, at 260.

Part III: The ICT in comparison to other accountability mechanisms

intention to shield a person from justice.[360] This approach is based on the intention of the state parties behind the creation of the ICC, which was aimed at ending impunity but not at establishing a mechanism to survey general due process in domestic proceedings.[361] Heller argues that the due process thesis is also not in line with the Rome Statute and its drafting history.[362] Article 17 explicitly determines that both criteria (unwillingness and inability) apply only whenever prosecutions are hampered due to due process deficits; they do not apply when the violation of fair trial standards leads to easier convictions.[363] Article 17(2) does not intend to protect the accused but to protect society from the impunity of the accused.[364] Moreover, it is argued that remedies for human rights violations should be sought primarily through the respective human rights bodies.[365]

The due process thesis also faces practical challenges regarding the definition of the degree of international standards that must be met before unwillingness or inability can be assumed. While it is already difficult to draw the exact line between fair und unfair, different legal cultures further complicate the determination.[366] Mégret and Samson argue that this line is definitely crossed when trials can no longer be considered trials because the outcome is predetermined or irrelevant.[367] In these cases, imprisonment and the death penalty equal arbitrary detention and extrajudicial executions.[368]

Intervention by the ICC in cases of fair trial standards violations can also create further conflicts. One of these is that it provides perpetrators of international crimes with priority treatment whereas low-level perpetrators or perpetrators of 'ordinary crimes' have to accept poor-quality domestic legal systems and the violation of their procedural rights. It also means that high-level perpetrators can escape the death penalty; a privilege others will be denied. This line of reasoning is also brought up frequently in the context of Bangladesh. The international community speaks up and criticises the flawed trials and the death penalty only with regard to the accused under the ICT Act. According to many Bangladeshis, however, the trials before the ICT re-

---

360 *Cryer et al.*, International Criminal Law, 3. edn, p. 157; *Carnero Rojo*, LJIL, 2005, 18(4), p. 829, at 853.
361 *Carnero Rojo*, LJIL, 2005, 18(4), p. 829, at 854.
362 *Heller*, CLF, 2006, 17(3), p. 255, at 260 ff.
363 *Heller*, CLF, 2006, 17(3), p. 255, at 261.
364 *Mégret*, in: *Stahn/El Zeidy* (eds), ICC and Complementarity, Vol. 1, p. 361, at 372; *Stigen*, ICC and National Jurisdictions, p. 221.
365 *Mégret/Samson*, JICL, 2013, 11(3), p. 571, at 578–579.
366 *Mégret/Samson*, JICL, 2013, 11(3), p. 571, at 579–580.
367 *Mégret/Samson*, JICL, 2013, 11(3), p. 571, at 586.
368 *Mégret/Samson*, JICL, 2013, 11(3), p. 571, at 586.

1 The different accountability mechanisms

flect the entire domestic judicial system and, against this background, it is incomprehensible why high-level perpetrators should enjoy privileges.[369]

Despite several problems arising from the due process thesis, its application also to cases in which due process deficits lead to faster convictions is preferable. In this way, the complementarity principle could function as an incentive to improve domestic legal systems in order to avoid the ICC's intervention. Nevertheless, an intervention by the ICC should be done cautiously and not lead to the Court exceeding its mandate. So far, there has been no admissibility challenge in which fair trial standards have become relevant. However, in the case against Saif Al-Islam Gaddafi the Pre-Trial Chamber found that Libya's judicial system lacked the capacity to provide adequate witness protection, to appoint an independent defence counsel for the accused, to obtain evidence and to transfer the accused to a governmental detention facility, and concluded that the judicial system was unavailable and, therefore, unable to carry out genuine proceedings at the domestic level.[370] The Chamber thus based its decision not on the absence of certain legal provisions but on the practical problems of the Libyan judicial system.[371]

The Appellate Division of the Supreme Court of Bangladesh dealt with this as a marginal issue. With regard to the principle of complementarity, the Division held that the legal system of Bangladesh is strong enough to try the perpetrators of the respective crimes at the domestic level.[372] It further argued that Bangladesh was not unwilling or unable to genuinely hold the trials because it had already started with the prosecution of perpetrators of international crimes through the ICT.[373]

To date, no investigations by the OTP have taken place in Bangladesh although some cases were brought to the attention of the ICC Prosecutor in 2014. British barrister Toby Cadman submitted a communication to the Prosecutor demanding the initiation of proceedings *proprio motu* regarding extrajudicial killings, torture and arbitrary detention against opposition supporters in 2013 in Bangladesh.[374] Cadman referred to the incidents of street violence and the brutal intervention by the police and the Rapid Action Battalion[375] (RAB) during the Shahbag protests but also to arbitrary detentions, forced disappearances and murder employed as measures to repress the

---

369 *Bergman*, Bangladesh War Trials: Justice or Politics?, Al Jazeera, 23 December 2014.
370 ICC (PTC), *Prosecutor v. Gaddafi and Al-Senussi*, Decision on the Admissibility of the Case against Saif Al-Islam Gaddafi, 31 May 2013, para. 205.
371 ICC (PTC), *Prosecutor v. Gaddafi and Al-Senussi*, Decision on the admissibility of the case against Saif Al-Islam Gaddafi, 31 May 2013, para. 205.
372 SC (AD), *Molla v. The Chief Prosecutor*, Appeal Judgment, 17 September 2013, p. 90.
373 SC (AD), *Molla v. The Chief Prosecutor*, Appeal Judgment, 17 September 2013, p. 92.
374 *Cadman*, Communication, 31 January 2014.
375 The RAB is a special paramilitary force of the Bangladesh Police established in 2004. Several human rights organisations have criticised the RAB and its systematic abuses. See

63

opposition.[376] According to Cadman, crimes against humanity and incitement to commit genocide were committed and supported by the government. Given that these cases are not investigated currently at the domestic level, there is scope for admissibility before the ICC. However, in 2016, the OTP of the ICC rejected the allegations in a letter to the Minister of Foreign Affairs of Bangladesh, arguing that there was no legal basis for the allegations.[377] However, the letter with the exact reasons for the rejection of the allegations was not published.

In cases in which perpetrators of international crimes are tried at the domestic level in the future, admissibility conflicts might arise if the trials are not held in accordance with fair trial standards. Nevertheless, an intervention would also depend on the scope of the due process thesis. However, even if the findings in Part IV show that the current trials before the ICT violate fair trial standards, it cannot be assumed that this will also hold true for future trials. Nonetheless, it might be an indication. At any rate, admissibility under Article 17 would require a careful examination of the specific circumstances.

1.2 Ad hoc international criminal tribunals

Two ad hoc international criminal tribunals have been established to date: the International Criminal Tribunal for the former Yugoslavia (ICTY) and the International Criminal Tribunal for Rwanda (ICTR). Both tribunals are subsidiary organs of the United Nations Security Council. The tribunals were created through UN Security Council Resolutions[378] under Chapter VII of the United Nations Charter to deal with serious violations of international humanitarian law committed on the territory of former Yugoslavia[379] and with the massacre of the Tutsi in Rwanda[380]. The Resolutions were passed on the basis of Article 39 of the UN Charter, which allows the Security Council to take measures to maintain and restore international peace and international security. An intervention of the Security Council thus requires a current threat to peace and, as a consequence, this form of accountability mechanism has a restricted scope of application. In post-conflict situations, the Security Council can intervene based on

---

Human Rights Watch, Letter to Bangladesh's Prime Minister Sheikh Hasina Wajed, Re: Bangladesh Rapid Action Battalion, 18 July 2014.
376 *Cadman*, Communication, 31 January 2014, paras. 18, 23.
377 *The Daily Star*, Int'l Court in Hague Rejects Allegations, 26 May 2016.
378 Security Council Resolution 827, 25 May 1993 (UN Doc. S/RES 827) for the ICTY; Security Council Resolution 955, 8 November 1994 (UN Doc. S/RES/955) for the ICTR.
379 Articles 1 and 8 of the ICTY Statute.
380 Articles 1 and 7 of the ICTR Statute.

Article 39 of the UN Charter under the condition that a renewed outbreak of violence is an effective risk.[381]

These requirements have evidently not been fulfilled in the case of Bangladesh. The Liberation War ended more than 40. For that reason, there is no typical post-conflict situation in the country. Beyond the legal requirements that remain unfulfilled, it is likely that there would also have been little political interest from the international community to establish an ad hoc international criminal tribunal in Bangladesh given the relatively insignificant impact of the Liberation War today and, of course, the horrendous costs that ad hoc tribunals incur.

1.3 Mixed tribunals

The idea of mixed or hybrid tribunals was developed during the negotiations between Cambodia and the United Nations concerning a tribunal for Cambodia in 1999 and was first implemented with the Special Panels for Serious Crimes in East Timor in 2000.[382] Mixed tribunals are composed of domestic and international judges and prosecutors, and they apply international as well as national law. The concept of mixed tribunals was mainly introduced to overcome several weak points of the ad hoc tribunals: the high costs, the long proceedings, their distance to the territories in which the crimes were committed and the resulting lack of impact on the population.[383]

A mixed tribunal would have been a feasible accountability mechanism to deal with the crimes from 1971. Although this possibility was discussed when debates about initiating trials arose, in practice, it was never seriously considered and no preparatory steps were taken. Unlike in other cases, e. g. in Cambodia or more recently in Sri Lanka, no UN Expert Group was ever established to assess the status of accountability in the country. Demands for a hybrid tribunal or, more generally, some form of international involvement were, if at all, raised only by individuals, but the idea never had broader support.

1.4 Domestic trials

Perpetrators of international crimes can also be prosecuted through domestic courts without international involvement. Whereas domestic trials have often been conducted through the ordinary domestic judicial system, the establishment of ad hoc tribunals at the domestic level has been realised only sporadically. At first glance, it

---

381 *Simma/Khan/Nolte/Paulus/Krisch*, UN Charter Commentary, Vol. 2, 3. edn, Article 39, marginal no. 13.
382 *Linton*, CLF, 2001, 12(2), p. 185, at 185.
383 *Cassese*, International Criminal Law, 3. edn, p. 265.

seems to be the accountability mechanism that requires less effort because no new infrastructure is required. As outlined above, domestic trials are also incentivised under the Rome Statute through the principle of complementarity. Prosecutions at the domestic level, however, require that the state in which the crimes were committed has the political will and the legal framework to try the respective perpetrators. Although domestic tribunals usually have a greater impact on society because they are closer to it, they also have to deal with the challenges arising from the fact that they directly form part of the domestic judiciary.

Problems arise whenever states have not implemented definitions of international crimes into domestic law and are thus forced to apply general criminal law. Likewise, domestic legislations often employ definitions of international crimes which differ from those that are internationally recognised and which extend the scope of application.[384] This can lead to strong divergence of international criminal law standards.[385]

In post-conflict situations, prosecutors and judges of the previous regime are often still in office and political influence on the trials is frequent.[386] Beyond that, domestic courts bear a higher risk of lacking impartiality because the judges are linked with the respective country and might be swayed by public reactions to the verdicts or political ideologies.[387] In contrast, for international staff it is easier to resist psychological pressure.[388]

In international criminal law, cases also tend to be extremely complex and the workload can be very high, exceeding the capacities of the domestic judicial system.[389] This becomes particularly relevant in states with an already overloaded and ailing judiciary.

1.5 Truth and reconciliation commissions

The establishment of a truth and reconciliation commission has not been considered in Bangladesh. It has certainly never been discussed as an alternative to trials. In the Bangladeshi context, it is particularly difficult to imagine that an accountability mechanism that does not impose punishment would find sufficient acceptance in society. The trial of war criminals is extremely emotionally charged in Bangladesh and, as outlined above, the call for the death penalty for war criminals formed the basis of the Shahbag movement. Nevertheless, as a complementary mechanism, a truth commis-

---

[384] For examples of extensions of the list of groups in the definition of genocide, see *Rikhof*, CLF, 2009, 20(1), p. 1, at 44.
[385] *Rikhof*, CLF, 2009, 20(1), p. 1, at 51.
[386] *Dickinson*, AJIL, 2003, 97(2), p. 295, at 301.
[387] *Cassese*, International Criminal Law, 3. edn, p. 267.
[388] *Cassese*, International Criminal Law, 3. edn, p. 268.
[389] *Williams*, Criminal Tribunals, p. 18.

sion could certainly help to improve the outreach of the trials and contribute to an open discourse on the events of 1971.

1.6 Trials in third states

Perpetrators of international crimes can also be brought to trial before a court in third states based on the principle of universal jurisdiction. The jurisdiction is triggered solely by the nature of the crime, and the state that prosecutes has no further link, that is, it can prosecute irrespective of the nationality of the accused and the victim, irrespective of the territory in which the crime was committed and without any other link to the crime.[390] The interests of the prosecuting state are thus not directly threatened by the crime committed.

With regard to Bangladesh, trials in third countries could take place under the principle of universal jurisdiction simultaneously to the trials before the ICT. The specific requirements for prosecutions depend on the implementation of universal jurisdiction in domestic law. This could require the presence of the suspect in the country in order to trigger investigations or the absence of a will to prosecute by the state with the stronger link, in this case Bangladesh.

In the past, alleged perpetrators of crimes committed in 1971 were investigated in the UK. A Channel 4 documentary named 'The War Crimes File' made this issue public in 1995.[391] The documentary reported on three alleged war criminals and former members of auxiliary forces: Chowdhury Mueen Uddin, Abu Sayeed and Lutfur Rahman. All of them resided in the UK and had acquired British citizenship. For this reason, these investigations were not linked to the principle of universal jurisdiction because a link existed due to the suspects being British nationals. However, the investigations did not result in charges. Chowdhury Mueen Uddin was sentenced to death in absentia by the ICT in 2013. It is not clear whether Bangladesh requested the extradition of the accused but, in any case, due to the possibility of the imposition of the death penalty, the UK would have denied such a request.

To date, no trial in a third country has taken place. Since most of the perpetrators reside in Bangladesh and Pakistan, it is also extremely unlikely that prosecutions will take place based on universal jurisdiction in the future.

---

390 *Cryer et al.*, International Criminal Law, 3. edn, p. 57.
391 The documentary was broadcast on 3 May 1995 by the British Channel 4.

1.7 Decision-making process in Bangladesh

Bangladesh opted for a domestic judicial body to try the perpetrators of crimes committed during the Liberation War.

Different accountability mechanisms were discussed, albeit mostly internally, before the ICT's establishment. Nevertheless, the debates were rather short-lived and it soon became apparent that international involvement was perceived as a drawback rather than a support.

Linton expressed concerns regarding fair trial standards in domestic trials given that the Liberation War is still a politically-sensitive issue and she considered an internationalised tribunal the best option to overcome the problems of the domestic judiciary.[392] She also highlighted that amnesties and pardons may create a problem with domestic law and recommended the revision of the 1973 Act.[393] At the same time, she acknowledged that a domestic tribunal might be more meaningful to the Bangladeshi population because national experts are more aware of the situation and more committed to their country.[394] Concerns were also expressed regarding the capacity of the Bangladeshi system to cope with the complex trials of those accused of international crimes due to the weakness of the domestic judicial system and the major problem of corruption.[395] In Cambodia, the same concerns were a crucial factor that led to the United Nations Group of Experts to strongly recommend the implementation of an international tribunal under the control of the United Nations. The Group of Experts came to the conclusion that the importance of corruption in the legal system and the political influence on the judiciary made it impossible for local judges to act independently from this pressure.[396]

At a very early stage of the debate on the trial of war criminals, involvement of the United Nations was considered and expressly requested. Bangladesh's law minister favoured international participation in order to ensure more transparency.[397] Assistance from the UN was sought in the form of international war crimes experts to assist the government in the process of prosecuting the war criminals.[398] However, this pro-

---

392 *Linton*, in: *Hoque* (ed.), Genocide Conference Papers, 2009, p. 155, at 159; *Linton*, CLF, 2010, 21(2), p. 191, at 210, n. 86.
393 *Linton*, in: *Hoque* (ed.), Genocide Conference Papers, 2009, p. 155, at 159.
394 *Linton*, in: *Hoque* (ed.), Genocide Conference Papers, 2009, p. 155, at 159.
395 *D'Costa*, Nationbuilding, p. 159.
396 Report of the Group of Experts for Cambodia established pursuant to General Assembly Resolution 52/135, 1999 (UN Doc. A/53/850), para 133.
397 Statement of Bangladesh's former Law Minister Shafiq Ahmed quoted in: *Ullah*, in: *Hoque* (ed.), Genocide Conference Papers, 2009, p. 139, at 141.
398 https://www.amnesty.org/en/latest/news/2009/04/un-provides-welcome-support-bangladesh-war-crimes-investigations-20090407/, accessed 18 August 2015.

cess was never initiated. There was soon a strong resistance to the idea of introducing international staff into the Bangladeshi judicial system[399] and international involvement in the trials was perceived as an affront to Bangladesh's sovereignty[400]. Others were concerned about the international politics that international participation would bring into play.[401]

International relations played a role in Bangladesh's decision against international involvement, too. There was very strong resistance from Pakistan and its allies, in particular Saudi Arabia which is an important commercial partner of Bangladesh due to the large number of Bangladeshi migrant workers under contract there.[402] Nevertheless, even the domestic trials have, though rather late, disturbed the diplomatic relations between Bangladesh and Pakistan. Pakistan reacted strongly to the execution of Chowdhury and Mujahid in 2015 after the delivery of the appeal judgments. In a first statement, the Ministry of Foreign Affairs of Pakistan expressed its deep concern regarding these executions and requested Bangladesh to comply with the approach of reconciliation taken in the Tripartite Agreement.[403] The government of Bangladesh protested against this inadequate statement and reminded Pakistan of its obligations to bring the 195 war criminals to justice in Pakistan.[404] It emphasised that the verdicts were the result of an independent, fair, impartial and transparent judicial process.[405] Pakistan thereupon delivered another statement denying its responsibility for the crimes committed in 1971.[406]

2 The domestic character of the International Crimes Tribunal in Bangladesh

Despite the mooted possibility of international involvement and the rather short-lived and mostly domestic debate on international involvement, the ICT in Bangladesh was ultimately set up as a purely domestic tribunal.

---

399 *Linton*, CLF, 2010, 21(2), p. 191, at 210, n. 86.
400 *Linton*, CLF, 2010, 21(2), p. 191, at 210, n. 86.
401 *Rahman/Billah*, in: *Hoque* (ed.), Genocide Conference Papers, 2009, p. 82, at 89.
402 *Linton*, CLF, 2010, 21(2), p. 191, at 210, n. 86.
403 http://www.mofa.gov.pk/pr-details.php?mm=MzI3MA, accessed 11 December 2015.
404 http://www.mofa.gov.bd/media/bangladesh-conveys-strong-protest-against-remarks-spokesperson-pakistan-foreign-ministry, accessed 11 December 2015.
405 http://www.mofa.gov.bd/media/bangladesh-conveys-strong-protest-against-remarks-spokesperson-pakistan-foreign-ministry, accessed 11 December 2015.
406 http://www.mofa.gov.pk/pr-details.php?mm=MzI5MQ, accessed 11 December 2015.

Part III: The ICT in comparison to other accountability mechanisms

2.1 Structure of the ICT

Although the ICT is part of the domestic judicial system, it is mostly independent and, apart from the absence of a separate appellate division, it comes with an infrastructure that is completely separate from the ordinary judiciary. It is situated in a separate building (the Old High Court Building), has a separate prosecution team, with judges working exclusively for the ICT and a separate Investigation Agency. It has its permanent seat in Dhaka. The ICT follows an adversarial system like all the other courts in Bangladesh.

Pursuant to Section 6(1) of the ICT Act, the government is entitled to set up one or more tribunals consisting of a chairman and not less than two and a maximum four members. In accordance with this provision, one tribunal currently operates, consisting of a chairman and two members appointed by the government. Also, Tribunal 2, deactivated since 15 September 2015, consisted of one chairman and two members. Those eligible are Supreme Court judges, former Supreme Court judges and judges who are qualified as Supreme Court judges.[407] The 2009 amendment of the ICT Act excluded from eligibility judges qualified as members of the General Court Martial pursuant to Section 80 of the Army Act.[408] In practice, senior Supreme Court judges work in the ICT. Age plays an important role in this context because, in Bangladeshi culture, respect is granted based on age and position and older persons automatically enjoy more authority. The Tribunal takes decisions by majority.[409] If one member is unable to attend a session in the course of a trial, the Tribunal is empowered to continue the trial with only one member.[410]

The government is also entitled to appoint the members of the prosecution.[411] The ICT Act provides no rules on their eligibility and also gives the government the power to determine the terms and conditions for the prosecution. Neither does the Act impose a limit on the number of prosecutors. One member of the prosecution team is appointed as Chief Prosecutor.[412] In practice, the age structure of the prosecution team is mixed and several young professionals form part of the team.

The Registrar of the Tribunal is responsible for the office of the Tribunal, that is, its administration and organisation. Its competences are determined in Chapter VII and Chapter VIII of the RoP. The office consists of the Registrar and a Deputy Regis-

---

407 Section 6(2) of the ICT Act.
408 For the full text of the Army Act, 1952, see http://bdlaws.minlaw.gov.bd/pdf_part.php?act_name=&vol=&id=248, accessed 26 September 2015.
409 Section 6(7) of the ICT Act.
410 On the problems arising from this provision, see p 232.
411 Section 8(1) of the ICT Act.
412 Section 8(2) of the ICT Act.

trar, Assistant Registrars and other personnel.[413] The Registrar receives all communications directed to the Tribunal and functions as the Tribunal's channel of communication.[414] The Registrar's office, among other duties, manages the case register and public access to the Tribunal, and is responsible for the custody of the case records.[415]

The Investigation Agency was established by the government, as provided for under the ICT Act. Officers of the Investigation are allowed to assist the Prosecution during trial.[416] Procedures of the Investigation Agency are set out in Chapter II of the RoP. After completion of the investigation, the Agency submits an investigation report.[417]

As pointed out above, the ICT has no separate appellate division. That is, the general Appellate Division of the Supreme Court covers this function. Bangladesh has no separate High Court. Instead, there is an integrated Supreme Court that is divided into an Appellate Division and a High Court Division. The Appellate Division consists of a Chief Justice and four members. It also decides on criminal review petitions, which can be filed against an appeal judgment. A review petition may be granted only in cases of apparent error.[418] Since the same division decides on the review petition, the impact of this legal remedy obviously is low.

In all working areas of the ICT, women are under-represented, if not absent. No female judge has ever been appointed and the prosecution team has only very few female members. However, this is certainly not an ICT-specific problem; in particular, the absence of female judges is also due to the fact that there are very few women who fulfil the eligibility criteria for the post. Yet, particularly in the context of sexual violence, this creates a difficult environment for witnesses and leads to an absence of women's perspectives in the entire judicial process.

2.2 Jurisdiction of the ICT

The ICT's jurisdiction as defined in the ICT Act is notably broad with regard to temporal and personal jurisdiction. This distinguishes the ICT clearly from many other national and international accountability mechanisms.

---

413 Rule 59(1) of the RoP.
414 Rule 60(2) of the RoP.
415 Rules 60(4) and 62(2) and 60(5) of the RoP.
416 Section 8(1) of the ICT Act.
417 Rule 11 of the RoP.
418 *Islam*, Constitutional Law, 3. edn, p. 901.

Part III: The ICT in comparison to other accountability mechanisms

2.2.1 Jurisdiction *ratione temporis*

Pursuant to Section 3(1) of the ICT Act, the Tribunal has jurisdiction over crimes committed before or after the commencement of the Act. The drafters of the ICT Act seem to have intended the establishment of the ICT as a permanent tribunal that can exercise jurisdiction also over crimes committed after the Liberation War. Nevertheless, it does not seem likely that the ICT will continue functioning as a permanent institution after completion of the trials related to 1971. There have also been no prosecutions of crimes committed in other contexts even though the Tribunal has stated that the 'minority oppression in 2001 was a pure example of crimes against humanity'.[419] In the absence of any prosecutions, this statement seems to be rather unfounded. Yet, apparently, the Tribunal does not consider these cases to fall under its jurisdiction.

However, due to practical political reasons, the Tribunal is not expected to have longevity. It is generally presumed that the trials will not continue once the BNP regains power.[420]

2.2.2 Jurisdiction *ratione personae*

Pursuant to Section 3(1), the ICT has jurisdiction over any individual, or group of individuals or organisation or any member of any armed, defence or auxiliary forces, irrespective of nationality. On the other hand, the ICT Act, 1973 restricted personal jurisdiction to any 'person irrespective of his nationality, who being a member of any armed, defence or auxiliary forces' committed any of the crimes under the Tribunal's jurisdiction.[421] The Section was completely revised with the first amendment in 2009, and the word 'organisation' was introduced with the third amendment in 2013. That is, while the ICT's jurisdiction was restricted originally to members of armed, defence or auxiliary forces who committed the crimes in such functions, this is no longer a requirement under the amended ICT Act. Personal jurisdiction was thus extended considerably. In accordance with the extension of the ICT's jurisdiction *ratione personae*, Article 47(3) of the Constitution was amended accordingly so that individuals or groups of individuals are also deprived of the rights guaranteed in Article 31(1) and (3), Article 35 and Article 44.

The Act does not establish a minimum age for criminal liability. This could become relevant if cases not related to the Liberation War are ever brought to trial. Re-

---

419 ICT 1, *The Chief Prosecutor v. Sayeedi*, case no. 01/2011, Judgment, 28 February 2013, para. 32(1).
420 *Adhikary*, Government Plan Not Welcome, The Daily Star, 17 August 2015.
421 Section 3(1) of the ICT Act, 1973.

course to domestic law would lead to a very low minimum age. The Penal Code of Bangladesh determines that acts committed by a child below nine years of age do not constitute an offence.[422] The criminal responsibility of children between nine and twelve years of age is excluded if they have not attained sufficient maturity to understand the nature and consequences of their conduct.[423] At 13 years of age, a person is thus fully criminally liable under domestic law. Nevertheless, many other statutes, such as the ICTY Statute, the ICTR Statute, and the Charter of the International Military Tribunal at Nuremberg (IMT Charter) also do not define a minimum age of criminal responsibility. Yet, no person below 18 has ever been tried before any international criminal tribunal.[424]

Beyond that, the ICT can exercise jurisdiction over perpetrators from both sides of the conflict and thus trials for those who fought for independence are not barred by the Act. However, the Indemnity Order is still in force and impedes the prosecution of any person who participated in the Liberation Struggle. In addition, there was never a political intention to prosecute any persons other than those who collaborated with the Pakistani army. Nevertheless, the Tribunal admitted that the freedom fighters might also have committed crimes in retaliation but argued that these crimes were negligible compared to the crimes committed by the Pakistani army.[425] With this reasoning, the Tribunal evidently ignores the fact that crimes must be investigated on a case-by-case basis and that the fact that the other side committed more serious crimes does not justify non-prosecution.

The Act also does not restrict personal jurisdiction to any nationality, and the trial of Pakistani or other foreign nationals would be possible. It was due to practical and political problems that the 195 Pakistani prisoners who were granted amnesty were not brought to trial. Although trials in absentia are allowed under the ICT Act, no Pakistani national has been tried to date. The trial of Pakistani nationals would inevitably lead to even stronger political tensions with Pakistan and its allies, and it is questionable whether Bangladesh would dare to take this step. Problems would also arise with regard to the Tripartite Agreement through which Bangladesh agreed to refrain from trying the 195 prisoners of war. Yet, as will be outlined below, the Tribunal considers this agreement void. However, with regard to foreign nationals, only one trial has been conducted against two co-defendants in absentia. Chowdhury Mueen Uddin and

---

422 Section 82 of the Penal Code.
423 Section 83 of the Penal Code.
424 *Cassese/Gaeta/Jones/Frulli*, Rome Statute Commentary, Vol. 1, p. 534.
425 ICT 1, *The Chief Prosecutor v. Azam*, case no. 06/2011, Judgment, 15 July 2013, para. 76. The Tribunal contended: 'Mukti Bahini may also have done [sic] [crimes] in retaliation but it [sic] was very negligible as compared to the atrocities committed by the Pakistani Army troops against the East Pakistani[s].'

Ashrafuzzaman Khan acquired foreign citizenship, but at least Chowdhury Mueen Uddin also still holds Bangladeshi citizenship.

Since the amendment in 2013, the ICT can exercise jurisdiction not only over natural persons but also over organisations. As outlined above, organisations have not been tried because the ICT Act does not establish a penalty for organisations. Yet, the ICT Act is in the course of being amended accordingly. Criminal liability of organisations is alien to the Bangladeshi Penal Code and the ICT Act is not exactly tailored to conducting trials against organisations. If the amendment is put into practice, it remains to be seen how the ICT deals with these challenges in practice.

2.2.3 Jurisdiction *ratione loci*

The territorial jurisdiction of the ICT is restricted to crimes committed on Bangladeshi territory.

2.2.4 Jurisdiction *ratione materiae*

Pursuant to Section 3(2) of the ICT Act, the ICT has jurisdiction over crimes against humanity; crimes against peace; genocide; war crimes; violation of any humanitarian rules applicable in armed conflicts laid down in the Geneva Conventions of 1949; any other crimes under international law; attempt, abetment or conspiracy to commit any such crimes; and complicity or failure to prevent commission of any such crimes. The Act contains definitions of the crimes, which differ from those employed in the Rome Statute, in the Genocide Convention or in other statutes.

Attempt, abetment, conspiracy, complicity and failure to prevent the commission of the crimes are listed as separate offences and not as modes of liability. This follows from the structure of Section 3(2) which determines the offences under the ICT's jurisdiction. Consequences following from this classification will be discussed below.

2.3 Applicable law and jurisprudence

From the domestic nature of the ICT, it follows that it applies mainly domestic law. On the other hand, Section 23 of the ICT Act excludes the entire Criminal Procedure Code, 1898 and the Evidence Act, 1872 from application. The RoP, therefore, constitute the Tribunal's only source of procedural law besides a few basic procedural provisions contained in the ICT Act. Both sources are relatively brief and thus do not provide sufficient guidance on all procedural and material legal aspects. Hence, the ICT is compelled to invoke other legal sources. Nevertheless, whether and under which conditions the ICT can apply international law to fill these gaps depends on the status of international law in Bangladesh.

As outlined above, the Constitution of Bangladesh contains some further provisions which restrict the fundamental rights of an accused under the ICT Act. It is, however, debatable whether the ICT is bound by these provisions.

2.3.1 Domestic sources

While it is clearly defined that the ICT shall apply the ICT Act as well as the RoP, the Act is silent on other sources that can be consulted in order to fill the gaps that derive from the fragmentary character of these two legal sources. Nevertheless, the applicability of the ICT Act is also not self-evident considering its enactment as post ex facto law.

2.3.1.1 Applicability of the ICT Act and its amendments

In Bangladesh, the ICT Act is usually regarded as a milestone of international criminal law. Those involved in the accountability movement often have a very strong emotional attachment to the Act and are proud that Bangladesh adopted this unique and, at its time, very progressive law.[426] For that reason, it is often considered that it has to be preserved and an entire review of the law is believed to be unnecessary.[427] Likewise, the Appellate Division of the Supreme Court of Bangladesh highlighted the uniqueness of this law, stating that it may be considered a 'model of due process'.[428] However, it is not self-evident that the Act is applicable to cases related to the Liberation War because it was enacted retroactively. To date, the ICT Act has been amended three times and the Tribunal confirmed the retroactive effect of these amendments. The fact that the crimes were committed more than 40 years ago might also create a problem in terms of statutory limitations.

2.3.1.1.1 The ICT Act, 1973 in the light of the principle of legality

The principle of legality is a fundamental principle of criminal law. It consists in the *nullum crimen sine lege* and the *nulla poena sine lege* principles. The *nullum crimen* principle comprises four different aspects: *nullum crimen sine lege scripta* (criminal offences must be provided for in written law), *nullum crimen sine lege stricta* (the principle of specificity), a ban on analogy and *nullum crimen sine praevia lege* (the principle of non-retroactivity). As for the *nulla poena* principle, a person must be sentenced in accordance with the law. The ICT Act appears to conflict with two of these aspects: the principle of non-retroactivity and the principle of specificity.

The principle of non-retroactivity was first internationally recognised by the Universal Declaration of Human Rights (UDHR) in 1948. Article 11(2) of the UDHR determines that no one shall be held guilty of a penal offence for an act or omission that did not constitute a penal offence under national or international law at the time of commission. Article 15(1) of the International Covenant on Civil and Political Rights

---

[426] *Linton*, CLF, 2010, 21(2), p. 191, at 208.
[427] *Linton*, CLF, 2010, 21(2), p. 191, at 208.
[428] SC (AD), *Molla v. The Chief Prosecutor*, Appeal Judgment, 17 September 2013, p. 87.

(ICCPR) also contains this provision but extends the applicability in sub-section (2), determining that the trial and punishment of a person for an act or omission, which at the time of commission was criminal according to general principles of law recognised by the community of nations, shall not be prejudiced. An ex post facto law that establishes liability for offences already recognised under customary international law thus does not infringe the principle of legality. Irrespective of whether an offence emerged as customary international law, the same also holds true for offences established by treaties as long as the treaty was not concluded in violation of *ius cogens*.[429]

The *nullum crimen* principle applies to criminal offences, general forms of individual liability and circumstances excluding criminal responsibility.[430] However, it does not apply to rules in favour of the accused[431] and to rules of procedure[432]. Neither is the principle applicable to the jurisdiction. It is therefore not affected if the court with jurisdiction over the respective crimes was established only after the commission of the crimes.[433]

The principle of non-retroactivity, nevertheless, leaves scope for judicial interpretation through the courts.[434] While courts cannot create new elements of crimes with their interpretation, they are allowed to adapt the provisions to changing social conditions.[435] An example of a changing interpretation is the ICTY's finding from 1995 that war crimes are punishable even if committed in internal armed conflicts.[436]

Given that international criminal law contains many undefined notions and broad provisions, the principle of specificity does not apply fully in this field of law.[437] Likewise, the *nulla poena* principle, which applies to the penalties, is construed in a restricted manner in international law and merely requires that no heavier penalty be applied than that established by law.[438]

---

429 ICTY (AC), *Prosecutor v. Tadić*, Decision on the Defence Motion for Interlocutory Appeal on Jurisdiction, 2 October 1995, para. 143.
430 Kreß in: *Wolfrum* (ed.), Max Planck Encyclopedia, Vol. 7, p. 889, at 894–895.
431 Kreß in: *Wolfrum* (ed.), Max Planck Encyclopedia, Vol. 7, p. 889, at 897.
432 ECtHR, *Coeme & others v. Belgium*, Judgment, 22 June 2000, paras. 148–151.
433 SCSL (AC), *Prosecutor v. Kallon et al.*, Decision on Constitutionality and Lack of Jurisdiction, 13 March 2004, para. 82; ICTY (AC), *Prosecutor v. Delalić et al.*, Judgment, 20 February 2001, paras. 179–180; ECCC (TC), *Prosecutor v. Kaing alias Duch*, Judgment, 20 February 2001, para. 34.
434 ICTY (AC), *Prosecutor v. Aleksovski*, Appeals Judgment, 24 March 2000, para. 127.
435 *Cassese*, International Criminal Law, 3. edn, p. 32.
436 ICTY (AC), *Prosecutor v. Tadić*, Decision on the Defence Motion for Interlocutory Appeal on Jurisdiction, 2 October 1995, paras. 94–137.
437 *Cassese*, International Criminal Law, 3. edn, p. 28.
438 Kreß in: *Wolfrum* (ed.), Max Planck Encyclopedia, Vol. 7, p. 889, at 898; *Ambos*, in: Haveman/Olusanya (eds), Sentencing and Sanctioning in Supranational Criminal Law, p. 17, at 25–26.

2 The domestic character of the International Crimes Tribunal in Bangladesh

The principle of legality is currently a peremptory norm of customary international law.[439] Sufficient evidence of the customary law character of the non-retroactivity principle can be found in numerous treaties and application through the ICC and the ad hoc Tribunals.[440] The exact point of time of emergence in customary international law is difficult to determine but this development certainly began, albeit gradually, after the trials of the IMT.[441]

In conclusion, the prosecution of international crimes based on an ex post facto law is admissible but the law has to reflect the status of international law at the time when the crimes were committed. The principle of legality, however, does not prevent a court from interpreting the crimes.

In Bangladesh, the principle of non-retroactivity is enshrined in the Constitution. Article 35 prohibits ex post facto laws and contains the *nulla poena* principle. As outlined above, Article 47A of the Constitution declares this provision inapplicable to the accused under the ICT Act. Beyond that, pursuant to Article 47(3), the ICT Act cannot be challenged for being unconstitutional. As a consequence, an accused under the ICT Act does not enjoy the protection of the principle of legality and neither can the ICT Act be challenged for being unconstitutional based on the infringement of the principle of legality.

Since the principle of legality is a peremptory norm of *ius cogens* that applies without exception, the constitutional provision contained in Article 47A violates customary international law. Though the exact point of time when the principle of legality emerged as a rule of customary international law is difficult to determine, it was most likely in existence in 1973 when the ICT Act came into force and when Article 47A was inserted. That is, Article 47A was contrary to the customary international law of the time.

It is, however, debatable whether the ICT Act was enacted in violation of the principle of legality. As outlined above, the prosecution of offences that were already recognised under international law does not run counter to non-retroactivity requirements. The ICT Act as an ex post facto law, therefore, infringes the principle only if it establishes offences or modes of liability that were not recognised under customary international law at the time when the crimes were committed or if it does not incorporate them in accordance with the status of customary international law of that time.

In order to determine whether the ICT Act infringes the prohibition of retroactivity, it is therefore crucial to determine the status of customary international law in 1971 and to define the limits between admissible interpretation of the elements of crimes and the creation of new offences. According to Article 38(1)(b) of the ICJ

---

439 *Cassese/Gaeta/Jones/Lamb*, Rome Statute Commentary, Vol. 1, p. 734; *Gallant*, Principle of Legality, p. 352.
440 *Gallant*, Principle of Legality, pp. 352–353.
441 *Cassese/Gaeta/Jones/Lamb*, Rome Statute Commentary, Vol. 1, pp. 735–742.

Statute, international custom is 'evidence of a general practice accepted as law'. That is, in order for customary international law to emerge, two elements need to be fulfilled: *opinio juris* and state practice.[442]

At first glance, retroactivity problems arise with regard to the possibility of prosecuting war crimes and crimes against peace committed in non-international armed conflicts.[443] Also the definition of genocide and crimes against humanity differ from the internationally recognised definitions. The latter contains also the crimes of imprisonment, abduction, confinement, torture and rape, and thus extends the scope of the offence beyond the definitions in force in 1971. The ICT Act is further silent on the requirement of a widespread and systematic attack or a war-connecting link.

Conflicts arise also in the context of the modes of liability. The ICT Act provides for the prosecution of superiors but the legal implementation differs significantly from the internationally recognised principle of command responsibility.[444] Beyond that, the application of the different modes of liability established under the Act might cause challenges. Contrary to the usual understanding, the ICT Act codifies several modes of liability as separate offences.[445] This has been confirmed also by the ICT which held that abetment is an independent offence under the ICT Act.[446]

The principle of legality is further affected in its specificity aspect. The Act contains vague formulations at several points. For instance, the ICT has jurisdiction over 'any crimes under international law' but the Act specifies neither the crimes nor the point of time when these crimes had to be defined under international law. This catch-all provision without any further definition infringes the principle of specificity.[447] Considering the crimes recognised under international law in 1971, it would open up the possibility to prosecute piracy and slavery, which were probably already crimes under customary law.[448] With regard to torture, it seems doubtful whether, in 1971, this was already a recognised international crime that established individual criminal responsibility because demands for its criminalisation arose only after the Liberation War.[449] Yet, the catch-all clause can be invoked also in order to partly overcome the incitement lacuna as incitement to commit genocide was undoubtedly already a crime under international law in 1971.[450]

---

442 Art. 38(1)(b) of the ICJ Statute.
443 *Linton*, CLF, 2010, 21(2), p. 191, at 214.
444 *Linton*, CLF, 2010, 21(2), p. 191, at 214.
445 *Forstein*, Special Issue No. 4 – Legal Conclusions Kamaruzzaman, p. 5
446 ICT 1, *The Prosecutor v. Azam*, case no. 06/2011, Charge Framing Order, 13 May 2012, p. 14.
447 *Linton*, CLF, 2010, 21(2), p. 191, at 268.
448 *Linton*, CLF, 2010, 21(2), p. 191, at 271.
449 *Linton*, CLF, 2010, 21(2), p. 191, at 272.
450 *Linton*, CLF, 2010, 21(2), p. 191, at 270.

2 The domestic character of the International Crimes Tribunal in Bangladesh

If regarded from this point of view, the provision does not seem to be too harmful despite the absence of a minimum specificity standard. Nevertheless, the catch-all clause has another dimension when considered in the context of Article 47A of the Constitution of Bangladesh. With the principle of retroactivity not being applicable to the accused under the ICT Act, the provision allows recourse to offences that were not recognised internationally at the time of commission of the crimes.

Not least, the ICT Act could also infringe the *nulla poena* principle considering that Section 20(2) allows the Tribunal to impose the death penalty or 'such other punishment proportionate to the gravity of the crime as appears to the Tribunal just and proper'. Nevertheless, if one considers the restricted scope of application of the *nulla poena* principle in international criminal law, Section 20(2) does not run counter to it. The heaviest penalty is expressly mentioned and there is thus no scope for a heavier penalty to be applied. Nevertheless, the provision is evidently problematic as it gives the Tribunal the power to impose a penalty that is not recognised under domestic law. In practice, however, the court invoked the penalties admitted under the Penal Code.[451]

The ICT dealt with the principle of legality only marginally. It rather briefly confirmed the admissibility of retroactive laws to prosecute crimes against humanity, genocide and systematic crimes committed in violation of customary international law.[452] It also referred to the ICTY, ICTR and SCSL (Special Court for Sierra Leone), pointing out that these tribunals were also based on ex post facto statutes.[453] This statement appears to ignore the core of the problem, which is not the admissibility of retroactivity in general but rather whether the retroactive law accords with the customary international law of the time when the criminal acts were committed. The ICT was established almost 40 years after the war based on a retroactive law that did not reflect entirely the status of international law at the time of drafting.

Tribunal 2 further held that it is immaterial for the trial whether the crimes formed part of customary international law in 1971 because they are listed in the ICT Act.[454] It emphasised that the Act cannot be barred by any domestic or international law be-

---

451 On the ICT's interpretation of this provision, see pp. 242 ff.
452 ICT 2, *The Chief Prosecutor v. Azad*, case no. 05/2012, Judgment, 21 January 2013, para. 14; ICT 1, *The Chief Prosecutor v. Sayeedi*, case no. 01/2011, Judgment, 28 February 2013, para. 52; ICT 2, *The Chief Prosecutor v. Molla*, case no. 02/2012, Judgment, 5 February 2013, para. 3. All judgments contain the same passage.
453 ICT 2, *The Chief Prosecutor v. Azad*, case no. 05/2012, Judgment, 21 January 2013, para. 14; ICT 1, *The Chief Prosecutor v. Sayeedi*, case no. 01/2011, Judgment, 28 February 2013, para. 52; ICT 2, *The Chief Prosecutor v. Molla*, case no. 02/2012, Judgment, 5 February 2013, para. 3.
454 ICT 2, *The Chief Prosecutor v. Sobhan*, case no. 06/2013, Charge Framing Order, 31 December 2013, p. 7.

cause of its status as a special law.⁴⁵⁵ As an additional argument, the Tribunal also invoked Articles 47(3) and 47A of the Constitution.⁴⁵⁶

Tribunal 1 also dealt with Article 15 of the ICCPR in the charge framing order against Chowdhury. It held that the requirements established by Article 15 of the ICCPR were met and that all the offences of the ICT Act formed part of the 'normal law' of Bangladesh in 1971.⁴⁵⁷ It is puzzling how the Tribunal comes to such a conclusion because, clearly, none of the international core crimes formed part of the domestic law in 1971. It then held that Article 15(1) of the ICCPR was overruled by Article 15(2) because the former was not applicable to international crimes.⁴⁵⁸ This finding, however, does not affect the non-retroactivity principle because even Article 15(2) requires acts or omissions to be recognised as criminal by the community of nations at the time of commission.

The Appellate Division confirmed this approach but based its findings on a different reasoning. Since the Division declared customary international law inapplicable for domestic courts, unless it is incorporated into domestic law, it also rejected the argument that the ICT Act would have to reflect the customary international law of 1971.⁴⁵⁹ With regard to the defence's argument that crimes against humanity require an international armed conflict because the offence has to be interpreted in accordance with the customary international law of 1971,⁴⁶⁰ the Division held that the ICT Act does not refer to an international armed conflict and, therefore, this element was not required⁴⁶¹. It then argued that, also in customary international law, an international armed conflict is not required for the commission of crimes against humanity and cited the relevant jurisprudence of the ICTY.⁴⁶² The Appellate Division thus ignored the fact that customary international law of the time of the commission of the crimes must be invoked.

In several aspects, the ICT Act does not reflect the customary international law of 1971 and therefore infringes the principle of legality. Article 47(3), which bars the

---

455 ICT 2, *The Chief Prosecutor v. Sobhan*, case no. 06/2013, Charge Framing Order, 31 December 2013, p. 7.
456 ICT 2, *The Chief Prosecutor v. Sobhan*, case no. 06/2013, Charge Framing Order, 31 December 2013, p. 7.
457 ICT 1, *The Chief Prosecutor v. Chowdhury*, case no. 02/2011, Charge Framing Order, 4 April 2012, p. 11.
458 ICT 1, *The Chief Prosecutor v. Chowdhury*, case no. 02/2011 Charge Framing Order, 4 April 2012, pp. 11–12.
459 SC (AD), *Molla v. The Chief Prosecutor*, Appeal Judgment, 17 September 2013, p. 158. On the role of customary international law in Bangladesh, see pp. 82 ff.
460 SC (AD), *Molla v. The Chief Prosecutor*, Appeal Judgment, 17 September 2013, p. 142.
461 SC (AD), *Molla v. The Chief Prosecutor*, Appeal Judgment, 17 September 2013, p. 579.
462 SC (AD), *Molla v. The Chief Prosecutor*, Appeal Judgment, 17 September 2013, p. 579.

application of the principle of legality to the accused under the ICT Act, was enacted in breach of customary international law and runs counter to Bangladesh's obligations under the ICCPR. Yet, the Tribunal considers the ICT Act, 1973 fully applicable.

2.3.1.1.2 Statutory limitations

The application of the ICT Act to crimes committed in 1971 also raises the question of whether statutory limitations could bar prosecution. The Convention on the Non-Applicability of Statutory Limitations to War Crimes and Crimes Against Humanity came into force on 11 November 1970. The Convention itself does not have retroactive effect as it determines that statutory limitations shall not apply to the crimes under the Convention, irrespective of the date of their commission.[463] To date, the Convention has only 55 member states, and Bangladesh is not among them.

Therefore, it becomes relevant whether the non-applicability of statutory limitations to international crimes ranks among customary international law. This is subject of heated debate. It is contended that statutory limitations are prohibited by customary international law at least for the core international crimes.[464] This view is also supported by the ICTY. With regard to torture, the ICTY determined that the inapplicability of statutory limitations is a consequence of the *ius cogens* character of the prohibition of torture.[465] Others instead consider the assumption of such a customary international rule to be premature.[466] In any event, statutory limitations require a positive provision in order to be applicable, and in the absence of such a positive rule in international law they cannot be applied to international crimes.[467]

The non-applicability of statutes of limitations at the international level contrasts with the domestic law of many countries which provide for statutory limitations; the conflict which emerges from this imbalance prevents states from ratifying the respective international conventions.[468] The European Convention on the Non-Applicability of Statutory Limitations to Crimes against Humanity and War Crimes did not come into force due to a lack of signatories. Unlike the Convention on the Non-Applicability of Statutory Limitations to War Crimes and Crimes Against Humanity, it was not given retroactive effect but was restricted to crimes committed after the Convention came into force.

---

463 Article I of the Convention on the Non-Applicability of Statutory Limitations to War Crimes and Crimes against Humanity.
464 *Cassese/Gaeta/Jones/Van den Wyngaert/Dugard*, Rome Statute Commentary, Vol. 1, p. 887.
465 ICTY (TC), *Prosecutor v. Furundžija*, Judgment, 10 December 1998, para. 157.
466 *Cryer et al.*, International Criminal Law, 3. edn, p. 84.
467 *Cryer et al.*, International Criminal Law, 3. edn, p. 84; *Schabas*, International Criminal Court, 4. edn, p. 247.
468 *Bassiouni*, Crimes against Humanity, p. 279.

Part III: The ICT in comparison to other accountability mechanisms

The defence raised this issue in several cases before the ICT, arguing that the unexplained delay of 41 years in initiating prosecutions casts doubts on the allegations in general but also leads to the acquittal of the accused.[469] The reason for the defence not invoking statutory limitations is based on the fact that limitation statutes are generally unknown in common law countries.[470] The issue is usually addressed under the abuse of process doctrine. Limitation statutes, nevertheless, do exist in a few common law systems but they usually do not include serious crimes.[471] The ICT countered that there is no time bar applicable to human rights crimes.[472] According to the Tribunal, this follows from the absence of any positive statutory limitations for crimes against humanity and war crimes in the Geneva Conventions.[473] It further invoked Article I of the Convention on the Non-Applicability of Statutory Limitations to War Crimes and Crimes Against Humanity of 26 November 1968.[474] Given that Bangladesh is not a party to the Convention, the ICT's reasoning based on this Convention is flawed although the result of non-applicability of statutory limitations to international crimes is certainly reasonable. With regard to the Convention on the Non-Applicability of Statutory Limitations to War Crimes and Crimes against Humanity, one could simply argue that the Convention was declaratory of customary international law in 1968. However, considering the extremely small number of signatories to the Convention, this argument is rather weak.[475]

The Appellate Division also addressed this issue. In contrast to the ICT's line of reasoning, it invoked domestic law to confirm that statutory limitations do not apply. It examined Sections 7, 8 and 9 of the ICT Act as well as the RoP and concluded that none of these provisions provided for any time bar.[476] The Division further argued that the delay in prosecution was based on the failure of the executive to establish a tribu-

---

469 ICT 2, *The Chief Prosecutor v. Kamaruzzaman*, case no. 03/2012, Judgment, 9 May 2013, para. 100; ICT 2, *The Chief Prosecutor v. Molla*, case no. 02/2012, Judgment, 5 February 2013, para. 78.
470 *Cassese/Gaeta/Jones/Van den Wyngaert/Dugard*, Rome Statute Commentary, Vol. 1, p. 885.
471 *Cassese/Gaeta/Jones/Van den Wyngaert/Dugard*, Rome Statute Commentary, Vol. 1, p. 885.
472 ICT 2, *The Chief Prosecutor v. Kamaruzzaman*, case no. 03/2012, Judgment, 9 May 2013, para. 101; ICT 2, *The Chief Prosecutor v. Molla*, case no. 02/2012, Judgment, 5 February 2013, para. 82.
473 ICT 2, *The Chief Prosecutor v. Kamaruzzaman*, case no. 03/2012, Judgment, 9 May 2013, para. 101; ICT 2, *The Chief Prosecutor v. Molla*, case no. 02/2012, Judgment, 5 February 2013, para. 82.
474 ICT 2, *The Chief Prosecutor v. Kamaruzzaman*, case no. 03/2012, Judgment, 9 May 2013, para. 101; ICT 2, *The Chief Prosecutor v. Molla*, case no. 02/2012, Judgment, 5 February 2013, para. 82.
475 *Cassese/Gaeta/Jones/Van den Wyngaert/Dugard*, Rome Statute Commentary, Vol. 1, p. 887.
476 SC (AD), *Molla v. The Chief Prosecutor*, Appeal Judgment, 17 September 2013, p. 285.

nal for many years and that this did not render the law ineffective.[477] The defence had referred to several decisions of the Appellate Division on the question of delay but the Division found them inapplicable to the present case because they were related to ordinary law.[478]

2.3.1.1.3 The ICT Act as amended in 2009

The first modifications of the ICT Act were realised through the International Crimes (Tribunals) (Amendment) Act in 2009[479] before the ICT was set up in 2010. Some minor changes were made with regard to the general definitions. The definition of the term 'armed forces' as utilised throughout the ICT Act was inserted and Section 2(d), which contained a definition of the term 'service law', was omitted.

As outlined above, the most significant modification was made in Section 3(1) with regard to the ICT's jurisdiction *ratione personae*. It was only this amendment that made the prosecution of individuals who did not act in their function as a member of any armed, defence or auxiliary forces and the trial of organisations possible.

An amendment to Section 6(2) introduced new criteria regarding the eligibility of judges, allowing only judges who are or were or have the qualification to be judges of the Supreme Court of Bangladesh to be appointed to the ICT. The original version of this section allowed also for the appointment of High Court judges and those qualified to be members of the General Court Martial. These amendments accommodate the reorganisation of the Bangladesh judicial system through which the separate High Court was converted into a High Court Division of the Supreme Court.

An important amendment with regard to the rights of the accused was realised with the newly inserted Section 6(2A). It determines that the Tribunal shall be independent in the exercise of its judicial functions and ensure a fair trial.

The spelling of 'Dacca' was modified to Dhaka (Section 6(3)) in accordance with the abrogation of colonial spellings. An amendment of great importance was the introduction of Bangla (Bengali) as an additional court language because English previously had been the only court language (Section 10(2)). In fact, the hearings are predominantly held in Bengali. Both languages are also used in written documents. The indictments and the transcripts of the witness testimonies are usually drafted in Bengali. Nevertheless, interim orders, judgments and the charge framing orders are drafted in English with the exception of parts that reproduce evidence in Bengali.

Section 21 on the right to appeal was extended in favour of the prosecution. A right to appeal for the prosecution did not exist in the initial version of the ICT Act. How-

---

477 SC (AD), *Molla v. The Chief Prosecutor*, Appeal Judgment, 17 September 2013, p. 285.
478 SC (AD), *Molla v. The Chief Prosecutor*, Appeal Judgment, 17 September 2013, p. 285.
479 Act no. LV of 2009.

ever, even with this amendment, the right to appeal was granted only in the case of an acquittal.

As outlined above, the principle of legality applies only to criminal offences, the forms of criminal liability and the circumstances excluding criminal responsibility. These elements were not affected by the 2009 amendments. In particular, the principle of legality does not apply to the jurisdiction of a tribunal. This also follows from the fact that the principle of legality does not bar the possibility to create new courts[480] and, therefore, clearly does not impede the extension of the jurisdiction of already-existing courts.

Contrary to the 2013 amendment, the first amendment does not specify whether a retroactive application was intended. In *Azad* and in *Sayeedi*, the defence argued that, in the absence of a clear provision showing the intention of retrospective effect, the amendment has only prospective effect.[481] As a consequence, only those perpetrators of crimes committed after the enactment could be brought to trial as 'individuals' or 'groups of individuals', over whom the ICT has had jurisdiction only since the 2009 amendment.[482] In *Sayeedi*, the defence also contended that the prosecution failed to prove the accused's membership of an auxiliary force.[483] On the other hand, in both cases, the ICT argued in favour of a retroactive effect, emphasising the rationale behind the extension of personal jurisdiction, which was clearly to avoid impunity for those who committed crimes under the ICT's jurisdiction.[484] It also invoked Article 47(3) and 47A(2) of the Constitution and affirmed that an accused does not have the right to call any provision of the ICT Act in question.[485]

---

480   *Gallant*, Principle of Legality, p. 394.
481   ICT 2, *The Chief Prosecutor v. Azad*, case no. 05/2012, Judgment, 21 January 2013, para. 55; ICT 1, *The Chief Prosecutor v. Sayeedi*, case no. 01/2011, Judgment, 28 February 2013, para. 51.
482   ICT 1, *The Chief Prosecutor v. Sayeedi*, case no. 01/2011, Judgment, 28 February 2013, para. 51.
483   ICT 1, *The Chief Prosecutor v. Sayeedi*, case no. 01/2011, Judgment, 28 February 2013, para. 51.
484   ICT 2, *The Chief Prosecutor v. Azad*, case no. 05/2012, Judgment, 21 January 2013, para. 58; ICT 1, *The Chief Prosecutor v. Sayeedi*, case no. 01/2011, Judgment, 28 February 2013, para. 53.
485   ICT 2, *The Chief Prosecutor v. Azad*, case no. 05/2012, Judgment, 21 January 2013, para. 59; ICT 1, *The Chief Prosecutor v. Sayeedi*, case no. 01/2011, Judgment, 28 February 2013, para. 54; ICT 2, *The Chief Prosecutor v. Molla*, case no. 02/2012, Judgment, 5 February 2013, para. 100; ICT 2, *The Chief Prosecutor v. Kamaruzzaman*, case no. 03/2012, Judgment, 9 May 2013, para. 111; ICT 1, *The Chief Prosecutor v. Sayeedi*, case no. 01/2011, Judgment, 28 February 2013, para. 54.

2.3.1.1.4 The amendments of 2012 and 2013

The first amendment was followed by the International Crimes (Tribunals) (Amendment) Ordinance in 2012,[486] the International Crimes (Tribunals) (Second Amendment) Act in 2012[487] and the International Crimes (Tribunals) (Amendment) Act, 2013 (with effect from 14 July 2009)[488].

The difference between these amendments and the amendment from 2009 is that, from 2010 onwards, cases were pending before the Tribunal and these amendments were applied to cases that were initiated under the Act as amended in 2009. Nevertheless, only the amendment of 2013 was given explicit retroactive effect from 14 July 2009.

With the Amendment Ordinance[489] in 2012, a new Section 11A was inserted into the Act. It allows for the transfer of cases between both tribunals whenever a transfer is considered just and convenient for proper dispensation of justice. Sub-section (2) determines that the Tribunal, to which the case has been transferred, shall proceed from the point of the transfer. The reason for this amendment was the establishment of Tribunal 2 in the same year. Section 11A facilitated the transfer of some cases to the newly set up Tribunal 2 without re-initiating the proceedings.

The second 2012 amendment inserted Section 10A. The Section frames the requirements for the ICT to initiate a trial in absentia, which were previously contained only in the RoP (Rule 32). Section 10A(2) allows the Tribunal to direct the engagement of a counsel for the defence of an accused in absentia. No equivalent provision is contained in the RoP and the amendment thus filled a gap and strengthened the rights of any of the accused tried in absentia. Another amendment with direct ramifications for the accused was the decrease of the period from 60 to 30 days for filing an appeal (Section 21(3)).

Two additional sub-sections were introduced into Section 20 regarding the issuance of certified copies of the judgment. While Rule 60(11) of the RoP determined that the Registrar should issue certified copies of a judgment upon an application and on payment of 10 taka per page, Sections 20(2A) and 20(2B) now provide for the issuance of certified copies without application and free of charge.

The most important modification introduced with the 2013 amendment was the extension of the prosecution's right of appeal. The right of appeal was further ex-

---

486 Act no. XXI of 2012.
487 Act no. XLIII of 2012.
488 Act no. III of 2013.
489 Article 93 of the Constitution allows the president to make and promulgate ordinances when Parliament stands dissolved or is not in session and the president is satisfied that an emergency situation requires a legal intervention.

tended and the prosecution was granted a right to appeal also against an order of sentence. The amendment further introduced that the Appellate Division shall dispose of an appeal within 60 days and that the appellant shall submit all the relevant documents at the time of filing the appeal. However, in practice, the deadline of 60 days has not been complied with. The idea behind this amendment was to ensure an expeditious trial. Nevertheless, given the complexity of the proceedings, a disposal within 60 days forces a compromise on quality.

These amendments had a powerful impact on the rights of the accused Molla. The prosecution's right to appeal was extended gradually from 2009. While in the ICT Act, 1973 the prosecution had no right to appeal at all, the 2009 amendment granted a right to appeal in the case of an acquittal. The amendment from 2013 finally extended the prosecution's right to appeal to cases in which there was a conviction. The bill for the amendment of the ICT Act was passed by Parliament on 17 February 2013 and given effect from 14 July 2009. The verdict against Molla was delivered on 5 February 2013. He was found guilty of five of the six charges and sentenced to life imprisonment. That is, the amendment was introduced after Molla's conviction. Based on the retroactive effect of the amendment, the prosecution filed an appeal despite the fact that the judgment had already been delivered at the time when the amendment was made. The prosecution requested the suspension of the acquittal for charge 4 and the imposition of the highest punishment for the other charges. The majority judgment followed this motion and imposed the death penalty.

The Appellate Division had to decide on the admissibility of the appeal from the prosecution based on the amendment. To this end, the Division considered the opinions of seven *amici curiae*.[490] All except one of the *amici curiae* pleaded for a retroactive applicability of the right to appeal even after the delivery of the judgment.[491]

The Division invoked its earlier decision in *Tarique Rahman v. Government of Bangladesh*[492] and argued that the ex-post facto law prohibition in Article 35(1) of the Constitution relates only to conviction under such a law but not to the trial of the offence or the procedure to be followed during investigation.[493] Based on *Bangladesh v. Sheikh Hasina*,[494] the Division concluded that the prohibition under Article 35(1) is

---

490 For a summary of the opinions submitted by the *amici curiae*, see SC (AD), *Molla v. The Chief Prosecutor*, Separate Opinion of Justice Choudhury, Appeal Judgment, 17 September 2013, pp. 538–559.
491 Parts of the submissions of the *amici curiae* are cited in: SC (AD), *Molla v. The Chief Prosecutor*, Separate Opinion of Justice Choudhury, Appeal Judgment, 17 September 2013, pp. 758 ff.
492 *Tarique Rahman v. Bangladesh*, 63 DLR (AD) (2011), pp. 18 ff.
493 SC (AD), *Molla v. The Chief Prosecutor*, Appeal Judgment, 17 September 2013, p. 167.
494 *Bangladesh v. Sheikh Hasina Wazed*, 60 DLR (AD) (2008), pp. 90 ff.

not applicable to procedural laws.[495] Since the amendment was specifically given retroactive effect from 14 July 2009, the Division found that there is no doubt regarding the legislator's aim to apply the amended Act retroactively, and the court has to give effect to this objective.[496] Beyond that, it held that the presumption against retroactive application does not apply to procedural rules and for that reason the amendment has to be applied also to concluded cases, even though it is not specifically mentioned in the amendment.[497] The Division argued that the principle of legality becomes relevant only when a retroactive law imposes a punishment or creates new offences.[498] The *amicus curiae* that rejected the admissibility of the appeal argued that Parliament would have had to specifically mention that the amendment applies also to cases which the ICT had already dealt with.[499]

According to the Appellate Division, the question of the appeal's admissibility is, beyond that, not of much practical relevance because it could also invoke Article 104 of the Constitution, which provides for the inherent power of the Division, equal to that of the ICT.[500] Article 104 of the Constitution of Bangladesh grants the Appellate Division the power to 'do complete justice':[501]

> *Article 104 of the Constitution*
> The Appellate Division shall have power to issue such directions, orders, decrees or writs as may be necessary for doing complete justice in any cause or matter pending before it, including orders for the purpose of securing the attendance of any person or the discovery or production of any document.

This power is extraordinary and can be exercised only in exceptional circumstances to remove injustice.[502] The scope of complete justice is, however, difficult to define, but in any case it should be restricted to the removal of strong injustice, whenever legal provisions to this end are absent.[503] It may thus not be exercised contrary to existing

---

495 SC (AD), *Molla v. The Chief Prosecutor*, Appeal Judgment, 17 September 2013, p. 168.
496 SC (AD), *Molla v. The Chief Prosecutor*, Appeal Judgment, 17 September 2013, p. 172; SC (AD), *Molla v. The Chief Prosecutor*, Dissenting Opinion of Justice Miah, Appeal Judgment, 17 September 2013, p. 264.
497 SC (AD), *Molla v. The Chief Prosecutor*, Appeal Judgment, 17 September 2013, p. 172.
498 SC (AD), *Molla v. The Chief Prosecutor*, Appeal Judgment, 17 September 2013, p. 172, 776.
499 SC (AD), *Molla v. The Chief Prosecutor*, Separate Opinion of Justice Choudhury, Appeal Judgment, 17 September 2013, p. 758.
500 SC (AD), *Molla v. The Chief Prosecutor*, Appeal Judgment, 17 September 2013, p. 174.
501 *Halim*, Legal System of Bangladesh, p. 92, *Islam*, Constitutional Law, 3. edn, p. 886.
502 *Islam*, Constitutional Law, 3. edn, p. 893.
503 *Islam*, Constitutional Law, 3. edn, p. 893.

legal provisions[504] or in violation of the fundamental rights guaranteed under Article 31 of the Constitution.[505]

According to the Division, Article 104 grants a very wide power of review and allows the Division to enhance the sentence, even without appeal by the prosecution.[506] Since the Appellate Division under Article 104 has the same powers as the ICT, it can also increase the penalty if it finds a sentence inadequate.[507]

The Division also relied on the argument made by one *amicus curiae* that, before the amendment of the ICT Act, there was a lack of parity regarding the right of appeal and the amendment thus merely equalised this imbalance.[508] However, the Appellate Division also pointed to Article 47(3) and Article 47A of the Constitution which excluded the possibility to declare the amendment of the ICT Act void or unlawful based on an inconsistency with the Constitution.[509]

Despite the fact that the principle of legality is not applicable to procedural law, the retroactive applicability of this amendment clearly raises strong fair trial concerns given that the accused was left only with the legal remedy of a review petition (decided on by the same Division) against the verdict. The point in time when this amendment was enacted also gives rise to the suspicion that it was a reaction to the calls for the death penalty by the Shahbag movement. It is not without reason that the Rome Statute clarifies that amendments to the Rules of Procedure and Evidence of the ICC shall not be applied retroactively to the detriment of an investigated, prosecuted or convicted person.[510] In order to ensure a fair trial, it would be essential for the ICT to adopt a similar approach.

In summary, the ICT as well as the Appellate Division consider the ICT Act and its amendments fully applicable to all cases.

2.3.1.2 Constitutional restrictions

As outlined above, there are several restrictions to the rights of the accused under the ICT Act that stem from the Constitution of Bangladesh. The Constitution is the country's supreme law.

---

504 *H. M. Ershad v. State*, 6 BLC (AD) (2001), pp. 18 ff., at 30.
505 *Islam*, Constitutional Law, 3. edn, p. 891.
506 SC (AD), *Molla v. The Chief Prosecutor*, Appeal Judgment, 17 September 2013, pp. 163, 777.
507 SC (AD), *Molla v. The Chief Prosecutor*, Appeal Judgment, 17 September 2013, p. 173.
508 SC (AD), *Molla v. The Chief Prosecutor*, Appeal Judgment, 17 September 2013, pp. 777–778.
509 SC (AD), *Molla v. The Chief Prosecutor*, Appeal Judgment, 17 September 2013, pp. 172, 180.
510 Article 51(4) of the Rome Statute.

2 The domestic character of the International Crimes Tribunal in Bangladesh

Article 47(3) and Article 47A of the Constitution deprive the accused under the ICT Act of several fundamental rights (the right to the protection of the law and to be treated in accordance with the law, the principle of legality, the right to a public and speedy trial by an independent or impartial court established by law, the right to move the High Court Division for the enforcement of fundamental rights conferred under Part IV of the Constitution) and, at the same time, curtail the right to challenge the ICT Act for being unconstitutional. As a consequence, no provision of the Act, whether contained since the beginning or inserted afterwards, can ever be declared unconstitutional. As outlined above, in the case of *Molla*, the Appellate Division adopted this approach and the constitutionality of the constitutional amendment that inserted Article 47(3) and 47A was never questioned.

However, it is not self-evident that these restrictions are lawful. Constitutional provisions can be void if they do not comply with the core values of a Constitution. That is, despite being part of the Constitution, constitutional amendments can be unconstitutional. This approach, however, is not adopted universally but is applied in Bangladesh and several constitutional amendments were challenged. Some have been declared illegal or partly illegal by the Supreme Court because they affected the basic structure of the Constitution.

The landmark decision in this regard concerned the Eighth Amendment of the Constitution. In *Anwar Hossain Chowdhury v. Bangladesh*,[511] the Eighth Constitutional Amendment was declared partly unconstitutional. The amendment modified Article 100 of the Constitution and allowed for the establishment of permanent High Court Division Benches outside the capital. It also gave the president the power to determine the territorial jurisdiction of the benches by notice. The president could thus restrain the High Court's territorial jurisdiction in the permanent seat. The Amendment was challenged for being unconstitutional because it modified the basic structure of the Constitution by abrogating the High Court Division with plenary judicial power over the entire republic.[512] In its original and now re-inserted version, Article 100 determines that the seat of the Supreme Court shall be in Dhaka but that the Chief Justice may, with approval of the president, determine that sessions of the High Court Division can be held in other places.

The Appellate Division had to deal with two major questions: whether constitutional amendments under Article 142 of the Constitution allow Parliament to modify the basic structure of the Constitution and whether the Eighth Amendment modified the Constitution's basic structure. The Division argued that amendments do not allow

---

511 *Anwar Hossain Chowdhury and others v. Bangladesh*, 41 DLR (AD) (1989), pp. 165 ff.
512 *Islam*, Constitutional Law, 3. edn, p. 525.

the destruction of the basic pillars of the Constitution.[513] It found that 'the term amendment implies such an addition or change within the lines of the original instrument as will effect an improvement or better carry out the purpose for which it was framed'[514] and argued that an amendment is aimed at improvement or at making the Constitution more effective or meaningful but not at eliminating or abrogating it.[515] Regarding the second question, the Appellate Division found that the High Court Division with plenary judicial power over the entire republic is a basic structure of the Constitution and the amendment was unconstitutional because it dissolved this structure.[516]

However, which principles belong to the basic structure of the Constitution is not clearly defined. The Appellate Division determined the basic structure of the Constitution by means of the Preamble. According to the Division, the basic features of the Constitution comprise the sovereignty of the people, supremacy of the Constitution, democracy, republican government, unitary state, separation of powers, independence of the judiciary, rule of law and fundamental rights.[517] In a later judgment, it also considered supremacy of law and separation of powers as basic features of the Constitution.[518] The First Constitutional Amendment, which inserted Articles 47(3) and 47A into the Constitution, has never been challenged. Islam concludes that the first three amendments do not affect the basic structure of the Constitution.[519]

Another landmark case on an amendment affecting the basic structure of the Constitution concerned the Fifth Constitutional Amendment. The High Court Division dealt with the legality of the Fifth Constitutional Amendment in *Italian Marble Works Ltd. v. Bangladesh*.[520] With the Fifth Constitutional Amendment, Parliament introduced Paragraph 18 into the Fourth Schedule of the Constitution and ratified all martial law proclamations that amended the Constitution and all the actions taken by the martial law authorities. It also declared all acts and amendments valid and excluded the possibility of challenging them in court. It is obvious that constitutional amend-

---

513 *Anwar Hossain Chowdhury and others v. Bangladesh*, 41 DLR (AD) (1989), pp. 165 ff., at 253.
514 *Anwar Hossain Chowdhury and others v. Bangladesh*, 41 DLR (AD) (1989), pp. 165 ff., at 221.
515 *Anwar Hossain Chowdhury and others v. Bangladesh*, 41 DLR (AD) (1989), pp. 165 ff., at 252.
516 *Anwar Hossain Chowdhury and others v. Bangladesh*, 41 DLR (AD) (1989), pp. 165 ff., at 270.
517 *Anwar Hossain Chowdhury and others v. Bangladesh*, 41 DLR (AD) (1989), pp. 165 ff., at 230–232.
518 *Sultana Kamal v. Bangladesh*, 14 BLC (HCD) (2009), pp. 141 ff.
519 *Islam*, Constitutional Law, 3. edn, pp. 539–540.
520 *Italian Marble Works Ltd. v. Bangladesh*, 62 DLR (HCD) (2010), pp. 70 ff.

ments through martial law proclamations are invalid because they do not follow the procedure determined in the Constitution for its amendment. With the Fifth Amendment, however, Parliament had ratified all the amendments through proclamations with a two-thirds majority. The High Court Division found this amendment to be ultra vires of the Constitution because it infringes basic constitutional features, such as judicial review and judicial independence.[521] The Appellate Division upheld the decision and confirmed that the amendment contravened the basic features of the Constitution and, for that reason, Parliament was not able to make such an amendment even though the amendment was formally admissible.[522]

Considering the judgment on the Eighth Amendment, the First Constitutional Amendment seems to be problematic, especially if one considers fundamental rights to be a part of the basic features of the Constitution. Article 47(3), however, must be regarded in the context of the entire provision.[523] Sub-sections (1) and (2) of the Article contain similar rules for other laws. Article 47(1) contains a list of matters and determines that any law providing for any of those matters shall not be deemed void on the ground that it is inconsistent with the rights guaranteed in Part III (i.e. the fundamental rights). The list includes, for example, the compulsory acquisition, nationalisation or requisition of any property. Sub-section (2) determines that no law specified in Schedule I of the Constitution, nor anything done or omitted to be done under the authority of such law shall be deemed void or unlawful on the grounds of inconsistency with any provision of the Constitution. Schedule I of the Constitution contains a list of different laws ranging from the Bangladesh Inland Water Transport Corporation Order, 1972 to the Bangladesh Shipping Corporation Order, 1972. While the laws referred to in Article 47(2) cannot be deemed void or unlawful on the ground of inconsistency with any provision of the Constitution, sub-section (1) is a bit more restrictive and 'merely' excludes the possibility to challenge the law based on inconsistency with fundamental rights. Beloff argues that Articles 47(3) and 47A are unconstitutional inasmuch as they abrogate the right to judicial review.[524] In the light of *Italian Marble Works Ltd. v. Bangladesh*, this conclusion is certainly difficult to dispute.

In the context of international human rights law, Article 47(3) and Article 47A are obviously highly problematic. Article 4(1) of the ICCPR determines that, in case of an emergency that threatens the life of a nation and the existence of which is officially proclaimed, derogations from some obligations assumed under the ICCPR may be made. Nevertheless, even in case of emergency, Article 4(2) of the ICCPR impedes

---

521 *Italian Marble Works Ltd. v. Bangladesh*, 62 DLR (HCD) (2010), pp. 70 ff., at 252, 283.
522 *Khondker Delwar Hossain v. Italian Marble Works Ltd.*, 62 DLR (AD) (2010), pp. 298 ff.
523 *Linton*, CLF, 2010, 21(2), p. 191, at 219.
524 *Beloff*, International Crimes (Tribunals) Act, 1973, p. 30.

the derogation from several rights, including the principle of legality enshrined in Article 15. However, it is evident that there was no case of emergency in 1973 when the ICT Act was enacted[525] and neither is there an emergency today. The constitutional curtailment of rights is, therefore, disproportionate.[526] Yet, even if, from the point of view of domestic law, the First Amendment is considered, the constitutional restrictions raise doubts regarding Bangladesh's compliance with the ICCPR.[527]

2.3.1.3 General domestic law

While Section 23 of the ICT Act expressly declares the provisions of the Criminal Procedure Code, 1898 and the Evidence Act, 1872 inapplicable to any proceedings before the ICT, the ICT Act is silent on other sources. This raises the question of whether the ICT can invoke domestic legal sources other than those expressly mentioned in Section 23 in order to fill the gaps of the ICT Act.

In practice, the question becomes relevant in particular with regard to certain legal concepts not further defined in the ICT Act. For example, the ICT Act neither defines the modes of liability nor provides definitions for the crimes that constitute crimes against humanity. Recourse to domestic law, however, runs the risk that domestic definitions differ from customary international law.

Since the ICT is a domestic court, it is evident that it applies domestic law. On various occasions, the ICT and the Appellate Division have invoked the Bangladesh Penal Code for definitions of legal terms not defined under the ICT Act. Given that the ICT and the Appellate Division have declared international law inapplicable on most occasions,[528] domestic law will always be applied in the first place for the interpretation of legal concepts.

In *Molla*, the Appellate Division invoked the Penal Code for the definition of rape and murder. The Division found that the Penal Code was applicable because its application was not expressly excluded by the ICT Act.[529] It further emphasised that all the laws of Bangladesh have been framed in accordance with concepts, principles, rules and traditions of English common law and that the definitions of these crimes, therefore, reflect English common law and so their validity is not doubtful.[530] On the other hand, the Appellate Division found the Police Regulations inapplicable to the investigation procedure under the ICT Act and the RoP even though there is no ex-

---

525 *Linton*, CLF, 2010, 21(2), p. 191, at 219.
526 *Linton*, CLF, 2010, 21(2), p. 191, at 219.
527 *Linton*, CLF, 2010, 21(2), p. 191, at 220.
528 On the applicability of international law, see pp. 82 ff.
529 SC (AD), *Molla v. The Chief Prosecutor*, Appeal Judgment, 17 September 2013, p. 143.
530 SC (AD), *Molla v. The Chief Prosecutor*, Appeal Judgment, 17 September 2013 p. 143–144.

2 The domestic character of the International Crimes Tribunal in Bangladesh

plicit provision that bars their applicability.[531] In *Chowdhury*, the Appellate Division applied the Code of Civil Procedure to determine the admissibility of an affidavit sworn abroad arguing that its applicability is neither barred by the ICT Act nor by the RoP.[532]

Based on the Appellate Division's findings, the ICT applied the Penal Code for the interpretation of Section 20(2) in *Jabbar Engineer*.[533] The ICT Act allows for the imposition of the death penalty or 'such other punishment proportionate to the gravity of the crime as appears to the Tribunal to be just and proper' but the Act does not contain any further provisions regarding the kind of penalties that can be imposed. The Tribunal dealt with the question of whether 'such other punishment' also allowed the Tribunal to impose a fine.[534] Invoking Section 53 of the Penal Code, it concluded that all the penalties mentioned there can be imposed and thus also a fine.[535] In conclusion, as a general rule, the ICT invokes domestic law for the interpretation of legal terms in the first place as long as this is not barred by the Act.

2.3.1.4 Rules of Procedure

The RoP are the ICT's main source of procedural law. The ICT Act contains very few procedural provisions. However, most of the rules only repeat what is already determined in the ICT Act.

The fact that each Tribunal frames its own rules can lead to different procedural law applicable to the cases depending on whether they are tried before Tribunal 1 or Tribunal 2. In practice, Tribunal 2 adopted the RoP of Tribunal 1 (including the amendments from 2010, 2011 and 2012) with some minor differences.[536] Since the

---

531 SC (AD), *Molla v. The Chief Prosecutor*, Appeal Judgment, 17 September 2013, p. 203.
532 SC (AD), *Chowdhury v. The Chief Prosecutor*, Appeal Judgment, 29 July 2015, p. 147.
533 ICT 1, *The Chief Prosecutor v. Jabbar Engineer*, case no. 01/2014, Judgment, 24 February 2015.
534 ICT 1, *The Chief Prosecutor v. Jabbar Engineer*, case no. 01/2014, Judgment, 24 February 2015, para. 313.
535 ICT 1, *The Chief Prosecutor v. Jabbar Engineer*, case no. 01/2014, Judgment, 24 February 2015, para. 316.
536 The RoP of Tribunal 1 determine in Rule 43(8) that the accused shall be issued a copy of the judgment free of cost, whereas this provision is not contained in the RoP of Tribunal 2. However, the provision is identical with Section 20(2A) of the ICT Act. Beyond that, Rule 26 of the RoP of Tribunal 1 has three further sub-rules regarding the filing of applications. Pursuant to Rule 26(4), the chairman or any member decides whether there are reasons for considering an application and only after a favourable decision is an application referred to the Tribunal. Sub-rule (5) determines that an application seeking review of an order has to be filed within 7 days and sub-rule (6) determines that applications have to be filed with the Registrar on working days until 3pm.

tribunals were merged and currently only one tribunal functions, the problem of diverging procedural law has now been settled. The jurisprudence considered hereinafter, however, dates from the period before this merge.

Although the possibility of framing differing rules has not become relevant in practice, it is evidently problematic if one considers that the RoP of the ICT do not contain mere organisational and technical rules but also determine the fundamental rights of the accused during trial that are not enshrined in the ICT Act. Rule 43 determines that the Tribunal must appoint a defence counsel for the defence of an unrepresented accused. The same rule also contains several fundamental procedural rights: the presumption of innocence; the *ne bis in idem* principle; the right to a fair and public hearing and the right to engage a defence counsel of his choice; the right to a trial without undue delay; the prohibition of punishment without giving the accused an opportunity to be heard; and the prohibition to compel any accused to testify against his will or to confess his guilt. Of these principles, the ICT Act only contains the right to defence counsel in Section 12. Section 17 of the ICT Act determines the rights of the accused during trial but does not include any of those contained in the RoP. Section 17 establishes the right of the accused to give any explanation relevant to the charge made against him; the right to conduct his own defence or to have the assistance of a counsel; the right to present evidence in a trial in support of his defence; and the right to cross-examine any witness called by the prosecution.

The regulation of the rights of the accused in the RoP is not only alarming in that they might differ depending on the tribunal but also because the tribunals themselves are empowered to frame and amend them. That is, the fundamental rights of the accused are not protected and can be modified without a parliamentary act.

Also, the lack of agreement between the RoP and the ICT Act causes practical problems as the Rules determine rights and obligations not contained in the ICT Act. This became relevant with regard to the question of whether the ICT could sentence an accused to pay compensation to the victims of the crimes he had committed. Rule 46(3) allows the Tribunal to order the accused to pay fit and proper reparations. In contrast, the ICT Act does not mention the possibility of imposing the payment of compensation or reparations to the victims but it does allow the Tribunal to impose 'such other punishment proportionate to the gravity of the crime'. The Tribunal rejected the prosecution's request to impose the payment of compensation and ruled that the RoP, as mere procedural rules enacted by the Tribunal itself, cannot override the main statute which was passed as a parliamentary act.[537] As a consequence, the ICT Act prevails in cases of conflict with the RoP.

---

[537] ICT 2, *The Chief Prosecutor v. Qaiser*, case no. 04/2013, Judgment, 23 December 2014, para. 981.

2.3.1.5 Domestic jurisprudence

The ICT applies domestic jurisprudence, i.e. besides its own jurisprudence, it also invokes jurisprudence of the Appellate Division of the Supreme Court. As a domestic court, it is bound not only by the Appellate Division's decisions delivered in the function of the Appellate Division for the ICT but also by the jurisprudence on general matters.

2.3.2 International and foreign sources

While the application of domestic legal sources follows from the nature of the ICT as a domestic tribunal, the application of international law or jurisprudence cannot be presumed. In contrast, the direct application of international law and jurisprudence by domestic courts depends on the legal system and the status of international law within the domestic judicial system. On the other hand, the application of foreign jurisprudence in domestic courts is common practice in common law systems.

2.3.2.1 Applicability of international law

The direct applicability of international law through the ICT depends on the status of international law in the domestic legal system.

Bangladesh's Constitution is silent on the status of international law in the domestic judicial system. It refers to international law in two articles but does not determine its relationship to domestic law. Article 25 incorporates some basic principles of customary international law as fundamental principles of state policy:[538]

> *Article 25 of the Constitution*
> The State shall base its international relations on the principles of respect for national sovereignty and equality, non-interference in the internal affairs of other countries, peaceful settlement of international disputes, and respect for international law and the principles enunciated in the United Nations Charter, and on the basis of those principles shall –
> (a) strive for the renunciation of the use of force in international relations and for general and complete disarmament;
> (b) uphold the right of every people freely to determine and build up its own social, economic and political system by ways and means of its own free choice; and
> (c) support oppressed peoples throughout the world waging a just struggle against imperialism, colonialism or racialism.

With regard to international treaties, Article 145A of the Constitution solely determines the procedure of accession of treaties:

---

[538] *Rahman Karzon/Al-Faruque*, BD JL, 1999, 3(1), p. 23, at 33.

Article 145A of the Constitution
All treaties with foreign countries shall be submitted to the President, who shall cause them to be laid before Parliament:
Provided that any such treaty connected with national security shall be laid in a secret session of Parliament.

Although there is an obligation to lay a treaty before Parliament, Parliament's approval is not required for its validity.[539] That is, treaty-making in Bangladesh is an executive act.[540] Nevertheless, the Constitution does not shed light on the status of international law within the legal system and thus does not provide a guideline for domestic courts on how to deal with international law.

The status of treaties under domestic law, though, can be deduced from the fact that Bangladesh's legal system is based on English common law and follows a dualist approach.[541] Unlike monist systems, dualist systems require the incorporation of treaties into domestic law in order for them to be applicable. Nevertheless, even in monist systems, not all treaties are applicable directly – a distinction is made between self-executing and non-self-executing treaties. The latter always require an implementation into domestic law. As a consequence of the dualist system in Bangladesh, regulations of treaties cannot be applied directly in domestic courts unless they are incorporated into domestic law. In view of the fact that many international treaties are not domestically implemented, discrepancies between international and domestic law are frequent.[542] In fact, in *State v. Md. Roushan Mondal Hashem*, the Supreme Court of Bangladesh expressed its concern for the government's practice of non-implementation with regard to the Convention on the Rights of the Child.[543]

On the other hand, customary international law is generally accepted to be part of the law of Bangladesh and to be of binding character as long as it is not inconsistent with domestic law.[544] The Constitution does not explicitly establish a hierarchy but declares the Constitution the supreme law of the country and any law inconsistent

---

539 *Islam*, Constitutional Law, 3. edn, p. 1026; *Rahman Karzon/Al-Faruque*, BD JL, 1999, 3(1), p. 23, at 37.
540 *Karim/Theunissen*, in: *Shelton* (ed.), International Law and Domestic Legal Systems, p. 98, at 100.
541 *Karim/Theunissen*, in: *Shelton* (ed.), International Law and Domestic Legal Systems, p. 98, at 101; *Linton*, CLF, 2010, 21(2), p. 191, at 220.
542 *Karim/Theunissen*, in: *Shelton* (ed.), International Law and Domestic Legal Systems, p. 98, at 103.
543 *State v. Md. Roushan Mondal Hashem*, 26 BLD (HCD) (2006), pp. 549 ff., at 571–572.
544 *Karim/Theunissen*, in: *Shelton* (ed.), International Law and Domestic Legal Systems, p. 98, at 106.

with it to be void.⁵⁴⁵ The Constitution, therefore, prevails in the case of conflict with international law.⁵⁴⁶

The Supreme Court of Bangladesh addressed the application of international law by domestic courts in several judgments.⁵⁴⁷ In *Bangladesh v. Sombon Asavhan*, the Appellate Division held that, wherever there is domestic law on a matter, the courts should apply exclusively domestic law even if the matter concerns international law.⁵⁴⁸ Nevertheless, domestic courts may invoke international law for interpretation if there is a need for interpretation of domestic law. In *Hussain Muhammad Ershad v. Bangladesh and others*, Justice Bimalendu Bikash Roy Chowdhury observed that:

> True it is that the Universal Human Rights norms, whether given in the Universal Declaration or in the Covenants, are not directly enforceable in national courts. But if their provisions are incorporated into the domestic law, they are enforceable in national courts. The local laws, both constitutional and statutory, are not always in consonance with the norms contained in international human rights instruments. The national court should not, I feel, straightway ignore the international obligations, which a country undertakes. If the domestic laws are not clear enough or there is nothing therein, the national courts should draw upon the principles incorporated in the international instruments. But in the cases where the domestic laws are clear and inconsistent with the international obligations of the state concerned, courts will be obliged to respect the national laws, but shall draw the attention of the law makers [sic] to such inconsistencies.⁵⁴⁹

Nonetheless, in practice, there is strong reluctance from Bangladeshi judges and lawyers to invoke international instruments, and international provisions are rarely considered.⁵⁵⁰ In *Bangladesh v. Sheikh Hasina*,⁵⁵¹ the Appellate Division observed that the domestic courts would not apply international treaties if they were ratified but not implemented into domestic law. According to the portrayal of the ICT on the Tribunal's official website:

> [...] the Tribunal shall never be precluded to seek guidance from the universally recognized norms and principles laid down in international law and International Criminal Law with a blend of national law, in trying the persons responsible for perpetration of crimes enumerated in the Act of 1973.⁵⁵²

---

545 Article 7(2) of the Constitution of Bangladesh.
546 *Karim/Theunissen*, in: *Shelton* (ed.), International Law and Domestic Legal Systems, p. 98, at 109.
547 For an overview of the relevant Supreme Court decisions, see *Alam*, Enforcement of International Human Rights Law, pp. 100–132 and *Rahman Karzon/Al-Faruque*, BD JL, 1999, 3(1), pp. 23–47.
548 *Bangladesh v. Sombon Asavhan*, 32 DLR (AD) (1980), pp. 194 ff., at 98.
549 *H. M. Ershad v. Bangladesh*, 21 BLD (AD) (2001), pp. 69 ff., at 70.
550 *Alam*, Enforcement of International Human Rights Law, pp. 102, 110; *Hoque/Naser*, Indian JIL, 2006, 46(2), p. 151, at 180.
551 *Bangladesh v. Sheikh Hasina Wazed*, 60 DLR (AD) (2008), pp. 90 ff., at 104.
552 http://ict-bd.org/ict1/, accessed 5 August 2014.

The ICT initially adopted this view and held that it should not be precluded from seeking guidance from the jurisprudence related to the international crimes.[553] Nevertheless, this does not shed light on the circumstances that have to be fulfilled in order for the Tribunal to invoke international law. In fact, the Appellate Division took the view that international law can be applied only restrictedly.

In *Molla*, the defence argued that the word 'international' in the title of the ICT Act as well as in Article 47(3) of the Constitution refers to international crimes and indicates that customary international law is applicable to cases under the ICT Act and has to be applied particularly for the definition of the crimes.[554] The Appellate Division objected to this reasoning and instead followed the previous domestic jurisprudence confirming that conventions, even if ratified, require incorporation into domestic law in order to be applicable.[555] It held that the fact that 'any other crimes under international law' are within the ICT's jurisdiction does not result in the conclusion that customary international law can be applied for the interpretation of the other crimes, too.[556] Nevertheless, it admitted that a person charged with 'any other crime under international law' is entitled to claim that customary international law be followed with regard to the definition.[557] Yet, in practice, the ICT has not complied with this finding.[558]

The Appellate Division heard seven *amici curiae* on the applicability of customary international law by the ICT.[559] Three argued in favour of applicability.[560] It was contended that the absence of definitions in the ICT Act as well as the fact that the respective crimes are international crimes oblige the Tribunal to invoke the definitions as established under customary international law.[561] It was also argued that, under inter-

---

[553] See, for instance, ICT 2, *The Chief Prosecutor v. Molla*, case no. 02/2012, Judgment, 5 February 2013, para. 72; ICT 2, *The Chief Prosecutor v. Ali*, case no. 03/2013, Judgment, 2 November 2014, para. 41.
[554] SC (AD), *Molla v. The Chief Prosecutor*, Appeal Judgment, 17 September 2013, pp. 79, 142.
[555] SC (AD), *Molla v. The Chief Prosecutor*, Appeal Judgment, 17 September 2013, p. 107; SC (AD), *Molla v. The Chief Prosecutor*, Dissenting Opinion of Justice Miah, Appeal Judgment, 17 September 2013, p. 259; SC (AD), *Molla v. The Chief Prosecutor*, Separate Opinion of Justice Choudhury, Appeal Judgment, 17 September 2013, p. 574.
[556] SC (AD), *Molla v. The Chief Prosecutor*, Appeal Judgment, 17 September 2013, p. 86.
[557] SC (AD), *Molla v. The Chief Prosecutor*, Appeal Judgment, 17 September 2013, p. 86.
[558] On the application of 'any other crimes under international law' by the ICT, see pp. 156 ff.
[559] Their opinions are partly cited in SC (AD), *Molla v. The Chief Prosecutor*, Separate Opinion of Justice Choudhury, Appeal Judgment, 17 September 2013, pp. 538 ff.
[560] SC (AD), *Molla v. The Chief Prosecutor*, Appeal Judgment, 17 September 2013, p. 83.
[561] SC (AD), *Molla v. The Chief Prosecutor*, Appeal Judgment, 17 September 2013, p. 83; also cited by Justice Choudhury in his Separate Opinion: SC (AD), *Molla v. The Chief*

2 The domestic character of the International Crimes Tribunal in Bangladesh

national law, customary international law has prevalence over domestic law and that a state does not have to formally accept a customary rule in order to be bound by it.[562]

In contrast, the Appellate Division adopted the findings of the *amici curiae* that rejected the applicability of customary international law by the ICT. It was held that the non-applicability of international law follows from the fact that crimes under customary international law do not impose any penal sanction on the individuals unless the crimes are incorporated into domestic law.[563] They also invoked Article 80(5) of the Bangladesh Constitution which requires the president to assent to a bill passed by Parliament in order for it to become law[564] and concluded, therefore, that international obligations do not have force of law unless incorporated into municipal law.[565] Yet, the *amici curiae* conceded that, whenever there is a gap in the provisions of the ICT Act, international law could be invoked but, although it appears that this is not the case with the definitions of the crimes in the ICT Act.[566] In any event, customary international law cannot be applied if it is inconsistent with the domestic law.[567] In line with this view, the Appellate Division clarified that, as long as there are domestic provisions such as in the case of rape and murder, these shall be applied and there is no scope for the application of customary international law.[568] The Division further affirmed that the provisions of the ICT Act are consistent with customary international law and absolutely unambiguous so that there is no need to invoke customary international law.[569] As outlined above, this finding is flawed as the ICT Act diverges from customary international law in several aspects. The ICT summed up the Appellate Division's findings as follows:

Prosecutor, Separate Opinion of Justice Choudhury, Appeal Judgment, 17 September 2013, p. 539.

562 SC (AD), *Molla v. The Chief Prosecutor*, Appeal Judgment, 17 September 2013, pp. 84, 85.
563 SC (AD), *Molla v. The Chief Prosecutor*, Appeal Judgment, 17 September 2013, p. 127; SC (AD), *Molla v. The Chief Prosecutor*, Separate Opinion of Justice Choudhury, Appeal Judgment, 17 September 2013, p. 544.
564 SC (AD), *Molla v. The Chief Prosecutor*, Appeal Judgment, 17 September 2013, p. 129.
565 SC (AD), *Molla v. The Chief Prosecutor*, Appeal Judgment, 17 September 2013, pp. 130, 131.
566 SC (AD), *Molla v. The Chief Prosecutor*, Separate Opinion of Justice Choudhury, Appeal Judgment, 17 September 2013, pp. 548, 549.
567 SC (AD), *Molla v. The Chief Prosecutor*, Separate Opinion of Justice Choudhury, Appeal Judgment, 17 September 2013, pp. 159, 551, 552.
568 SC (AD), *Molla v. The Chief Prosecutor*, Appeal Judgment, 17 September 2013, p. 262.
569 The Division concurred on this: SC (AD), *Molla v. The Chief Prosecutor*, Appeal Judgment, 17 September 2013, p. 159; SC (AD), *Molla v. The Chief Prosecutor*, Dissenting Opinion of Justice Miah, Appeal Judgment, 17 September 2013, p. 261; SC (AD), *Molla v. The Chief Prosecutor*, Separate Opinion of Justice Choudhury, Appeal Judgment, 17 September 2013, p. 574.

Part III: The ICT in comparison to other accountability mechanisms

> The Act of 1973 is a codified law, thus, it is not needed to travel to seek assistance from other trials held or being held by the tribunals/courts either under the charter of agreements of the nations or under other arrangements under the mandate of [the] United Nations or [an]other International body, such as [the] Nuremburg trial and the Balkan trials.[570]

Yet, in such a general and absolute manner, this summary does not reflect precisely the findings of the Appellate Division.

Considering the Appellate Division's restrictive position, the ICT is left with little freedom to apply international law. Nevertheless, to date, neither the ICT nor the Appellate Division have complied with Justice Bimalendu Bikash Roy Chowdhury's suggestion in *Hussain Muhammad Ershad v. Bangladesh and others* that the courts shall draw the attention of the law-makers to inconsistencies between domestic and international law. As outlined above, the ICT Act provides sufficient grounds for this.

In summary, it can be concluded that the ICT, like all other domestic courts of Bangladesh, primarily applies domestic law and, if at all, invokes international law only in the absence of domestic provisions or ambiguity of domestic law. In the case of inconsistency of international law with municipal law, its applicability is, nevertheless, excluded.

2.3.2.2 International criminal law jurisprudence

The ICT Act also does not shed light on the applicability of jurisprudence from international criminal tribunals. For the interpretation of the crimes under the ICT Act, international jurisprudence is crucial. While the Tribunal stated that it would not be precluded from invoking modern jurisprudence on the offences,[571] the Appellate Division questioned the relevance of international jurisprudence. The Division held that they are not applicable to the ICT Act because they refer only to provisions of specific statutes and these differ greatly from the ICT Act.[572] At the same time, it applied the same approach as to the applicability of international law and affirmed that as long as there are domestic provisions then international jurisprudence is not to be invoked.[573] However, Justice Choudhury adopted a broader approach and argued that decisions of

---

570 ICT 1, *The Chief Prosecutor v. Khokon*, case no. 04/2013, Judgment, 13 November 2014, para. 39; ICT 1, *The Chief Prosecutor v. Hossain*, case no. 01/2013, Judgment, 24 November 2014, para. 42.
571 ICT 1, *The Chief Prosecutor v. Azam*, case no. 06/2011, Judgment, 15 July 2013, para. 42; ICT 1, *The Chief Prosecutor v. Chowdhury*, case no. 02/2011, Judgment, 1 October 2013, para. 274.
572 SC (AD), *Molla v. The Chief Prosecutor*, Appeal Judgment, 17 September 2013, p. 159.
573 SC (AD), *Kamaruzzaman v. The Chief Prosecutor*, Appeal Judgment, 3 November 2014, p. 193.

international tribunals could be taken into consideration whenever they do not conflict with the domestic law.[574]

2.3.2.3 Foreign jurisprudence

The interpretation of the law by means of jurisprudence from other common law countries in the domestic courts of Bangladesh is common practice and therefore applies to the ICT as well. This is in line with the widespread practice of common law courts.

In fact, the Tribunal clarified that it considers settled and recognised jurisprudence from around the world.[575] In practice, the ICT frequently invokes British and Indian jurisprudence for the interpretation of general legal concepts.

Likewise, the Appellate Division invokes Indian, British and American jurisprudence in the discussion of legal issues,[576] and Justice Choudhury emphasised that the courts of Bangladesh consider the jurisprudence of the common law countries because of the similarity of the legal provisions[577]. Nevertheless, the scope of foreign jurisprudence for the interpretation of the offences under the ICT Act is clearly limited.

2.4 Amnesties

The domestic character of the ICT also determines the scope of amnesties granted at the domestic level. In the context of the ICT, amnesties become relevant for the trials in different ways. First, the amnesties provided to those prosecuted or investigated under the Collaborators Order might bar prosecutions before the ICT. Second, the clemency agreed on in the Tripartite Agreement in 1974 might constitute a bar to the prosecution of the 195 Pakistani prisoners. This aspect is, of course, more theoretical because, as pointed out, the trial of Pakistani nationals is hampered by the refusal of Pakistan to extradite them. Finally, provided that the clemency granted to the main perpetrators in 1974 is valid, it might bar the prosecution of the low-level perpetrators.

The government proclaimed a general amnesty on 30 November 1973, releasing most of those arrested under the Collaborators Order. The Collaborators Order was

---

574 SC (AD), *Molla v. The Chief Prosecutor*, Dissenting Opinion of Justice Choudhury, Appeal Judgment, 17 September 2013, p. 575.
575 ICT 2, *Molla v. The Chief Prosecutor*, case no. 02/2012, Judgment, 5 February 2013, para. 40.
576 SC (AD), *Molla v. The Chief Prosecutor*, Appeal Judgment, 17 September 2013, p. 101, p. 106.
577 SC (AD), *Molla v. The Chief Prosecutor*, Separate Opinion of Justice Choudhury, Appeal Judgment, 17 September 2013, p. 585.

afterwards repealed in 1975 and the Repeal Ordinance determined that all ongoing trials under the Collaborators Order should be called off.[578]

However, it would be very difficult to argue that this amnesty bars prosecutions under the ICT Act. It was explicitly granted for those accused under the Collaborators Order and thus only for the commission of crimes punishable under the Order.[579] The Collaborators Order penalised collaboration in the commission of different crimes defined in the Penal Code but did not include international crimes. Beyond that, the General Amnesty Order explicitly excluded perpetrators of murder, culpable homicide not amounting to murder, rape, mischief by fire of explosive, mischief by fire of explosive substance with intent to destroy a house, or mischief by fire of explosive substance to any vessel.[580] The General Amnesty Order thus did not grant a blanket amnesty. Since it was expressly restricted to some crimes, it can be concluded that it was not intended to cover the core international crimes.

In the cases considered, the ICT had to deal with this issue only in the case of *Yusuf*. The accused died before the delivery of a judgment but after the trial was concluded. The accused was convicted under the Collaborators Order for: (1) waging war or attempting to do so or abetting the waging of war against Bangladesh; (2) attempting to bring into hatred or attempting to excite disaffection towards the government of Bangladesh; and (3) attempting to aid or aiding the occupation army in furthering its design of perpetrating the forcible occupation of Bangladesh.[581] During the pendency of the appeal, he was released based on the general amnesty granted by the government.[582] The accused benefited from the amnesty because he was not convicted of murder or of any other offence excluded by the Amnesty Order. The Tribunal rightly clarified that this clearly does not exclude a trial for murder today.[583] This applies all the more in view of the fact that the General Amnesty Order was not a blanket amnesty.

The second question regarding the effect of amnesties concerns the Tripartite Agreement reached between India, Pakistan and Bangladesh on 9 April 1974. As mentioned above, Bangladesh agreed to repatriate the 195 Pakistani prisoners held in India and decided not to proceed with the trials as an act of clemency:

---

578 Section 2(2) of the Repeal Ordinance.
579 *Matas*, in: *Hoque* (ed.), Genocide Conference Papers, 2009, p. 33, at 41.
580 Cited by *Matas*, in: *Hoque* (ed.), Genocide Conference Papers, 2009, p. 33, at 41.
581 ICT 2, *The Chief Prosecutor v. A. K. M. Yusuf*, case no. 02/2013, Order no. 76, 12 February 2014, para. 9.
582 ICT 2, *The Chief Prosecutor v. A. K. M. Yusuf*, case no. 02/2013, Order no. 76, 12 February 2014, para. 9.
583 ICT 2, *The Chief Prosecutor v. A. K. M. Yusuf*, case no. 02/2013, Charge Framing Order, 1 August 2013, para. 25.

2 The domestic character of the International Crimes Tribunal in Bangladesh

Para. 13 (Sentence 2) of the Agreement on the Repatriation of Prisoners of War and Civilian Internees
The Foreign Minister of Bangladesh stated that the excesses and manifold crimes committed by these prisoners of war constituted, according to the relevant provisions of the U.N. General Assembly Resolutions and International Law, war crimes, crimes against humanity and genocide, and that there was universal consensus that persons charged with such crimes as the 195 Pakistani prisoners of war should be held to account and subjected to the due process of law.

Para. 15 of the Agreement on the Repatriation of Prisoners of War and Civilian Internees
In the light of the forgoing and, in particular, having regard to the appeal of the Prime Minister of Pakistan to the people of Bangladesh to forgive and forget the mistakes of the past, the Foreign Minister of Bangladesh stated that the Government of Bangladesh had decided not to proceed with the trials as an act of clemency. It was agreed that the 195 prisoners of war may be repatriated to Pakistan along with the other prisoners of war now in the process of repatriation under the Delhi Agreement.

In order to examine the possibility of trying the 195 Pakistani prisoners, it becomes pivotal to determine whether the amnesty provided in the Tripartite Agreement is valid. The Tribunal dealt with the question in various judgments. The ICT argued that the amnesty was granted through an executive act. This derogated to international regulations and the domestic law in force at that time (the ICT Act), which implemented the obligation to prosecute international crimes.[584] The Tribunal held that the agreement was contrary to *ius cogens* and as an executive act it cannot bar the obligations assumed under the UDHR and under the ICT Act to try international crimes.[585] The Tribunal reiterated that, as a state party to the UDHR and the Geneva Conventions, Bangladesh cannot escape its obligations to provide justice to the victims of international crimes.[586] It also invoked Article 53 of the Vienna Convention on the Law of Treaties (Vienna Convention), pursuant to which a treaty is void if it is contrary to *ius cogens*.[587] The

---

[584] See, for instance, ICT 2, *The Chief Prosecutor v. Azad*, case no. 05/2012, Judgment, 21 January 2013, para. 62; ICT 1, *The Chief Prosecutor v. Sayeedi*, case no. 01/2011, Judgment, 28 February 2013, para. 46; ICT 2, *Molla v. The Chief Prosecutor*, case no. 02/2013, Judgment, 5 February 2013, para 105; ICT 2, *The Chief Prosecutor v. Kamaruzzaman*, case 03/2012, Judgment, 9 May 2013, para. 118; ICT 2, *The Chief Prosecutor v. Alim*, case no. 01/2012, Judgment, 9 October 2013, para 93. The reasoning in the judgment in *Sayeedi* was adopted in all the judgments that followed.

[585] ICT 1, *The Chief Prosecutor v. Sayeedi*, case no. 01/2011, Judgment, 28 February 2013, para. 47; ICT 2, *Molla v. The Chief Prosecutor*, case no. 02/2013, Judgment, 5 February 2013, para. 106; ICT 2, *The Chief Prosecutor v. Kamaruzzaman*, case 03/2012, Judgment, 9 May 2013, para. 121; ICT 2, *The Chief Prosecutor v. Alim*, case no. 01/2012, Judgment, 9 October 2013, para 96.

[586] ICT 1, *The Chief Prosecutor v. Sayeedi*, case no. 01/2011, Judgment, 28 February 2013, para. 48.

[587] ICT 2, *The Chief Prosecutor v. Kamaruzzaman*, case no. 03/2012, Judgment, 9 May 2013, para. 121.

Tribunal concluded that the agreement was contrary to *ius cogens* and, therefore, no state obligation arises from it.[588] The Appellate Division dealt with this issue only marginally. Justice Choudhury argued in his separate opinion that, since the amnesty was granted through an executive order and not by a court, the courts are not bound by it.[589] Justice Miah corroborated parts of the ICT's findings and held that the clemency did not make the ICT Act void and the failure of the government to act in accordance with the Act did not give the accused the right to be exonerated.[590]

The findings of the ICT are inconsistent in several ways. First, the Tribunal appears to mistake the nature of the UDHR because it is not a treaty. Rather, it was adopted as a Resolution by the UN General Assembly and, unlike a treaty, does not have binding legal effect. Nevertheless, its universal validity has been confirmed frequently in the past. It is widely accepted that the UDHR, at least in some parts,[591] has become part of customary international law. Many of the rights enshrined in it have even achieved the status of *ius cogens*.[592] However, it does not contain a prohibition on granting amnesties.

Secondly, the Tribunal also invoked the Vienna Convention from 1969. Pursuant to Article 53 of the Convention, a treaty is void if, at the time of its conclusion, it conflicts with a peremptory norm of international law. Interestingly, the Tribunal omitted a further explanation on the applicability of this treaty, to which Bangladesh is not a state party even today and which came into force only in 1980. In any event, the Vienna Convention does not apply to Bangladesh. While Article 53 has become a rule of customary international law today, it is disputed whether this was already the case prior to the Convention.[593]

Third, the Geneva Conventions do not establish a general duty to prosecute international crimes but rather a duty to prosecute grave breaches of the Conventions.[594] Yet, the Geneva Conventions do not establish individual responsibility for grave

---

588 ICT 1, *The Chief Prosecutor v. Sayeedi*, case no. 01/2011, Judgment, 28 February 2013, para. 48.
589 SC (AD), *Molla v. The Chief Prosecutor*, Separate Opinion of Justice Choudhury, Appeal Judgment, 17 September 2013, p. 750.
590 SC (AD), *Molla v. The Chief Prosecutor*, Dissenting Opinion of Justice Miah, Appeal Judgment, 17 September 2013, p. 279.
591 *Kaczorowska*, Public International Law, 4. edn, p. 508 argues, for instance, that violations of equality of men and women and of the right to nationality are not strongly condemned by the international community and thus do not form part of customary international law.
592 *Kaczorowska*, Public International Law, 4. edn, p. 508.
593 *Corten/Klein/Suy*, Commentary Vienna Conventions on the Law of Treaties, Vol. 2, p. 1226.
594 *Tomuschat*, in: *Cremer/Giegerich/Richter/Zimmermann* (eds), FS Steinberger, p. 315, at 333.

2 The domestic character of the International Crimes Tribunal in Bangladesh

breaches in non-international armed conflicts.[595] Common Article 3 and Additional Protocol I, both applicable to internal armed conflicts, do not mention individual responsibility.[596] It was only with the creation of the ICTR Statute that violations of Common Article 3 of the Geneva Conventions and of Article 4(2) of Additional Protocol II committed in internal armed conflicts were officially recognised.[597] As a consequence, at the time when the amnesty was granted, individual criminal liability for grave breaches was recognised only when committed in international armed conflicts. As will be outlined below, the Liberation War was a national conflict and became international only after the intervention of India.[598] The reasoning of the Tribunal thus holds true only with regard to a specific period of the war.

While a duty to prosecute can arise from treaties, it is only binding for the member states. A duty to prosecute is broadly accepted with regard to the crimes of genocide, torture and those war crimes that constitute grave breaches of the Geneva Conventions.[599] For other crimes, such as crimes against humanity, there is no treaty that establishes such duty. However, in the case of Bangladesh, there was no such treaty in 1974 that could have imposed a duty to prosecute. Notably, Bangladesh acceded to the Genocide Convention only in 1998. The Tribunal assumed that, already in 1974, when the clemency was granted, a duty to prosecute international crimes was part of *ius cogens*. Nevertheless, whether such a duty forms part of customary international law continues to be debated even today.[600] It can be said with certainty that in 1974 when the amnesty was granted, customary law did not impose a general duty to prosecute international crimes.

It is questionable whether, as stated by the Tribunal, the amnesty was contrary to the ICT Act. It would certainly be difficult to argue that the ICT Act contains a duty to prosecute, especially if one considers that the ICT Act itself allows for conditional amnesties. Although the Tribunal has not made use of this provision, Section 15 empowers it to grant amnesties in exchange for full and true disclosure of an accused. The same provision was also contained in the Collaborators Order.[601] Section 15 calls

---

595 *International Commission of Jurists*, Events in East Pakistan, p. 54.
596 *Boed*, CLF, 2002, 13(3), p. 293, at 298.
597 *Werle/Jessberger*, International Criminal Law, 3. edn, marginal no. 1068.
598 For further details on the nature of the conflict, see p. 153.
599 *Ambos*, in: *Ambos/Large/Wierda* (eds), Building a Future, p. 19, at 30; *Gropengießner/ Meißner*, ICLR, 2005, 5(2), p. 267, at 273–274; *Robinson*, EJIL, 2003, 14(3), p. 481, at 490–491; *Stahn*, IJCJ, 2005, 13(3), p. 695, at 703.
600 On the discussion, see *Cassese*, International Criminal Law, 3. edn, pp. 309–312; *Bassiouni*, Crimes against Humanity, pp. 213–218; *Cryer et al.*, International Criminal Law, 3. edn, pp. 77–79; *Tomuschat*, in: *Cremer/Giegerich/Richter/Zimmermann* (eds), FS Steinberger, pp. 315–349.
601 Section 10 of the Collaborators Order.

this a 'pardon' but this is rather a confusion of notions because pardons are granted after convictions.[602] Section 15 thus provides for the possibility of granting amnesties but this power belongs to the Tribunal.[603] Nevertheless, if one invokes Justice Choudhury's findings, courts in Bangladesh are bound by amnesties only if granted by a court.[604]

However, if one considers Bangladesh's obligations under the international law of today, amnesties under Section 15 certainly contravene the duty to prosecute.[605] The ICTY found that the *ius cogens* prohibition of torture necessarily also bars amnesties for torture.[606] As a consequence, an amnesty granted for torture would not bar prosecutions in another state or under a subsequent regime in the state in which it was granted.[607] It must be kept in mind, though, that these are rather recent developments.

If one invokes the above-outlined reasoning of Ziauddin that the president does not have any right to grant amnesties at all under the Constitution, one would further come to the conclusion that the amnesty granted to the 195 prisoners of war was unconstitutional. The validity of the clemency granted to the 195 prisoners of war was questioned in the context of the possibility of trying low-level perpetrators as aiders and abettors despite the fact that the high-level perpetrators were granted amnesties.[608] The ICT Act was enacted more than a year after the Collaborators Order. It was aimed at bringing high-ranking perpetrators of core international crimes to trial.[609] In various cases, the defence, therefore, argued that the ICT Act was exclusively created to bring the 195 Pakistani prisoners to trial and, as a consequence of the amnesty awarded to the main perpetrators through the Tripartite Agreement, it would be impossible to prosecute the accused as an aider or abettor under the ICT Act.[610] Although the Tribunal found the amnesty invalid, it brought forward further arguments to underline the possibility of prosecuting the perpetrators even if the amnesty was valid.

---

602 *Linton*, CLF, 2010, 21(2), p. 191, at 286.
603 *Linton*, CLF, 2010, 21(2), p. 191, at 286.
604 SC (AD), *Molla v. The Chief Prosecutor*, Separate Opinion of Justice Choudhury, Appeal Judgment, 17 September 2013, p. 750.
605 *Linton*, CLF, 2010, 21(2), p. 191, at 287.
606 ICTY (TC), *Prosecutor v. Furundžija*, Judgment, 10 December 1998, para. 155.
607 ICTY, (TC II), *Prosecutor v. Furundžija*, Judgment, 10 December 1998, para. 155.
608 See, for instance, ICT 2, *The Chief Prosecutor v. Kamaruzzaman*, case no. 03/2012, Charge Framing Order, 4 June 2012, p. 6.
609 *Linton*, CLF, 2010, 21(2), p. 191, at 228.
610 See, for instance, ICT 2, *The Chief Prosecutor v. Molla*, case no. 02/2013, Judgment, 5 February 2013, para. 59; ICT 2, *The Chief Prosecutor v. Alim*, case no. 01/2012, Judgment, 9 October 2013, para. 73; ICT 2, *The Chief Prosecutor v. Kamaruzzaman*, case no. 03/2012, Charge Framing Order, 4 June 2012, p. 6. The line of reasoning is the same in all these cases.

2 The domestic character of the International Crimes Tribunal in Bangladesh

The Tribunal found that the Tripartite Agreement did not intend to prevent any possible future trials other than those concerning the 195 Pakistani prisoners.[611] It further interpreted the clemency to the effect that it was decided merely not to try the prisoners in Bangladesh but that, nevertheless, the Pakistani prisoners can be brought to trial.[612] The Tribunal further pointed to the wording of the ICT Act which expressly gives the ICT the power to prosecute members of auxiliary forces and individuals.[613] It also stressed the possibility of prosecuting an accused for abetment under the ICT Act and concluded that there is thus no need to prosecute the main perpetrator in order to hold a perpetrator liable as an abettor.[614]

These arguments are certainly relevant. Nevertheless, it should not be disregarded that, even if, in practice, the Pakistani prisoners cannot be tried, be it due to the amnesty or mere practical impossibility, the focus on trying lower-level perpetrators due to the impossibility of holding high-level perpetrators accountable can tarnish the process.[615]

2.5 Ne bis in idem

The *ne bis in idem* principle establishes that nobody can be tried for the same criminal conduct more than once. In the context of the trials in Bangladesh, the principle might be affected if the accused under the ICT Act were already tried under the Collaborators Order.

The *ne bis in idem* principle is enshrined in the Bangladeshi Constitution in Article 35(2), which determines that no person shall be punished for the same offence more than once. It is further contained in Section 403 of the Code of Criminal Procedure although this provision is not applicable to cases under the ICT Act. The *ne bis in idem* principle is also contained in the RoP. Rule 43(3) determines that no person shall be tried twice for the same offence described under Section 3(2) of the Act. To date, there have been no cases in which the principle has become relevant with regard to a second

---

611 ICT 2, *The Chief Prosecutor v. Kamaruzzaman*, case no. 03/2012, Judgment, 9 May 2013, para. 42.
612 See, for instance, ICT 2, *The Chief Prosecutor v. Kamaruzzaman*, case 03/2012, Judgment, 9 May 2013, para. 118; ICT 2, *The Chief Prosecutor v. Alim*, case no. 01/2012, Judgment, 9 October 2013, para. 93; ICT 2, *The Chief Prosecutor v. Ali*, case no. 03/2013, Judgment, 2 November 2014, para. 92.
613 ICT 1, *The Chief Prosecutor v. Sayeedi*, case no. 01/2011, Judgment, 28 February 2013, para. 49.
614 ICT 2, *The Chief Prosecutor v. Molla*, case no. 02/2013, Judgment, 5 February 2013, para. 121.
615 *Linton*, CLF, 2010, 21(2), p. 191, at 229.

trial under the ICT Act. Nevertheless, there were some accused who had been investigated or tried under the Collaborators Order.

For instance, in *Azad*, the defence held that the accused could have been tried under the Collaborators Order in 1972 and a prosecution of the same offences before the ICT would, therefore, be barred.[616] In the particular case, there was, however, no scope of application for the principle of double jeopardy because there was no proof that the accused was actually prosecuted under the Collaborators Order.[617] The mere possibility that a trial could have taken place certainly does not conflict with the *ne bis in idem* principle. On the other hand, the accused Alim was tried under the Collaborators Order in 1972 and later released[618] but there was no proof that the accused was released after a trial under the Order.[619] The Tribunal held that the earlier trial must have been concluded with a final determination of the facts at issue, i.e. there must have been a final verdict of acquittal or conviction.[620] For this reason, it rejected the applicability of the *ne bis in idem* principle.[621] In both cases, the ICT further clarified that the offences under the Collaborators Order and under the ICT Act are not identical and thus do not constitute 'the same offence' as would be required for the *ne bis in idem* principle to be applicable.[622] The Tribunal argued that the word 'offence' referred to the legal characteristics of an offence but not to the facts on which it is based.[623] It clarified that it must be considered whether the crime charged in the later indictment is the same, is in effect the same, or is substantially the same as the crime charged in the former indictment, and that whether the facts under examination or the witnesses called in later proceedings coincide with those of the earlier proceedings is irrelevant.[624] The same reasoning was also applied in the case of *Sayeedi* in which two incidents of the charges were already under investigation and criminal cases were pending simultaneously in the magistrate court.[625]

---

616 ICT 2, *The Chief Prosecutor v. Azad*, case no 05/2012, Judgment, 21 January 2013, para. 65.
617 ICT 2, *The Chief Prosecutor v. Azad*, case no. 05/2012, Judgment, 21 January 2013, para. 66.
618 ICT 2, *The Chief Prosecutor v. Alim*, case no. 01/2012, Judgment, 9 October 2013, para. 57.
619 ICT 2, *The Chief Prosecutor v. Alim*, case no. 01/2012, Judgment, 9 October 2013, para. 103.
620 ICT 2, *The Chief Prosecutor v. Alim*, case no. 01/2012, Charge Framing Order, 11 June 2012, p. 9.
621 ICT 2, *The Chief Prosecutor v. Alim*, case no. 01/2012, Judgment, 9 October 2013, para. 109.
622 ICT 2, *The Chief Prosecutor v. Alim*, case no. 01/2012, Judgment, 9 October 2013, para. 105; ICT 2, *The Chief Prosecutor v. Azad*, case no. 05/2012, Judgment, 21 January 2013, para. 69.
623 ICT 2, *The Chief Prosecutor v. Alim*, case no. 01/2012, Judgment, 9 October 2013, para. 110.
624 ICT 2, *The Chief Prosecutor v. Azad*, case no. 05/2012, Judgment, 21 January 2013, para. 67.
625 ICT 1, *The Chief Prosecutor v. Sayeedi*, case no. 01/2011, Judgment, 28 February 2013, para. 63.

2 The domestic character of the International Crimes Tribunal in Bangladesh

Qaiser was tried in absentia under the Collaborators Order but acquitted after trial.[626] The Tribunal, though, rejected the applicability of the *ne bis in idem* principle with the same argumentation.[627]

2.6 Funding

The absence of international assistance also has far-reaching consequences for the funding of a tribunal. Although a domestic tribunal is less cost-intensive than international criminal tribunals, financial challenges are a major problem for the ICT. The ICT is extremely well equipped in comparison to ordinary courts in the country. Nonetheless, its infrastructure is poor. The beautiful Old High Court building in Dhaka is old and in some aspects does not fit the needs of a modern court. The courtroom of Tribunal 2 is extremely small and this forces victims to stand very close to the accused while testifying. This certainly creates an intimidating atmosphere. Also, the Investigation Agency works with rather basic standards. There is no proper accommodation for the victims who, in most cases, have long journeys from rural areas to Dhaka in order to testify before the ICT. In the absence of proper facilities, they are accommodated in the premises of the Investigation Agency.

The lack of human resources and technical equipment also causes challenges with regard to the archiving process and documentation. Apart from the judgments and the charge framing orders, case records are not available in soft copy; a situation probably resulting from a lack of human resources, technical equipment and expert knowledge.

The recent decision to merge both tribunals is also likely to be based on financial constraints. Given that the Investigation Agency has received allegations against more than 3,000 people, the decision does not seem to be led by practical considerations.[628] In part, this might also be a political decision because the trials of the most prominent suspects have been completed and the government's interest in the trials has decreased.

The ICT started with an initial budget of approximately 10 crore taka (around US$10 million) for the trials.[629] However, even in the domestic context, the initial budget was too low to cover all expenses and, in addition, what exactly the budget was expected to cover was not disclosed.[630] Beyond that, no further information on the budget is available and relevant sources are not public.

---

626 ICT 2, *The Chief Prosecutor v. Qaiser*, case no. 04/2013, Judgment, 23 December 2014, para. 56.
627 ICT 2, *The Chief Prosecutor v. Qaiser*, case no. 04/2013, Judgment, 23 December 2014, para. 61.
628 *Adhikary*, Government Plan Not Welcome, The Daily Star, 17 August 2015.
629 *Bina D'Costa*, Nationbuilding, p. 159; *Reiger*, ICTJ Briefing Paper, p. 4.
630 *Bina D'Costa*, Nationbuilding, p. 159.

2.7 Interim findings

As a domestic tribunal, the ICT has several advantages in comparison to international or mixed tribunals. The trials feel closer to society and, therefore, certainly find better acceptance in the country. The process of establishing the Tribunal was also extremely fast due to the availability of the entire infrastructure and the fact that no agreements at the international level had to be reached. The bureaucracy of the entire process was comparatively low. These circumstances have also contributed partially to the Tribunal's high judgment quota. Since its establishment in March 2010 until April 2015, the ICT has delivered 17 judgments.

However, from the domestic character it also follows that the ICT is part of the domestic judicial system and is, therefore, confronted with severe practical challenges and flaws. Corruption constitutes a major problem. Bangladesh's public sector is among the most corrupt in the world. According to Transparency International's Corruption Perception Index from 2015, the country is ranked 139 of 167.[631] The domestic judicial system is also chronically overloaded with an enormous case backlog. Moreover, the political tensions in the country have a strong impact on the judicial system. Judges, prosecutors and lawyers are usually affiliated to political parties and there is a high risk of political influence on the judiciary.

Beyond the practical challenges, major problems arise from the applicable legal sources. The ICT Act's non-compliance with the principle of legality is certainly not a good starting point for the trials and the observance of fair trial standards. Further constitutional restrictions curtail important fundamental rights of the accused; a problem that the Tribunal does not appear to recognise. The reluctance of the ICT and the Appellate Division to consider international criminal law causes further challenges since most legal concepts of the ICT Act do not exist under domestic law. Furthermore, the fragmentary character of the ICT Act and the RoP creates significant legal ambiguity.

---

631 *Transparency International*, Corruption Perceptions Index, 2015, http://www.transparency.org/cpi2015/#results-table, accessed 23 September 2015.

Part IV: Compliance of the ICT Act, the Rules of Procedure and the ICT's jurisprudence with international standards

The ICT's domestic character and the very restrictive applicability of international law in Bangladesh do not weaken the binding effect of international human rights treaties and the obligation to implement international standards. It should be noted that Bangladesh acceded to several international human rights treaties that contain binding provisions on procedural aspects. Further, definitions of international crimes and the modes of liability, as well as many principles of criminal law, have become part of customary international law.

This part scrutinises whether and to what extent the ICT Act and the RoP, as well as the application of these sources in the jurisprudence of the ICT and the Appellate Division, reflect internationally established standards. To this end, the crimes within the jurisdiction and the modes of liability, as well as procedural aspects, will be scrutinised.

1 Criteria of investigation

The criteria of investigation are defined by the binding international standards that apply to Bangladesh. The call from the international community for the application of international standards by the ICT usually encounters questions over the meaning of the term 'international standard'. The National Human Rights Commission of Bangladesh considers the international standard to be an 'orchestrated delaying tactic to save the alleged war criminals'[632] and points out that 'there is no concrete definition in international criminal law of [an] international standard as such'[633]. Tribunal 1 uses a similar argument when it points out that the 'international standard itself is a fluid concept' that changes with time and the development of international criminal law.[634] On the basis of the foregoing argument, the ICT concludes that 'one can look at the concept of "standard" from entirely a technical perspective; whereas, others can see it as a matter of inherent spirit'.[635] While it is unclear what exactly the Tribunal intends

---

632 *Rahman*, Trial of Crimes against Humanity FAQs, Question 18, 19.
633 *Rahman*, Trial of Crimes against Humanity FAQs, Question 18, 19.
634 This was first stated in ICT 1, *The Chief Prosecutor v. Sayeedi*, case no. 01/2011, Judgment, 28 February 2013, para. 18. Later this argument was repeated in several judgments of Tribunal 1. See, for instance, ICT 1, *The Chief Prosecutor v. Azam*, case no. 06/2011, Judgment, 15 July 2013; ICT 1, *The Chief Prosecutor v. Nizami*, case no. 03/2011, Judgment, 29 October 2014, para. 22.
635 ICT 1, *The Chief Prosecutor v. Sayeedi*, case no. 01/2011, Judgment, 28 February 2013, para. 18; ICT 1, *The Chief Prosecutor v. Azam*, case no. 06/2011, Judgment, 15 July 2013;

to express with this statement, it is evident that it considers international standards to be rather vague and undefined. The argument that international standards are a 'fluid concept' and that there is no definition of them was also employed by Tureen Afroz, now prosecutor of the ICT, at the European Parliament Session on the ICT in Bangladesh in 2012.[636]

The concerns regarding the international standards resemble those expressed during the preparatory debates about international involvement in the establishment of a tribunal. The international community is perceived as a danger rather than a support. It appears that there is a strong fear in Bangladesh of the international community imposing rules and interfering in domestic matters. Some cultural aspects are certainly also of influence in this aversion towards international standards. In Bangladesh, criticism is generally seen as something negative and its direct expression is easily perceived as offending rather than contributing. This perception is even stronger when the criticism comes from western countries. A common fear in Bangladesh is also the negative portrayal of the country at the international level.

Another reason for the scepticism towards international standards is certainly that these standards are set by western countries with their respective financial means. It is evidently more difficult for a legal system of a developing country to meet these standards. In the context of Bangladesh, it is argued that the expectations towards the standard are set too high[637] and that the ICT should not be prevented from developing its own procedural rules[638]. Certainly, perfection cannot be expected and cannot be the applied standard. Instead, the trials before the ICT have to be viewed in a broader context; local factors with regard to the legal system but also cultural aspects have to be respected.

Nevertheless, this does not allow the conclusion that minimum standards do not have to be met. The claim that there is no international standard or that it is not definable certainly does not reflect the reality. Several international treaties as well as customary international law contain binding provisions which determine standards to be applied during criminal trials. Also, the definitions and elements of the core crimes as well as of the modes of liability have developed and form part of customary international law. Although a standard is something that develops and progresses over time,

---

ICT 1, *The Chief Prosecutor v. Nizami*, case no. 03/2011, Judgment, 29 October 2014, para 22.
636 See the video of the Parliamentary Session on the ICT Bangladesh, 31 January 2012, https://www.youtube.com/watch?v=buO7i25WBEw, accessed 14 July 2016.
637 *Rahman*, Trial of Crimes against Humanity FAQs, Question 18.
638 *Islam*, in: *Hoque/Wara* (eds), Journal of the 1st Winter School, p. 51, at 64; *Islam*, in: *Sellars* (ed.) Trials for International Crimes in Asia, p. 301, at 317.

many basic provisions have been long-established internationally and have changed little over time. This holds true, for instance, for Article 14 of the ICCPR.

Moreover, Alam rightly points out that the ICT in Bangladesh, despite being a domestic institution, 'does not exist in an international legal vacuum'; arguments that reject the applicability of international standards to the ICT ignore the fact that the law the ICT applies is international law.[639]

International standards arise from relevant treaties as well as from customary international law. With regard to the elements of crimes and the modes of liability, the jurisprudence of international criminal law becomes relevant because it defines the current construction under customary international law.

1.1 International treaties

Since its independence, Bangladesh has acceded to several international treaties. The country is a party to eight of the nine major international human rights treaties: the International Covenant on Civil and Political Rights (acceded to in 2000); the International Covenant on Economic, Social and Cultural Rights (acceded to in 1998); the International Convention on the Elimination of All Forms of Racial Discrimination (acceded to in 1979); the Convention on the Elimination of All Forms of Discrimination against Women (acceded to in 1984); the Convention on the Rights of the Child (acceded to in 1990); the Convention against Torture and Other Cruel Inhuman or Degrading Treatment or Punishment (acceded to in 1998); the Convention on the Protection of Rights of all Migrant Workers and Members of their Families (acceded to in 2011); and the International Convention on the Rights of Persons with Disabilities (acceded to in 2008). The International Convention for the Protection of all Persons from Enforced Disappearances has not been ratified as of today. Further, Bangladesh did not sign most of the Optional Protocols to these international treaties.

For the purpose of examining the trials before the ICT, the ICCPR, which establishes in Article 14 several rights of the accused in criminal proceedings, will be relevant. Article 15 contains the principle of legality. Article 9 establishes fundamental rights on arrest and detention. With regard to the death penalty, Article 6(2) determines some minimum standards for countries that impose the death penalty.

On the other hand, the Optional Protocols to the ICCPR are not applicable to Bangladesh. The First Optional Protocol came into force in 1976 and recognises the Human Rights Committee established under Part IV of the ICCPR as an individual complaint mechanism. The Optional Protocol enables the Human Rights Committee to receive and consider communications from individuals who claim to be victims of violations of the Convention. While this Protocol has no bearing on the trials under

---

639 *Alam*, Women and Transitional Justice, p. 68.

the ICT Act, it could become relevant for those convicted by the ICT if violations of the rights established in the ICCPR take place. Nevertheless, Bangladesh has not acceded to the Protocol[640] even though the Tribunal erroneously states that the government has ratified the ICCPR along with its Optional Protocol[641].

The Second Optional Protocol to the ICCPR aims at the abolition of the death penalty and therefore runs counter to Bangladesh's state practice. Beyond that, Bangladesh also signed the ICCPR with a reservation and provided declarations on some articles. It reserves the application of Article 14(3)(d) of the ICCPR with regard to the right of an accused to be tried in his presence. While, in general, the domestic law of criminal procedure requires the presence of the accused during trial, it also provides for trials in absentia in cases in which the accused is a fugitive or, despite his obligation to be present, fails to present himself or to explain the reasons for his non-appearance. Article 10(3) of the ICCPR establishes, inter alia, that the penitentiary system should concern itself with the treatment of prisoners. Bangladesh declared in this regard that, due to a lack of financial resources, the country does not have the facilities to address this. Another declaration was made with regard to Article 11 based on exceptional situations in which the domestic law provides for civil imprisonment for the default in complying with a decree. Article 14(6) of the ICCPR establishes that, in the case of miscarriage of justice, compensation shall be awarded. Bangladesh declared that, despite the acceptance of this provision, it was unable to comply with it at the time of accession but that it aimed to comply in the near future.

The country further acceded to the Geneva Conventions in 1972 and the Additional Protocols to the Geneva Conventions from 1977 in 1980. The International Convention on the Suppression and Punishment of the Crime of Apartheid was acceded to in 1985. Yet, it was only in 1998 that the country also became a state party to the Genocide Convention.

As already mentioned, Bangladesh is also a state party to the Rome Statute. Despite the prevalence of domestic prosecutions under the Rome Statute, it does not oblige states parties to implement its regulations into domestic law but simply encourages them to do so.[642] In case a state party does not have the legal tool to prosecute, it risks an intervention of the ICC under the principle of complementarity.[643] Even in

---

640 https://treaties.un.org/pages/ViewDetails.aspx?src=TREATY&mtdsg_no=IV-5&chapter=4&lang=en#4, accessed 14 January 2016.
641 ICT 2, *The Chief Prosecutor v. Molla*, case no. 02/2012, Judgment, 5 February 2013, para. 4.
642 *Schabas*, HRLJ, 1999, 20(4–6), p. 157, at 160; *Cryer et al.*, International Criminal Law, 3. edn, p. 163; *Cassese/Gaeta/Jones/Robinson*, Rome Statute Commentary, Vol. 2, pp. 1860–1861.
643 *Werle/Jessberger*, International Criminal Law, 3. edn, marginal no. 375.

monist legal cultures, the Rome Statute cannot be invoked directly because an immediate application of international law requires a treaty to be self-executing, a characteristic that is not given in the case of the Rome Statute.[644] The ICT denied the applicability of the definitions of crimes employed in the Rome Statute, arguing that the Statute expressly establishes the definitions 'for the purpose of the Statute'.[645] While this argument is legitimate, it ignores the fact that the definitions in the Rome Statute to a large extent reflect customary international law. Nevertheless, the Rome Statute does not conform to customary international law in all aspects,[646] and establishes further requirements for some offences. The Appellate Division confirmed the ICT's approach and rejected the universality of the definitions of the Statute. Nevertheless, the reasoning is quite different from that of the ICT. The Division argued that the definitions under the Rome Statute are valid only for seven years because, pursuant to Article 121 of the Statute, states parties are allowed to submit proposals for amendments to the Statute after seven years and are also entitled to withdraw from the Rome Statute.[647] The Division concluded that, for these reasons, the Rome Statute is a piece of temporary legislation and thus has no binding effect.[648]

Despite the fact that Bangladesh acceded to several international treaties, many of them lack domestic implementation. Yet, according to Article 27 of the Vienna Convention, internal law cannot be invoked as a justification for non-compliance with international treaty obligations. As mentioned, Bangladesh has not acceded to the Vienna Convention but the content of Article 27 forms part of customary international law[649] and is thus binding also upon Bangladesh.

In general, accession to a treaty is not always necessary for its content to have binding effect because the content of several international treaties has become customary international law over time. In many cases, treaties also regulate what was already in existence in customary international law prior to their entry into force. In these cases, accession is thus not relevant for the binding effect of their content upon Bangladesh.

International treaties also come into play for the determination of the status of customary international law at a specific point in time. Treaties often constitute evidence for the emergence of customary rules and can thus be invoked to determine the

---

644 *Ryngaert*, in: *Stahn/El Zeidy* (eds), ICC and Complementarity, Vol. 2, p. 855, at 867.
645 ICT 1, *The Chief Prosecutor v. Sayeedi*, case no. 01/2011, Judgment, 28 February 2013, para. 61. See Articles 6–8 bis of the Rome Statute.
646 *Cassese*, International Criminal Law, 3. edn, p. 29.
647 SC (AD), *Molla v. The Chief Prosecutor*, Appeal Judgment, 17 September 2013, p. 94.
648 SC (AD), *Molla v. The Chief Prosecutor*, Appeal Judgment, 17 September 2013, p. 95.
649 ICJ, *Djibouti v. France*, 4 June 2006, para. 124.

status of international law at the relevant time.[650] In the case of Bangladesh, this is of great relevance for the determination of the status of customary international law in 1971.

1.2 Customary international law

International standards also find expression in customary international law. According to Article 38(1)(b) of the ICJ Statute, for the emergence of customary international law a respective *opinio juris* and state practice are required.[651]

For the present study, international customary law becomes relevant in two separate ways. First, some legal principles and procedural rights are enshrined in international customary law. Second, the definitions of the core international crimes form part of customary international law. Certainly, some of these definitions have changed over the past few decades and for the trials before the ICT their definition under customary international law of 1971 would be relevant.

Among the several general principles of international criminal law and public international law that have become customary international law are, for instance, the principle of legality, the presumption of innocence, the principle of equality of arms and the principle of command responsibility.[652] Also, the modes of liability originally derived from general principles of law but form part of customary international law today.[653]

1.3 Jurisprudence of international criminal law

The jurisprudence in international criminal law has contributed and still contributes significantly to the interpretation of international criminal law and, therefore, becomes relevant for the construction of the offences, the modes of liability and numerous procedural aspects. With regard to several legal concepts and definitions, the jurisprudence also identified the point in time of their emergence as customary law.

Although the jurisprudence in international criminal law does not have any binding effect beyond the specific tribunal, it is clearly indispensable for the construction of the offences, the modes of liability and other legal concepts. To a great extent, it thus further determines the international standard and the customary international law. Since many legal concepts do not exist in domestic law, it is of great importance for the scrutiny of the ICT Act and the ICT jurisprudence.

---

650 *Cassese*, International Criminal Law, 3. edn, p. 13.
651 Art. 38(1)(b) of the ICJ Statute.
652 *Cassese*, International Criminal Law, 3. edn, p. 15.
653 *O'Keefe*, International Criminal Law, marginal no. 5.3.

2 The crimes within the ICT's jurisdiction

Pursuant to Article 3(2) of the ICT Act, the ICT has jurisdiction over genocide, crimes against humanity, crimes against peace, war crimes, violations of any humanitarian rules applicable in armed conflicts laid down in the Geneva Conventions of 1949, and any other crimes under international law. In practice, only genocide, crimes against humanity and the catch-all clause of any other crimes under international law have been prosecuted. The offences have remained without amendments since the enactment of the ICT Act in 1973.

2.1 Genocide

Several accused under the ICT Act have been found guilty of genocide. The crime of genocide is defined in the Genocide Convention, which came into force in 1951. The crime of genocide as defined therein has three requirements: (1) the commission of an act listed in the definition ('killing members of the group, causing serious bodily or mental harm to members of the group, deliberately inflicting on the group conditions of life calculated to bring about its physical destruction in whole or in part, imposing measures intended to prevent births within the group, forcibly transferring children of the group to another group'); (2) the direction of this act against a national, ethnic, racial or religious group; (3) the intent to destroy the group in whole or in part. The internationally recognised definition of genocide has been consistent since its definition in the Genocide Convention and is also employed in the Rome Statute. It is recognised that this definition enjoys the status of customary international law.[654] The fact that Bangladesh acceded to the Convention only in 1998 thus does not hinder the applicability of the definition to crimes committed in 1971. Pursuant to Article III of the Convention, also conspiracy to commit genocide, direct and public incitement to commit genocide, attempt to commit genocide and complicity in genocide shall be punishable. Article I of the Convention clarifies that genocide can be committed in times of peace as well as in times of war so that no link to an armed conflict is required.

2.1.1 Genocide under the ICT Act and customary international law

While the definition employed in the ICT Act encompasses all elements of the definition under the Genocide Convention, it contains two slight differences which have significant consequences.

First, it includes 'political groups' as a protected group and, second, the words 'as such' are reversed. The definition thus reads 'with intent to destroy, in whole or in

---

654 *Ratner/Abrams/Bischoff*, Accountability for Human Rights Atrocities, 3. edn, p. 43.

part, a national, ethnic, racial, religious, or political group, such as[655]' before listing the acts and thereby modifies the exhaustive list of acts into a non-exhaustive list.[656] It is likely that this mix-up of words was an unintended mistake by the drafters.[657] The same substitution can also be found in the English version of the Cambodian Genocide Law in which it seems to be a translation mistake from the official French version into English.[658] Nevertheless, the consequences of this mix-up are significant. On the one hand, given that the list of acts is non-exhaustive, the crime of genocide can be committed through other acts than those listed. On the other hand, this drafting mistake also weakens the intent requirement because the group does not have to be attacked 'as such'. The element 'as such' establishes the requirement that the accused must act with the intent to destroy the respective group in its quality as that group.[659] The ICTR found that the element 'as such' clarifies the specific intent and serves to draw the line between mass murder and genocide.[660] The ICT did not deal with these legal problems but merely disregarded the discrepancies and, against all evidence, stated that the definition of genocide in the ICT Act was in conformity with the definition in the Rome Statute.[661]

Also, the inclusion of political groups is not covered by the internationally recognised definition and, therefore, does not reflect prevailing customary international law, neither at the time when the crimes were committed nor today.[662] The inclusion of political groups as a protected group is, however, not merely a Bangladeshi phenomenon but was discussed internationally when the definition of genocide was framed. In 1946, in preparation for the Genocide Convention, the UN General Assembly unanimously passed Resolution 96(I).[663] The Resolution, as well as earlier drafts of the Genocide Convention, recognised the commission of genocide against political groups. It was in the debates following Resolution 96(I) that the inclusion of political groups was rejected. The international community was divided on this issue.[664] While

---

655 My emphasis.
656 *Bergsmo/Novic*, JGR, 2011, 13(4), 503, at 507; *Linton*, CLF, 2010, 21(2), p. 191, at 246; *Nersessian*, Genocide and Political Groups, p. 114.
657 *Linton*, CLF, 2010, 21(2), p. 191, at 245.
658 *Nersessian*, Genocide and Political Groups, p. 55.
659 *O'Keefe*, International Criminal Law, marginal no. 4.80.
660 ICTR (AC), *Prosecutor v. Niyitegeka*, Appeal Judgment, 9 July 2004, para. 53.
661 ICT 2, *The Chief Prosecutor v. Azad*, case no. 05/2012, Judgment, 21 January 2013, para. 156; ICT 1, *The Chief Prosecutor v. Jabbar Engineer*, case no. 01/2014, Judgment, 24 February 2015, para. 184; ICT 2, *The Chief Prosecutor v. Alim*, case no. 01/2012, Judgment, 9 October 2013, para. 68.
662 *O'Keefe*, International Criminal Law, marginal no. 9.70.
663 General Assembly Resolution 96(I), 11 December 1946.
664 *Schabas*, Genocide in International Law, 2. edn, pp. 158–159.

demands for the inclusion of political groups were also expressed by some delegations during the preparation of the Rome Statute,[665] this did not provoke a serious debate[666]. The reason for this decision lies in the absence of stable attributes of political groups and the fact that they are joined on a voluntary basis, which differentiates them from the other protected groups.[667] Nevertheless, in several other countries, political groups are likewise protected under the genocide definition in domestic law.[668] For instance, the French definition allows recourse to any other group that can be defined by any arbitrary criterion.[669] On the other hand, the Spanish definition does not include political groups but the Audiencia Nacional found that political as well as social groups fall under the term national groups.[670] Despite the protection of political groups in some domestic legal instruments, there is not sufficient state practice that would allow the conclusion that this is an emerging rule of customary international law.[671] The extension of the domestic provisions in this regard is, nonetheless, admissible under public international law.[672] Yet, given that the ICT Act was enacted as an ex post facto law, it has to reflect the customary international law of 1971 and the inclusion of political groups remains problematic as the application in practice would be a violation of the principle of legality.[673] On the other hand, this does not count for the very unlikely case that crimes committed after the enactment of the ICT Act are ever prosecuted.

In this context, the ICTR held that the list of groups is not necessarily exhaustive and considered that other groups could be included as long as they are of a permanent and stable character.[674] It argued that the intention of the drafters was to protect any stable and permanent group.[675] This extensive approach, though, has never been applied in practice. Nevertheless, even if one follows the view of the ICTR, political groups would not fall into the scope of the definition because they lack permanence.

---

665 Report of the Ad Hoc Committee on the Establishment of an International Criminal Court, 30 March 1995, para. 61 (UN Doc. A/50/22); Report of the Preparatory Committee on the Establishment of an International Criminal Court, Vol. I, 1996, para. 59 (UN Doc. A/51/22).
666 *Schabas*, Genocide in International Law, 2. edn, p. 164.
667 *Ratner/Abrams/Bischoff*, Accountability for Human Rights Atrocities, 3. edn, p. 36.
668 In total, there are 11 states, see *Nersessian*, Genocide and Political Groups, Apendix A, Table I, pp. 268–272.
669 Article 211-1 of the French Code Penal.
670 Audiencia Nacional, Judgment, 5 November 1998, in: ILR, 2002, 119, p. 331, at 341.
671 *Nersessian*, Genocide and Political Groups, p. 128.
672 *Werle*/Jessberger, International Criminal Law, 3. edn, marginal no. 804.
673 *Linton*, CLF, 2010, 21(2), p. 191, at 245.
674 ITCR (TC), *Prosecutor v. Akayesu*, Trial Judgment, 2 September 1998, para. 516.
675 ITCR (TC), *Prosecutor v. Akayesu*, Trial Judgment, 2 September 1998, para. 516.

Part IV: Compliance of the ICT Act, the Rules of Procedure and the ICT's jurisprudence

The ICT Act does not include the modes of liability and the inchoate crimes of Article III of the Genocide Convention. Nevertheless, the Act penalises attempt, complicity and conspiracy in relation to any of the crimes under the ICT's jurisdiction. For the prosecution of direct and public incitement to commit genocide, the Tribunal invoked the catch-all clause 'any other crimes under international law' of Section 3(2)(f) of the ICT Act.

Further practical challenges arise with regard to recent developments in the jurisprudence of international criminal law. For instance, rape was recognised as an act of genocide only in 1998 with the ICTR judgment in *Akayesu*. Nevertheless, there was no indictment based on rape as genocide and so the Tribunal did not need to discuss the scope of the definition of genocide under the ICT Act in relation to this. In one case, however, the prosecution argued that rape as genocide was committed but, as will be outlined below, this allegation did not have any legal basis.

2.1.2 The definition in the ICT jurisprudence

Among the examined cases, 22 charges of genocide were brought against the accused.[676] However, only nine of the charges were actually proven beyond reasonable doubt.[677] In many cases, the prosecution failed to produce sufficient evidence to prove the charges beyond reasonable doubt and the accused were acquitted for lack of evidence.[678] Nevertheless, in several cases, the accused were also acquitted based on legal grounds.

---

676 The following cases contain charges of genocide: ICT 2, *The Chief Prosecutor v. Azad*, case no. 05/2012, Judgment, 21 January 2013; ICT 2, *The Chief Prosecutor v. Mujahid*, case no. 04/2012, Judgment, 17 July 2013; ICT 1, *The Chief Prosecutor v. Chowdhury*, case no. 02/2011, Judgment, 1 October 2013; ICT 2, *The Chief Prosecutor v. Alim*, case no. 01/2012, Judgment, 9 October 2012; ICT 1, *The Chief Prosecutor v. Nizami*, case no. 03/2011, Judgment, 29 October 2014; ICT 1, *The Chief Prosecutor V. Khokon*, case no. 04/2013, Judgment, 13 November 2014; ICT 2, *The Chief Prosecutor v. Qaiser*, case no. 04/2013, Judgment, 23 December 2014; ICT 1, *The Chief Prosecutor v. Islam*, case no. 05/2013, Judgment, 30 December 2014; ICT 2, *The Chief Prosecutor v. Sobhan*, case no. 01/2014, Judgment, 18 February 2015; ICT 1, *The Chief Prosecutor v. Jabbar Engineer*, case no. 01/2014, Judgment, 24 February 2015.
677 In the following cases, the accused were found guilty of genocide: ICT 2, *The Chief Prosecutor v. Azad*, case no. 05/2012, Judgment, 21 January 2013; ICT 1, *The Chief Prosecutor v. Chowdhury*, case no. 02/2011, Judgment, 1 October 2013; ICT 2, *The Chief Prosecutor v. Alim*, case no. 01/2012, Judgment, 9 October 2012; ICT 1, *The Chief Prosecutor v. Islam*, case no. 05/2013, Judgment, 30 December 2014; ICT 1, *The Chief Prosecutor v. Jabbar Engineer*, case no. 01/2014, Judgment, 24 February 2015.
678 See, for instance, ICT 1, *The Chief Prosecutor v. Sayeedi*, case no. 01/2011, Judgment, 28 February 2013, paras. 86, 184, 198. Sayeedi was indicted for genocide in four cases. On two charges, the Prosecution failed to produce any witness and on the other two charges it failed to prove the involvement of the accused in the events.

The scope of the protected groups and the requirements of specific intent also constitute the most significant challenges in the cases before the ICT. This becomes evident from a glance at the charges which show major imprecisions in the application of these elements in practice.

Some formulations indicate that the prosecution as well as the Tribunal consider the genocidal intent already fulfilled if the perpetrator acts with intent to destroy the targeted victims. The specific intent of the offence of genocide instead requires that the perpetrator acts with intent to destroy the targeted group as such and not only the targeted victims. For instance, Sayeedi allegedly acted 'with intent to destroy in whole or in part members of [the] Hindu religious group'[679]. The charge framing order in the case of *Nizami* contains similar formulations. Nizami allegedly acted 'in order to destroy in whole or in part the members of [the] Hindu religious group'[680] and 'intended to eliminate the above victims and others, in whole or in part, as members of national, ethnic and racial group [sic] as [the] crime of genocide'[681]. Despite the ambiguous formulation with regard to the specific intent, the latter charge also concerned the killing of professionals and intellectuals. The assumption that intellectuals and professionals form a national, ethnic and racial group is evidently inaccurate and thus, already, the indictment lacks sufficient substance. Interestingly, the ICT accepted the charges in the charge framing order.

Further challenges arise also with the utilisation of the term 'genocide' in the context of witness statements. For instance, in *Azam*, witnesses testified that the Pakistani army committed genocide.[682] Also, in *Chowdhury*, a prosecution witness testified that, under the leadership of the accused, the Pakistani armed forces 'committed genocide and persecuted numerous Hindu people targeting [this] religious group'.[683] While it is not recognisable whether the witnesses really utilised these terms or whether the Tribunal introduced them in the reproduction of their testimonies, these legal qualifications clearly exceed the capacities of a witness. Another explanation of this phenomenon could also be, as discussed previously, the general tendency in Bangladesh to utilise the term 'genocide' to refer to mass killings.

---

679   ICT 1, *The Chief Prosecutor v. Sayeedi*, case no. 01/2014, Charge Framing Order, 3 October 2011, p. 11.
680   ICT 1, *The Chief Prosecutor v. Nizami*, case no. 03/2011, Charge Framing Order, 28 May 2012, p. 22.
681   ICT 1, *The Chief Prosecutor v. Nizami*, case no. 03/2011, Charge Framing Order, 28 May 2012, p. 27.
682   ICT 1, *The Chief Prosecutor v. Azam*, case no. 06/2011, Judgment, 15 July 2013, paras. 123, 125.
683   ICT 1, *The Chief Prosecutor v. Chowdhury*, case no. 02/2011, Judgment, 1 October 2013, para. 131.

Part IV: Compliance of the ICT Act, the Rules of Procedure and the ICT's jurisprudence

2.1.2.1 Acts of genocide

Despite the possibility under the domestic definition (due to the wording 'such as'), in none of the relevant cases did the ICT extend the definition of genocide to acts not listed in the ICT Act. In practice, there were convictions for acts of killing members of the group and a few for causing serious bodily or mental harm to members of the group because the intended killing failed.

Nevertheless, an attempt to classify rape as an act of genocide was made by the prosecution in the case of *Kamaruzzaman*. The prosecution argued that the commission of murder and rape, originally indicted as crimes against humanity, amounted to genocide because the accused acted with intent to destroy, in whole or in part, the 'women community or group' of the specific village.[684] The prosecution invoked the ICTR case of *Akayesu* in order to argue that rape could constitute genocide but apparently failed to understand that the ICTR in *Akayesu* found that the accused acted with the intent to destroy a protected group under the definition. The Tribunal rejected the allegation of genocide and argued that the prosecution failed to prove the specific intent as well as the group requirement.[685] It affirmed that mere multiplicity of victims does not amount to genocide.[686]

2.1.2.2 A national, ethnic, racial, religious or political group

In the jurisprudence of the ICT, only national, religious and political groups have been discussed. Despite the inclusion of political groups in the definition of genocide under the ICT Act, there has not been a single judgment by the ICT in which a political group was explicitly recognised as the targeted group. In all cases in which genocide was found proved, the perpetrator targeted the Hindu community and thus a religious group. Whether ethnic or racial groups were targeted in the course of the Liberation War was not discussed at all. In several cases, the prosecution tried to extend the definition by including a variety of other groups not protected by the offence of genocide. However, the Tribunal did not follow this approach.

In a general manner, Tribunal 1 held that, during the Liberation War, a group protected under the Genocide Convention was attacked:

> It is not correct to say that during the War of Liberation, no protected group as required under the Genocide Convention was targeted by the Pakistani occupation forces and its allied forces

---

684 ICT 2, *The Chief Prosecutor v. Kamaruzzaman*, case no. 03/2012, Judgment, 9 May 2013, para. 308.
685 ICT 2, *The Chief Prosecutor v. Kamaruzzaman*, case no. 03/2012, Judgment, 9 May 2013, para. 346.
686 ICT 2, *The Chief Prosecutor v. Kamaruzzaman*, case no. 03/2012, Judgment, 9 May 2013, para. 346.

to commit offences of genocide. It is gathered from common facts of knowledge [sic] that the occupation forces launched war in the night following 25th March 1971 against a protected Bangalee nation who sided for the independence of Bangladesh.[687]

However, it remains unclear which group under the Genocide Convention the Tribunal actually referred to. It can only be assumed that reference was made to a political group or a national group, although the former does not form part of the definition under the Genocide Convention. The Tribunal omitted further explanations. In other cases, it reiterated that the killing of individuals based on their membership of a specific national, ethnic, racial, religious or political group during the Liberation War is a fact of common knowledge that does not need to be proved through evidence.[688]

Whether political groups could constitute a target group of the offence of genocide was discussed marginally in some cases. The accused Alim was charged with genocide for killing 26 detained freedom fighters who were unarmed at the time they were killed. The indictment stated that the accused acted with the intent to destroy the 'group of pro-liberation youths',[689] and he was charged with 'abetting and contributing to the actual commission of [the] offence of "killing a group" which is an offence of "genocide"'[690]. The charges do not shed light on the specific group that allegedly was targeted and, at the same time, the targeted groups are significantly extended because it is held that the 'killing of a group' constitutes genocide. The Tribunal, however, found that the victims did not belong to any stable group and, at the same time, emphasised that political groups are protected under the ICT Act.[691] It found that the victims belonged to 'a group of freedom fighters'.[692] The Tribunal did not further discuss the notion of a 'political group' but held that it had found earlier (under charge 9) that the killing of unarmed freedom fighters constituted the offence of murder as crimes against humanity and that this was, therefore, also the

---

687 ICT 1, *The Chief Prosecutor v. Nizami*, case no. 03/2011, Judgment, 29 October 2014, para. 77.
688 ICT 1, *The Chief Prosecutor v. Islam*, case no. 05/2013, Judgment, 30 December 2014, para. 190; ICT 1, *The Chief Prosecutor v. Jabbar Engineer*, case no. 01/2014, Judgment, 24 February 2015, para. 180.
689 ICT 2, *The Chief Prosecutor v. Alim*, case no. 01/2012, Charge Framing Order, 11 June 2012, p. 21.
690 ICT 2, *The Chief Prosecutor v. Alim*, case no. 01/2012, Charge Framing Order, 11 June 2012, p. 21; see also the summary of the charges in ICT 2, *The Chief Prosecutor v. Alim*, case no. 01/2012, Judgment, 09 October 2012, para. 443.
691 ICT 2, *The Chief Prosecutor v. Alim*, case no. 01/2012, Judgment, 9 October 2012, para. 469.
692 ICT 2, *The Chief Prosecutor v. Alim*, case no. 01/2012, Judgment, 9 October 2012, para. 469.

case under this charge.[693] On the other hand, the offence of genocide was not discussed in the adjudication of charge 9 and neither was it indicted. The line of reasoning is rather confusing and does not shed light on the criteria for the definition of a political group employed by the ICT. The Tribunal also left unanswered the question of whether it considers the 'stability' of a group a general requirement that generally excludes genocide against political groups.

The case of *Khokon*, however, suggests that at least Tribunal 1 considers political groups to be protected under the ICT Act. In this case, the Tribunal emphasised that the offence of genocide requires that the victims be targeted because they belong to a particular group and that mere systematic killings do not fall under the notion of genocide.[694] In the specific case, however, the problem was a lack of evidence that the victims were in fact Awami League supporters and the Tribunal thus rejected the charge of genocide.[695] Nevertheless, Tribunal 1 seems to have recognised indirectly that political groups can be a targeted group under the definition of genocide as it discussed whether the victims actually belonged to that group.

In conclusion, it remains unclear whether the ICT considers political groups to be protected under the offence of genocide. Although the latter judgment seems to affirm that this is the case, there are no examples of an application in practice.

Genocide against a national group was discussed in some cases but did not lead to convictions. The Tribunal omitted to establish elements for the definition of a national group. Problems arise in this context with regard to the fact that many of those who collaborated with the Pakistani army as Razakars or Peace Committee leaders themselves belonged to the same national group as the victims, that is, the Bengalis.[696] The concept of a so-called 'auto-genocide' has been discussed controversially in the context of Cambodia.[697] The Khmer Rouge, however, lacked specific intent because belonging to the ethnic group of the Khmer was not critical for the targeting of the victims but rather other factors such as social position or level of education played a major role.[698]

Also, in the context of the Liberation War, it seems doubtful whether Bengalis were really targeted 'as such'. This is rather difficult to establish because the entire

---

693 ICT 2, *The Chief Prosecutor v. Alim*, case no. 01/2012, Judgment, 9 October 2012, para. 469.
694 ICT 1, *The Chief Prosecutor v. Khokon*, case no. 04/2013, Judgment, 13 November 2014, para. 184.
695 ICT 1, *The Chief Prosecutor v. Khokon*, case no. 04/2013, Judgment, 13 November 2014, para. 184.
696 *Bose*, JGR, 2011, 13(4), p. 393, at 398.
697 *Schabas*, Genocide in International Law, 2. edn, p. 138.
698 *Werle/Jessberger*, International Criminal Law, 3. edn, marginal no. 844.

2 The crimes within the ICT's jurisdiction

region of East Pakistan was predominantly inhabited by Bengalis.[699] Though not discussed by the Tribunal, the targeting of the Bengalis as an ethnic or racial group clearly leads to the same difficulties. Another challenge would certainly be the specific intent because the perpetrators did not intend to destroy the national group 'as such' but rather selected victims based on their political affiliation.[700]

Sobhan was indicted for murder as a crime against humanity and for the commission of genocide based on the allegation that he acted 'with intent to destroy, in whole or in part, a Bengali national group and a Hindu religious group'.[701] Nevertheless, in the charge framing order, it is stated that the victims were workers of the Awami League, Hindus and supporters of the Liberation War.[702] This broad pattern of targets raises doubts about the charge of genocide and indeed shows that the victims were not targeted based on their membership of the national group. This was also observed by the Tribunal as it rejected the classification of the crimes as genocide due to the absence of evidence that a specific group was targeted and that the accused acted with the specific intent.[703]

The prosecution employed the same argument in *Islam* and stated that the Bengalis were targeted as a national group and the Hindus as a religious group.[704] The Tribunal held that, in the specific case, not all those killed were Hindus and so it rejected the allegations.[705] However, the Tribunal did not elucidate on why it did not consider the Bengalis to be targeted as a national group.

Mujahid was indicted for genocide based on the killing of intellectuals with intent to destroy, in whole or in part, the 'intellectual group' or alternatively for the crime against humanity of murder.[706] The ICT came to the conclusion that the crime against humanity of extermination was committed but observed that, other than murder, extermination must be directed against a group of individuals.[707] In this specific case, the ICT argued that the killings were aimed at annihilating the 'Bengali intellectual group,

---

699 *Bose*, JGR, 2011, 13(4), p. 393, at 398.
700 *International Commission of Jurists*, Events in East Pakistan, p. 56.
701 ICT 2, *The Chief Prosecutor v. Sobhan*, case no. 01/2014, Charge Framing Order, 31 December 2013, p. 16.
702 ICT 2, *The Chief Prosecutor v. Sobhan*, case no. 01/2014, Charge Framing Order, 31 December 2013, p. 16.
703 ICT 2, *The Chief Prosecutor v. Sobhan*, case no. 01/2014, Judgment, 18 February 2015, para. 420.
704 ICT 1, *The Chief Prosecutor v. Islam*, case no. 05/2013, Judgment, 30 December 2014, para. 129.
705 ICT 1, *The Chief Prosecutor v. Islam*, case no. 05/2013, Judgment, 30 December 2014, para. 129.
706 ICT 2, *The Chief Prosecutor v. Mujahid*, case no. 04/2012, Charge Framing Order, 21 June 2012, p. 13.
707 ICT 2, *The Chief Prosecutor v. Mujahid*, case no. 04/2012, Judgment, 17 July 2013, para. 495.

Part IV: Compliance of the ICT Act, the Rules of Procedure and the ICT's jurisprudence

a part of [a] national group'.[708] The elements applied here are a combination of the crime of genocide and extermination as crimes against humanity. While genocide requires a specific group to be targeted, this is not a requirement for extermination.[709] On the contrary, extermination as a crime against humanity targets a group of persons but this group does not have to share any common characteristics.[710] Despite the conclusion that a national group was targeted, the Tribunal failed to examine further elements of genocide. Nevertheless, 'intellectuals' do not constitute a national group but rather a social group that is not protected by the definition. The mere fact that they also formed part of the national group of Bengalis does not allow the conclusion that they were targeted as a national group. Also, Nizami was indicted for genocide based on the killing of intellectuals but the prosecution held that the professionals and intellectuals were part of a national, ethnic and racial group.[711] This shows that there is little consistency in the application of the notions in the indictments. Nevertheless, also in this case, the Tribunal rejected the genocide charges. In a later order on framing charges, the killing of intellectuals was directly indicted as a crime against humanity.[712]

All convictions for genocide were based on killings directed against Hindus. The term 'religious group' did not provoke further problems, but whether the Hindu community was really targeted was discussed and rejected in the case of *Qaiser*. The accused was indicted for the commission of genocide or, alternatively, for the crime against humanity of extermination. The prosecution argued that the victims targeted by the accused were mainly Hindus and that this suggests that Hindus were targeted based on their religion.[713] The Tribunal rejected the charges for genocide. It found that, based merely on the high number of victims, genocide was not fulfilled and concluded that the targeted victims were pro-liberation civilians and that there were also many Muslims among the victims.[714] It held that the intent was to commit a large-scale killing of pro-liberation civilians.[715] Based on these findings, it would have been

---

708 ICT 2, *The Chief Prosecutor v. Mujahid*, case no. 04/2012, Judgment, 17 July 2013, para. 495.
709 *Werle/Jessberger*, International Criminal Law, 3. edn, marginal no. 922.
710 ICTY (AC), *Prosecutor v. Lukić & Lukić*, Appeal Judgment, 4 December 2012, para. 538.
711 ICT 1, *The Chief Prosecutor v. Nizami*, case no. 03/2011, Charge Framing Order, 28 May 2011, p. 27.
712 ICT 2, *The Chief Prosecutor v. Uddin et al.*, case no. 01/2013, Charge Framing Order, 24 June 2013, p. 14
713 ICT 2, *The Chief Prosecutor v. Qaiser*, case no. 04/2013, Judgment, 23 December 2014, para. 850.
714 ICT 2, *The Chief Prosecutor v. Qaiser*, case no. 04/2013, Judgment, 23 December 2014, para. 897.
715 ICT 2, *The Chief Prosecutor v. Qaiser*, case no. 04/2013, Judgment, 23 December 2014, para. 897.

difficult to establish that the accused acted with the intent to destroy a religious group. Nevertheless, the Tribunal again omitted to explain why it did not consider the pro-liberation civilians to fall under the term 'political group'.

2.1.2.3 The specific intent

The crime of genocide requires two different mental elements: the general intent as well as the specific intent to destroy, in whole or in part, the targeted group. However, in international jurisprudence, it is settled that the standard varies according to the mode of liability. The modes of liability that became relevant in the jurisprudence of the ICT were aiding and abetting as well as participation in a joint criminal enterprise (JCE). Whereas a participant in a joint criminal enterprise (JCE I and II) has to share the same criminal intent, including the specific intent,[716] an ordinary aider and abettor only has to know or have reason to know the genocidal intent of the principal[717].

Since the Tribunal did not find groups targeted other than the religious group of Hindus, the intent was examined only in this context. Nevertheless, for the determination of the specific intent, the ICT provided criteria only in some judgments. The examination of the specific intent remains rather vague or even absent.

In *Azad*, the Tribunal established criteria for the proof of the genocidal intent. It argued that intent as a mental factor can only be inferred from certain facts.[718] For this purpose, the Tribunal considered the following factors to be relevant: (1) the scale and pattern of atrocities; (2) the fact that individuals belonging to a group were systematically targeted; (3) the political dogma of the perpetrators; and (4) the extent and repetition of the destructive and discriminatory acts.[719] In the specific case, the intent was found to be proven based on the fact that a village predominantly populated by Hindus was attacked and that all crimes were committed against members of the Hindu community in a structured way.[720] The Tribunal found that the accused substantially provided practical assistance to the principals and encouraged them but it did not specify the mode of liability and its relevance in the context of the specific intent. The Tribu-

---

716 *Ambos*, 2009, IRRC, 91(876), p. 833, at 853; *Cassese*, International Criminal Law, 3. edn, p. 164.
717 See, for instance, ICTY (AC), *Prosecutor v. Krstić*, Appeal Judgment, 19 April 2004, para. 140; ICTY (AC), *Prosecutor v. Krnojelac*, Appeal Judgment, 17 September 2003, para. 152.
718 ICT 2, *The Chief Prosecutor v. Azad*, case no. 05/2012, Judgment, 21 January 2013, para. 161.
719 ICT 2, *The Chief Prosecutor v. Azad*, case no. 05/2012, Judgment, 21 January 2013, para. 161.
720 ICT 2, *The Chief Prosecutor v. Azad*, case no. 05/2012, Judgment, 21 January 2013, paras. 148–150, 153.

nal also held that 'in whole or in part' means that 'in the event that the plan to destroy all members of the group fails, the successful destruction of part of the group also constitutes genocide'.[721] The interpretation of the Tribunal suggests that the perpetrator always needs to act with the intent to destroy the entire group. It invoked the example of Hitler who failed to kill all Jews in accordance with his plan but still committed genocide.[722] While there are different approaches to the interpretation of the term 'in part',[723] the Tribunal adopted an extremely narrow interpretation. This approach is also irreconcilable with the words of the offence of genocide.[724] The ICTY Trial Chamber found that 'in part' requires the perpetrator to act with intent to destroy at least a substantial part of the group.[725] Nevertheless, contradicting its own finding, the Tribunal at the same time recognised that genocide can be committed in a limited geographical zone.[726]

A different approach was adopted in *Jabbar Engineer* in which the Tribunal held that, in order to establish the specific intent, it is not necessary to prove that the accused intended to achieve the complete annihilation of the group.[727]

In *Azad*, the Tribunal held that the genocidal intent was 'indicated' by the fact that, after the crimes committed against the Hindu community, the members of this community left the country and fled to India.[728] The reactions of the community after the commission of a crime clearly cannot be invoked to prove the specific intent of the perpetrator at the time when the crime was committed.

In *Alim*, the Tribunal argued that the victims were chosen because they belonged to the Hindu community and concluded therefrom that the accused acted with intent

---

721 ICT 2, *The Chief Prosecutor v. Alim*, case no. 01/2012, Judgment, 9 October 2012, para. 163, reaffirmed in: ICT 1, *The Chief Prosecutor v. Islam*, case no. 05/2013, Judgment, 30 December 2014, para. 195.
722 ICT 2, *The Chief Prosecutor v. Alim*, case no. 01/2012, Judgment, 9 October 2012, para. 163.
723 For an overview of the different approaches, see: *Schabas*, Genocide in International Law, 2. edn, pp. 277–286.
724 *Schabas*, Genocide in International Law, 2. edn, p. 278.
725 ICTY (TC), *Prosecutor v. Jelisić*, Judgment, 14 December 1999, para. 77.
726 ICT 2, *The Chief Prosecutor v. Alim*, case no. 01/2012, Judgment, 9 October 2012, para. 150; ICT 1, *The Chief Prosecutor v. Islam*, case no. 05/2013, Judgment, 30 December 2014, paras. 186, 188; ICT 1, *The Chief Prosecutor v. Jabbar Engineer*, case no. 01/2014, Judgment, 24 February 2015, para. 177.
727 ICT 1, *The Chief Prosecutor v. Jabbar Engineer*, case no. 01/2014, Judgment, 24 February 2015, para. 184.
728 ICT 2, *The Chief Prosecutor v. Qaiser*, case no. 04/2013, Judgment, 23 December 2014, para. 319.

2 The crimes within the ICT's jurisdiction

to destroy this religious group, in whole or in part.[729] The Tribunal found that the accused acted as part of a JCE but invoked jurisprudence on aiding and abetting as an accessory for the establishment of the criteria of examination.[730] Nevertheless, it did not draw any conclusions from the mode of liability for the specific intent. With regard to another charge, the accused was indicted for inciting, abetting and contributing to the commission of genocide,[731] and the Tribunal held that he shared the genocidal intent of the principals based on his inciting speech.[732] At the time of the commission of the crimes, the accused ordered his followers to 'loot whatever belongings the Hindus had'.[733] In the same case, the Tribunal often referred to the 'discriminatory intent' in the context of genocide.[734] This is not in conformity with the definition of genocide which does not require a perpetrator of genocide to act with discriminatory intent. On the contrary, the intent to commit individual discriminatory acts against members of the group does not amount to genocidal intent.[735]

In *Islam*, the Tribunal held that the 'intent to destroy a group may, in principle, be established if the destruction is related to a significant section of the group'.[736] In the specific case, four Hindu college professors were targeted while Muslim professors of the same campus were ignored.[737] The Tribunal did not further elucidate on whether this amounted to a significant section of the group. However, it emphasised that the victims of genocide must be targeted for the reason of their membership to the specific community[738] and saw this requirement as fulfilled because Muslim professors were spared from the killings. It affirmed that a plan is not a legal element of the offence of

---

729 ICT 2, *The Chief Prosecutor v. Alim*, case no. 01/2012, Judgment, 9 October 2012, paras. 262–263.
730 ICT 2, *The Chief Prosecutor v. Alim*, case no. 01/2012, Judgment, 9 October 2012, paras. 267–269.
731 ICT 2, *The Chief Prosecutor v. Alim,* case no. 01/2012, Charge Framing Order, 11 June 2012, p. 20.
732 ICT 2, *The Chief Prosecutor v. Alim*, case no. 01/2012, Judgment, 9 October 2012, para. 408.
733 ICT 2, *The Chief Prosecutor v. Alim*, case no. 01/2012, Judgment, 9 October 2012, para. 408.
734 ICT 2, *The Chief Prosecutor v. Alim*, case no. 01/2012, Judgment, 9 October 2012, paras. 218, 240, 251, 271.
735 ICTY (TC), *Prosecutor v. Jelisić*, Judgment, 14 December 1999, para. 79.
736 ICT 1, *The Chief Prosecutor v. Islam*, case no. 05/2013, Judgment, 30 December 2014, para. 186.
737 ICT 1, *The Chief Prosecutor v. Islam*, case no. 05/2013, Judgment, 30 December 2014, para. 97.
738 ICT 1, *The Chief Prosecutor v. Islam*, case no. 05/2013, Judgment, 30 December 2014, para. 188.

Part IV: Compliance of the ICT Act, the Rules of Procedure and the ICT's jurisprudence

genocide but that it plays an important role in determining the intent.[739] In the specific case, it was found that Jamaat-e-Islami and Islami Chhatra Sangha (the student organisation of Jamaat-e-Islami) held a hostile attitude which found expression in several public declarations.[740] It held that the accused, as a leader of Islami Chhatra Sangha, executed the common plan and policy and acted with intent to destroy, in whole or in part, the Hindus.[741] Islam was found guilty of abetting members of the Pakistani army in the commission of genocide.[742] Although the Tribunal quoted SCSL jurisprudence,[743] according to which an aider or abettor must be aware of the specific intent of the perpetrator but does not need to act with the specific intent himself,[744] it did not comment further on the consequences of this finding for the specific case. Since the Tribunal invoked a combination of jurisprudence on ordinary aiding and abetting and participation in a JCE, it remains unclear which standard with regard to the specific intent the Tribunal ultimately intended to apply.[745] The Tribunal, however, held that 'no person of normal human prudence will come to a conclusion that at the time of [an] incident of part of [a] systematic attack, the accused who accompanied the principal perpetrators had a different or innocent intent',[746] and concluded that the accused and the principals acted with common intent[747]. Only from this finding, it can be assumed that the Tribunal based its findings on JCE.

Though the Tribunal found the specific intent given in *Jabbar Engineer*, it also invoked jurisprudence related to the role of motive for the crime of genocide[748] and

---

739 ICT 1, *The Chief Prosecutor v. Islam*, case no. 05/2013, Judgment, 30 December 2014, para. 197.
740 ICT 1, *The Chief Prosecutor v. Islam*, case no. 05/2013, Judgment, 30 December 2014, paras. 202–206.
741 ICT 1, *The Chief Prosecutor v. Islam*, case no. 05/2013, Judgment, 30 December 2014, para. 206.
742 ICT 1, *The Chief Prosecutor v. Islam*, case no. 05/2013, Judgment, 30 December 2014, para. 210.
743 Even though the case cited by the ICT does not contain the relevant quote, this has been confirmed frequently in international jurisprudence. See, for instance, ICTY (AC), *Prosecutor v. Krstić*, Appeal Judgment, 19 April 2004, para. 140; ICTY (AC), *Prosecutor v. Krnojelac*, Appeal Judgment, 17 September 2003, para. 152
744 ICT 1, *The Chief Prosecutor v. Islam*, case no. 05/2013, Islam, Judgment, 30 December 2014, para. 173.
745 ICT 1, *The Chief Prosecutor v. Islam*, case no. 05/2013, Judgment, 30 December 2014, paras. 168–173.
746 ICT 1, *The Chief Prosecutor v. Islam* case no. 05/2013, Judgment, 30 December 2014, para. 178.
747 ICT 1, *The Chief Prosecutor v. Islam*, case no. 05/2013, Judgment, 30 December 2014, para. 178.
748 ICTR (TC), *Prosecutor v. Muvunyi*, Judgment, 12 September 2006, para. 479.

2 The crimes within the ICT's jurisdiction

therefrom concluded that 'it is not necessary to have criminal intent within the vicinity of the accused in committing an offence of genocide'[749]. However, this seems to be a misinterpretation with regard to the distinction of motive and intent. The personal motive of the perpetrator can go beyond the criminal intent to commit genocide but this does not affect the requirement of the specific intent with which the perpetrator has to act.

Also, in *Chowdhury*, the Tribunal did not draw a clear line between the specific intent and motive. Chowdhury was indicted for committing genocide[750] and was found guilty of 'substantially contributing [sic] the actual commission of the offence of genocide'.[751] The Tribunal did not specify the mode of liability. The convict acted together with members of the Pakistani army and it can thus be concluded that he acted as a co-perpetrator in a JCE. However, the Tribunal defined the specific intent regardless of the mode of liability and did not outline the standard that must be applied for the specific intent. Instead, it omitted to examine the specific intent and stated that the accused acted on a religious grudge against the Hindu minority because his father had been defeated in the elections for the National Assembly by a young candidate of the Awami League and, driven by this grudge, the accused killed five Hindus and injured one seriously.[752] The Tribunal concluded that the accused acted with 'intent to destroy, in whole or in part, the members of [the] Hindu religious group which is genocide'.[753] The defeat in the elections may well have been a motivation for the act but it does not necessarily amount to the specific intent to destroy the group, in whole or in part. Although one witness testified that the accused entered the village and ordered via microphone that all the Hindus of the village should remain in their houses,[754] the Tribunal did not discuss this further to establish the intent. Nevertheless, the Tribunal also did not discuss the fact that all of the victims belonged to one particular family. The Appellate Division affirmed the findings without further explanation.[755]

---

749   ICT 1, *The Chief Prosecutor v. Jabbar Engineer*, case no. 01/2014, Judgment, 24 February 2015, para. 171.
750   ICT 1, *The Chief Prosecutor v. Chowdhury*, case no. 02/2011, Charge Framing Order, 4 April 2012, p. 16.
751   ICT 1, *The Chief Prosecutor v. Chowdhury*, case no. 02/2011, Judgment, 1 October 2013, para. 88.
752   ICT 1, *The Chief Prosecutor v. Chowdhury*, case no. 02/2011, Judgment, 1 October 2013, para. 87.
753   ICT 1, *The Chief Prosecutor v. Chowdhury*, case no. 02/2011, Judgment, 1 October 2013, para. 88.
754   ICT 1, *The Chief Prosecutor v. Chowdhury*, case no. 02/2011, Judgment, 1 October 2013, para. 82.
755   SC (AD), *Chowdhury v. The Chief Prosecutor*, Appeal Judgment, 29 July 2015, p. 217.

In the adjudication of the other charges, the intent was not examined further but rather deduced from the fact that the victims were Hindus.[756]

2.1.3 Conclusion

In conclusion, it can be said that the ICT applies the elements of the definition as recognised under international law. Nevertheless, the interpretation and application of these elements differ greatly from common practice in international criminal law. In fact, the jurisprudence of the ICT reveals an imprecise application and a general assumption with regard to the specific intent of the crime. Linguistic imprecisions in the context of the specific intent (such as the reference to it as discriminatory intent) further contribute to a vague construction of the intent. Further problems arise in terms of the modes of liability and the absence of concrete criteria for the intent in this context.

Moreover, the jurisprudence of the ICT has not clarified which groups are actually protected by the offence of genocide under the ICT Act. The findings of the ICT are rather contradictory in this regard and no consistent practice can be deduced therefrom. The Tribunal also abstained from providing precise definitions of the protected groups and their application in the context of the Liberation War. The submissions of the prosecution show a clear tendency to arbitrarily amplify the genocide definition and to include social groups or to consider the offence of genocide as fulfilled in cases in which no specific group was targeted. This approach, however, has not been adopted by the Tribunal.

Though not discussed by the ICT, the unintentional mix-up of the words 'as such' does not seem to have had any practical consequences because the Tribunal did not consider any other acts than those listed in the definition. Nevertheless, the Tribunal also did not clarify that it considers this to be a drafting mistake so that future extensions of the definition are not prevented. At the same time, the Tribunal also recognised that the targeted groups must be targeted 'as such' and thus apparently also ignored the differing text of the ICT Act in this regard. This, at least, contributes to an interpretation that is closer to international standards.

2.2 Crimes against humanity

Crimes against humanity was the offence the accused under the ICT Act were most often charged with and, also, of which all of them were found guilty. It is only the crimes against humanity of enslavement and imprisonment that have not been indicted and thus no jurisprudence exists on these offences.

---

[756] ICT 1, *The Chief Prosecutor v. Chowdhury*, case no. 02/2011, Judgment, 1 October 2013, paras. 125, 138, 140, 158.

2 The crimes within the ICT's jurisdiction

The definitions of crimes against humanity contained in the different statutes of international criminal law vary in several aspects. Nevertheless, a standardised definition has developed through the international jurisprudence in international criminal law. The offence of crimes against humanity consists of the following elements: (1) one of the listed acts was committed (murder, extermination, enslavement, deportation or forcible transfer of population, imprisonment, torture, sexual violence, enforced disappearance of persons, other inhumane acts, persecution on political, racial, national, ethnic or cultural grounds); (2) the act formed part of an attack; (3) the attack was widespread or systematic in nature; (4) the attack was directed against any civilian population; (5) the perpetrator acted with the mens rea proper to the underlying offence; and (6) he had knowledge of the existence of a widespread or systematic attack and of the fact that his act forms part of this attack.

The definition of crimes against humanity contained in the Rome Statute goes beyond customary international law as it requires an additional proof of policy.[757]

2.2.1 Crimes against humanity under the ICT Act and customary international law

The definition of crimes against humanity under the ICT Act differs significantly from the internationally established definition. The wording of the Act suggests that the listed crimes can be qualified as crimes against humanity solely based on the fact that they were committed against any civilian population because the ICT Act does not require the acts to be committed as part of a systematic and widespread attack nor does it establish any further requirements, such as an armed conflict.[758] The definition of the Act conforms mainly to the definition of the IMT Charter but omits the prerequisite of the crimes being committed in connection with crimes against peace or war crimes. While this war-connecting link was still a requirement under the IMT Charter, it started to disappear gradually and was also removed from the definition of crimes against humanity under Control Council Law No. 10 (CCL).[759] In customary international law, it began to disappear in the late 1960s.[760] Proof of this development are the Convention on the Non-Applicability of Statutory Limitations to War Crimes and Crimes against Humanity from 1968, which refers expressly to crimes against humanity whether committed in time of war or in time of peace, as well as the Convention on the Suppression and Punishment of the Crime of Apartheid from 1973.[761] Like-

---

757 Article 7(2)(a) of the Rome Statute.
758 *Linton*, CLF, 2010, 21(2), p. 191, at 233.
759 *Cassese*, International Criminal Law, 3. edn, p. 90.
760 *Cassese*, JICJ, 2006, 4(2), p. 410, at 413.
761 *Cassese*, International Criminal Law, 3. edn, p. 90.

wise, the International Commission of Jurists argued that the war link was no longer in existence in 1972.[762]

In 1993, the ICTY Statute introduced the element of an international or internal armed conflict for crimes against humanity. Yet, the ICTY confirmed that the Statute defined crimes against humanity more narrowly than under customary international law and that a nexus to an armed conflict might not be a requirement at all.[763] Nevertheless, even if at least an internal armed conflict was a requirement in 1971 for crimes against humanity to be committed, it would be of less practical relevance for the case of Bangladesh because, undisputedly, there was an armed conflict in 1971 in East Pakistan.[764]

As a consequence, it becomes relevant whether the requirement that the act be committed as part of a 'systematic or widespread attack' already formed part of customary international law in 1971. This seems very likely if one considers that Article 5 of the Law on the Establishment of the Extraordinary Chambers in the Courts of Cambodia (ECCC Law) establishes this element as part of the definition of crimes against humanity that applies to crimes committed during the period between 1975 and 1979. Beyond that, in practice, the ECCC affirmed that a 'widespread or systematic attack' was a chapeau element.[765]

It is necessary to scrutinise whether the crimes listed in the ICT Act as crimes against humanity reflect the status of the customary international law of 1971. Section 3(2)(a) of the ICT Act lists the following offences: murder, extermination, enslavement, deportation, imprisonment, abduction, confinement, torture, rape, and other inhumane acts, as well as persecution. While some of these crimes were already established in the IMT Charter, imprisonment, abduction, confinement, torture and rape were not. However, imprisonment, torture and rape were recognised as crimes against humanity under CCL and also form part of the definition of crimes against humanity under the customary international law of today.

Yet, even today, confinement and abduction are not among the listed crimes. Considering that imprisonment and confinement are listed as separate crimes in the Act, the term confinement can only be understood as referring to a deprivation of liberty that cannot be considered official imprisonment. Nevertheless, in international criminal law, this understanding of confinement falls under the notion of imprisonment

---

762 *International Commission of Jurists*, Events in East Pakistan, p. 61.
763 ICTY (AC), *Prosecutor v. Tadić*, Decision on the Defence Motion for Interlocutory Appeal on Jurisdiction, 2 October 1995, para. 141.
764 *Linton*, CLF, 2010, 21(2), p. 191, at 238.
765 ECCC (TC), *Prosecutor v. Kaing Guek Ean alias Duch*, Judgment, 26 July 2010, para. 300; ECCC (SCC), *Prosecutor v. Kaing Guek Ean alias Duch*, Appeal Judgment, 31 February 2012, para. 106.

2 The crimes within the ICT's jurisdiction

which comprises, in general, any arbitrary deprivation of liberty without due process of law[766].

Instead, abduction constitutes a form of enforced disappearance. The Rome Statute in Article 7(2)(i) defines enforced disappearance as:

> [T]he arrest, detention or abduction of persons by, or with the authorisation, support or acquiescence of, a State or a political organisation, followed by a refusal to acknowledge that deprivation of freedom or to give information on the fate or whereabouts of those persons, with the intention of removing them from the protection of law for a prolonged period of time.

However, it must be determined whether these specific offences were already recognised as crimes against humanity under customary international law in 1971.

Enforced disappearance was first considered a crime against humanity in 1996 in the Draft Code of Crimes Against Peace and Security of Mankind.[767] It was only with the Rome Statute that the crime was recognised as a crime against humanity by an international criminal tribunal.[768] It can thus be concluded that the ICT Act does not comply with the customary international law of 1971 with regard to the inclusion of abduction. Nevertheless, enforced disappearances could be prosecuted as 'other inhumane acts'. In fact, the ECCC found that enforced disappearance could be qualified as 'other inhumane acts' despite the fact that it was not a recognised crime against humanity in 1975. This is because the underlying conduct itself does not need to have had the status of a crime against humanity in order to qualify as another inhumane act.[769] Also, the ICTY found that other inhumane acts undoubtedly encompass enforced disappearances.[770]

Imprisonment did not form part of the definition of crimes against humanity in the IMT Charter but it was listed already in CCL and forms part of the definition of the ad hoc tribunals' Statutes as well as of the ECCC Law and the Rome Statute. Confinement has never been recognised as a distinct crime against humanity, and the ICT Act conflicts with customary international law in this regard. However, the relevant criminal conduct would fall under imprisonment because imprisonment also encompasses other forms of deprivation of liberty.[771] The ICTY Trial Chamber found that imprisonment and unlawful confinement are identical in their elements of crime.[772]

---

766 ICTY (AC), *Prosecutor v. Kordić et al.*, Appeal Judgment, 17 December 2004, para. 116; ICTY (TC), *Prosecutor v. Kordić et al.*, Judgment, 26 February 2001, para. 302.
767 *Bassiouni*, Crimes against Humanity, p. 450.
768 *Bassiouni*, Crimes against Humanity, p. 450.
769 ECCC (SCC), *Prosecutor v. Kaing Guek Ean alias Duch*, Appeal Judgment, 31 February 2012, paras. 436, 443.
770 ICTY (TC), *Prosecutor v. Kupreškić et al.*, Judgment, 14 January 2000, para. 566.
771 *Bassiouni*, Crimes against Humanity, p. 444.
772 ICTY (TC), *Prosecutor v. Kordić*, Judgment, 26 February 2001, para. 301.

Torture was not included in the definition of the IMT Charter but, at that time, it had already been subsumed under other inhumane acts.[773] The ECCC Supreme Court Chamber confirmed that torture had emerged as a distinct crime against humanity under customary international law by 1975 and based its findings on post World War II cases.[774] It can thus be concluded that this was also the case in 1971 and the ICT Act reflects customary international law in this regard. Nevertheless, challenges arise with regard to the definition of torture because it has changed significantly over time. The first international definition of torture under the Declaration on the Protection of All Persons from Being Subjected to Torture and Other Cruel, Inhuman or Degrading Treatment or Punishment (Declaration on Torture) from 1975 is more restrictive than the definition contained in the United Nations Convention against Torture and Other Cruel, Inhuman or Degrading Treatment or Punishment (UNCAT) from 1984.[775] The Supreme Court Chamber of the ECCC found that the definition of the former was declaratory of customary international law and thus relevant for the crimes committed between 1975 and 1979.[776] From this, it follows that this definition must also be taken as a basis for the definition of torture in the context of the Liberation War.

The recognition of rape as a distinct crime against humanity started only with the ad hoc tribunals' statutes. Though rape was already listed as a crime against humanity in CCL, the first conviction for rape as a crime against humanity took place only in 1998 before the ICTR.[777] The Supreme Court Chamber of the ECCC confirmed that, under customary law, rape had not yet crystallised as an independent crime against humanity in 1975 but had been established as a war crime.[778] Nevertheless, the ECCC ruled that the definition of torture employed in the Declaration on Torture from 1975 reflected the customary international law of that time and that rape constitutes torture under this definition.[779] From the lack of recognition of rape as a crime against humanity in 1971, it follows that the ICT cannot prosecute rape as a distinct crime against humanity but that it would have to follow the ECCC's path.

---

773 *Bassiouni*, Crimes against Humanity, p. 415.
774 ECCC (SCC), *Prosecutor v. Kaing Guek Ean alias Duch*, Appeal Judgment, 31 February 2012, para. 188.
775 ECCC (SCC), *Prosecutor v. Kaing Guek Ean alias Duch*, Appeal Judgment, 31 February 2012, para. 192.
776 ECCC (SCC), *Prosecutor v. Kaing Guek Ean alias Duch*, Appeal Judgment, 31 February 2012, para. 205.
777 *Askin*, Berkeley JIL, 2003, 21, p. 288, at 318.
778 ECCC (SCC), *Prosecutor v. Kaing Guek Ean alias Duch*, Appeal Judgment, 3 February 2012, para. 180.
779 ECCC (SCC), *Prosecutor v. Kaing Guek Ean alias Duch*, Appeal Judgment, 3 February 2012, paras. 196, 208.

2 The crimes within the ICT's jurisdiction

The wording of the ICT Act suggests that the discriminatory intent ('on political, racial, ethnic or religious grounds') applies only to the offence of persecution. This is in line with the customary international law of 1971. The ECCC found that this was already suggested by the wording of the IMT Charter and the CCL, and thus no change of interpretation has taken place in this regard.[780] Although persecution based on ethnic grounds was not contained in the IMT Charter definition, the inclusion of ethnic grounds does not really exceed customary international law because there is little independent scope for application on ethnic grounds,[781] that is, grounds that are considered 'ethnic' would also fall under 'racial'.

In summary, it can be held that several aspects of the definition of crimes against humanity differ from the customary international law of 1971. The major challenge exists in the absence of any nexus requirement to a widespread or systematic attack. Nevertheless, these loopholes can be overcome through an interpretation in accordance with international jurisprudence.

2.2.2 The ICT's jurisprudence on crimes against humanity

The definition of crimes against humanity under the ICT Act has been discussed by the ICT in several cases. The Tribunal held that there is no consistency between the definitions in the different statutes (referring to the ICTY Statute, the ICTR Statute and the Rome Statute) and thus found that no uniform definition exists.[782] Although this observation is correct if one considers the different provisions contained in the Statutes, it overlooks the fact that there is consensus regarding the interpretation in international jurisprudence.

Tribunal 1 made clear determinations on the requirements under the definition of the ICT Act:
(1) an armed conflict is not required and crimes against humanity can be committed even in peacetime but undoubtedly there was an armed conflict in 1971;
(2) a discriminatory intent is only required for the crime of persecution and not for the other crimes listed in the definition;
(3) the ICT Act does not require the crimes to be part of a widespread and systematic attack but the element 'against any civilian population' implies that the crime is part of a widespread or systematic attack;

---

780 ECCC (SCC), *Prosecutor v. Kaing Guek Ean alias Duch*, Appeal Judgment, 3 February 2012, para. 238.
781 *Werle/Jessberger*, International Criminal Law, 3. edn, marginal no. 1002.
782 ICT 2, *The Chief Prosecutor v. Azad*, case no. 05/2012, Judgment, 21 January 2013, para. 74.

Part IV: Compliance of the ICT Act, the Rules of Procedure and the ICT's jurisprudence

(4) the term 'widespread' refers to the large-scale nature of the crime whereas 'systematic' establishes the organised nature of the crimes, and it suffices if one of these elements is fulfilled;
(5) the element 'civilian population' intends to exclude isolated acts and the criminal acts thus have to be on a large-scale so there must be some form of governmental, organisational or group policy to commit these acts and the perpetrator must know the context (knowledge and intent) in which the crimes are committed;
(6) only persecution has to be committed on discriminatory grounds;
(7) the term 'civilian population' has to be construed broadly and requires the population to be only predominantly civilian in nature; that is, a population can be civilian even if armed combatants or former combatants are among them.[783]

After outlining the requirements of crimes against humanity under the ICT Act, the Tribunal concluded that the definition of crimes against humanity in the ICT Act is consistent with the internationally established definition.[784] However, it is mainly the application of these elements in jurisprudence that differs greatly from international practice. Beyond that, the Appellate Division has not fully confirmed these criteria. The Tribunal also did not deal with the problem that the listed crimes in the definition of the ICT Act do not coincide entirely with the internationally recognised crimes.

2.2.2.1 Chapeau requirements

Although the definition of crimes against humanity in the ICT Act contains merely the chapeau requirement that the attack be directed against any civilian population, the Tribunal dealt also with the prerequisite of a systematic or widespread attack.

As outlined above, the Tribunal found that an armed conflict is not a requirement for crimes against humanity because of the absence of such a requirement under the definition of the ICT Act.[785] Since the Tribunal found itself not bound by the principle of legality, it did not consider the customary international law of 1971. As a consequence, it did not discuss whether the (international) armed conflict requirement was in existence in 1971. Nevertheless, it clarified that there was an armed conflict in

---

783 These determinations were first made in ICT 1, *The Chief Prosecutor v. Sayeedi*, case no. 01/2011, Judgment, 28 February 2013, paras. 30–32. In later judgments, the Tribunal repeated the exact same passage. See, for instance, ICT 1, *The Chief Prosecutor v. Azam*, case no. 06/2011, Judgment, 15 July 2013, paras. 30–32.
784 ICT 1, *The Chief Prosecutor v. Sayeedi*, case no. 01/2011, Judgment, 28 February 2013, para. 32.
785 ICT 1, *The Chief Prosecutor v. Sayeedi*, case no. 01/2011, Judgment, 28 February 2013, para. 32; ICT 1, *The Chief Prosecutor v. Chowdhury*, case no. 02/2011, Charge Framing Order, 4 April 2012, p. 11.

1971.[786] The Tribunal interpreted the element 'directed against any civilian population' as comprising the requirements that the act forms part of a widespread and systematic attack and that the population is civilian in nature.

Although Tribunal 1 generally rejected the requirement of a widespread and systematic attack based on the wording of the ICT Act,[787] it held simultaneously that the element 'civilian population' indicates that the act has to be part of a widespread and systematic attack[788] and then concluded that 'it is now well-settled that the attack in 1971 was widespread and systematic in nature'[789]. The Tribunal seems to consider the widespread and systematic character of the attack automatically fulfilled if the attack was directed against a civilian population.[790] This view is also confirmed by the Tribunal's response to the defence's argument that crimes against humanity require a nexus to an armed conflict. It confirmed that a 'nexus is not required during armed conflict, when such [an] attack is directed against [a] civilian population to cause crimes against humanity or genocide'.[791] However, this finding overlooks the fact that the context requirement of crimes against humanity does not apply to the offence of genocide.

Tribunal 2 adopted a slightly different approach. In *Azad*, it appears that it found that the acts have to form part of a systematic attack. Nevertheless, the Tribunal held that this requirement was already fulfilled if the crimes were committed in the context of the Liberation War because the war itself was a systematic attack against the 'Bangladeshi self-determined population'.[792] It further held that this was a fact of common knowledge and took judicial notice thereof in accordance with Section 19(3) of the ICT Act.[793] Judicial notice of the existence of an attack was also taken in *Azam*. The Tribunal affirmed

---

786 ICT 1, *The Chief Prosecutor v. Sayeedi*, case no. 01/2011, Judgment, 28 February 2013, para. 32. See also SC (AD), *Molla v. The Chief Prosecutor*, Separate Opinion of Justice Choudhury, Appeal Judgment, 17 September 2013, p. 579.
787 ICT 1, *The Chief Prosecutor v. Sayeedi*, case no. 01/2011, Judgment, 28 February 2013, para. 30(3); ICT 1, *The Chief Prosecutor v. Azam*, case no. 06/2011, Judgment, 15 July 2013, para. 30(3).
788 ICT 1, *The Chief Prosecutor v. Sayeedi*, case no. 01/2011, Judgment, 28 February 2013, para. 30(2); ICT 1, *The Chief Prosecutor v. Azam*, case no. 06/2011, Judgment, 15 July 2013, para. 30(3).
789 ICT 1, *The Chief Prosecutor v. Sayeedi*, case no. 01/2011, Judgment, 28 February 2013, para. 30(2); ICT 1, *The Chief Prosecutor v. Azam*, case no. 06/2011, Judgment, 15 July 2013, para. 30(3).
790 *Taylor*, Special Issue No. 5 – Legal Conclusions Azam, p. 6.
791 ICT 1, *The Chief Prosecutor v. Azam*, case no. 06/2011, Judgment, 15 July 2013, paras. 65, 288.
792 ICT 2, *The Chief Prosecutor v. Azad*, case no. 05/2012, Judgment, 21 January 2013, para. 78.
793 ICT 2, *The Chief Prosecutor v. Azad*, case no. 05/2012, Judgment, 21 January 2013, para. 78, 186.

that 'it is the [sic] fact of common knowledge that thousands of incidents happened throughout the country as a part of organised and planned attack'.[794] The Tribunal also took judicial notice of the fact that the Al-Badr, Al-Shams, Razakars and Peace Committees acted as auxiliary forces of the Pakistani army and participated in the crimes.[795]

The Tribunal provided different definitions of the term 'attack'. In *Qaiser*, it defined 'attack' as 'a course of conduct involving the multiple commission of acts referred to in Section 3(2) of the Act' in the context of the scrutiny of the chapeau requirements.[796] In the same judgment, it suddenly provided a definition of an 'unlawful attack on civilians' in the adjudication of a charge for other inhumane acts as crimes against humanity although the chapeau elements were scrutinised at the end of the judgment. There seems to be some confusion here, and the Tribunal apparently considers that the act of the perpetrator itself has to constitute an 'unlawful attack' and not merely form part of it. It held that an unlawful attack has to result in deaths or serious injuries of civilians, destruction of private property of civilians or a combination thereof and that the attack has to be directed against the civilian population or individual civilians.[797] In earlier cases, it found that the notion of attack 'embodies the notion of acting purposefully to the detriment of the interest or well being [sic] of a civilian population'.[798]

Also, the requirement of a link between the perpetrator's act and the attack was discussed by the Tribunal within the scope of the element 'directed against any civilian population'. According to the Tribunal, 'directed against any civilian population' means that the civilian population is the main target and that isolated acts are excluded.[799] The Tribunal held that a crime constitutes an isolated act if 'it is so far removed from the attack'.[800] With this criterion, the Tribunal seems to intend to refer to a find-

---

794 ICT 1, *The Chief Prosecutor v. Azam*, case no. 06/2011, Judgment, 15 July 2013, para. 43.
795 *Taylor*, Special Issue No. 5 – Legal Conclusions Azam, p. 5; ICT 1, *The Chief Prosecutor v. Azam*, case no. 06/2011, Judgment, 15 July 2013, para. 43.
796 ICT, *The Chief Prosecutor v. Qaiser*, case no. 04/2013, Judgment, 23 December 2014, para. 925. Similarly, ICT 2, *The Chief Prosecutor v. Kamaruzzaman*, case no. 03/2012, Judgment, 9 May 2013, para. 503.
797 ICT 2, *The Chief Prosecutor v. Qaiser*, case no. 04/2013, Judgment, 23 December 2014, para. 184.
798 ICT 2, *The Chief Prosecutor v. Azad*, case no. 05/2012, Judgment, 21 January 2013, para. 320; ICT 2, *The Chief Prosecutor v. Molla*, case no. 02/2013, Judgment, 5 February 2013, paras. 383.
799 ICT 2, *The Chief Prosecutor v. Azad*, case no. 05/2012, Judgment, 21 January 2013, para. 76, 311; ICT 2, *The Chief Prosecutor v. Kamaruzzaman*, case no. 03/2012, Judgment, 9 May 2013, para. 510; ICT 2, *The Chief Prosecutor v. Molla*, case no. 02/2013, Judgment, 5 February 2013, para. 374.
800 ICT 2, *The Chief Prosecutor v. Azad*, case no. 05/2012, Judgment, 21 January 2013, para. 311; ICT 2, *The Chief Prosecutor v. Kamaruzzaman*, case no. 03/2012, Judgment,

2 The crimes within the ICT's jurisdiction

ing of the ICTY Trial Chamber but it omitted the most relevant part of the sentence. The Trial Chamber held that the act or the acts 'may not be so far removed from the attack that, having considered the context and circumstances in which it occurred, the act or acts cannot reasonably be said to have been part of the attack'.[801] The criterion 'so far removed from the attack' as established by the Tribunal does not constitute a useful tool to examine the nexus because of the absence of a point of reference. The sentence is clearly incomplete.

The Tribunal further held that the fact that the acts were part of a government policy or the policy of an organisation could be considered to determine the relevant context of the crimes.[802] However, it also clarified that a policy is not a required element of crimes against humanity.[803] The Tribunal emphasised that there is no need for a multiplicity of victims and that even a single crime can constitute a crime against humanity if it forms part of an attack that targets a civilian population.[804] It clarified that the crime against humanity of murder does not necessarily require an attack on a number of victims but rather can be fulfilled if just one person is murdered, provided that the act forms part of an attack against a civilian population.[805]

In several judgments, the Tribunal also explained why the Liberation War amounted to a systematic attack. Referring to *Blaškić*,[806] the Tribunal determined that the following elements need to be fulfilled to give an attack a systematic character: (1) there must be a political objective, a plan pursuant to which the attack is perpetrated or an ideology to destroy, persecute or weaken a community; (2) a criminal act on a large scale must be committed repeatedly and continuously against a group of civilians; (3) significant public or private resources must be used, whether military or other; and (4) high-level political and/or military authorities must be involved in the definition and establishment of the methodical plan.[807] Applying these elements to the

---

9 May 2013, para. 510; ICT 2 case no. 02/2013, *The Chief Prosecutor v. Molla*, Judgment, 5 February 2013, paras. 374.
801 ICTY (TC), *Prosecutor v. Blagojević et al.*, Judgment, 17 January 2005, para. 547.
802 ICT 2, *The Chief Prosecutor v. Azad*, case no. 05/2012, Judgment, 21 January 2013, para. 312; ICT 2, *The Chief Prosecutor v. Molla*, case no. 02/2013, Judgment, 5 February 2013, para. 375.
803 ICT 2, *The Chief Prosecutor v. Azad*, case no. 05/2012, Judgment, 21 January 2013, para. 312; ICT 2, *The Chief Prosecutor v. Kamaruzzaman*, case no. 03/2012, Judgment, 9 May 2013, para. 510; ICT 2, *The Chief Prosecutor v. Molla*, case no. 02/2013, Judgment, 5 February 2013, paras. 123, 375.
804 ICT 1, *The Chief Prosecutor v. Azam*, case no. 06/2011, Judgment, 15 July 2013, para. 306.
805 ICT 1, *The Chief Prosecutor v. Azam*, case no. 06/2011, Judgment, 15 July 2013, para. 306.
806 ICTY (TC), *Prosecutor v. Blaškić*, Judgment, 03 March 2000, para. 203.
807 ICT 2, *The Chief Prosecutor v. Azad*, case no. 05/2012, Judgment, 21 January 2013, para. 313; ICT 2, *The Chief Prosecutor v. Kamaruzzaman*, case no. 03/2012, Judgment,

context of Bangladesh, the Tribunal found that: (1) the policy was to target the self-determined Bangladeshi civilian population; (2) high-level political or military authorities were involved in the implementation of the policy; (3) auxiliary forces were established to assist the implementation of the policy; and (4) a regular and continuous pattern of atrocities existed to target the non-combatant civilian population.[808] Next, the Tribunal held that the Pakistani army acted in execution of the government's plan and policy in collaboration with the local anti-liberation forces and that 'the unarmed civilian Bangalee population, pro-liberation people, Hindu community' were the target of this policy.[809]

With regard to the civilian character of the population, the Tribunal clarified that it is sufficient if the targeted population was predominantly civilian in nature.[810] It held that the situation of the victim at the time of the attack but not the general status of the victim is relevant to determine whether a civilian population was targeted.[811] Relying on *Blaškić*,[812] the Tribunal held that anyone who is no longer an active combatant in the 'specific situation' at the time of the commission of the crimes is a civilian.[813] The same argument was employed in *Alim* in which the victims were freedom fighters but, due to their detention, they were placed *hors de combat* at the time the murder was committed.[814] This finding corresponds with the finding by the ICTY Appeals Chamber in *Martić* that members of armed forces placed *hors de combat* could be victims of crimes against humanity, provided that the act is committed in the context of a

---

9 May 2013, para. 511; ICT 2, *The Chief Prosecutor v. Molla*, case no. 02/2012, Judgment, 5 February 2013, para. 376.

808   ICT 2, *The Chief Prosecutor v. Azad*, case no. 05/2012, Judgment, 21 January 2013, para. 314; ICT 2, *The Chief Prosecutor v. Kamaruzzaman*, case no. 03/2012, Judgment, 9 May 2013, para. 513; ICT 2, *The Chief Prosecutor v. Molla*, case no. 02/2012, Judgment, 5 February 2013, para. 377. See also: ICT, *The Chief Prosecutor v. Qaiser*, case no. 04/2013, Judgment, 23 December 2014, para. 929.

809   ICT 2, *The Chief Prosecutor v. Azad*, case no. 05/2012, Judgment, 21 January 2013, para. 316; ICT 2, *The Chief Prosecutor v. Kamaruzzaman*, case no. 03/2012, Judgment, 9 May 2013, para. 515; ICT 2, *The Chief Prosecutor v. Molla*, case no. 02/2012, Judgment, 5 February 2013, para. 379.

810   ICT 2, *The Chief Prosecutor v. Molla*, case no. 02/2012, Judgment, 5 February 2013, para. 291.

811   ICT 2, *The Chief Prosecutor v. Molla*, case no. 02/2012, Judgment, 5 February 2013, para. 292.

812   ICTY (TC), *Prosecutor v. Blaškić*, Judgment, 3 March 2000, para. 214.

813   ICT 2, *The Chief Prosecutor v. Molla*, case no. 02/2012, Judgment, 5 February 2013, para. 290.

814   ICT 2, *The Chief Prosecutor v. Alim*, case no. 01/2012, Judgment, 9 October 2013, para. 468. See also ICT 1, *The Chief Prosecutor v. Hossain*, case no. 01/2013, Judgment, 24 November 2014, paras. 73, 74, 75.

systematic and widespread attack against a civilian population.[815] Nevertheless, the Tribunal's finding is certainly problematic against the background that it does not consider a systematic and widespread attack a requirement for crimes against humanity.

The Appellate Division generally followed the Tribunal's approach but rejected the application of the internationally established elements. It found that crimes against humanity as defined under the ICT Act do not require the crimes to be committed as part of a widespread or systematic attack and criticised the ICT for invoking international case law instead of relying on the wording of the domestic provision.[816] According to the Appellate Division, it is sufficient to prove that the crimes were committed during the period of the Liberation War or during Operation Searchlight in cooperation with the Pakistani army against unarmed civilians with the aim of frustrating the result of the 1970 General Assembly election.[817] Nevertheless, the Appellate Division did not further illustrate what 'in cooperation with the Pakistani army' means. In practice, the finding is equivalent to that of the ICT because it also considers the Liberation War sufficient to comply with the context requirement of crimes against humanity.

The fact that the Appellate Division relies on 'cooperation with the Pakistani army' instead of a nexus between the acts and the attack could give rise to problems with regard to the intellectual killings. The Tribunal itself, relying on the Hamoodur Rahman Commission Report,[818] found that the Pakistani army was not connected with these killings but that they were in fact committed exclusively by the Al-Badr.[819] According to the Appellate Division's finding, the committed act must be committed in cooperation with the Pakistani army in order for the chapeau requirements to be fulfilled. Whether this would be the case with the intellectual killings is thus questionable. Neither the Appellate Division nor the Tribunal discussed this issue further. However, as outlined above, the reliability and neutrality of the Hamoodur Rahman Commission Report is highly questionable. It is, therefore, surprising that the Tribunal relied on this source to determine the involvement of the Pakistani army. Yet, in *Uddin*

---

815 ICTY (AC), *Prosecutor v. Martić*, Appeal Judgment, 8 October 2008, para. 313.
816 SC (AD), *Molla v. The Chief Prosecutor*, Appeal Judgment, 17 September 2013, p. 240; the same approach was taken by Justice Choudhury: SC (AD), *Molla v. The Chief Prosecutor*, Separate Opinion of Justice Choudhury, Appeal Judgment, 17 September 2013, p. 585.
817 SC (AD), *Molla v. The Chief Prosecutor*, Appeal Judgment, 17 September 2013, pp. 241–242.
818 *Hamoodur Rahman Commission*, Report, p. 27.
819 ICT 2, *The Chief Prosecutor v. Mujahid*, case no. 04/2012, Judgment, 17 July 2013, para. 429. Likewise, Bose contends that no connection between the Pakistani army and these killings has been established to date, see *Bose*, JGR, 2001, 13(4), p. 393, at 407.

Part IV: Compliance of the ICT Act, the Rules of Procedure and the ICT's jurisprudence

et al., the Tribunal modified its finding and held that the Pakistani army provided 'organizational backup and endorsement in carrying out the planned killing mission that resulted in [the] dreadful and barbaric event of intellectuals killing [sic]'.[820]

With regard to the mens rea, the Tribunal applied the internationally established requirement that the perpetrator needs to know that his acts were part of the attack against the targeted population.[821] Although the Tribunal established in a general manner that the discriminatory intent is only a requirement for persecutions, it made some contradictory findings in this regard. Tribunal 2 found that the ICT Act requires the acts to be committed against any civilian population or persecution on political, racial, ethnic or religious grounds.[822] While this indicates that only persecutions must be based on political, racial, ethnic or religious grounds, the Tribunal's further considerations seem to indicate the opposite. It held that 'the acts enumerated in Section 3(2)(a) of the act must be committed against the 'civilian population' on national, political, ethnic, racial or religious grounds' in order to qualify as crimes against humanity.[823] It remains unclear how Tribunal 2 comes to this conclusion. Beyond that, the definition of the ICT Act does not contain 'national grounds' for the crime of persecution. Nevertheless, the discriminatory intent was not discussed further in the adjudication of the charges because they were not related to persecution.

2.2.2.2 Murder

Murder as a crime against humanity was not defined in any of the judgments. As discussed above, the Appellate Division found the domestic definition of murder applicable, arguing that the ICT Act does not explicitly bar the application of the Penal Code.[824]

---

820 ICT 2, *The Chief Prosecutor v. Uddin et al.*, case no. 01/2013, Judgment, 3 November 2013, para. 221.
821 ICT 2, *The Chief Prosecutor v. Azad*, case no. 05/2012, Judgment, 21 January 2013, para. 321; ICT 2, *The Chief Prosecutor v. Molla*, case no. 02/2012, Judgment, 5 February 2013, para. 384; ICT 2, *The Chief Prosecutor v. Kamaruzzaman*, case no. 03/2012, Judgment, 9 May 2013, para. 521; ICT 1, *The Chief Prosecutor v. Islam*, case no. 05/2013, Judgment, 30 December 2014, para. 37.
822 ICT 2, *The Chief Prosecutor v Azad*, case no. 05/2012, Judgment, 21 January 2013, para. 79; ICT 2, *The Chief Prosecutor v. Molla*, case no. 02/2013, Judgment, 5 February 2013, para. 131.
823 ICT 2, *The Chief Prosecutor v. Azad*, case no. 05/2012, Judgment, 21 January 2013, para. 79; ICT 2, *The Chief Prosecutor v. Molla*, case no. 02/2013, Judgment, 5 February 2013, para. 131.
824 SC (AD), *Molla v. The Chief Prosecutor*, Appeal Judgment, 17 September 2013, p. 143.

2 The crimes within the ICT's jurisdiction

Section 300 of the Penal Code
Except in the cases hereinafter excepted, culpable homicide is murder, if the act by which the death is caused is done with the intention of causing death, or –
Secondly – If it is done with the intention of causing such bodily injury as the offender knows to be likely to cause the death of the person to whom the harm is caused, or –
Thirdly – If it is done with the intention of causing bodily injury to any person and the bodily injury intended to be inflicted is sufficient in the ordinary course of nature to cause death, or –
Fourthly – If the person committing the act knows that it is so imminently dangerous that it must, in all probability, cause death, or such bodily injury as is likely to cause death, and commits such act without any excuse for incurring the risk of causing death or such injury as aforesaid.

In the context of international criminal law, the mental element established under the domestic definition becomes relevant. In international criminal law, murder requires that: (1) the perpetrator has caused the death of another person through his unlawful conduct; and (2) the perpetrator is aware of the substantial likelihood that the conduct will result in the death of the victim.[825] Regarding the mental element, it is sufficient if the perpetrator caused the victim's serious injury in reckless disregard for human life.[826] The domestic definition, however, coincides with the internationally recognised definition with regard to the mens rea because it also does not require premeditation. Although not discussed by the Tribunal, the definition of the Penal Code would also have to be applied to the notion of 'killing' in the offence of genocide and 'murder' in the context of war crimes.

2.2.2.3 Extermination

Extermination has been discussed by the Tribunal in the context of the intellectual killings during the Liberation War. In international criminal law, extermination is defined as killing on a large scale and encompasses also indirect methods of causing death.[827] The mens rea of extermination requires that the accused act with 'the intention to kill on a large scale or to systematically subject a large number of people to conditions of living that would lead to their deaths'.[828]

The Tribunal found that the offence of extermination as a crime against humanity requires proof that it was committed on a large scale.[829] It established that, in order to

---

825 *Werle/Jessberger*, International Criminal Law, 3. edn, marginal no. 919.
826 ICTR (TC), *Prosecutor v. Akayesu*, Judgment, 2 September 1998, paras. 589–590; ICTY (TC), *Prosecutor v. Kupreškić*, Judgment, 14 January 2000, para. 561.
827 ICTY (AC), *Prosecutor v. Stakić*, Appeal Judgment, 22 March 2006, para. 259; ICTR (AC), *Prosecutor v. Ntakirutimana*, Appeal Judgment, 13 December 2004, paras. 515, 522.
828 ICTY (AC), *Prosecutor v. Stakić*, Appeal Judgment, 22 March 2006, paras. 259, 260.
829 ICT 2, *The Chief Prosecutor v. Mujahid*, case no. 04/2012, Judgment, 17 July 2013, para. 494; ICT 2, *The Chief Prosecutor v. Qaiser*, case no. 04/2013, Judgment, 23 Decem-

differentiate extermination from murder, there must be a large number of killings and the attack must be directed against a group.[830] In *Mujahid*, the Tribunal found that the 'Bengali intellectual group' that formed part of the national group was targeted.[831] However, other than genocide, extermination does not require a specific group to be targeted but rather a civilian population, as such.[832] The targeted group does not have to share any common characteristics.[833]

Likewise, in *Uddin et al.*, the Tribunal established the criterion of large scale[834] to differentiate extermination from murder. It established two key factors for the qualification of murder as extermination: (1) the accused persons knew the designed scheme of collective murder; and (2) they took part in it to enforce the murderous scheme.[835] These elements relate to the mental elements of JCE I but do not constitute criteria to differentiate extermination from murder. Nevertheless, the Tribunal did not explicitly say throughout the entire judgment that the accused were liable for participation in a JCE and the accused were finally found guilty of 'participation by abetting and complicity' with regard to the eleven charges.[836]

The Tribunal also dealt with the question of whether the killing of 18 persons could amount to extermination and merely held that 'it is needless in the present case to determine whether 18 deaths [...] alone satisfy this requirement of scale'.[837] However, it omitted to elucidate on why it considered extermination to have been so clearly fulfilled. Although it cited the ICTR Appeals Chamber's decision in the case of *Ndindabahizi* in which the Chamber held that extermination does not require a numerical minimum but that particularly large numbers of victims can be considered as

---

ber 2014, paras. 896, 899; ICT 2, *The Chief Prosecutor v. Sobhan*, case no. 01/2014, Judgment, 18 February 2015, paras. 420, 421; ICT 2, *The Chief Prosecutor v. Uddin et al.*, case no. 01/2013, Judgment, 3 November 2013, para. 189.

830 ICT 2, *The Chief Prosecutor v. Mujahid*, case no. 04/2012, Judgment, 17 July 2013, para. 495.
831 ICT 2, *The Chief Prosecutor v. Mujahid*, case no. 04/2012, Judgment, 17 July 2013, para. 495.
832 *Werle/Jessberger*, International Criminal Law, 3. edn, marginal no. 922.
833 ICTY (AC), *Prosecutor v. Kristić and Kristić*, Appeal Judgment, 4 December 2012, para. 538.
834 ICT 2, *The Chief Prosecutor v. Uddin et al.*, case no. 01/2013, Judgment, 3 November 2013, para. 189.
835 ICT 2, *The Chief Prosecutor v. Uddin et al.*, case no. 01/2013, Judgment, 3 November 2013, para. 190.
836 ICT 2, *The Chief Prosecutor v. Uddin et al.*, case no. 01/2013, Judgment, 3 November 2013, para. 432.
837 ICT 2, *The Chief Prosecutor v. Uddin et al.*, case no. 01/2013, Judgment, 3 November 2013, para. 194.

an aggravating factor,[838] it did not apply this finding to the case. However, it is evident that there was no scope of application for an aggravating factor based on 18 victims.

The 18 victims are the sum of the victims of the 11 charges for extermination.[839] The ICTY Trial Chamber held that the number of victims of separate incidents could be aggregated in order to establish the large-scale character of the killings.[840] Nevertheless, the Tribunal did not find all the incidents together to be one count of extermination but rather found the accused guilty of extermination in 11 cases.[841]

In the same case, the Tribunal appeared to establish a specific intent requirement for the crime of extermination as a crime against humanity. It held that the accused acted with 'intent to exterminate the intellectual class of the nation'[842] even though a specific intent is not required for the offence of extermination[843].

2.2.2.4 Deportation

There have been a few cases in which the Tribunal dealt with the crime of deportation. International jurisprudence defines deportation as 'forced displacement of the persons concerned by expulsion or other coercive acts from the area in which they are lawfully present, across a de jure state border and, in certain circumstances, a de facto state border, without grounds permitted under international law'.[844] Under customary international law, 'deportation' requires a transfer beyond state borders whereas 'forcible transfer' of a population comprises displacement within a state.[845] However, forcible transfer does not amount to deportation and thus has to be prosecuted under 'other inhumane acts' by the ICT Act. With regard to the mens rea, the ICTY Appeals Chamber found that intent to displace the individual across the border permanently is not required.[846]

Also, the Tribunal made a distinction between deportation and forcible transfer.[847] In the cases examined, however, only deportation became relevant because the vic-

---

838 ICTR (AC), *Prosecutor v. Ndindabahizi*, Appeal Judgment, 16 January 2007, para. 135.
839 ICT 2, *The Chief Prosecutor v. Uddin et al.*, case no. 01/2013, Judgment, 3 November 2013, para. 194.
840 ICTY (TC), *Prosecutor v. Brđanin*, Judgment, 1 September 2004, paras. 391.
841 ICT 2, *The Chief Prosecutor v. Uddin et al.*, case no. 01/2013, Judgment, 3 November 2013, para. 432.
842 ICT 2, *The Chief Prosecutor v. Uddin et al.*, case no. 01/2013, Judgment, 3 November 2013, para. 190.
843 ICTY (TC), *Prosecutor v. Krstić*, Judgment, 2 August 2001, para. 499.
844 ICTY (AC), *Prosecutor v. Stakić*, Appeal Judgment, 22 March 2006, para. 278.
845 ICTY (TC), *Prosecutor v. Krstić*, Judgment, 2 August 2001, para. 521.
846 ICTY (AC), *Prosecutor v. Stakić*, Appeal Judgment, 22 March 2006, para. 278.
847 ICT 2, *The Chief Prosecutor v. Alim*, case no. 01/2012, Judgment, 9 October 2013, para. 211.

tims always fled to India and thus beyond state borders. Nevertheless, the Tribunal did not define the crime of deportation.

In *Alim*, the prosecution argued that deportation does not require physical force but that it can be committed through the creation of a coercive climate by criminal activities that force an 'individual to deport [sic]'.[848] This approach was adopted by the Tribunal.[849] This finding is in line with the jurisprudence of international criminal law, according to which the deportation is still forcible if the victims flee from a territory for fear of discrimination.[850] In the specific case, the perpetrators aided in the looting of the house of a local Awami League leader and in setting it ablaze so that the victim and his family 'had to deport [sic] to India'.[851] The Tribunal emphasised that the return of the victim and his family to Bangladesh after the Liberation War ended does not exclude the offence of deportation.[852]

Ambiguities also arise from the Tribunal's flawed use of the verb 'to deport'. It frequently utilises formulations such as the victims 'deported to India'[853] as if the offence of deportation always required an act of the victim. However, this might also be a mere linguistic problem.

The findings on the mens rea remain rather vague. The Tribunal found that the act created a climate of coercion and terror and that this 'validly suggests that the intention of the attackers was to displace the victim and his inmates from their own place'.[854] With regard to the accused who presumably was found guilty of abetting, the Tribunal held that he accompanied the main perpetrators with 'intent to consciously share the intent of the perpetrators [Pakistani army]'.[855] It is unclear which standard for the mens rea of abetting the Tribunal applied here.

---

[848] ICT 2, *The Chief Prosecutor v. Alim*, case no. 01/2012, Judgment, 9 October 2013, para. 67.

[849] ICT 2, *The Chief Prosecutor v. Alim*, case no. 01/2012, Judgment, 9 October 2013, para. 212.

[850] ICTY (TC), *Prosecutor v. Krstić*, Judgment, 2 August 2001, para. 528.

[851] ICT 2, *The Chief Prosecutor v. Alim*, case no. 01/2012, Judgment, 9 October 2013, para. 208.

[852] ICT 2, *The Chief Prosecutor v. Alim*, case no. 01/2012, Judgment, 9 October 2013, para. 215.

[853] See, for instance, ICT 1, *The Chief Prosecutor v. Chowdhury*, case no. 02/2011, Judgment, 1 October 2013, para. 159: 'the other member[s] of Sotish Chandra Palit [were] deported to India for their safety'. In ICT 2, *The Chief Prosecutor v. Alim*, case no. 01/2012, Judgment, 9 October 2013, para. 213, the Tribunal held that 'the victims and his inmates had no other option excepting [sic] to avail deportation'.

[854] ICT 2, *The Chief Prosecutor v. Alim*, case no. 01/2012, Judgment, 9 October 2013, para. 208.

[855] ICT 2, *The Chief Prosecutor v. Alim*, case no. 01/2012, Alim, Judgment, 9 October 2013, para. 216.

In *Khokon*, the Tribunal rejected deportation in charge 11 in which the victim left the country in order to receive training as a freedom fighter.[856] It is evident that the latter does not amount to deportation. Also, Chowdhury was found guilty of the crime against humanity of deportation. The Tribunal held that, as a consequence of genocide committed by the accused in a Hindu village, some members of the Hindu community were forced to take shelter in India as refugees and the offence of deportation was, therefore, fulfilled.[857] No further clarifications were made and no definition of deportation was provided.

2.2.2.5 Abduction

The Tribunal dealt with abduction as a crime against humanity in several cases. Since abduction is not a distinct crime against humanity under international criminal law, there is no definition on which to rely. As outlined above, abduction is criminalised as forced disappearance in the Rome Statute if the further elements of the crime are fulfilled.

The Tribunal, however, did not define the crime of abduction in any of the judgments. The analysis of the cases suggests that it considers abduction equal to 'forcible capture' and that the interpretation of the offence is not related to enforced disappearance at all. The offence of enforced disappearance requires inter alia 'a refusal to acknowledge the deprivation of freedom or to give information on the fate or whereabouts of those persons'.[858] This element was not discussed in the judgments and thus was not a decisive criterion for classification as abduction.

It can only be assumed that the Tribunal based its findings on the definition of abduction under the Penal Code. Nevertheless, the Tribunal does not explicitly mention this. Abduction is defined in Section 362 of the Penal Code.

> *Section 362 of the Penal Code*
> Whoever by force compels, or by any deceitful means induces, any person to go from any place, is said to abduct that person.

However, under the Penal Code, mere abduction is not punishable. Instead, the act of abduction has to be committed with a specific purpose. For instance, Section 364 of the Penal Code criminalises abduction 'in order that such person may be murdered or may be so disposed of as to be put in danger of being murdered'. Likewise, Section 365 criminalises abduction with 'intent to cause that person to be secretly and wrong-

---

856 ICT 1, *The Chief Prosecutor v. Khokon*, case no. 04/2013, Judgment, 13 November 2014, para. 197.
857 ICT 1, *The Chief Prosecutor v. Chowdhury*, case no. 02/2011, Judgment, 1 October 2013, para. 158.
858 Article 7(2)(i) of the Rome Statute.

Part IV: Compliance of the ICT Act, the Rules of Procedure and the ICT's jurisprudence

fully confined'. Nevertheless, with regard to the Penal Code, the Appellate Division found that, if the murder intended in accordance with Section 364 is in fact realised, the charges must be for murder under Section 302.[859] The indictments for abduction under the ICT Act and also the application of abduction by the Tribunal do not reflect this jurisprudence.

In *Chowdhury*, the accused was found guilty of abduction and murder as crimes against humanity based on the fact that the two victims were captured and brought to an army camp where they were subsequently killed.[860] The Tribunal did not explain why abduction was fulfilled in this case. The wife of one of the victims testified that her brother-in-law had requested information about the whereabouts of the victims and that they were informed that both were held detained at the army camp.[861] The family members requested their release, which was refused, and, at a later point, they were informed that the two had been killed.[862] The Tribunal did not further elucidate on which exact conduct it considers to be the abduction. In the summary of a witness testimony, it stated that the whereabouts of the victims could not be ascertained.[863] It seems as if this holds true only with regard to the corpses because the witnesses had testified that they knew that the victims were held at the army camp. Beyond that, it does not become clear whether the lack of information about the whereabouts constitutes an element of the crime of abduction.

Considering domestic law, the act of abduction must be committed with a specific intention. Given that the victims were killed later on, the requirements of Section 364 would be fulfilled in this case. The Tribunal, however, omitted to discuss this. Beyond that, considering the abovementioned domestic jurisprudence of the Appellate Division, the charges would have to be under murder as a crime against humanity and not under abduction because the murder was ultimately committed.

In the same case, the accused was also found guilty of abduction, confinement and torture regarding another charge.[864] Three victims were arrested and taken to an army camp where they were tortured; afterwards, they were sent to prison until the end of

---

859 *Mazharul Huq v. Crown*, 1 DLR (1949), pp. 173 ff., at 174.
860 ICT 1, *The Chief Prosecutor v. Chowdhury*, case no. 02/2011, Judgment, 1 October 2013, para. 175.
861 ICT 1, *The Chief Prosecutor v. Chowdhury*, case no. 02/2011, Judgment, 1 October 2013, para. 168.
862 ICT 1, *The Chief Prosecutor v. Chowdhury*, case no. 02/2011, Judgment, 1 October 2013, paras. 170, 172, 173.
863 ICT 1, *The Chief Prosecutor v. Chowdhury*, case no. 02/2011, Judgment, 1 October 2013, para. 174.
864 ICT 1, *The Chief Prosecutor v. Chowdhury*, case no. 02/2011, Judgment, 1 October 2013, para. 202.

the war.⁸⁶⁵ It seems as though the Tribunal considers the act of apprehension to constitute abduction.⁸⁶⁶ The consideration of the apprehension of a person as a separate offence from confinement seems contradictory because it is in fact an essential requirement for the offence of confinement.

In *Uddin et al.*, the accused were indicted for abduction or, alternatively, extermination as crimes against humanity in all 11 charges.⁸⁶⁷ The Tribunal assumed that abduction was fulfilled but it did not provide a definition.⁸⁶⁸ The victims were picked up at gun point.⁸⁶⁹ This judgment suggests strongly that, again, the Tribunal considers abduction equal to forcible capture.⁸⁷⁰ Other than in *Chowdhury*, the accused were not found guilty of extermination and abduction simultaneously but only of extermination.⁸⁷¹

The qualification of forcible capture as abduction also becomes clear in the case against Ali, who was indicted for abduction, confinement and torture. The Tribunal held that the respective charge consisted of three phases and listed them as follows: forcible capture, confinement and causing torture.⁸⁷² In the same judgment, the Tribunal depicted the testimony of a witness with the words: 'In narrating the event of abduction or forcible picking up [...]'.⁸⁷³ In this case, the victim was blindfolded and taken to a torture camp.⁸⁷⁴

Likewise, in *Sobhan*, the offence of abduction was applied without scrutiny to forcible capture, after which the accused killed the victims.⁸⁷⁵ As in *Uddin et al.*, the

---

865 ICT 1, *The Chief Prosecutor v. Chowdhury*, case no. 02/2011, Judgment, 1 October 2013, para. 202.
866 ICT 1, *The Chief Prosecutor v. Chowdhury*, case no. 02/2011, Judgment, 1 October 2013, para. 202.
867 ICT 2, *The Chief Prosecutor v. Uddin et al.*, case no. 01/2013, Charge Framing Order, 24 June 2013.
868 ICT 2, *The Chief Prosecutor v. Uddin et al.*, case no. 01/2013, Judgment, 3 November 2013, paras. 164, 214–215.
869 ICT 2, *The Chief Prosecutor v. Uddin et al.*, case no. 01/2013, Judgment, 3 November 2013, para. 165.
870 See also ICT 2, *The Chief Prosecutor v. Uddin et al.*, case no. 01/2013, Judgment, 3 November 2013, paras. 214–215. In this case, the Tribunal first mentioned the forcible capture and then referred to it as the 'event of abduction'.
871 ICT 2, *The Chief Prosecutor v. Uddin et al.*, case no. 01/2013, Judgment, 3 November 2013, para. 432.
872 ICT 2, *The Chief Prosecutor v. Ali*, case no. 03/2013, Judgment, 2 November 2014, para. 624.
873 ICT 2, *The Chief Prosecutor v. Ali*, case no. 03/2013, Judgment, 2 November 2014, para. 265.
874 ICT 2, *The Chief Prosecutor v. Ali*, case no. 03/2013, Judgment, 2 November 2014, para. 282.
875 ICT 2, *The Chief Prosecutor v. Sobhan*, case no. 01/2014, Judgment, 18 February 2015, para. 159.

Tribunal abstained from cumulative conviction for abduction and murder although it did find the accused's participation in the abduction to be proven.[876]

The interpretation of abduction by the Tribunal goes far beyond enforced disappearance under international law. The absence of a definition and the non-application of the domestic provision pose the risk of an extensive application of the crime against humanity of abduction.

2.2.2.6 Confinement

The offence of confinement has been dealt with little by the Tribunal. As outlined above, under international criminal law, imprisonment encompasses confinement.

In international criminal law, imprisonment only amounts to a crime against humanity if it is arbitrary and thus requires the deprivation of liberty without due process of law.[877] In domestic law, wrongful confinement is defined in Section 340.

> *Section 340 of the Penal Code*
> Whoever wrongfully restrains any person in such a manner as to prevent that person from proceeding beyond certain circumscribing limits, is said 'wrongfully to confine' that person.

In the same way as under international criminal law, the domestic provision clearly restricts confinement to 'wrongful confinement'.

The Tribunal did not deal with a definition of confinement in any of the judgments. For instance, the Tribunal found Mujahid guilty of the crime against humanity of confinement without examining the legal requirements.[878] In this case, the victim was arrested and kept confined to a house in the Bihari colony in the morning and managed to escape at night.[879] The victim was thus kept in a non-official detention establishment. In *Chowdhury*, the accused was found guilty of confinement as a crime against humanity based on the fact that the two victims, who were Awami League supporters, were kept detained at an army camp.[880] Also, in this case, the offence of confinement was merely assumed. The Tribunal also omitted to establish criteria to circumscribe confinement from imprisonment.

---

876 ICT 2, *The Chief Prosecutor v. Sobhan*, case no. 01/2014, Judgment, 18 February 2015, paras. 171, 192
877 ICTY (AC), *Prosecutor v. Kordić et al.*, Appeal Judgment, 17 December 2004, para. 116; ICTY (TC), *Prosecutor v. Kordić et al.*, Judgment, 26 February 2001, para. 302.
878 ICT 2, *The Chief Prosecutor v. Mujahid*, case no. 04/2012, Judgment, 17 July 2013, paras. 295–318.
879 ICT 2, *The Chief Prosecutor v. Mujahid*, case no. 04/2012, Judgment, 17 July 2013, para. 297.
880 ICT 1, *The Chief Prosecutor v. Chowdhury*, case no. 02/2011, Judgment, 1 October 2013, para. 175.

2 The crimes within the ICT's jurisdiction

2.2.2.7 Torture

Torture was dealt with extensively by the Tribunal. Nevertheless, the jurisprudence barely examined which concrete acts constitute torture. This is due to the fact that in most of the cases the Tribunal stated that the victims were tortured without mentioning the specific conduct of the perpetrators.[881] For instance, in *Ali*, the accused was indicted for torture in 12 of the 14 charges but the conduct was not disclosed in any of the charges.[882] Instead, the indictment states that torture was committed and thus employs the legal term without the need to refer to an action.[883]

In domestic law in Bangladesh, a general prohibition of torture is enshrined in Article 35(5) of the Constitution. In 2013, the Torture and Custodial Death (Prevention) Act was enacted in order to implement the provisions of the UNCAT from 1984, to which Bangladesh acceded to in 1998. The domestic act incorporates parts of the UNCAT definition of torture.[884] However, it omits some essential elements. For instance, it does not explicitly state that the act has to be committed intentionally and it does not restrict the conduct to acts which cause severe pain.

The international definition has changed over time and the UNCAT definition from 1984 is broader than that of the Declaration on Torture from 1975.[885] The 1984 definition extends the list of purposes and includes also coercing as well as any reason based on discrimination of any kind as additional purposes of torture. It also broadens significantly the public official requirement.[886] Whereas the Declaration required severe pain or suffering to be inflicted by or at the instigation of a public official, under the definition of the Convention, it can be 'inflicted by or at the instigation of or with the consent or acquiescence of a public official or other person acting in an official

---

881 See, for instance, ICT 1, *The Chief Prosecutor v. Nizami*, case no. 03/2011, Judgment, 29 October 2014, paras. 202–215. In this case, the charges already state that the accused was 'inhumanly tortured' without referring to specific acts. Also, the parts of the witness testimonies reproduced in the judgment do not contain further details.
882 ICT 1, *The Chief Prosecutor v. Ali*, case no. 03/2013, Charge Framing Order, 5 September 2013, pp. 9–18.
883 See ICT 1, *The Chief Prosecutor v. Ali*, case no. 03/2013, Charge Framing Order, 5 September 2013, except charges 11 and 12.
884 For two unofficial translations, see http://www.humanrights.asia/countries/bangladesh/laws/legislation/Torture-CustodialDeath-ActNo50of2013-English.pdf/view, accessed 17 December 2017 and *Blast*, Review of the Torture and Custodial Death (Prevention) Act, p. 4. However, both translations are imprecise.
885 ECCC (SCC), *Prosecutor v. Kaing Guek Ean alias Duch*, Appeal Judgment, 31 February 2012, para. 192.
886 ECCC (SCC), *Prosecutor v. Kaing Guek Ean alias Duch*, Appeal Judgment, 31 February 2012, para. 193.

capacity'. As outlined above, the 1975 definition would certainly be relevant for the ICT in light of the principle of legality.

Nevertheless, today's definition of torture in international criminal law differs from the Convention's notion. Therefore, within the scope of crimes against humanity, torture must be defined separately.[887] In international humanitarian law, torture consists of the following requirements: (1) the infliction, by act or omission, of severe pain or suffering, whether physical or mental; (2) the act or omission must be intentional; (3) the act or omission must aim at obtaining information or a confession, or at punishing, intimidating or coercing the victim or a third person, or at discriminating, on any ground, against the victim or a third person.[888] Therefore, the public official requirement does not form part of the definition. On the other hand, the definition of torture in the Rome Statute also renounces the requirement that torture must be committed for a particular purpose and, therefore, exceeds customary international law in this regard.[889]

The Tribunal almost adopts the definition established under customary international law. In *Ali*, it held that the following three elements must be fulfilled: (1) the presence of an act or omission inflicting or causing relentless pain or suffering, whether physical or mental; (2) the act or omission must be deliberate or intentional; and (3) the act or omission must have been carried out with a specific purpose, such as to obtain information or a confession, to punish, intimidate or coerce the victim or a third person.[890] While the first two elements reflect customary international law, the last differs slightly because it lists the purposes as examples ('such as') and thereby suggests that the Tribunal considers the list non-exhaustive. An extension of the list of grounds is problematic because these grounds have become part of customary international law.[891]

In practice, the Tribunal does not always disclose the specific purpose.[892] In the adjudication of one charge, however, it concluded in a general manner that torture and inhumane mistreatment were used to extract information about the freedom fighters.[893] Nevertheless, details on the specific torture cases remain absent from all charges. That is, the testimonies are either given or reproduced without details regarding the acts of torture that were committed.

---

887 ICTY (TC), *Prosecutor v. Kunarac et al.*, 22 February 2001, para. 482.
888 ICTY (TC), *Prosecutor v. Kunarac et al.*, Judgment, 22 February 2001, para. 497.
889 Werle/Jessberger, International Criminal Law, marginal no. 968.
890 ICT 2, *The Chief Prosecutor v. Ali*, case no. 03/2013, Judgment, 2 November 2014, para. 176.
891 ICTY (TC), *Prosecutor v. Kunarac et al.*, Judgment, 22 February 2001, paras. 485, 497.
892 For example: ICT 2, *The Chief Prosecutor v. Ali*, case no. 03/2013, Judgment, 2 November 2014, paras. 183–217 (charge 3) and paras. 218–240 (charge 4).
893 ICT 2, *The Chief Prosecutor v. Ali*, case no. 03/2013, Judgment, 2 November 2014, para. 296.

In *Khokon*, the Tribunal contended that forced conversions fall under torture, arguing that torture does not require physical harm but rather can be committed through 'mental pressure, forceful conversion, intimidation for deportation, even by way of making loudly [sic] sound of horn [sic]'.[894] However, in listing these acts, the Tribunal omitted to mention that severe pain or suffering must be caused through the acts in order for them to amount to torture. Tribunal 1 instead found that forceful conversions constitute 'other inhumane acts' in a case in which the indictment classified this as persecution.[895] There is thus no consistency in the application of the offence of torture to forceful conversions.

2.2.2.8 Rape

There have only been a few convictions for rape before the ICT. The definition of crimes against humanity in the ICT Act includes only rape; other forms of sexual violence or forced pregnancy are not listed. In the jurisprudence of the Tribunal, problems arise with regard to the definition of rape but also with respect to the general perception of rape.

The Appellate Division held that the Penal Code must be invoked for the definition of rape.[896]

> *Section 375 of the Penal Code*
> A man is said to commit 'rape' who except in the case hereinafter excepted, has sexual intercourse with a woman under circumstances falling under any of the five following descriptions –
> First – Against her will.
> Secondly – Without her consent.
> Thirdly – With her consent, when her consent has been obtained by putting her in fear of death, or of hurt.
> Fourthly – With her consent, when the man knows that he is not her husband, and that her consent is given because she believes that he is another man to whom she is or believes herself to be lawfully married.
> Fifthly – With or without her consent, when she is under fourteen years of age.
> Explanation – Penetration is sufficient to constitute the sexual intercourse necessary to the offence of rape.
> Exception – Sexual intercourse by a man with his own wife, the wife not being under thirteen years of age, is not rape.

---

894 ICT 2, *The Chief Prosecutor v. Khokon*, case no. 04/2013, Judgment, 13 November 2014, para. 90.
895 ICT 1, *The Chief Prosecutor v. Jabbar Engineer*, case no. 01/2014, Charge Framing Order, 14 August 2014, p. 16; ICT 1, *The Chief Prosecutor v. Jabbar Engineer*, case no. 01/2014, Judgment, 24 February 2015, para. 219.
896 SC (AD), *Molla v. The Chief Prosecutor*, Appeal Judgment, 17 September 2013, p. 143.

The definition is very narrow and criminalises rape only if committed against women. That is, rape committed against men or transgender persons is not encompassed by it. It further defines sexual intercourse as the penetration of the male reproductive organ and does not comprise penetration through objects or other organs.[897]

These shortcomings become evident if one compares the domestic definition to that established under international criminal law. In *Kunarac et al.*, the ICTY Appeal Chamber confirmed that the actus reus of rape consisted of the following elements: the sexual penetration, however slight: (a) of the vagina or anus of the victim by the penis of the perpetrator or any other object used by the perpetrator; or (b) of the mouth of the victim by the penis of the perpetrator or any other object used by the perpetrator, where such sexual penetration occurs without the consent of the victim.[898]

Since other forms of sexual violence are not listed in the ICT Act (and other forms of sexual violence were also not distinct crimes against humanity under customary international law in 1971), the Tribunal would have to invoke the catch-all clause of other inhumane acts for prosecution. The Penal Code defines only outraging the modesty of a woman by assault or criminal force (Section 354) and so-called unnatural offences (Section 377) as sexual offences other than rape. The latter criminalises voluntary 'carnal intercourse against the order of nature with any man, woman or animal' but fails to distinguish between consensual and non-consensual acts[899]. The Prevention of Oppression against Women and Children Act from 2010[900] criminalises sexual oppression against women and provides a broader definition of sexual violence in Section 10. Nevertheless, with regard to rape, the Act adopts the definition of the Penal Code (Section 2(e)). In spite of this, the Tribunal has not dealt with the definition of sexual violence.

In *Sayeedi*, the Tribunal invoked the definition of rape as determined by the ICTR in *Akayesu* (a physical invasion of a sexual nature committed on a person under circumstances that are coercive) as well as the definition of sexual violence (any act of a sexual nature that is committed on a person under circumstances that are coercive).[901] It remains unclear why the Tribunal did not rely on the Penal Code. However, this judgment was delivered before the Appellate Division's findings on the applicability of the domestic provision. Although the Tribunal provided a definition of sexual vio-

---

897 *Ahmed/Sunga*, Critical Appraisal of Laws Relating to Sexual Offences in Bangladesh, p. 18.
898 ICTY (AC), *Prosecutor v. Kunarac et al.*, Appeal Judgment, 12 June 2002, para. 127.
899 *Ahmed/Sunga*, Critical Appraisal of Laws Relating to Sexual Offences in Bangladesh, p. 17.
900 For an unofficial translation, see http://www.hsph.harvard.edu/population/trafficking/bangladesh.traf.00.pdf, accessed 17 December 2016.
901 ICT 1, *The Chief Prosecutor v. Sayeedi*, case no. 01/2011, Judgment, 28 February 2013, para. 191.

lence, this did not become relevant in the specific case because the victim was actually raped.

In *Islam*, the prosecution brought forward that, under international law, not only rape but also indecent assault, sexual slavery, enforced prostitution, forced pregnancy, enforced sterilisation and other forms of sexual violence are recognised.[902] The Tribunal, without further argument, adopted these submissions and found the accused guilty of aiding and abetting in 'sexual violence including rape' as crimes against humanity.[903] It appears, therefore, that the Tribunal considers sexual violence a distinct crime against humanity even though this interpretation runs counter to the wording of the ICT Act. The Tribunal also did not elucidate on which acts constituted sexual violence. It rather found in a general manner that the victim was 'sexually abused'[904] but ultimately it remains unclear whether the victim was raped or whether other sexual violence was committed.

In *Qaiser*, the Tribunal frequently classified pregnancy resulting from rape as forced pregnancy.[905] However, it did not provide a definition for this term and the accused was not found guilty of forced pregnancy as a crime against humanity. Nevertheless, not every pregnancy resulting from rape is a forced pregnancy. To date, the term has only been included in the Rome Statute but differs greatly from the Tribunal's understanding. The Statute defines it as 'the unlawful confinement of a woman forcibly made pregnant, with the intent of affecting the ethnic composition of any population or carrying out other grave violations of international law'.[906] Also, in *Azad*, the accused was found guilty of rape[907] but the judgment does not define the term nor does it examine the details of the act of the rape.

A fundamental problem in the context of sexual violence arises from the general portrayal of rape in jurisprudence. The absence of sensitive vocabulary does not contribute to breaking the antiquated view of considering rape a loss of dignity but rather strengthens these perspectives. For instance, the Tribunal held that the rape victims did not merely lose their chastity but that they 'fought by laying their highest self-

---

902 ICT 1, *The Chief Prosecutor v. Islam*, case no. 05/2013, Judgment, 30 December 2014, para. 263.
903 ICT 1, *The Chief Prosecutor v. Islam*, case no. 05/2013, Judgment, 30 December 2014, para. 266
904 ICT 1, *The Chief Prosecutor v. Islam*, case no. 05/2013, Judgment, 30 December 2014, para. 238.
905 ICT 2, *The Chief Prosecutor v. Qaiser*, case no. 04/2013, Judgment, 23 December 2014, paras. 665, 686.
906 Article 7(2)(f) of the Rome Statute.
907 ICT 1, *The Chief Prosecutor v. Azad*, case no. 05/2012, Judgment, 21 January 2013, para. 273.

worth, for the cause of our independence'.[908] Also, in *Kamaruzzaman*, the Appellate Division refers to rape as a loss of chastity.[909] This shows clearly that the Tribunal adopts the prevailing perception of sexual violence in Bangladesh. Rape is frequently regarded as a crime against the dignity and honour of women rather than a crime that violates the mental and physical integrity of a person.[910] In the national narrative, rape is usually described as the loss of *izzat* (dignity, honour, chastity).[911] This is also based on the misconception that honour is something that can be taken away by the perpetrator and leads to victimisation. The portrayal of rape in jurisprudence thus rather strengthens the concept of the loss of honour and thereby contributes to the stigmatisation of rape victims.

The Tribunal also reinforces the term '*birangona*' although this identity is refused by many rape victims precisely because it is strongly linked to the loss of *izzat*[912]. Although the '*birangona* approach' might have been a suitable way of dealing with sexual violence in the specific societal context of 1971, it had already failed to help women overcome the stigma in 1971.[913] The continued survival of the *birangona* concept is also strongly linked to the glorification of its creator, Sheikh Mujibur Rahman, usually referred to as 'the father of the nation'. In fact, the proposal to change the term *birangona* to '*birankonya*' (which can be translated as valiant/heroic daughter) was rejected with the argument that it was Rahman who introduced the concept of *birangona*.[914] Public discourse on a new approach with the strong participation of women and victims is undoubtedly required.

In a very emotional manner, the Tribunal held that the rape victims are 'the greatest mothers and sisters of the soil'.[915] This also reflects a common phenomenon in dealing with rape victims in Bangladeshi society whereby they are usually deprived of their individuality and merely appear in relation to others (as sisters and mothers) in the national narrative.[916]

---

908 ICT 2, *The Chief Prosecutor v. Qaiser*, case no. 04/2013, Judgment, 23 December 2014, para. 720.
909 SC (AD), *Kamaruzzaman vs. The Chief Prosecutor*, Appeal Judgment, 3 November 2014, p. 65.
910 *Hossain*, in: *Hoque* (ed.), Genocide Conference Papers, 2009, p. 98, at 99.
911 *Hossain*, in: *Hoque* (ed.), Genocide Conference Papers, 2009, p. 98, at 99.
912 *Hossain*, in: *Hoque* (ed.), Genocide Conference Papers, 2009, p. 98, at 100.
913 *D'Costa*, Nationbuilding, p. 120; *Hossain*, in: *Hoque* (ed.), Genocide Conference Papers, 2009, p. 98, at 100.
914 *Basher Anik*, Birangonas Get Freedom Fighter Status, Dhaka Tribune, 13 October 2015.
915 ICT 2, *The Chief Prosecutor v. Qaiser*, case no. 04/2013, Judgment, 23 December 2014, para. 989.
916 *Hossain*, in: *Hoque* (ed.), Genocide Conference Papers, 2009, p. 98, at 99.

2 The crimes within the ICT's jurisdiction

The fact that women continue to be almost completely absent from the whole judicial process contributes to the lack of gender-sensitive perspectives in the judgments and excludes them from the process of coming to terms with the past. The appointment of women, especially as judges, is crucial to overcome this problem. In the context of the ICTR, it was, to a large extent, the appointment of women that contributed significantly to the sensitiveness of the Tribunal towards gender-based crimes.[917] The fact that women are underrepresented in the courtroom of the ICT certainly creates an intimidating atmosphere for rape victims during their testimony.

2.2.2.9 Other inhumane acts

The catch-all clause 'other inhumane acts' has been invoked in several judgments. Nevertheless, only in a few cases has a definition been properly applied.

In international criminal law, other inhumane acts are defined in accordance with the definition of the Rome Statute and comprise acts of 'a similar character intentionally causing great suffering, or serious injury to body or to mental or physical health'.[918]

While the offence was invoked in several cases without further clarification, the Tribunal provided a definition in *Kamaruzzaman*. It clarified that the term 'other inhumane act' is recognised under customary international law and that it has the function of a residual category for crimes not listed in the definition.[919] It held that it encompasses 'a treatment which is detrimental to [the] physical or mental wellbeing of an individual who is predominantly an unarmed civilian'.[920] Based on the fact that the term is listed after murder and torture, among others, the Tribunal concluded that it must be a coercive act which injures the victim's physical or mental well-being.[921] It also held that the acts must be of a similar seriousness to the listed crimes.[922] According to the Tribunal, this element must be evaluated considering all factual circumstances: the nature of the act or omission, the context of its commission, the individual circumstances of the victim and the physical and mental impact on the vic-

---

917 *Charlesworth/Chinkin*, Boundaries of International Law, p. 312.
918 Article 7(1)(k) of the Rome Statute.
919 ICT 2, *The Chief Prosecutor v. Kamaruzzaman*, case no. 03/2012, Judgment, 9 May 2013, para. 286; reiterated in: ICT 2, *The Chief Prosecutor v. Qaiser*, case no. 04/2013, Judgment, 23 December 2014, para. 186.
920 ICT 2, *The Chief Prosecutor v. Kamaruzzaman*, case no. 03/2012, Judgment, 9 May 2013, para. 282.
921 ICT 2, *The Chief Prosecutor v. Kamaruzzaman*, case no. 03/2012, Judgment, 9 May 2013, para. 282.
922 ICT 2, *The Chief Prosecutor v. Kamaruzzaman*, case no. 03/2012, Judgment, 9 May 2013, para. 285.

Part IV: Compliance of the ICT Act, the Rules of Procedure and the ICT's jurisprudence

tim.[923] It further clarified that acts do not necessarily need to have a long-term effect on the victim but a long-term effect can become relevant for the determination of 'similar seriousness'.[924] In order to determine the seriousness and the extent of the acts, the Tribunal held that context, the reason for targeting the victim, the age and status of the victim and the pattern of the acts are factors to be considered.[925]

Nevertheless, the relevant case did not meet the requirements the Tribunal itself established. The victim was shaved and afterwards coerced to walk through the town with ink and lime on his face and with a rope tied around his waist.[926] The Tribunal found that the elements of an inhumane act had been fulfilled despite the fact that, contrary to the indictment, it was not proven that the victim was almost undressed and that he was constantly whipped.[927] The Appellate Division affirmed this finding. It argued that the victim had been physically and mentally humiliated and that this humiliation was an attack on human dignity and honour.[928] It held that the accused acted with the intention to show that those who disobey orders would not be spared in the future.[929] Justice Miah argued in his separate opinion that, in the absence of a definition of 'inhumane acts' in domestic law, the dictionary definition would have to be invoked, but he failed to provide any definition.[930] Nevertheless, he concluded that the offence was fulfilled without further explanation.[931] While the act certainly was an attack on human dignity and honour, one would have to admit that it clearly fails to pass the 'similar seriousness test' also recognised by the Tribunal.

In *Qaiser*, the Tribunal did not deal with the definition but held that the intentional destruction of houses and shops through arson and plundering is an 'attack to [sic]

---

923 ICT 2, *The Chief Prosecutor v. Kamaruzzaman*, case no. 03/2012, Judgment, 9 May 2013, para. 285.
924 ICT 2, *The Chief Prosecutor v. Kamaruzzaman*, case no. 03/2012, Judgment, 9 May 2013, para. 285.
925 ICT 2, *The Chief Prosecutor v. Kamaruzzaman*, case no. 03/2012, Judgment, 9 May 2013, para. 288.
926 ICT 2, *The Chief Prosecutor v. Kamaruzzaman*, case no. 03/2012, Judgment, 9 May 2013, para. 284.
927 ICT 2, *The Chief Prosecutor v. Kamaruzzaman*, case no. 03/2012, Charge Framing Order, 4 June 2013, p. 14; ICT 2, *The Chief Prosecutor v. Kamaruzzaman* case no. 03/2012, Judgment, 9 May 2013, para. 284.
928 SC (AD), *Kamaruzzaman v. The Chief Prosecutor*, Appeal Judgment, 3 November 2014, p. 42.
929 SC (AD), *Kamaruzzaman v. The Chief Prosecutor*, Appeal Judgment, 3 November 2014, p. 42.
930 SC (AD), *Kamaruzzaman v. The Chief Prosecutor*, Dissenting Opinion of Justice Miah, Appeal Judgment, 3 November 2014, p. 194.
931 SC (AD), *Kamaruzzaman v. The Chief Prosecutor*, Dissenting Opinion of Justice Miah, Appeal Judgment, 3 November 2014, p. 289.

2 The crimes within the ICT's jurisdiction

human dignity, [the] right to live in happiness and it caused great suffering to the victims of the attack'.[932] It then found that the intention of these attacks was to terrorise innocent civilians and that this was an inhumane act 'as it substantially affected their fundamental right to property and safety, in violation of humanitarian law'[933]. It emphasised the malicious intent behind the extensive destruction.[934] While the Tribunal applied the requirement of intentionally causing great suffering, it did not broach the similar gravity requirement at all.

Likewise, in *Khokon*, plundering and arson were classified as other inhumane acts without further discussion.[935] Regarding a different charge under which the accused shot at the victim with the intention to kill or seriously injure and caused a bullet injury on the elbow of the victim, the Tribunal further elaborated on whether this would fall under the residual category.[936] It invoked the case of *Savić*[937] before the War Crimes Chamber in the Court of Bosnia and Herzegovina, in which the Chamber referred to ICTY case law[938] according to which beatings and other acts of violence and serious injuries to physical or mental integrity constituted other inhumane acts.[939] The Tribunal classified this act as an 'other inhumane' act and simultaneously as torture.[940] It remains unclear why the Tribunal invoked the catch-all clause if it considered the crime of torture to have been fulfilled. Also, the attempt to murder was not discussed further although the Tribunal held that the accused had the 'intention to kill or inflict serious physical injuries' and 'knew that his act of shooting was likely to cause grievous injury, even to [sic] death'.[941]

---

932 ICT 2, *The Chief Prosecutor v. Qaiser*, case no. 04/2013, Judgment, 23 December 2014, para. 186.
933 ICT 2, *The Chief Prosecutor v. Qaiser*, case no. 04/2013, Judgment, 23 December 2014, para. 187.
934 ICT 2, *The Chief Prosecutor v. Qaiser*, case no. 04/2013, Judgment, 23 December 2014, para. 188.
935 ICT 1, *The Chief Prosecutor v. Khokon*, case no. 04/2013, Judgment, 13 November 2014, paras. 127, 155, 184.
936 ICT 1, *The Chief Prosecutor v. Khokon*, case no. 04/2013, Judgment, 13 November 2014, para. 193.
937 War Crimes Chamber in the Court of Bosnia and Herzegovina, *Prosecutor v. Savić*, Judgment, 3 July 2009, p. 53.
938 ICTY (TC), *Prosecutor v. Kvočka et al.*, Judgment, 2 November 2001, para. 208; ICTY (TC), *Prosecutor v. Blaškić*, Judgment, 3 March 2000, para. 523.
939 ICT 1, *The Chief Prosecutor v. Khokon*, case no. 04/2013, Judgment, 13 November 2014, para. 194.
940 ICT 1, *The Chief Prosecutor v. Khokon*, case no. 04/2013, Judgment, 13 November 2014, para. 195.
941 ICT 1, *The Chief Prosecutor v. Khokon*, case no. 04/2013, Judgment, 13 November 2014, para. 195.

Part IV: Compliance of the ICT Act, the Rules of Procedure and the ICT's jurisprudence

In several other cases, the Tribunal merely assumed that a certain act constituted an inhumane act but did not discuss any details in this regard. In *Islam*, the Tribunal considered arson to fall under the residual category.[942] In *Jabbar Engineer*, it qualified forceful conversions as other inhumane acts.[943] Likewise, in *Kamaruzzaman*, the accused was indicted for torture, murder and other inhumane acts but the charges do not clarify what the 'other inhumane act' consists of.[944] Also, the Tribunal did not make any further findings in this regard.

2.2.2.10 Persecution

The ICT Act criminalises persecution on political, racial, ethnic and religious grounds. In practice, only persecutions based on political and religious grounds have been prosecuted before the ICT. In international criminal law, persecutions are defined as the intentional and severe deprivation of fundamental rights contrary to international law by reason of the identity of the group or collectivity.[945]

In *Mujahid*, the Tribunal clarified that persecution under customary international law was defined as an act or omission that: (1) discriminates in fact and denies or infringes upon a fundamental right laid down in customary or treaty law (actus reus); and (2) was carried out deliberately with the intention to discriminate on one of the listed grounds, specifically race, religion or politics (mens rea).[946] With regard to the mens rea, the Tribunal specified that a 'specific intent to cause injury to a human being because he belongs to a particular community or group' is required.[947] The definition corresponds to that established by the ICTY Trial Chamber.[948] However, the Tribunal omitted to clarify further that only severe deprivations of fundamental rights can amount to persecution[949] and that the acts must be of equal gravity to the listed crimes[950].

---

942 ICT 1, *The Chief Prosecutor v. Islam*, case no. 05/2013, Judgment, 30 December 2014, paras. 115, 136, 129.
943 ICT 1, *The Chief Prosecutor v. Jabbar Engineer*, case no. 01/2014, Judgment, 24 February 2015, para. 219.
944 ICT 2, *The Chief Prosecutor v. Kamaruzzaman*, case no. 03/2012, Charge Framing Order, 4 June 2013, p. 14.
945 Article 7(2)(g) of the Rome Statute. The definition reflects customary international law.
946 ICT 2, *The Chief Prosecutor v. Mujahid*, case no. 04/2012, Judgment, 17 July 2013, para. 564.
947 ICT 2, *The Chief Prosecutor v. Mujahid*, case no. 04/2012, Judgment, 17 July 2013, para. 565.
948 ICTY (AC), *Prosecutor v. Blaskić*, Appeal Judgment, 29 July 2004, para 131.
949 ICTY (TC), *Prosecutor v. Kupreškić*, Judgment, 14 January 2000, para. 618.
950 ICTY (AC), *Prosecutor v. Blaskić*, Appeal Judgment, 29 July 2004, para 138.

2 The crimes within the ICT's jurisdiction

In this specific case, the Tribunal determined that persecution on religious grounds was committed through 'displacement' because several crimes (rape, murder, arson and looting) were committed against members of the Hindu community and, as a consequence, many Hindus fled to India.[951] The cumulative effect of criminal acts in the specific village infringed upon the fundamental rights of the members of the Hindu community.[952] It further invoked the decision by the Appeals Chamber in *Blaskić*[953] to argue that deportation, forcible transfer and forcible displacement could amount to persecution, but failed to apply these findings to the specific case. It also cited the parts of *Blaskić*[954] in which the Appeals Chamber confirmed that the destruction of property could amount to persecution if committed on discriminatory grounds and if it constituted a destruction of the livelihood of a certain population.[955] Nevertheless, the Tribunal did not further scrutinise whether, in this specific case, the destruction of property equalled the destruction of livelihood.

Also, in *Chowdhury*, the Tribunal found that the looting and arson of houses of the Hindu community constituted persecution, though without examining any elements of the offence.[956] Since the Tribunal found that, at the same time, genocide was committed, it appears that it infers the mental element for persecution from the genocidal intent.[957] In *Nizami*, the accused was found guilty of persecution but the grounds were mentioned neither in the charges nor in the adjudication.[958] While it can be inferred from the names of the victims that they were Hindus, the Tribunal also failed to deal with the definition of further elements of the offence of persecution, including the mens rea.

In *Jabbar Engineer*, the Tribunal dealt with the question of which acts can amount to persecution. It invoked the ICTY case of *Kvočka et al.* in which the Trial Chamber listed acts of persecution.[959] These acts comprise imprisonment; unlawful detention of

---

951 ICT 2, *The Chief Prosecutor v. Mujahid*, case no. 04/2012, Judgment, 17 July 2013, para. 544.
952 ICT 2, *The Chief Prosecutor v. Mujahid*, case no. 04/2012, Judgment, 17 July 2013, para. 544.
953 ICTY (AC), *Prosecutor v. Blaskić*, Appeal Judgment, 29 July 2004, paras. 152–153.
954 ICTY (AC), *Prosecutor v. Blaskić*, Appeal Judgment, 29 July 2004, para. 146; ICTY (TC), *Prosecutor v. Kupreskić*, Judgment, 14 January 2000, para. 631.
955 ICT 2, *The Chief Prosecutor v. Mujahid*, case no. 04/2012, Judgment, 17 July 2013, para. 567.
956 ICT 1, *The Chief Prosecutor v. Chowdhury*, case no. 02/2011, Judgment, 1 October 2013, para. 125.
957 ICT 1, *The Chief Prosecutor v. Chowdhury*, case no. 02/2011, Judgment, 1 October 2013, para. 125.
958 ICT 1, *The Chief Prosecutor v. Nizami*, case no. 03/2011, Judgment, 29 October 2014, para. 178; ICT 1, case no. 03/2011, Charge Framing Order, 28 May 2012, p. 20.
959 ICTY (TC), *Prosecutor v. Kvočka et al.*, Judgment, 2 November 2001, para. 186.

civilians or infringement upon individual freedom; murder; deportation or forcible transfer; seizure, collection, segregation and forced transfer of civilians to camps; comprehensive destruction of homes and property; the destruction of towns, villages and other public or private property and the plunder of property; attacks upon cities, towns and villages; trench digging and the use of hostages and human shields; the destruction and damage of religious or educational institutions; and sexual violence, all of which could constitute persecution if committed with discriminatory intent.[960]

With regard to the mens rea, the Tribunal held that the intent of the perpetrators was to 'destroy the Hindu group or community' and that targeting a particular community is substantial enough to infer the discriminatory intent.[961] It concluded that the victims were targeted because they belonged to the Hindu community.[962]

Similar findings with regard to the mens rea were made in *Sayeedi* in which the Tribunal found that persecution on political and religious grounds were committed. The accused had raided shops and houses belonging to the Hindu community and supporters of the Liberation War.[963] Since the mode of liability was not specified, it remains unclear which standard for the mens rea the Tribunal applied in this case. However, it found that the accused 'substantially contributed and facilitated' and acted with full knowledge.[964] The Tribunal established, in a general manner, that all attacks by the Pakistani army, together with Peace Committees and Razakars, were directed against the 'Hindu community' and 'liberation loving people' and, it appears that, on this basis, assumed that persecution was committed. However, no specifications on the mental element were made and it remains unclear which standard the Tribunal ultimately applied with regard to the discriminatory intent. The Tribunal also did not specify the grounds on which the persecution was allegedly committed. Within the adjudication of another charge of persecution, the Tribunal stated that the looting was directed against a civilian population with intent to destroy a political group[965] and also held that the accused 'substantially contributed' and acted with 'full knowledge'.[966]

---

960 ICTY (TC), *Prosecutor v. Kvocka et al.*, Judgment, 02 November 2001, para. 186.
961 ICT 2, *The Chief Prosecutor v. Mujahid*, case no. 04/2012, Judgment, 17 July 2013, para. 553.
962 ICT 2, *The Chief Prosecutor v. Mujahid*, case no. 04/2012, Judgment, 17 July 2013, para. 553.
963 ICT 1, *The Chief Prosecutor v. Sayeedi*, case no. 01/2011, Judgment, 28 February 2013, para. 126.
964 ICT 1, *The Chief Prosecutor v. Sayeedi*, case no. 01/2011, Judgment, 28 February 2013, para. 126.
965 ICT 1, *The Chief Prosecutor v. Sayeedi*, case no. 01/2011, Judgment, 28 February 2013, para. 137.
966 ICT 1, *The Chief Prosecutor v. Sayeedi*, case no. 01/2011, Judgment, 28 February 2013, para. 139.

2 The crimes within the ICT's jurisdiction

Only in *Jabbar Engineer* did the Tribunal further determine the mens rea requirements of persecution. Based on *Blaskić*,[967] it held that the accused must act with the specific intent to cause injury to a human being because he belongs to the particular group.[968] The Tribunal, then, invoked the discriminatory intent from the finding that the accused held a meeting and publicly declared that freedom fighters, 'freedom loving people' and Hindus were the enemies of Pakistan and that the Razakars should annihilate them.[969] Nevertheless, also in this case, the grounds of persecution with regard to 'freedom loving people' remain unclear. However, since the Razakars plundered houses in two Hindu villages, captured 37 Hindu civilians, killed 22 and injured eight,[970] the accused was found guilty of persecution merely on religious grounds[971].

In conclusion, it can be observed that the standards for persecution applied in the judgments differ greatly. While in some judgments the elements of persecution are defined in accordance with international jurisprudence, in most cases the findings with regard to persecution remain rather vague.

2.2.3 Conclusion

The elements of crimes against humanity applied by the ICT differ greatly from the internationally recognised elements. With regard to many elements of crime, however, the problem lies mainly in the practical application rather than in the fact that the Tribunal does not consider internationally established definitions.

With regard to the chapeau requirements, the waiver of a widespread and systematic attack by the Tribunal as well as by the Appellate Division significantly extends the scope of application of the offence of crimes against humanity. The extensive use of judicial notice in this context further broadens the scope of application because it exempts the prosecution from producing evidence. Beyond that, the criteria established by the Tribunal in order to determine the nexus between the attack and the specific act are problematic because the formula 'so far removed from the attack' is not a workable standard.

With regard to the different offences, the major problem lies in the absence of clear definitions of the legal terms or, in cases in which definitions are provided, in their

---

967 ICTY (AC), *Prosecutor v. Blaskić*, Appeal Judgment, 29 July 2004, para. 165.
968 ICT 1, *The Chief Prosecutor v. Jabbar Engineer*, case no. 01/2014, Judgment, 24 February 2015, paras. 272, 274, 275.
969 ICT 1, *The Chief Prosecutor v. Jabbar Engineer*, case no. 01/2014, Judgment, 24 February 2015, para. 274.
970 ICT 1, *The Chief Prosecutor v. Jabbar Engineer*, case no. 01/2014, Judgment, 24 February 2015, para. 274.
971 ICT 1, *The Chief Prosecutor v. Jabbar Engineer*, case no. 01/2014, Judgment, 24 February 2015, para. 281.

unsatisfactory application. A detailed scrutiny of the mental elements is often entirely omitted and leads to a very extensive application of the offences. Overall, with regard to most of the distinct crimes against humanity, there is no systematic application in practice. The application of the elements of crimes in the different judgments also varies significantly.

In conclusion, the definition of crimes against humanity applied by the ICT is, to a great extent, not in accordance with international criminal law. The absence of clear definitions and the failure to apply them precisely to the cases creates a high risk of arbitrary application of the law.

2.3 War crimes

The definition of war crimes in Section 3(2)(d) of the ICT Act is identical to the definition employed in the IMT Charter, with the exception of the restriction to crimes committed in the territory of Bangladesh and the additional words 'and detenues' behind the 'killing of hostages'. The definition itself undoubtedly incorporates the international customary law of the time. Section 3(2)(d) of the ICT Act criminalises the violation of laws or customs of war and contains an illustrative list of such violations.

Nevertheless, the application to crimes committed in the context of the Liberation War is problematic because, in 1971, the prosecution of war crimes was linked to an international armed conflict. The International Commission of Jurists had already argued in 1972 in favour of the applicability of war crimes to internal conflicts and, referring to Common Article 3 of the Geneva Conventions, the Commission demanded the consideration of at least breaches of Common Article 3 as war crimes when committed in internal conflicts.[972] It based its argument on the adoption of Common Article 3 of the Geneva Conventions, which shows that international laws extend to internal conflicts, and on the intention of the United Nations to give these principles a very wide scope.[973] Nevertheless, this opinion did not reflect customary international law in 1971.

Undoubtedly, the Liberation War became international in the course of time. For the prosecution of war crimes, the point at which the conflict became international would have to be defined. This clearly became the case after India directly intervened on 3 December 1971. However, it is not so evident with regard to earlier stages of the war. Linton argues that there were three stages of the Liberation War.[974] While, initially, the conflict was entirely internal in character, it became an internationalised conflict due to the assistance provided by India to the freedom fighters and finally in-

---

972 *International Commission of Jurists*, Events in East Pakistan, pp. 59–60.
973 *International Commission of Jurists*, Events in East Pakistan, p. 59.
974 *Linton*, CLF, 2010, 21(2), p. 191, at 246.

2 The crimes within the ICT's jurisdiction

ternational when India intervened directly.[975] For the classification of a conflict, it is crucial to identify the parties involved. The ICTY Appeals Chamber applied the criterion of 'overall control' for the determination of the parties involved in a conflict.[976] In order to characterise a national conflict as international, a foreign state must exercise overall control over the military or paramilitary forces of one party in the conflict.[977] However, to this end, mere financial contributions and the provision of equipment do not suffice.[978] In contrast, organising and coordinating activities as well as influence in the planning and in military actions are required.[979] Nevertheless, whether and from which point in time the assistance of India to the freedom fighters increased to such an extent that the conflict became international would have to be determined in detail by the ICT.

The quest for an extension of the notion of international armed conflicts that includes liberation movements emerged in the 1960s and was first officially recognised by a United Nations Resolution in 1973.[980] This extension was later incorporated into Article 1(4) of Additional Protocol I to the Geneva Conventions in 1977. The provision establishes that armed conflicts arising from peoples fighting against colonial domination, alien occupation or racist regimes amount to international conflicts. Yet, at the time of the Liberation War, no such provision was in force and there is insufficient evidence to prove that the qualification of liberation wars as international conflicts had already gained the status of customary international law in 1971.[981] Likewise, there is not enough state practice to allow the conclusion that captured freedom fighters were considered prisoners of war and would therefore benefit from the application of the Geneva Conventions.[982] The scope of application of war crimes is thus limited to the period after which the conflict became international due to increasing involvement from India.

Further problems arise with regard to individual responsibility. In order to lead to individual responsibility, a norm must determine what act or omission would lead to criminal responsibility.[983] The International Commission of Jurists acknowledged this problem in 1972 with regard to the Geneva Conventions and pointed out that they do

---

975 *Linton*, CLF, 2010, 21(2), p. 191, at 247.
976 ICTY (AC), *Prosecutor v. Tadić*, Appeal Judgment, 15 July 1999, para. 131.
977 ICTY (AC), *Prosecutor v. Tadić*, Appeal Judgment, 15 July 1999, para. 131.
978 ICTY (AC), *Prosecutor v. Tadić*, Appeal Judgment, 15 July 1999, para. 137.
979 ICTY (AC), *Prosecutor v. Tadić*, Appeal Judgment, 15 July 1999, para. 137.
980 *La Haye*, War Crimes in Internal Armed Conflicts, p. 14; General Assembly Resolution 3103 (XXVIII), 12 December 1973 (UN Doc. A/RES/3103).
981 *Linton*, CLF, 2010, 21(2), p. 191, at 257.
982 *Linton*, CLF, 2010, 21(2), p. 191, at 257.
983 ICTY (TC), *Prosecutor v. Vasiljević*, Judgment, 29 November 2002, para. 193.

Part IV: Compliance of the ICT Act, the Rules of Procedure and the ICT's jurisprudence

not provide for individual responsibility in case of breaches of Common Article 3.[984] In fact, the Geneva Conventions and the Additional Protocol I establish individual responsibility but non-international conflicts are exempted from the grave breaches regime. Common Article 3 and the Additional Protocol I, which are both applicable to internal armed conflicts, do not mention individual responsibility.[985] Also, none of the international treaties between 1949 and 1995 that referred to non-international armed conflicts established individual responsibility.[986]

It was only with the creation of the ICTR Statute in 1994 that violations of Common Article 3 of the Geneva Conventions and of Article 4(2) of Additional Protocol II committed in internal armed conflicts were officially recognised as leading to criminal responsibility.[987] In practice, it was the ICTY that first confirmed that violations of Common Article 3 in internal conflicts amounted to violations of the laws and customs of war and could thus be prosecuted as war crimes. In *Tadić*, the Appeals Chamber invoked a finding of the IMT according to which the absence of an explicit provision of punishment in a treaty does not exclude individual responsibility and that only by punishing individuals who committed crimes under international law is it possible to enforce international law.[988] In accordance with the IMT, the Appeals Chamber concluded that individual responsibility is engendered when rules are unequivocally established in international law and state practice, expressed through statements by government officials and international organisations and punishments by national courts or military tribunals, which indicate the intention to punish violations of these rules.[989] Nevertheless, these developments in international jurisprudence took place long after the Liberation War. Linton, nonetheless, holds that there are grounds for the criminalisation of breaches of Common Article 3 that occurred in 1971 but also admits that proof would need to be found of state *praxis* and *opinio juris* on this matter.[990]

Beyond that, it also seems questionable whether Section 3(2)(d) of the ICT Act actually intended to include the Geneva Conventions of 1949 as laws of war. The is due to the placement of this provision before 'violation of any humanitarian rules applicable in armed conflicts laid down in the Geneva Conventions of 1949' in the ICT Act.[991] Linton suggests that, considering this context, the idea of the drafters was ap-

---

984 *International Commission of Jurists*, Events in East Pakistan, p. 54.
985 *Boed*, CLF, 2002, 13(3), p. 293, at 298.
986 *O'Keefe*, International Criminal Law, marginal no. 4.16.
987 *Werle/Jessberger*, International Criminal Law, 3. edn, marginal no. 1068.
988 The Trial of German Major War Criminals: Proceedings of the International Military Tribunal sitting at Nuremberg, 1950, Part 22, pp. 445, 447.
989 ICTY (AC), *Prosecutor v. Tadić*, Decision on the Defence Motion for Interlocutory Appeal on Jurisdiction, 2 October 1995, para. 128.
990 *Linton*, CLF, 2010, 21(2), p. 191, at 263–264.
991 *Linton*, CLF, 2010, 21(2), p. 191, at 261.

parently to cover the Hague law with the war crimes provision whereas Geneva law was intended to be covered by Section 3(2)(d).[992] However, also with regard to the Hague law, the absence of an international conflict limits the scope of application.

In conclusion, it is possible to prosecute for war crimes in the context of the Liberation War but only from the time the internal armed conflict in Bangladesh became international.[993] To date, there has been no indictment for war crimes before the ICT.

2.4 Crimes against peace

The definition of crimes against peace under the ICT Act (Section 3(2)(b)) coincides with the definition under the IMT Charter. As indicated above, at the time of the IMT it was difficult to establish individual responsibility for crimes against peace based on customary international law and the IMT Charter did not reflect the customary international law of that time in this regard. Nevertheless, the IMT convicted several persons for crimes against peace. However, even if individual responsibility could be established, the applicability of this offence in the context of Bangladesh's Liberation War would be restricted to the time from when the conflict became international. Yet, in the context of Bangladesh, crimes against peace have no scope of application[994] as no war of aggression was initiated by Bangladesh. Consequently, there has also been no prosecution for crimes against peace before the ICT.

2.5 Violation of any humanitarian rules applicable in armed conflicts laid down in the Geneva Conventions of 1949

The ICT Act further gives the ICT jurisdiction over 'violations of any humanitarian rules applicable in armed conflicts laid out in the Geneva Conventions of 1949' in Section 3(2)(e). The wording of this provision is somewhat confusing because all of the rules of the Geneva Conventions are humanitarian in nature.[995]

Nevertheless, not every violation of rules of the Geneva Conventions leads to criminal responsibility.[996] On the contrary, only grave breaches of the Geneva Conventions lead to individual criminal responsibility and, as outlined above, in 1971 they were linked to the context of an international armed conflict.[997] This leads to the question of whether breaches of Common Article 3 can be classified as grave breaches.

---

992 *Linton*, CLF, 2010, 21(2), p. 191, at 265.
993 *Linton*, CLF, 2010, 21(2), p. 191, at 266.
994 *Linton*, CLF, 2010, 21(2), p. 191, at 242.
995 *Linton*, CLF, 2010, 21(2), p. 191, at 264.
996 *Linton*, CLF, 2010, 21(2), p. 191, at 265.
997 *Linton*, CLF, 2010, 21(2), p. 191, at 265.

However, the ICTY Appeals Chamber rejected this possibility in 1994[998] and the customary international law of 1971 would, therefore, not allow for such a classification.

In conclusion, the scope of application of Section 3(2)(e) of the ICT Act is likewise limited to the period after the conflict became international. Among the considered cases, there are no examples of indictments under this provision.

2.6 Any other crimes under international law

Despite the problems regarding the principle of specificity arising from the catch-all clause 'any other crimes under international law' in Section 3(2)(f) of the ICT Act, the scope of application is limited because, in 1971, very few crimes were recognised under international law and those recognised do not become relevant in the context of the Liberation War.

2.6.1 Other crimes under international law in 1971

The international crimes recognised under customary international law in 1971 were probably only piracy, genocide, crimes against humanity and war crimes.[999] Linton holds that there is also the possibility that slavery and terrorism were international crimes in 1971.[1000] Nevertheless, in the context of the Liberation War, they are not of further relevance. Only direct and public incitement to commit genocide becomes relevant because it is not contained in the ICT Act.

2.6.2 Application of the clause in the jurisprudence of the ICT

In practice, the Tribunal has barely dealt with the interpretation of the scope of this catch-all clause. Rather, it was invoked to prosecute incitement and planning regardless of the scope of application under customary international law.

2.6.2.1 Incitement

Incitement to commit genocide was already established as an offence in Article 3(c) of the Genocide Convention. Also, the Rome Statute and the Statutes of the ICTY and the ICTR criminalise direct and public incitement to commit genocide.[1001] With re-

---

998 ICTY (AC), *Prosecutor v. Tadić*, Decision on the Defence Motion for Interlocutory Appeal on Jurisdiction, 2 October 1995, para. 83.
999 *Linton*, CLF, 2010, 21(2), p. 191, at 271.
1000 *Linton*, CLF, 2010, 21(2), p. 191, at 269–271.
1001 Article 25(3)(e) of the Rome Statute; Article 4(3)(c) of the ICTY Statute; Article 2(3)(c) of the ICTR Statute.

gard to genocide, its application by the ICT does not provoke any conflicts with the principle of legality because it has formed part of customary international law since before 1971. On the other hand, this is not the case with incitement to commit crimes against humanity.

The material act consists of public and direct incitement to commit genocide. The direct character of the incitement must be viewed in the context, and even coded language can still be direct as long as it is not ambiguous for the specific audience.[1002] The public element of incitement requires it to be made in a public place or through respective means, such as mass media, to address the general public.[1003] The mens rea requires the intentional and knowing commission of the material elements as well as the intent to destroy a group in whole or in part.[1004]

In *Azam*, the accused was indicted for incitement to commit crimes under Section 3(2) of the ICT Act.[1005] In the adjudication of the charges, the Tribunal, however, reduced the charge to incitement to commit crimes against humanity and genocide.[1006] The Tribunal merely stated that incitement to commit crimes against humanity and genocide are established crimes under customary international law and, therefore, fall under Section 3(2)(f) ICT Act.[1007] The judgment also contains several contradictions and it does not become clear whether the accused is ultimately found guilty of incitement to commit genocide or crimes against humanity, or both.[1008]

In order to determine the requirements for incitement, the Tribunal invoked the definition contained in the Draft Criminal Code for England and Wales as well as the definitions of direct and public incitement to commit genocide as established by the ICTR.[1009]

1002 ICTR (AC), *Prosecutor v. Nahimana et al.*, Appeal Judgment, 28 November 2007, para. 701.
1003 ICTR (TC), *Prosecutor v. Akayesu*, Judgment, 2 September 1998, para. 556.
1004 ICTR (TC), *Prosecutor v. Akayesu*, Judgment, 2 September 1998, para. 560.
1005 See charge 3 in ICT 1, *The Chief Prosecutor v. Azam*, case no. 06/2011, Charge Framing Order, 13 May 2012, p. 34.
1006 ICT 1, *The Chief Prosecutor v. Azam*, case no. 06/2011, Judgment, 15 July 2013, para. 135.
1007 ICT 1, *The Chief Prosecutor v. Azam*, case no. 06/2011, Judgment, 15 July 2013, para. 135.
1008 In ICT 1, *The Chief Prosecutor v. Azam*, case no. 06/2011, Judgment, 15 July 2013, para. 215, the accused was found guilty of incitement to commit genocide, whereas later, at para. 387, he was found guilty of incitement to commit crimes under Section 3(2).
1009 ICT 1, *The Chief Prosecutor v. Azam*, case no. 06/2011, Judgment, 15 July 2013, paras. 136–137; the same criteria were also invoked later in: ICT 1, *The Chief Prosecutor v. Nizami*, case no. 03/2011, Judgment, 29 October 2014, para. 256.

Part IV: Compliance of the ICT Act, the Rules of Procedure and the ICT's jurisprudence

Clause 47 of the Draft Criminal Code for England and Wales
A person is guilty of incitement to commit an offence or offences if –
(a) he incites another to do or cause to be done an act or acts which, if done, will involve the commission of the offence or offences by the other; and
(b) he intends or believes that the other, if he acts as incited, shall or will do so with the fault required for the offence or offences.

This definition has little to do with the international crime of public and direct incitement to commit genocide. Instead, it defines the mode of liability of prompting somebody to commit a crime, which amounts to instigation. In fact, the criteria 'direct' and 'public' distinguish the inchoate crime from this mode of liability.[1010] In the context of public and direct incitement to commit genocide, the definition of the Draft Criminal Code for England and Wales is thus not helpful. Its application is also contradictory because the charges are under 'any other crime under international law'. Despite the ICT's reluctance to apply international law in cases in which 'crimes under international law' are prosecuted, international law must be necessarily applied because the respective crime exists only under international law. As outlined above, this approach was also confirmed by the Appellate Division which emphasised that for 'any other crimes under international law', international law must be invoked.[1011]

The Tribunal further established the following requirements for direct and public incitement to commit genocide: (1) the accused incites others to commit genocide; (2) the incitement was direct; (3) the incitement was public; and (4) the accused acted with the specific intent to commit genocide, i.e. the intent to destroy, in whole or in part, a national, ethnic, racial or religious group.[1012] Interestingly, this definition does not encompass political groups. The Tribunal further confirmed that incitement to commit genocide is an inchoate offence and, therefore, is already completed when the discourse is published.[1013] It also clarified that the context of a particular speech is relevant to the assessment of whether incitement to commit genocide was fulfilled.[1014]

The application of these criteria in the case of *Azam* is contradictory on several points. The indictment contains 28 counts, and the evidence consists exclusively of

---

1010 *Cassese*, International Criminal Law, 3. edn, p. 203.
1011 SC (AD), *Molla v. The Chief Prosecutor*, Appeal Judgment, 17 September 2013, p. 86.
1012 ICT 1, *The Chief Prosecutor v. Azam*, case no. 06/2011, Judgment, 15 July 2013, para. 137; ICT 1, *The Chief Prosecutor v. Nizami*, case no. 03/2011, Judgment, 29 October 2014, para. 256.
1013 ICT 1, *The Chief Prosecutor v. Azam*, case no. 06/2011, Judgment, 15 July 2013, para. 138; ICT 1, *The Chief Prosecutor v. Nizami*, case no. 03/2011, Judgment, 29 October 2014, para. 256.
1014 ICT 1, *The Chief Prosecutor v. Nizami*, case no. 03/2011, Judgment, 29 October 2014, para. 265.

newspaper clippings. Many of these sources, however, do not disclose any inciting activity. Nevertheless, problems arise also from the inexact reproduction of the sources. Since the Tribunal did not clarify whether it scrutinises incitement to commit crimes against humanity or to commit genocide, it remains unclear which criteria are actually applied. In the context of crimes against humanity, the Tribunal did not invoke any specific definition and it remains unclear whether it considers the definition of the Draft Criminal Code for England and Wales applicable. Under Count 2, the accused gave a speech aired over Radio Pakistan in which he stated that:

> [...] by sending armed intruders, India has challenged the patriotism of the East Pakistani People. India should keep it in mind that it should not interfere for the freedom of a country. I believe that these intruders will never get any assistance from the Muslims of East Pakistan.[1015]

The Tribunal concluded from this that the followers of the accused were 'incited to commit atrocities during the Liberation War and at his influence and instigation many unarmed Bangalees including a group of Hindus, supporters of [the] Awami League who had sided with an independent Bangladesh, were also killed'.[1016] This finding is contradictory based on several aspects. First, it seems to ignore the inchoate character of public and direct incitement because it emphasises the crimes that were committed afterwards. Second, the incitement is not direct because the accused does not call for the commission of crimes. Third, if the Tribunal referred to incitement to commit genocide, it further failed to establish the specific intent.

The evidence of Count 10 proves that the accused stated in public that 'there is no documentary evidence to show that the Hindus are the friends of Muslims'.[1017] The accused further said that Hindus 'always were the enemies of Muslims'.[1018] The Tribunal interprets these statements to the effect that the accused 'expressed hatred and communal feeling towards [the] Hindu Community with intent to destroy or deport this religious group from this country'.[1019] Nevertheless, it again failed to discuss the requirement of the incitement being direct.

Regarding Count 15, the Tribunal found that the speech of the accused 'amounts to clear incitement to commit crimes against humanity and genocide'.[1020] According to the evidence, the accused participated in a meeting and said that '[...] Bengalee Muslims will get their rights one day if Pakistan exists. And Bengalee Muslims will not exist if Pakistan [is] extinct. Those who do not understand this truth, they must be

---

1015 ICT 1, *The Chief Prosecutor v. Azam*, case no. 06/2011, Judgment, 15 July 2013, para. 141.
1016 ICT 1, *The Chief Prosecutor v. Azam*, case no. 06/2011, Judgment, 15 July 2013, para. 142.
1017 ICT 1, *The Chief Prosecutor v. Azam*, case no. 06/2011, Judgment, 15 July 2013, para. 161.
1018 ICT 1, *The Chief Prosecutor v. Azam*, case no. 06/2011, Judgment, 15 July 2013, para. 162.
1019 ICT 1, *The Chief Prosecutor v. Azam*, case no. 06/2011, Judgment, 15 July 2013, para. 211.
1020 ICT 1, *The Chief Prosecutor v. Azam*, case no. 06/2011, Judgment, 15 July 2013, para. 212.

eradicated from the soil of East Pakistan'.[1021] The Tribunal found that 'those who do not understand this truth' referred to the pro-liberation people and therefrom concluded that the accused incited genocide and crimes against humanity.[1022] Nevertheless, it is not clear how the Tribunal established the specific intent because no mental elements of the crime were discussed. It appears that it assumed that the accused acted with the intent to destroy, in whole or in part, a political group. However, political groups were not included in the definition of public and direct incitement that the Tribunal provided.

Another incident involved a statement by the accused before the media urging the government to supply the latest automatic weapons to all patriots, members of Peace Committees and Razakars in order to establish peace in Pakistan.[1023] This incident clearly lacks the character of incitement because there is no evidence of any persons that the accused incited. The ICT concluded that the accused publicly and directly incited 'his subordinates to wipe out Bangalee people by using the alleged automatic weapons'[1024] and thus incited crimes against humanity and genocide.[1025]

The ICT further found the charge proven based on a meeting held between the accused and the president of Pakistan. The content of this meeting was published in a newspaper but the accused did not address the public. In this meeting, the accused called the freedom fighters an 'enemy force' and stated that the number of Razakars was sufficient to counter the freedom fighters but urged that the number of Razakars be increased.[1026] The Tribunal held that the accused had a superior status and, by his statement, incited the Razakars, who were subordinate to him, to commit crimes against humanity and genocide.[1027] The Tribunal found also that this amounted to incitement to commit crimes against humanity and genocide.

In *Nizami*, the Tribunal also invoked Section 3(2)(f) of the ICT Act but found that the elements of incitement to commit genocide were not fulfilled.[1028] The four charges already lack any basis for direct and public incitement to commit genocide[1029] because the accused allegedly declared that Pakistan was the house of Allah and that no

---

1021 ICT 1, *The Chief Prosecutor v. Azam*, case no. 06/2011, Judgment, 15 July 2013, para. 174.
1022 ICT 1, *The Chief Prosecutor v. Azam*, case no. 06/2011, Judgment, 15 July 2013, para. 212.
1023 ICT 1, *The Chief Prosecutor v. Azam*, case no. 06/2011, Judgment, 15 July 2013, para. 213.
1024 ICT 1, *The Chief Prosecutor v. Azam*, case no. 06/2011, Judgment, 15 July 2013, para. 214.
1025 ICT 1, *The Chief Prosecutor v. Azam*, case no. 06/2011, Judgment, 15 July 2013, para. 214.
1026 ICT 1, *The Chief Prosecutor v. Azam*, case no. 06/2011, Judgment, 15 July 2013, para. 215.
1027 ICT 1, *The Chief Prosecutor v. Azam*, case no. 06/2011, Judgment, 15 July 2013, para. 215.
1028 ICT 1, *The Chief Prosecutor v. Nizami*, case no. 03/2011, Judgment, 29 October 2014, para. 271.
1029 ICT 1, *The Chief Prosecutor v. Nizami*, case no. 03/2011, Charge Framing Order, 28 May 2012, pp. 23–26.

one could destroy Pakistan.[1030] The Tribunal rightly concluded that this utterance was an incorrect interpretation of the Quran but that it did not contain any inciting element to commit crimes against a specific group.[1031]

2.6.2.2 Planning

Planning is not listed in the ICT Act as a mode of liability. It appears merely in the offence of crimes against peace (planning of a war of aggression or a war in violation of international treaties, agreements or assurances) in Section 3(2)(b). Yet, in the context of an act of aggression, planning constitutes a form of commission.[1032]

Planning is also mentioned in Section 4(2) of the ICT Act which establishes criminal liability of superior officers and commanders who are connected with plans involving the commission of crimes under Section 3(2). If one considers this context, one might argue that invoking planning as a crime under international law runs counter to the ICT Act because the drafters apparently intended to criminalise planning only if superior officers and commanders are involved.

Nevertheless, the qualification of planning as a 'crime under international law' under Section 3(2)(f) is flawed. Contrary to 'incitement to commit genocide', which is an established offence under international law, there is no offence of 'planning'. Although there are good reasons why planning should be classified as an inchoate crime,[1033] it is actually treated as a mode of liability in international criminal law. The primary characteristic that distinguishes an inchoate crime from a mode of criminal liability is that the former does not depend on the completion of further activities in order to ground criminal liability.[1034] In fact, the ICTY Appeals Chamber found that liability for planning requires a crime to be committed in execution of the accused's plan.[1035] This reflects the Statutes of the ad hoc tribunals which list planning as a mode of liability.[1036]

Given that planning is not a crime under international law, the catch-all clause of the ICT Act cannot be invoked for the prosecution of planning a crime within the jurisdiction of the ICT Act. Nevertheless, the ICT disregards international law. Yet, since the Tribunal applies planning as an inchoate crime, the actual commission of the

---

1030 ICT 1, *The Chief Prosecutor v. Nizami*, case no. 03/2011, Charge Framing Order, 28 May 2012, p. 23.
1031 ICT 1, *The Chief Prosecutor v. Nizami*, case no. 03/2011, Judgment, 29 October 2014, para. 267.
1032 *O'Keefe*, International Criminal Law, marginal no. 5.50.
1033 *Cassese*, International Criminal Law, 3. edn, p. 199.
1034 *Boas/Bischoff/Reid*, Forms of Responsibility, p. 283.
1035 ICTY (AC), *Prosecutor v. Kordić et al.*, Appeal Judgment, 17 December 2004, para. 26.
1036 Article 7(1) of the ICTY Statute; Article 6(1) of the ICTR Statute.

offence is not required. On the contrary, international jurisprudence stipulates that the crime must be perpetrated after the planning and that the planning must contribute substantially to the commission of the crime.[1037] The mens rea requires the direct intent to commit the crime or have it committed by others in accordance with the plan or, at least, the awareness of the substantial likelihood that a crime will be committed in execution of the planned acts or omissions.[1038]

Azam was indicted for planning to commit crimes under Section 3(2) of the ICT Act as other international crime pursuant to Section 3(2)(f).[1039] The Tribunal failed to specify the crimes that were actually planned. In the absence of a definition of planning in the ICT Act, the Tribunal invoked jurisprudence of the ICTY[1040] and concluded that planning means that one or more persons design the commission of a crime at both the preparatory and the execution phases.[1041] No further requirements of planning were established and the specific intent was not discussed at all.

The Tribunal evaluated the evidence of Charge 1 (conspiracy) and Charge 2 (planning) together and apparently considered conspiracy as well as planning to be inchoate offences.[1042] Yet, it was emphasised that, as a consequence of planning and conspiracy, massive crimes were committed throughout Bangladesh.[1043] Again, the Tribunal seems to have come to this conclusion because it took judicial notice of the fact that crimes against humanity and genocide were committed during the Liberation War.[1044]

Also, the conduct that the Tribunal qualified as planning is not covered by the definition. It found the accused guilty of planning based on the fact that Azam and others held a meeting with General Tikka Khan (then Martial Law Administrator) for the formation of the Peace Committee in order to support the Pakistani army.[1045] The

---

1037 ICTY (AC), *Prosecutor v. D. Milosević*, Appeal Judgment, 12 November 2009, para. 268.
1038 ICTY (AC), *Prosecutor v. D. Milosević*, Appeal Judgment, 12 November 2009, para. 268.
1039 ICT 1, *The Chief Prosecutor v. Azam*, case no. 06/2011, Charge Framing Order, 13 May 2012, p. 20.
1040 ICTY (TC), *Prosecutor v. Naletilić and Martinović*, Judgment, 21 March 2003, para. 59; ICTY (TC), *Prosecutor v. Krstić*, Judgment, para. 601. However, the definition invoked in these judgments of the Trial Chamber was established by the ICTR in ICTR (TC), *Prosecutor v. Akayesu*, Judgment, 2 September 1998, para. 480.
1041 ICT 1, *The Chief Prosecutor v. Azam*, case no. 06/2011, Judgment, 15 July 2013, para. 110.
1042 *Taylor*, Special Issue No. 5 – Legal Conclusions Azam, p. 10.
1043 ICT 1, *The Chief Prosecutor v. Azam*, case no. 06/2011, Judgment, 15 July 2013, para. 134.
1044 *Taylor*, Special Issue No. 5 – Legal Conclusions Azam, p. 10; ICT 1, *The Chief Prosecutor v. Azam*, case no. 06/2011, Judgment, 15 July 2013, para. 43.
1045 ICT 1, *The Chief Prosecutor v. Azam*, case no. 06/2011, Judgment, 15 July 2013, para. 114.

accused further participated in several meetings aimed at the formation of the Central and local Peace Committees.[1046] However, the Tribunal did not disclose any specific content of the meetings from which a precise act of planning became apparent. None of the invoked evidence explicitly shows that the formation of these groups encompassed a plan to commit genocide or crimes against humanity.[1047] Here, again, the Tribunal seems to have relied on the fact of common knowledge that the Peace Committees committed crimes during the Liberation War and of which it had taken judicial notice. The accused was found guilty of conspiracy (Charge 1) and planning (Charge 2) that allegedly resulted in 'massive crimes against humanity and genocide in [sic] a large scale in all over [sic] Bangladesh by his subordinate para milita [sic] forces'.[1048]

In *Sobhan*, Tribunal 2 seems to have considered planning a mode of liability that is not restricted to superiors because it rejected the prosecution's submission that the accused incurred liability as a civilian superior[1049] but, at the same time, it discussed his liability for planning, which was ultimately rejected with the argument that a conviction cannot be based on planning and commission at the same time.[1050] Nevertheless, it argued that involvement in the planning could be considered an aggravating factor.[1051] The latter finding is in consonance with the jurisprudence of the ICTY.[1052] Ultimately, however, the Tribunal did not consider involvement in the planning to be an aggravating factor in this case.

2.6.2.3 Conclusion

Section 3(2)(f) has certainly helped to fill the gap in the ICT Act with regard to public and direct incitement to commit genocide. Nevertheless, the Tribunal applied international law beyond its scope in all cases and thus did not merely apply crimes under international law but also modes of liability. The catch-all clause has thus led to arbitrary application of the law. This problem, however, is not rooted in the lack of speci-

---

1046 ICT 1, *The Chief Prosecutor v. Azam*, case no. 06/2011, Judgment, 15 July 2013, para. 120.
1047 *Taylor*, Special Issue No. 5 – Legal Conclusions Azam, p. 13.
1048 ICT 1, *The Chief Prosecutor v. Azam*, case no. 06/2011, Judgment, 15 July 2013, para. 134.
1049 ICT 2, *The Chief Prosecutor v. Sobhan*, case no. 01/2014, Judgment, 18 February 2015, para. 277.
1050 ICT 2, *The Chief Prosecutor v. Sobhan*, case no. 01/2014, Judgment, 18 February 2015, para. 275.
1051 ICT 2, *The Chief Prosecutor v. Sobhan*, case no. 01/2014, Judgment, 18 February 2015, para. 274.
1052 ICTY (TC), *Prosecutor v. Brđanin*, Judgment, 1 September 2004, para. 268; ICTY (TC), *Prosecutor v. Stakić*, 31 July 2003, Judgment, para. 443.

Part IV: Compliance of the ICT Act, the Rules of Procedure and the ICT's jurisprudence

ficity of the catch-all clause as such, but rather in the incorrect application of international law through the Tribunal.

2.7 Inchoate crimes

The ICT Act criminalises two inchoate crimes: conspiracy and attempt to commit are listed in Section 3(2)(g) and refer to any of the crimes under the ICT's jurisdiction.

2.7.1 Conspiracy and attempt under customary international law

Conspiracy to commit genocide is explicitly criminalised in the Genocide Convention, the ICTY Statute and the ICTR Statute. The ICT Act in Section 3(2)(g) goes beyond that and criminalises conspiracy to commit any crime under the ICT's jurisdiction.

Yet, Section 3(2)(g) of the ICT Act resembles the regime of liability for conspiracy under the IMT Charter. Article 6 of the Charter established criminal responsibility for 'leaders, organisers, instigators and accomplices participating in the formulation or execution of a common plan or conspiracy to commit any of the foregoing crimes'. That is, conspiracy was criminalised with regard to crimes against peace, war crimes and crimes against humanity. However, this does not reflect customary international law. While conspiracy to commit genocide forms part of customary international law,[1053] this is not the case with conspiracy to commit war crimes or crimes against humanity[1054]. In this regard, the IMT Charter incorporated ex post facto law,[1055] although the IMT applied conspiracy only in connection with crimes against peace[1056]. The ICT Act thus goes beyond the customary international law of 1971 and today insofar as it criminalises conspiracy to commit crimes other than genocide.

The Act also criminalises the attempt to commit any of the crimes under the ICT's jurisdiction in Section 3(2)(g). The ad hoc tribunals' Statutes criminalise attempt only with regard to genocide, but no cases have been tried under the respective provisions. In general, attempt has not played a major role in the jurisprudence but it is accepted as forming part of international criminal law.[1057] Likewise, in the jurisprudence of the ICT, attempt has had no practical significance.

1053 *Cassese*, International Criminal Law, 3. edn, p. 202.
1054 *Werle/Jessberger*, International Criminal Law, 3. edn, marginal no. 696.
1055 *Cassese*, International Criminal Law, 3. edn, p. 202.
1056 The Trial of Major German War Criminals: Proceedings before the International Military Tribunal sitting at Nuremberg, Germany, 1950, Part 22, p. 449.
1057 *Cassese*, International Criminal Law, 3. edn, p. 200.

2.7.2 Conspiracy and attempt in the jurisprudence of the ICT

In practice, there have been only a few indictments for conspiracy. While the Tribunal initially invoked definitions of conspiracy from British law and from international criminal law, this practice changed entirely in *Jabbar Engineer* when the Tribunal, for the first time, relied on the domestic definition of the Penal Code.

According to international jurisprudence, conspiracy to commit genocide requires an agreement between two or more persons[1058] with each needing to be aware of the agreement and act with the specific intent of genocide.[1059]

In *Azam*, the Tribunal affirmed that conspiracy is a separate crime and not a mere mode of liability[1060] and dealt with four charges of conspiracy to commit crimes under the ICT Act. Nevertheless, the charge framing order does not specify which crimes the accused allegedly conspired in but rather indicts him for conspiracy to commit the 'above mentioned [sic] crimes in Bangladesh'.[1061] Only from the context can it be concluded that, with the 'above mentioned [sic] crimes', reference is made to the general historical background provided in the order.[1062] Nevertheless, the historical background does not provide a specific classification of the crimes and thus the standards applied by the Tribunal remain unclear. This also leads to problems with regard to attribution and the scope of the agreement that forms part of the offence of conspiracy.

The Tribunal invoked the British Criminal Law Act 1977 in its amended version from 1981 for the definition of conspiracy.[1063]

> *Section 1(1) of the Criminal Law Act, 1977, as amended through the Criminal Attempts Act in 1981*
> Subject to the following provisions of this Part of this Act, if a person agrees with any other person or person that a course of conduct shall be pursued which, if the agreement is carried out in accordance with their intentions, either –
> (a) will necessarily amount to or involve the commission of any offences by one or more of the parties to the agreement;

1058 ICTR (AC), *Prosecutor v. Nahimana et al.*, Appeal Judgment, 28 November 2007, para. 894; ICTR (AC), *Prosecutor v. Ntagerura et al.*, Appeal Judgment, 7 July 2006, para. 92.
1059 ICTY (TC), *Prosecutor v. Tolimir*, Judgment, 12 December 2012, para. 787.
1060 ICT 1, *The Chief Prosecutor v. Azam*, case no. 06/2011, Judgment, 15 July 2013, para. 96.
1061 ICT 1, *The Chief Prosecutor v. Azam*, case no. 06/2011, Charge Framing Order, 15 May 2012, p. 17.
1062 ICT 1, *The Chief Prosecutor v. Azam*, case no. 06/2011, Charge Framing Order, 15 May 2012, pp. 2–6.
1063 ICT 1, *The Chief Prosecutor v. Azam*, case no. 06/2011, Judgment, 15 July 2013, para. 93.

Part IV: Compliance of the ICT Act, the Rules of Procedure and the ICT's jurisprudence

(b) or would do so but for the existence of facts which render the commission of the offence or any of the offences impossible, he is guilty of the crime of conspiracy to commit the offence or offences in question.

The Tribunal then defined the actus reus by means of criteria that constitute exceptions to the crime:[1064] '(1) The conspirators will not be liable when they never acted on their own plan. (2) The fact that the conspirators give a second thought and withdraws [sic] does not provide any defence'.[1065] Concerning the mens rea, the Tribunal established that 'the partner must intend that the crime will be carried out'.[1066] Then, the Tribunal defined the actus reus as the agreement itself, which must be manifested by acts, and held that the mens rea requires: (a) an intention to agree; (b) an intention to carry out the agreement; and (c) intention or knowledge as to any circumstances forming part of the substantive offence.[1067] The Tribunal further clarified that conspiracy should be limited to agreements to commit criminal offences and confirmed that conspiracy is an inchoate offence.[1068]

For the definition of conspiracy to commit genocide, however, the Tribunal invoked the elements established by the ICTR: (1) concerted agreement to act; and (2) specific intent (to destroy, in whole or in part, a national, ethnic, racial or religious group).[1069] With regard to the specific case, the Tribunal once again did not clarify whether it considers political groups to be encompassed within this. The Tribunal further omitted to specify the requirements of conspiracy to commit crimes against humanity. The applicability of the Penal Code for the definition of conspiracy was not discussed at all.

Nevertheless, the provided definitions were not applied in practice. The evidence consisted of newspaper articles that proved that the accused participated in several meetings in which he, for instance, affirmed his support for the Peace Committees and demanded the extension of the Razakars and for the further supply of arms.[1070] From the latter, the Tribunal concluded that the accused conspired to kill intellectuals but the evidence does not corroborate such an agreement.[1071] The judgment does not scrutinise the mens rea but rather assumes that the evidence proves the accused's 'direct

---

1064 *Taylor*, Special Issue No. 5 – Legal Conclusions Azam, p. 8.
1065 ICT 1, *The Chief Prosecutor v. Azam*, case no. 06/2011, Judgment, 15 July 2013, para. 93.
1066 ICT 1, *The Chief Prosecutor v. Azam*, case no. 06/2011, Judgment, 15 July 2013, para. 93.
1067 ICT 1, *The Chief Prosecutor v. Azam*, case no. 06/2011, Judgment, 15 July 2013, para. 95.
1068 ICT 1, *The Chief Prosecutor v. Azam*, case no. 06/2011, Judgment, 15 July 2013, para. 94; reaffirmed in ICT 1, *The Chief Prosecutor v. Jabbar Engineer*, case no. 01/2014, Judgment, 24 February 2015, para. 244.
1069 ICT 1, *The Chief Prosecutor v. Azam*, case no. 06/2011, Judgment, 15 July 2013, para. 97.
1070 ICT 1, *The Chief Prosecutor v. Azam*, case no. 06/2011, Judgment, 15 July 2013, paras. 98–109.
1071 ICT 1, *The Chief Prosecutor v. Azam*, case no. 06/2011, Azam, Judgment, 15 July 2013, para. 109.

2 The crimes within the ICT's jurisdiction

knowledge' of the crimes committed by the Pakistani army.[1072] This does not reflect the mental elements of conspiracy as established by the Tribunal earlier.

In several cases, the Tribunal found the accused guilty of conspiracy to commit genocide or crimes against humanity and, simultaneously, of complicity in the commission of the same offences.[1073] The judgments, however, do not specify the elements of complicity and do not reveal the respective conduct that led to the finding that conspiracy was committed. Also, Nizami was found guilty of conspiracy to commit the crime against humanity of murder and simultaneously of committing the offence.[1074] Although the Tribunal did not discuss the elements of conspiracy, it seems that this finding was gathered from the fact that the crime was committed in a planned manner.

That there can or must be convictions for the inchoate crime of conspiracy when the person is also found guilty of committing genocide is controversial. The ICTR Appeals Chamber in *Gatete* found that convictions must be based on both crimes simultaneously.[1075] The ICT's approach to convicting for both crimes appears also to be in line with the practice of the Appellate Division under domestic law in Bangladesh.[1076]

It was only in the case of *Jabbar Engineer* that the Tribunal, for the first time, invoked the Penal Code for the definition of conspiracy[1077] and complied with the Appellate Division's findings on the primary application of the Penal Code.

> *Section 120A of the Penal Code: Definition of criminal conspiracy*
> When two or more persons agree to do, or cause to be done; –
> (1) an illegal act, or
> (2) an act which is not illegal by illegal means, such an agreement is designated a criminal conspiracy:
> Provided that no agreement except an agreement to commit an offence shall amount to a criminal conspiracy unless some act besides the agreement is done by one or more parties to such agreement in pursuance thereof.

1072 ICT 1, *The Chief Prosecutor v. Azam*, case no. 06/2011, Judgment, 15 July 2013, para. 131.
1073 In ICT 1, *The Chief Prosecutor v. Chowdhury*, case no. 02/2011, Judgment, 1 October 2013, para. 125, the accused was found guilty of conspiracy and complicity in genocide as well as the crime against humanity of persecution. In ICT 1, *The Chief Prosecutor v. Hossain*, case no. 01/2013, Judgment, 24 November 2014, para. 84, the accused was found guilty of conspiracy to and complicity in the crimes against humanity of murder, torture and abduction.
1074 ICT 1, *The Chief Prosecutor v. Nizami*, case no. 03/2011, Judgment, 29 October 2014, para. 145.
1075 ICTR (AC), *Prosecutor v. Gatete*, Appeal Judgment, 9 October 2012, paras. 260–264.
1076 *Major Bazlul Huda v. State*, 62 DLR (AD) (2010), pp. 1 ff., at 70.
1077 ICT 1, *The Chief Prosecutor v. Jabbar Engineer*, case no. 01/2014, Judgment, 24 February 2015, para. 242.

> Explanation – It is immaterial whether the illegal act is the ultimate object of such agreement, or is merely incidental to that object.

This definition also establishes the requirement of an agreement. In the context of international crimes, Section 120A(2) evidently has no scope of application. The domestic definition unmistakeably defines conspiracy as an inchoate crime.[1078] In contrast, the Tribunal held that the concept of conspiracy extends liability to individuals who did not directly participate in the commission of the crime and that it thus establishes indirect liability for crimes against humanity.[1079] The characterisation of conspiracy as a mode of liability is untenable against the backdrop of the domestic definition.

The Tribunal then held that conspiracy consists of the following elements: (1) an agreement between the perpetrators aimed at the achievement of an illegal goal; (2) the perpetrators have knowledge of the nature of the conspiracy and nevertheless participate in it; and (3) at least one member of the group has to commit an overt act in furtherance of the conspiracy.[1080] The Tribunal further held that 'the lack of a direct agreement between the defendant and the physical perpetrator is no bar to applying the conspiracy doctrine as long as the chain of overlapping agreements connects them'.[1081]

The findings of the Tribunal are a combination of two different notions of conspiracy. The Penal Code differentiates between criminal conspiracy under Section 120A and abetment by conspiracy under Section 107. Section 107 determines that a person abets the doing of a thing, inter alia, if he or she 'engages with one or more other person or persons in any conspiracy for the doing of that thing, if an act or illegal omission takes place in pursuance of that conspiracy, and in order to the doing of that thing'. That is, under the Penal Code, conspiracy amounts to abetment when the crime is committed in pursuance of the conspiracy.[1082] If no crime is committed, conspiracy amounts to criminal conspiracy under Section 120A. Therefore, the notion of conspiracy in Section 120A of the Penal Code equals the inchoate crime of conspiracy in international criminal law. Criminal conspiracy as a form of abetment is not an inchoate crime but rather extends the liability of an abettor to the pre-perpetration stage of a crime. The further findings of the Tribunal show that, in this specific case,[1083] it re-

---

1078 *Md Yaqub v. Crown*, 7 DLR (1955), pp. 75 ff., at 81.
1079 ICT 1, *The Chief Prosecutor v. Jabbar Engineer*, case no. 01/2014, Judgment, 24 February 2015, para. 246.
1080 ICT 1, *The Chief Prosecutor v. Jabbar Engineer*, case no. 01/2014, Judgment, 24 February 2015, para. 247.
1081 ICT 1, *The Chief Prosecutor v. Jabbar Engineer*, case no. 01/2014, Judgment, 24 February 2015, para. 251.
1082 *Major Bazlul Huda v. State*, 62 DLR (AD) (2010), pp. 1 ff., at 206.
1083 ICT 1, *The Chief Prosecutor v. Jabbar Engineer*, case no. 01/2014, Judgment, 24 February 2015, para. 244.

fers to conspiracy as a form of abetment even though conspiracy was initially classified as an inchoate crime.

The Tribunal then determined the criteria that must be fulfilled for a person to be 'concerned' with conspiracy: (1) the person agrees with another person or other persons that they or one of them will engage in an act that constitutes a crime; or (2) the person agrees to aid the other person or persons in the planning or commission of a crime or attempt or solicitation to commit a crime; or (3) the person's purpose was to promote or facilitate the commission of the crime.[1084] As will be outlined in the context of the modes of liability,[1085] the standard 'concerned with the commission of the crime' is frequently utilised by the Tribunal to establish whether the accused can be held liable for the respective crime. Nevertheless, it remains unclear on which basis the Tribunal established these criteria. However, it concluded from the criteria that criminal conspiracy also encompasses planning.[1086]

The Tribunal also quoted the *Bangabandhu* murder case[1087] in which the Appellate Division dealt extensively with the distinction between conspiracy under Section 120A and abetment. However, the parts of the judgment quoted by the Tribunal do not fit into the concept of conspiracy as an inchoate offence in international criminal law. With regard to conspiracy as a form of abetment, the Appellate Division found in the *Bangabandhu* murder case that not every party of the conspiracy is required to undertake an overt act towards the fulfilment of the object of the conspiracy.[1088] The Tribunal finally found that the accused 'conspired, abetted [and] facilitated' the commission of abduction, murder, persecution and other inhumane acts as crimes against humanity.[1089] Ultimately, it remains unclear how the Tribunal defines conspiracy. The concluding finding creates even more confusion because it mentions conspiracy alongside abetment and thus indicates that the Tribunal considers conspiracy as something different from abetment.

There are no indictments for attempts to commit any crimes under the ICT Act. The definition would, however, be challenging because the Penal Code does not contain a general definition of 'attempt'. Section 511, in a general manner, punishes an attempt to commit an offence only if the respective offence is 'punishable with imprisonment for

---

1084 ICT 1, *The Chief Prosecutor v. Jabbar Engineer*, case no. 01/2014, Judgment, 24 February 2015, para. 253.
1085 See pp. 172 ff.
1086 ICT 1, *The Chief Prosecutor v. Jabbar Engineer*, case no. 01/2014, Judgment, 24 February 2015, para. 254.
1087 ICT 1, *The Chief Prosecutor v. Jabbar Engineer*, case no. 01/2014, Judgment, 24 February 2015, para. 173 citing: *Major Bazlul Huda v. State*, 62 DLR (AD) (2010), pp. 1 ff.
1088 *Major Bazlul Huda v. State*, 62 DLR (AD) (2010), pp. 1 ff., at 206–207.
1089 ICT 1, *The Chief Prosecutor v. Jabbar Engineer*, case no. 01/2014, Judgment, 24 February 2015, para. 281.

life or imprisonment'. For that reason, the Penal Code defines attempt only in relation to the specific crimes (for instance, murder) for which attempt is penalised but does not contain a general definition that could be invoked for the crimes under the ICT Act.

2.7.3 Conclusion

The application of the inchoate crime of conspiracy runs counter to any established doctrine at the domestic as well as at the international level. As the case of *Jabbar Engineer* shows, it ultimately remains unclear whether the Tribunal considers conspiracy to be an inchoate crime or rather a form of abetment.

2.8 Interim findings

The application of the offences under the ICT's jurisdiction in the jurisprudence is fraught with problems. The main problems consist of the absence of definitions and imprecise definitions as well as their flawed application to the cases. Despite the finding of the Tribunal that domestic law prevails, there are several occasions in which domestic provisions were not considered at all. While it is certainly positive that the Tribunal relies on international jurisprudence, the absence of a systematic approach as to when international law is applied leads to arbitrary application of the law.

The application of the catch-all clause 'other crimes under international law' reveals a lack of familiarity with international law. In fact, prosecution under the clause has led to the creation of new crimes and clearly infringes the principle of legality.

3 The modes of liability of the ICT Act

The ICT Act establishes different modes of liability, whereas direct commission as a main perpetrator is not listed separately but contained in Section 3(1) of the ICT Act ('who commits'). Section 3(2)(g) criminalises abetment to commit any of the crimes listed in Section 3(2); and Section 3(h) establishes liability for complicity or failure to prevent the commission of any of these crimes. However, several modes of liability are missing in the ICT Act. There are no provisions for ordering (except in Section 4(2), which refers to superior officers and commanders), planning and instigation and no explicit reference to JCE is made. Section 4(2) establishes liability of commanders and superior officers.

For its part, the Penal Code does not contain definitions of all of these notions but only defines abetment (Section 107) and includes a provision on joint commission in furtherance of common intention (Section 34).

3 The modes of liability of the ICT Act

3.1 The modes of liability of the ICT Act and customary international law

The system of individual criminal liability in the ICT Act differs greatly from the provisions in the Statutes of the international criminal tribunals. Contrary to the usual understanding of criminal law, the ICT Act codifies several modes of liability as separate offences because they are listed in Section 3, which defines the jurisdiction of the Tribunal.[1090] This was affirmed in *Azam* in which the Tribunal held that abetment is framed as an independent offence in the ICT Act.[1091]

Inasmuch as the ICT Act criminalises complicity in any of the crimes within the ICT's jurisdiction, the Act exceeds customary international law which recognises complicity only in the context of genocide. Section 4(1) of the ICT Act determines that, in the case of a joint commission of a crime, each person is liable for the crime as if it was committed by them alone. According to the ICT, Section 4(1) implements the concept of JCE.[1092] Yet, the exact wording of the provision does not seem to define a mode of liability but rather to clarify the individual nature of criminal liability.[1093] However, the applicability of JCE in the context of the Liberation War in the first place depends on whether and to what extent the doctrine formed part of customary international law in 1971. The findings of the ECCC Trial Chamber on the emergence of the concept of JCE and the conclusion that it was already in existence during the period 1975–1979[1094] suggest strongly that the concept could be applied to the period of the Liberation War. The Trial Chamber held that the IMT Charter as well as CCL already recognised the liability of persons who did not directly perpetrate a crime but who intentionally participated in the formulation or execution of a common plan or enterprise involving the commission of crimes.[1095] It further invoked several post-World War II cases and concluded that there is no doubt that JCE I and II emerged during the post-World War II period.[1096] In contrast, with regard to JCE III, the Trial

---

1090 *Forstein*, Special Issue No. 4 – Legal Conclusions Kamaruzzaman, p. 5
1091 ICT 1, *The Chief Prosecutor v. Azam*, case no. 06/2011, Charge Framing Order, 13 May 2012, p. 14.
1092 See, for instance, ICT 1, *The Chief Prosecutor v. Chowdhury*, case no. 02/2011, Judgment, 1 October 2013, para. 155; ICT 1, *The Chief Prosecutor v. Nizami*, case no. 03/2011, Judgment, 29 October 2014, para. 108; ICT 1, *The Chief Prosecutor v. Ali*, case no. 01/2013, Judgment, 24 November 2014, para. 166; ICT 2, *The Chief Prosecutor v. Qaiser*, case no. 04/2013, Judgment, 23 December 2014, para. 889.
1093 *Linton*, CLF, 2010, 21(2), p. 191, at 275.
1094 ECCC (PTC), *Prosecutor v. Ieng Thirith et al.*, Decision on the Appeals against the Co-Investigative Judges Order on Joint Criminal Enterprise, 20 May 2010, para. 57.
1095 ECCC (PTC), *Prosecutor v. Ieng Thirith et al.*, Decision on the Appeals against the Co-Investigative Judges Order on Joint Criminal Enterprise, 20 May 2010, para. 58.
1096 ECCC (PTC), *Prosecutor v. Ieng Thirith et al.*, Decision on the Appeals against the Co-Investigative Judges Order on Joint Criminal Enterprise, 20 May 2010, para. 69.

Chamber contended that there is not sufficient evidence that it had crystallised as customary international law in 1975.[1097] For the trials in Bangladesh, this means that the ICT would have to refrain from the application of JCE III to the period of the Liberation War. With regard to JCE I and II, the Tribunal could contemplate the application of Section 34 of the Penal Code (acts done by several persons in furtherance of common intention) if it could be concluded that the provision has the same scope as JCE.

Section 4(2) has been invoked by the ICT to apply the doctrine of command responsibility.[1098] This is, however, debatable and must be examined from two aspects. First, the time of emergence of the principle of command responsibility in international law must be determined in order to establish whether the provision reflects the customary international law of 1971. Second, whether the provision really incorporates the principle of command responsibility must be scrutinised.

With regard to the first question, no conflicts arise because the doctrine of command responsibility of military as well as of civilian leaders emerged as a customary rule only a few years after World War II.[1099] In fact, the ICTY Appeals Chamber held that command responsibility was recognised under customary international law before the adoption of Additional Protocol I to the Geneva Conventions of 1949, which was not constitutive for the doctrine.[1100] This finding rejected the defence's contention that the doctrine applies merely to international armed conflicts because it is mentioned in Additional Protocol I to the Geneva Conventions but not in Additional Protocol II, which refers to internal armed conflicts.[1101] The ICTY Trial Chamber found that command responsibility was already recognised in the context of crimes not committed in armed conflict before the establishment of the ICTY.[1102]

Nevertheless, it is questionable whether Section 4(2) of the ICT Act actually incorporates superior responsibility as recognised under customary international law. The rationale behind command responsibility is to establish liability of superiors for crimes committed by their subordinates based on their duty to punish or prevent. However, the

---

1097 ECCC (PTC), *Prosecutor v. Ieng Thirith et al.*, Decision on the Appeals against the Co-Investigative Judges Order on Joint Criminal Enterprise, 20 May 2010, para. 83.
1098 ICT 2, *The Chief Prosecutor v. Kamaruzzaman*, case no. 03/2012, Judgment, 9 May 2023, paras. 618–619. The Appellate Division has confirmed this finding in SC (AD), *Kamaruzzaman v. The Chief Prosecutor*, Appeal Judgment, 3 November 2014, p. 120.
1099 *Cassese*, International Criminal Law, 3. edn, p. 186.
1100 ICTY (AC), *Prosecutor v. Hadžihasanović et al.*, Decision on Interlocutory Appeal Challenging Jurisdiction in Relation to Command Responsibility, 16 July 2003, para. 29.
1101 ICTY (AC), *Prosecutor v. Hadžihasanović et al.*, Decision on Interlocutory Appeal Challenging Jurisdiction in Relation to Command Responsibility, 16 July 2003, para. 28.
1102 ICTY (TC), *Prosecutor v. Hadžihasanović et al.*, Decision on Joint Challenge to Jurisdiction, 12 November 2002, para. 93.

wording of Section 4(2) of the ICT Act suggests strongly that it does not make reference to this doctrine.[1103] The provision establishes criminal responsibility of superior officers or commanders who order, permit, acquiesce or participate in the commission of a crime under Section 3(2) or are connected with any plans and activities involving the commission of such crime. It further establishes liability of commanders and superior officers who fail or omit to discharge their duty to maintain discipline, or to control or supervise the actions of the persons under their command or their subordinates, whereby such persons or subordinates or any of them commit any such crimes, or who fail to take necessary measures to prevent the commission of such crimes. This Section establishes a mode of criminal liability that is entirely alien to international criminal law.[1104] The first part of the provision refers to direct individual responsibility for ordering or even participation, which does not fall under command responsibility, whereas the second part relies on a failure or omission to discharge the duty to maintain discipline.[1105] Although this formulation shows similarities with the Yamashita Standard, which was applied in the trial of the Japanese general Yamashita who was charged with having failed to discharge his duty to control the operations of his subordinates, the concept of the ICT Act greatly exceeds even this controversial standard. Section 4(2) also fails to determine a mental element. While the application of superior responsibility does not lead to problems with the principle of legality, Section 4(2), if applied in this context, would have to be construed in accordance with customary international law, especially with regard to the mental element.

The ICT Act establishes omission liability in Section 3(2)(h) and criminalises the failure to prevent the commission of any of the crimes under Section 3(2). This omission liability goes far beyond internationally recognised standards because, under customary international law, omission liability arises only when there is a failure to comply with a legal duty to act.[1106] While several modes of liability can be committed through omission, the ICT Act seems to establish omission as a separate mode of liability but does not expressly introduce the requirement of a legal duty to act. However, this pertains mainly to the interpretation rather than to the compliance of the Act with customary international law. Beyond that, the ICT Act also recognises omission liability for commanders and superior officers in Section 4(2) in the context of superior responsibility.

1103 *Linton*, CLF, 2010, 21(2), p. 191, at 276.
1104 *Linton*, CLF, 2010, 21(2), p. 191, at 276.
1105 *Linton*, CLF, 2010, 21(2), p. 191, at 276–278.
1106 *Cassese*, International Criminal Law, 3. edn, p. 181.

Part IV: Compliance of the ICT Act, the Rules of Procedure and the ICT's jurisprudence

3.2 The modes of liability in the jurisprudence of the ICT

The application of the modes of liability under the ICT Act, in practice, is characterised by a rather unsystematic approach. The Tribunal invokes mainly international jurisprudence for the definition of the modes of liability. Nevertheless, the notions the Tribunal applies to the different forms of participation are not always in line with international practice and, at several points, it appears that the Tribunal rather relies on concepts of domestic law.

Section 16(1) of the ICT Act determines the elements that must be contained in the charges: the name and particulars of the accused person, the crime with which the accused is charged, and such particulars of the alleged crime as are reasonably sufficient to give the accused person notice of the matter with which he is charged. In *Kamaruzzaman*, the prosecution argued that Section 16(1) of the ICT Act does not require the determination of the mode of liability in the charges.[1107] This argument was advanced in order to hold the accused liable for superior responsibility under Section 4(2), which was not mentioned in the charges. The Tribunal adopted this view, arguing that the mode of liability can be determined only during the trial on the basis of evidence.[1108] This reasoning is clearly not persuasive because the mode of liability is a basic requirement to hold somebody liable and thus must be investigated right from the beginning. The mode of liability links the accused to the crime and is, therefore, essential 'to give the accused person notice of the matter with which he is charged', as required under Section 16(1). However, the finding of the Tribunal explains the imprecision of several charge framing orders when it comes to the modes of liability. In most indictments and judgments, the mode of liability is not specified at all. The accused are rather indicted for or found guilty of 'participating, abetting, facilitating and substantially contributing' to the commission of the respective offences.[1109] This formulation does not even reveal whether the accused acted as an accessory or as the main perpetrator.

1107 ICT 2, *The Chief Prosecutor v. Kamaruzzaman*, case no. 03/2012, Judgment, 9 May 2013, para. 496.
1108 ICT 2, *The Chief Prosecutor v. Kamaruzzaman*, case no. 03/2012, Judgment, 9 May 2013, para. 498.
1109 ICT 2, *The Chief Prosecutor v. Azad*, case no. 05/2012, Judgment, 21 January 2013, para. 186; ICT 1, *The Chief Prosecutor v. Sobhan*, case no. 06/2013, Charge Framing Order, 31 December 2013, pp. 11–19; ICT 2, *The Chief Prosecutor v. Qaiser*, case no. 04/2014, Charge Framing Order, 2 February 2014, pp. 11–18; ICT 1, *The Chief Prosecutor v. Jabbar Engineer*, case no. 01/2014, Charge Framing Order, 14 August 2014, p. 14. In ICT 2, *The Chief Prosecutor v. Ali*, case no. 03/2013, Charge Framing Order, 5 September 2013, pp. 9–18. All the charges refer to 'abetting and facilitating' the respective offences but the Tribunal found that the accused acted as a superior and participated in a JCE, see ICT, *The Chief Prosecutor v. Ali*, case no. 03/2013, Judgment, 2 November 2014, paras. 620–621.

3 The modes of liability of the ICT Act

Beyond that, the use of notions in the judgments is inconsistent and does not reflect the wording of the ICT Act. Many of the definitions provided overlap and are applied simultaneously, which leads to contradictory results. In particular, this concerns the notions of 'participation', 'complicity' and 'facilitating' which have been used as umbrella terms for several forms of accessory liability, as well as participation in a JCE. For instance, Mujahid was indicted for 'participating, abetting and facilitating the commission of [the] offence of murder as [a] crime against humanity'.[1110] In its deliberations, the Tribunal defined participation as 'approval or instigation or encouragement or aiding or abetment',[1111] and for the further interpretation of 'participation', it cited international jurisprudence that deals with JCE[1112]. The same definition was invoked in *Qaiser* but, ultimately, it was held that the act of the accused amounted to participation, abetment and complicity.[1113] In the adjudication of charge 12, the Tribunal defined abetment as 'approval, encouragement, assistance or support that contributes substantially to the accomplishment of the actual crime'.[1114] In *Nizami*, the accused was found guilty of 'participation in abetting, facilitating and complicity to the actual commission'.[1115] From this practice, it can be concluded that the term 'participation' as employed by the Tribunal encompasses any mode of liability. Nevertheless, the definition of the term 'participation' by the Tribunal contravenes the wording of the ICT Act because participation is only mentioned in Section 4(2) in the context of superiors.

Beyond that, the term 'facilitating' is frequently employed in the sense of aiding. Mujahid was charged with participating in and facilitating the commission of murder as a crime against humanity.[1116] In its findings, the Tribunal scrutinised abetment by means of the criteria it had established in earlier cases.[1117]

1110 See charge 5 in ICT 2, *The Chief Prosecutor v. Mujahid*, case no. 04/2012, Charge Framing Order, 21 June 2012, p. 12.
1111 ICT 2, *The Chief Prosecutor v. Mujahid*, case no. 04/2012, Judgment, 17 July 2013, para. 361. The same definition is invoked in ICT 2, *The Chief Prosecutor v. Qaiser*, case no. 04/2013, Judgment, 23 December 2014, para. 396.
1112 ICT 2, *The Chief Prosecutor v. Mujahid*, case no. 04/2012, Judgment, 17 July 2013, para. 596.
1113 ICT 2, *The Chief Prosecutor v. Qaiser*, case no. 04/2013, Judgment, 23 December 2014, paras. 395, 396.
1114 ICT 2, *The Chief Prosecutor v. Qaiser*, case no. 04/2013, Judgment, 23 December 2014, para. 718.
1115 ICT 1, *The Chief Prosecutor v. Nizami*, case no. 03/2011, Judgment, 29 October 2014, para. 201.
1116 See charge 7 in ICT 2, *The Chief Prosecutor v. Mujahid*, case no. 04/2012, Charge Framing Order, 21 June 2012, p. 13.
1117 ICT 2, *The Chief Prosecutor v. Mujahid*, case no. 04/2012, Judgment, 17 July 2013, para. 572.

Overall, it can be stated that the inaccuracies with regard to the terms related to the modes of liability make it difficult to determine a general practice with regard to the standards applied by the Tribunal.

3.2.1 Abetment

While the ICT Act merely contains abetment as a mode of liability, the Tribunal considers several other modes of liability covered by this term even though their derivation is unclear. The Penal Code defines abetment in Section 107:

> *Section 107 of the Penal Code: Abetment of a thing*
> A person abets the doing of a thing, who –
> First – Instigates any person to do that thing; or,
> Secondly – Engages with one or more other person or persons in any conspiracy for the doing of that thing, if an act or illegal omission takes place in pursuance of that conspiracy, and in order to the doing of that thing; or,
> Thirdly – Intentionally aids, by any act or illegal omission, the doing of that thing.
> Explanation 1 – A person who, by wilful misrepresentation, or by wilful concealment of a material fact which he is bound to disclose, voluntarily causes or procures, or attempts to cause or procure, a thing to be done, is said to instigate the doing of that thing.
> Explanation 2 – Whoever, either prior to or at the time of the commission of an act, does anything in order to facilitate the commission of that act, and thereby facilitates the commission thereof, is said to aid the doing of that act.

The definition of abetment in the Penal Code is relatively broad and encompasses instigation and conspiracy as well as aiding. It is a potential reason for which the Tribunal, as a matter of course, considers abetment an umbrella term that comprises several modes of liability, such as instigation and ordering, which, in the Statutes of the international criminal tribunals, are listed separately. In *Molla*, Judge Choudhury of the Appellate Division, in his separate opinion, emphasised that the definition of abetment in Section 109 of the Penal Code shall be invoked.[1118] Nevertheless, no reference to the domestic provision has been made in the judgments of the ICT.

In the jurisprudence of international criminal law, it is established that aiding and abetting require practical assistance, encouragement or moral support that has a substantial effect on the commission of the crime by the physical perpetrator.[1119] With regard to the mental elements, the aider and abettor must act intentionally with knowledge or awareness that his act will lend assistance, encouragement or moral support to

---

1118 SC (AD), *Molla v. The Chief Prosecutor*, Separate Opinion of Justice Choudhury, Appeal Judgment, 17 September 2013, p. 748.
1119 ICTY (TC), *Prosecutor v. Simić et al.*, Judgment, 28 November 2006, para. 85; ICTY (AC), *Prosecutor v. Blaškić*, Appeal Judgment, 29 July 2004, para. 46.

3 The modes of liability of the ICT Act

the physical perpetrator.[1120] The aider and abettor must further be aware of the essential elements of the committed crime.[1121] With regard to specific intent crimes, the aider and abettor must merely know the intent of the main perpetrators but does not necessarily have to share it.[1122]

In consonance with international jurisprudence, the Tribunal found that the actus reus of abetting encompasses assistance, encouragement or moral support that has a substantial effect on the commission of the crimes.[1123] In *Qaiser*, the Tribunal relied on the same definition but also found that abetting encompasses inciting, soliciting, inducing, influencing and encouraging the main perpetrator.[1124] In the case of *Azad*, aiding was defined as providing assistance or help to another person in the commission of a crime.[1125] The Tribunal further found that aiding and abetting do not require the participation in all aspects of the criminal act and that it may occur before, during or after the actual commission of the crime.[1126]

According to the Tribunal, mere presence at the crime scene can be sufficient contribution as an aider or abettor[1127] but the presence needs to have a direct and substantial effect[1128]. Based on this, the Tribunal rejected the charges in *Azad* because it found that the mere fact that the accused had a close association with the Pakistani army and visited the army camp regularly did not ipso facto prove substantial encouragement to torture and confinement.[1129]

1120 ICTY (AC), *Prosecutor v. Blaškić*, Appeal Judgment, 29 July 2004, para. 49.
1121 ICTY (AC), *Prosecutor v. Simić et al.*, Appeal Judgment, 28 November 2006, para. 86.
1122 ICTY (AC), *Prosecutor v. Krnojelac*, Appeal Judgment, 17 September 2003, para. 52.
1123 See, for instance, ICT 2, *The Chief Prosecutor v. Molla*, case no. 02/2012, Judgment, 5 February 2013, para. 358; ICT 2, *The Chief Prosecutor v. Qaiser*, case no. 04/2013, Judgment, 23 December 2014, para. 221.
1124 ICT 2, *The Chief Prosecutor v. Qaiser*, case no. 04/2013, Judgment, 23 December 2014, para. 154.
1125 ICT 2, *The Chief Prosecutor v. Azad*, case no. 05/2012, Judgment, 21 January 2013, para. 166.
1126 ICT 2, *The Chief Prosecutor v. Molla*, case no. 02/2012, Judgment, 5 February 2013, para. 211; ICT 2, *The Chief Prosecutor v. Ali*, case no. 03/2013, Judgment, 2 November 2014, para. 126.
1127 ICT 2, *The Chief Prosecutor v. Molla*, case no. 02/2012, Judgment, 5 February 2013, para. 330; ICT 1, *The Chief Prosecutor v. Hossain*, case no. 01/2013, Judgment, 24 November 2014, para. 76.
1128 ICT 2, *The Chief Prosecutor v. Molla*, case no. 02/2012, Judgment, 5 February 2013, para. 362.
1129 ICT 2, *The Chief Prosecutor v. Azad*, case no. 05/2012, Judgment, 21 January 2013, paras. 210, 211.

Part IV: Compliance of the ICT Act, the Rules of Procedure and the ICT's jurisprudence

In several cases, the Tribunal relied on the ICTY Trial Chamber decision in *Tadić*[1130] to determine that actual physical presence during the commission of the crime is not required. However, the quoted passage does not exactly reproduce the Trial Chamber's findings[1131] because it omits a sentence of the finding which confirms that, in any case, a direct and substantial effect of the acts is required to establish liability for aiding and abetting.[1132]

With regard to the mens rea for aiding and abetting, the Tribunal relied on SCSL jurisprudence and determined that the accused needs to know that his acts will assist the commission of the crime or that he must be aware of the substantial likelihood that his acts will assist the commission of the crime[1133] and that the accused must also be aware of the specific intent if it forms part of the offence.[1134] This approach was affirmed in *Khokon*.[1135]

Aiding and abetting through omission were discussed by the Tribunal in *Alim*. The Tribunal found that the accused abetted and instigated the crime against humanity of murder through omission[1136] by arguing that, based on his position of authority, he incurred liability for his 'inaction' under Section 4(2) because, despite 'knowing the foreseeable consequence', he refused to prevent the crime.[1137] It further clarified that abetment or instigation can both be committed through omission and found that, in this case, the accused had provided moral support and encouragement through omission.[1138] The accused had rejected a request from family members of victims to release them from detention at an army camp and the victims were later killed.[1139] The

---

1130 ICTY (TC), *Prosecutor v. Tadić*, Judgment, 7 May 1997, para. 691.
1131 ICT 2, *The Chief Prosecutor v. Mujahid*, case no. 04/2012, Judgment, 17 July 2013, para. 382; ICT 2, *The Chief Prosecutor v. Ali*, case no. 03/2013, Judgment, 2 November 2014, para. 127.
1132 ICTY (TC), *Prosecutor v. Tadić*, Judgment, 7 May 1997, para. 691.
1133 ICT 2, *The Chief Prosecutor v. Molla*, case no. 02/2012, Judgment, 5 February 2013, para. 356. See also ICT 1, *The Chief Prosecutor v. Islam*, case no. 05/2013, Judgment, 30 December 2014, para. 110.
1134 ICT 2, *The Chief Prosecutor v. Molla*, case no. 02/2012, Judgment, 5 February 2013, para. 356.
1135 ICT 1, *The Chief Prosecutor v. Khokon*, case no. 01/2013, Judgment, 24 November 2014, para. 76.
1136 ICT 2, *The Chief Prosecutor v. Alim*, case no. 01/2012, Judgment, 9 October 2013, para. 373.
1137 ICT 2, *The Chief Prosecutor v. Alim*, case no. 01/2012, Judgment, 9 October 2013, para. 370.
1138 ICT 2, *The Chief Prosecutor v. Alim*, case no. 01/2012, Judgment, 9 October 2013, para. 373.
1139 ICT 2, *The Chief Prosecutor v. Alim*, case no. 01/2012, Judgment, 9 October 2013, para. 371.

3 The modes of liability of the ICT Act

Tribunal concluded that the refusal to release them was an inaction that constituted a 'signal' or 'approval' of the principals[1140] because the accused had a position of authority as he was part of the 'local elite and a leader of [the] Convention Muslim League having [the] profile of a legal practitioner too in Joypurhat'.[1141] From the accused's position as an influential Peace Committee leader, the Tribunal further concluded that Razakars were bound to act on his decision with regard to the release of the victims.[1142] It is unclear how the Tribunal drew a line between superior responsibility and abetment or instigation through omission in this case. Ultimately, the accused was held liable only under Section 4(1) for abetting through omission.[1143] Nevertheless, the Tribunal concluded, in general, at the end of the judgment for all charges that the accused also incurred liability as a superior.[1144] The criteria applied in this case are a combination of abetment and instigation.

Jurisprudence in international criminal law has established that an accused is liable for instigation if he prompts another person to commit a crime and to act with intent or awareness of substantial likelihood that the crime will be committed or if he prompts an action or omission in the awareness of the substantial likelihood that a crime will be committed.[1145] Instigation requires more than aiding and abetting for which facilitating the commission of the crime can suffice.[1146] Contrary to the discussion of the Tribunal, instigation does not require a superior position.

In other cases, the Tribunal also found instigation to be a mode of liability encompassed by aiding and abetting but did not provide definitions to circumscribe both terms.[1147] The assumption that instigation is a form of aiding and abetting can certainly be deduced from the definition in the Penal Code although this was not clarified by the Tribunal.

1140 ICT 2, *The Chief Prosecutor v. Alim*, case no. 01/2012, Judgment, 9 October 2013, para. 371.
1141 ICT 2, *The Chief Prosecutor v. Alim*, case no. 01/2012, Judgment, 9 October 2013, para. 368.
1142 ICT 2, *The Chief Prosecutor v. Alim*, case no. 01/2012, Judgment, 9 October 2013, para. 369.
1143 ICT 2, *The Chief Prosecutor v. Alim*, case no. 01/2012, Judgment, 9 October 2013, para. 373.
1144 ICT 2, *The Chief Prosecutor v. Alim*, case no. 01/2012, Judgment, 9 October 2013, para. 624.
1145 ICTY (AC), *Prosecutor v. Kordić et al.*, Appeal Judgment, 17 December 2014, paras. 27, 29, 30.
1146 ICTY (TC), *The Chief Prosecutor v. Orić*, Judgment, 30 June 2006, para. 271.
1147 ICT 2, *The Chief Prosecutor v. Alim*, case no. 01/2012, Judgment, 9 October 2012, paras. 556, 561.

In *Mujahid*, the Tribunal found that providing advice was a form of abetment and instigation.[1148] In this case, the accused had advised army personnel to kill detainees.[1149] After finding that the accused instigated, the Tribunal observed that he also participated in a JCE but merely stated that, by his conduct, the accused was part of a common plan.[1150] The elements of instigation were not further defined. The Appellate Division defined instigation as 'to goad urge forward, provoke, incite or encourage to do an act' and further stated that 'a person is said to instigate another when he actively suggests or stimulates him to the act by any means, or language, direct or indirect whether it takes the form of express solicitation or of hints, insinuation or encouragement'.[1151] This approach also fails to clarify to what extent instigation differs from aiding and abetting and it contravenes the Tribunal's definition of abetting, which comprises encouragement. Beyond that, the definition is very broad as it encompasses also mere suggesting.

In *Alim*, the Tribunal defined instigation in line with international jurisprudence as an 'act of prompting another person to commit an offence'[1152] and clarified that there is no requirement to prove that the crime would not have been committed without the accused[1153]. It argued that the act of inciting can consist of words, threats or pressure as well as persuasion,[1154] whereas persuasion requires a suggestion, proposal or request.[1155] Although the accused was simultaneously held liable for incitement and aiding, and for participating in a JCE,[1156] the mental element for incitement was not clearly defined. In fact, the Tribunal drew the conclusion that the accused was a 'consenting party' to the criminal enterprise.[1157] This mix-up of JCE and aiding and abet-

---

1148 ICT 2, *The Chief Prosecutor v. Mujahid*, case no. 04/2012, Judgment, 17 July 2013, para. 364.
1149 ICT 2, *The Chief Prosecutor v. Mujahid*, case no. 04/2012, Judgment, 17 July 2013, para. 382.
1150 ICT 2, *The Chief Prosecutor v. Mujahid*, case no. 04/2012, Judgment, 17 July 2013, para. 384.
1151 SC (AD), *Mujahid v. The Chief Prosecutor*, Appeal Judgment, 16 June 2013, p. 156.
1152 ICT 2, *The Chief Prosecutor v. Alim*, case no. 01/2012, Judgment, 9 October 2012, para. 556.
1153 ICT 2, *The Chief Prosecutor v. Alim*, case no. 01/2012, Judgment, 9 October 2012, para. 556.
1154 ICT 2, *The Chief Prosecutor v. Alim*, case no. 01/2012, Judgment, 9 October 2012, para. 257.
1155 ICT 2, *The Chief Prosecutor v. Alim*, case no. 01/2012, Judgment, 9 October 2012, para. 257.
1156 ICT 2, *The Chief Prosecutor v. Alim*, case no. 01/2012, Judgment, 9 October 2012, paras. 263, 269, 270.
1157 ICT 2, *The Chief Prosecutor v. Alim*, case no. 01/2012, Judgment, 9 October 2012, para. 270.

3 The modes of liability of the ICT Act

ting is a frequent practice of the Tribunal[1158] and is problematic given that the requirements for a conduct to amount to participation in a JCE are broader than those for aiding and abetting and that there are different mental prerequisites as well.

The Tribunal also dealt with ordering as a form of aiding and abetting in several judgments but did not further explain how it arrived at the conclusion that this mode of liability falls under aiding and abetting. Section 107 of the Penal Code does not refer to ordering, whereas the ICT Act lists ordering only in Section 4(2) if committed by a commander or superior officer. In international jurisprudence, ordering means that a person of authority instructs another person to commit a crime.[1159] The person has to act with intent or awareness of the substantial likelihood that a crime will be committed in the execution of the order.[1160] A formal superior-subordinate relationship is not required.[1161] However, other than under the ICT Act, ordering is listed as a separate mode of liability in the Statutes of the international criminal tribunals.

In *Mujahid*, the Tribunal stated that an order can be given verbally, in writing or through signs.[1162] It further argued that there are two forms of orders: (1) 'formal orders' in the form of provisions, directives and commands; and (2) 'orders based on real effectiveness', comprising signals, gestures, concrete actions or various similar expressions.[1163] However, the notion of ordering employed by the Tribunal in this case is contradictory. It held that ordering means that a person in a position of authority uses this position 'to convince or instigate or encourage' another person to commit an offence.[1164] This, again, confuses several different modes of liability because encouraging is encompassed by aiding and abetting and does not require authority. The Tribunal acknowledged that a mere position of authority does not amount to ordering as aiding and abetting but that the acts must have a substantial effect.[1165] With regard to the accused, his meeting with army officials was an indication of his position of

---

1158 See, for instance, ICT 1, *The Chief Prosecutor v. Islam*, case no. 05/2013, Judgment, 30 December 2014, para. 210; ICT 2, *The Chief Prosecutor v. Qaiser*, case no. 04/2013, Judgment, 23 December 2014, para. 158.
1159 ICTY (AC), *Prosecutor v. Kordić et al.*, Appeal Judgment, 17 December 2014, para. 28.
1160 ICTY (AC), *Prosecutor v. Kordić et al.*, Appeal Judgment, 17 December 2014, para. 30.
1161 ICTY (AC), *Prosecutor v. Kordić et al.*, Appeal Judgment, 17 December 2014, para. 28.
1162 ICT 2, *The Chief Prosecutor v. Mujahid*, case no. 04/2012, Judgment, 17 July 2013, para. 307.
1163 ICT 2, *The Chief Prosecutor v. Mujahid*, case no. 04/2012, Judgment, 17 July 2013, para. 307.
1164 ICT 2, *The Chief Prosecutor v. Mujahid*, case no. 04/2012, Judgment, 17 July 2013, para. 310.
1165 ICT 2, *The Chief Prosecutor v. Mujahid*, case no. 04/2012, Judgment, 17 July 2013, para. 309.

authority, 'even over the occupation army',[1166] but did not establish criteria to define a position of authority. The accused was at the army camp when a victim was taken there and gave a signal to the Razakars, who subsequently tortured the victim and kept him confined.[1167] The mens rea was discussed under the requirements of the actus reus, and the Tribunal held that the aider must be aware of the consequence of his act.[1168] This standard is clearly imprecise.

In *Jabbar Engineer*, the Tribunal relied on ICTR jurisprudence and found that no formal superior-subordinate relationship is required but that the person who orders must have de facto or de jure authority to order the commission of a crime.[1169] It acknowledged that the order does not need to be given directly to the person who commits the crime and that no specific form needs to be met by the order.[1170] The Tribunal invoked ICTR jurisprudence[1171] on the requirement of a direct and substantial effect of the order[1172] but did not further apply this prerequisite to the specific case. It concluded that the accused, as a Razakar commander, had de jure as well as de facto authority,[1173] whereas the mental element was entirely omitted.

3.2.2 Complicity

Section 3(2)(g) of the ICT Act establishes liability for complicity in the commission of any crime under the ICT's material jurisdiction.

The definition of complicity has proven challenging also for international criminal tribunals because complicity is listed only in the international definition of genocide, whereas aiding and abetting are modes of liability applicable to all offences. The jurisprudence has been divided on the interpretation of these notions. The ICTR found that there are two criteria that distinguish complicity in genocide from aiding and abetting genocide. In *Akayesu*, the Trial Chamber held that complicity requires a pos-

---

1166 ICT 2, *The Chief Prosecutor v. Mujahid*, case no. 04/2012, Judgment, 17 July 2013, para. 307.
1167 ICT 2, *The Chief Prosecutor v. Mujahid*, case no. 04/2012, Judgment, 17 July 2013, para. 297.
1168 ICT 2, *The Chief Prosecutor v. Mujahid*, case no. 04/2012, Judgment, 17 July 2013, para. 311.
1169 ICT 1, *The Chief Prosecutor v. Jabbar Engineer*, case no. 01/2014, Judgment, 24 February 2015, para. 91.
1170 ICT 1, *The Chief Prosecutor v. Jabbar Engineer*, case no. 01/2014, Judgment, 24 February 2015, para. 94.
1171 ICTR (AC), *Prosecutor v. Kamubanda*, Appeal Judgment, 19 September 2005, para. 75.
1172 ICT 1, *The Chief Prosecutor v. Jabbar Engineer*, case no. 01/2014, Judgment, 24 February 2015, para. 90.
1173 ICT 1, *The Chief Prosecutor v. Jabbar Engineer*, case no. 01/2014, Judgment, 24 February 2015, para. 99.

3 The modes of liability of the ICT Act

itive act, whereas aiding and abetting 'may consist in failing to act or refraining from action'.[1174] With regard to the mental element, the Chamber found that a person could only incur liability as an aider and abettor if he or she acts with genocidal intent.[1175] For complicity, on the other hand, the knowledge that the act lends assistance to the main perpetrator in the commission of genocide suffices.[1176] In contrast, the ICTY Appeals Chamber did not follow this approach but held that there is no difference between both terms apart from the fact that complicity encompasses conduct broader than aiding and abetting.[1177]

The same problem arises in the context of the ICT Act which does not establish complicity merely in relation to genocide but considers it a mode of liability for all crimes under the ICT's jurisdiction; the same applies to abetment. In contrast to the international debate, the differentiation under the ICT Act thus becomes relevant not only in the context of genocide. In practice, the Tribunal has applied complicity in relation to crimes against humanity and genocide. The Penal Code does not define complicity so no domestic provision can be consulted.

In *Azam*, the accused was charged with complicity but the charge framing order does not specify in which offences under the ICT's jurisdiction.[1178] In the adjudication of the charges, the Tribunal relied on a definition of complicity in an American free legal online dictionary, USLEGAL.[1179] According to this definition, complicity means:

> Complicity in criminal law refers to when someone is legally accountable, or liable for a criminal offense, based upon the behaviour of another. Criminal complicity may arise in the following situations:
> With the intent to promote or assist the commission of the offense:
> 1. a person procures, induces or causes such other person to commit the offense; or
> 2. a person aids or abets such other person in committing the offence; or
> 3. having a legal duty to prevent the commission of the offence, a person fails to make an effort he is legally required to make.[1180]

While the relevance of this source in the context of the ICT is certainly dubious, this definition employs complicity as an umbrella term that includes also aiding and abetting. In line with the above outlined jurisprudence, the Tribunal clarified that complic-

---

1174 ITCR (TC), *Prosecutor v. Akayesu*, Trial Judgment, 2 September 1998, para. 548.
1175 ITCR (TC), *Prosecutor v. Akayesu*, Trial Judgment, 2 September 1998, para. 485.
1176 ITCR (TC), *Prosecutor v. Akayesu*, Trial Judgment, 2 September 1998, para. 538.
1177 ICTY (AC), *Prosecutor v. Krstić*, Appeal Judgment, 19 April 2004, para. 139.
1178 ICT 1, *The Chief Prosecutor v. Azam*, case no. 06/2011, Charge Framing Order, 13 May 2012, p. 47.
1179 http://uslegal.com, accessed 17 December 2017.
1180 http://definitions.uslegal.com/c/complicity/, accessed 17 December 2017.

ity by aiding and abetting requires a positive action and that it cannot be committed by a failure to act or an omission.[1181]

With regard to complicity in genocide, the Tribunal held that it could be committed by the following means: '(1) complicity by procuring means, such as weapons, instruments or any other means, used to commit genocide, with the accomplice knowing that such means would be used for such a purpose; (2) complicity by knowingly aiding or abetting a perpetrator of a genocide in the planning or enabling acts thereof; and (3) complicity by instigation, for which a person is liable who, though not directly participating in the crime of genocide, gave instructions to commit genocide, through gifts, promises, threats abuse of authority or power, machinations or culpable artifice, or who directly incited to commit genocide'.[1182]

The Tribunal did not further clarify that these forms of complicity were based on findings of the ICTR in *Akayesu* in which the Trial Chamber declared the Rwandan domestic definition of complicity applicable and defined these forms of complicity in the light of Article 91 of the Rwandan Penal Code[1183].

It appears that the Tribunal considered different standards for complicity in crimes against humanity and complicity in genocide. Nevertheless, since in the adjudication of the charges the Tribunal omitted to specify the offence, it remains unclear which standard was ultimately applied to the case. The Tribunal appears to have based its findings on the accused's complicity in all crimes committed during the Liberation War. It argued that the accused incurred liability for complicity because he urged the government to supply modern weapons to Razakars and praised the Pakistani army and Razakars despite knowing about the crimes that were committed by them.[1184] Again, the Tribunal relied on the 'fact of common knowledge' that international crimes were committed during the Liberation War and, therefore, failed to establish a link between the accused's acts and a specific crime.

The Tribunal concluded that the accused 'contributed to the commission of crimes against humanity and genocide by aiding, abetting and incitement' and found him guilty 'for his complicity with [sic] the commission of those offences as specified in Section 3(2)(h) of the Act'.[1185] The finding suggests that complicity is employed as an umbrella term for aiding, abetting and incitement.

The case of *Azam* is also problematic with regard to attribution. The Tribunal found that the participation of the accused in a meeting with the Chief Martial Law

---

1181 ICT 1, *The Chief Prosecutor v. Azam*, case no. 06/2011, Judgment, 15 July 2013, para. 217.
1182 ICT 1, *The Chief Prosecutor v. Azam*, case no. 06/2011, Judgment, 15 July 2013, para. 218.
1183 ICTR (TC), *Prosecutor v. Akayesu*, Judgment, 2 September 1998, para. 537.
1184 ICT 1, *The Chief Prosecutor v. Azam*, case no. 06/2011, Judgment, 15 July 2013, paras. 285, 286.
1185 ICT 1, *The Chief Prosecutor v. Azam*, case no. 06/2011, Judgment, 15 July 2013, para. 290.

3 The modes of liability of the ICT Act

Administrator of Pakistan, in which he assured his full cooperation with the aim of returning the country to normality, indicates his complicity in 'all above-mentioned crimes committed in Bangladesh'[1186] and thereby makes reference to all crimes committed in Bangladesh during the Liberation War.

Complicity was also discussed in *Kamaruzzaman* in which the Tribunal took an entirely different approach. The accused was indicted for complicity in the crime against humanity of murder.[1187] In the adjudication of the charges, the Tribunal cited jurisprudence on aiding and abetting as well as on participation in a JCE.[1188] Thus, it appears that, in this case, the ICT interpreted complicity as an umbrella term for aiding and abetting as well as JCE[1189] although, at the same time, it clarified that complicity encompasses 'conduct broader than aiding and abetting'[1190]. Nevertheless, it failed to differentiate both modes of liability in relation to the case. The accused led a group of Al-Badr in abducting a victim who was then taken to an army camp where he was tortured and killed.[1191] The Tribunal argued that, in leading the group during the abduction, the accused provided assistance or encouragement that amounted to complicity[1192] and concluded that he directly and substantially assisted the perpetrators.[1193]

Other judgments indicate that the Tribunal does not differentiate at all between complicity and abetment. In *Ali*, the Tribunal defined abetment as 'encouragement, providing moral support or assistance'[1194] but found the accused liable under Section 3(2)(g) and 3(2)(h) without clarification of whether this amounted to complicity or abetment[1195].

1186 ICT 1, *The Chief Prosecutor v. Azam*, case no. 06/2011, Judgment, 15 July 2013, para. 225.
1187 Charges 1, 2, 3, 4, 5, 7 in ICT 2, *The Chief Prosecutor v. Kamaruzzaman*, case no. 03/2012, Charge Framing Order, 4 June 2012, pp. 13–17.
1188 ICT 2, *The Chief Prosecutor v. Kamaruzzaman*, case no. 03/2012, Judgment, 9 May 2013, paras. 235, 240, 243.
1189 *Forstein*, Special Issue No. 4 – Legal Conclusions Kamaruzzaman, p. 14.
1190 ICT 2, *The Chief Prosecutor v. Kamaruzzaman*, case no. 03/2012, Judgment, 9 May 2013, para. 609.
1191 ICT 2, *The Chief Prosecutor v. Kamaruzzaman*, case no. 03/2012, Judgment, 9 May 2013, para. 244.
1192 ICT 2, *The Chief Prosecutor v. Kamaruzzaman*, case no. 03/2012, Judgment, 9 May 2013, para. 244.
1193 ICT 2, *The Chief Prosecutor v. Kamaruzzaman*, case no. 03/2012, Judgment, 9 May 2013, para. 245.
1194 ICT 2, *The Chief Prosecutor v. Ali*, case no. 03/2013, Judgment, 2 November 2013, para. 212.
1195 ICT 2, *The Chief Prosecutor v. Ali*, case no. 03/2013, Judgment, 2 November 2013, para. 217. Likewise, in *Hossain*, the Tribunal discussed the requirements of aiding and abetting and the term of complicity without further explanation, see ICT 1, *The Chief Prosecutor v. Hossain*, case no. 01/2013, Judgment, 24 November 2014, para. 76.

Part IV: Compliance of the ICT Act, the Rules of Procedure and the ICT's jurisprudence

The Tribunal's practice of combining jurisprudence on different legal concepts also leads to contradictory results with regard to the mental prerequisites. Concerning the mens rea, the Tribunal held that the accused acted with intent to accomplish the commission of the crime of murder.[1196] At the same time, it found that it was immaterial whether the accused intended to facilitate or contribute to the actual commission of the principal offence of murder.[1197] For this finding, the Tribunal relied on ICTY jurisprudence but ignored the fact that the respective judgment deals with a case of JCE. The Tribunal also found that the 'intent requirement may be well deduced from the mode of participation'[1198] but ultimately failed to establish a standard for the mens rea.[1199]

In *Azam*, the Tribunal held that the accomplice must act knowingly, that is, he must know that he assists the principal to commit the offence at the moment he is acting.[1200] Although this is in line with the jurisprudence of international criminal law, this standard was not applied to the case because the crimes were not specified. As a consequence, the Tribunal also failed to outline the requirements of the mens rea with regard to the specific intent of genocide. Ultimately, the Tribunal merely held that the accused had knowledge of the crimes committed against unarmed civilians in Bangladesh.[1201]

An entirely different standard for complicity was applied in *Molla*. The Tribunal explicitly declared that a substantial contribution is not required to establish liability and defined complicity as a liability based on 'culpable association' with the principle offenders.[1202] The Tribunal found the accused liable based on his association with the perpetrators, despite the fact that there was no proof that he was involved in the murder or even knew about it. The Tribunal stated: 'It is to be noted that instead of focusing on the substantial contribution of an accused's criminal conduct to the perpetration of a crime, focus should also be put on the accused's culpable association with the perpetrators, as a manifestation of willingness to be associated with a crime and his support to the principal perpetrator of the crime.'[1203] According to the charges, the

---

1196 ICT 2, *The Chief Prosecutor v. Kamaruzzaman*, case no. 03/2012, Judgment, 9 May 2013, para. 245.
1197 ICT 2, *The Chief Prosecutor v. Kamaruzzaman*, case no. 03/2012, Judgment, 9 May 2013, para. 246.
1198 ICT 2, *The Chief Prosecutor v. Kamaruzzaman*, case no. 03/2012, Judgment, 9 May 2013, para. 235.
1199 ICT 2, *The Chief Prosecutor v. Kamaruzzaman*, case no. 03/2012, Judgment, 9 May 2013, para. 235.
1200 ICT 1, *The Chief Prosecutor v. Azam*, case no. 06/2011, Judgment, 15 July 2013, para. 219.
1201 ICT 1, *The Chief Prosecutor v. Azam*, case no. 06/2011, Judgment, 15 July 2013, para. 284.
1202 ICT 2, *The Chief Prosecutor v. Molla*, case no. 02/2012, Judgment, 5 February 2013, para. 210.
1203 ICT 2, *The Chief Prosecutor v. Molla*, case no. 02/2012, Judgment, 5 February 2013, para. 196.

accused gave the order to his accomplices to kill the victim[1204] but this was not proven during trial[1205]. This finding establishes criminal liability based on mere membership, although this is not criminalised under the ICT Act.

3.2.3 Joint criminal enterprise

JCE has been applied in several cases before the ICT. The Tribunal invoked Section 4 of the ICT Act. As outlined above, despite the fact that the existence of JCE III under customary international law in 1971 is doubtful, the Tribunal found that all three forms of JCE are enshrined in the ICT Act.

International jurisprudence has established three physical elements for all forms of JCE: (1) a plurality of persons involved in the commission of a crime; (2) the existence of a common plan, design or purpose that involves the commission of a crime; and (3) the participation of the accused in the common plan, design or purpose involving the perpetration of a crime in the form of a significant contribution. The significant contribution is what distinguishes participation in a JCE from conspiracy or membership in a criminal organisation.[1206] The mental elements differ for the three forms of JCE. JCE I requires that all co-perpetrators act pursuant to a common design and share the same intent.[1207] The second category of JCE relates to cases in which the crimes are committed within an institutional framework of a concentration or detention camp and requires personal knowledge of the system of ill-treatment and the intent to further this common system of ill-treatment.[1208] The third category of JCE refers to cases in which one perpetrator commits a crime that was not within the common design but was a natural and foreseeable consequence.[1209]

As outlined above, the ICT invokes Section 4(1) of the ICT Act for JCE liability. The Appellate Division held that Section 4(1) of the ICT Act resembles Section 34 of the Penal Code.[1210]

1204 ICT 2, *The Chief Prosecutor v. Molla*, case no. 02/2012, Judgment, 5 February 2013, para. 153.
1205 ICT 2, *The Chief Prosecutor v. Molla*, case no. 02/2012, Judgment, 5 February 2013, para. 159.
1206 ICTY (AC), *Prosecutor v. Milutinović et al.*, Decision on Dragoljub Ojdanić's Motion Challenging Jurisdiction – Joint Criminal Enterprise, 21 May 2003, para. 26.
1207 ICTY (AC), *Prosecutor v. Tadić*, Appeal Judgment, 15 July 1999, para. 196.
1208 ICTY (AC), *Prosecutor v. Tadić*, Appeal Judgment, 15 July 1999, para. 202.
1209 ICTY (AC), *Prosecutor v. Tadić*, Appeal Judgment, 15 July 1999, para. 204.
1210 SC (AD), *Kamaruzzaman v. The Chief Prosecutor*, Appeal Judgment, 3 November 2014, p. 168.

Part IV: Compliance of the ICT Act, the Rules of Procedure and the ICT's jurisprudence

> *Section 34 of the Bangladesh Penal Code: Acts done by several persons in furtherance of common intention*
> When a criminal act is done by several persons, in furtherance of the common intention of all, each of such persons is liable for that act in the same manner as if it were done by him alone.

Unlike Section 4(1), the provision of the Penal Code contains the element 'in furtherance of the common intention of all'. The Division argued that the rationale behind the absence of this requirement in Section 4(1) is that the objective of the Pakistani army and its auxiliary forces was already determined and it was clear that they acted with a common intention.[1211] This explanation is debatable because the amended version of Section 3(1) extended the personal jurisdiction over individuals irrespective of their membership in auxiliary forces or the Pakistani army. Beyond that, the ICT Act, in general, differs significantly from the system of participation in domestic law and it is unlikely that the drafters took the Penal Code as an orientation for the wording of Section 4(1). The Division further clarified that Section 4(1) intends to overcome difficulties in distinguishing between the acts of individual members and in proving what part each co-perpetrator took[1212] because Section 4(1) requires only the proof that the criminal act was committed by one of the accused persons.[1213] This interpretation of Section 4(1) is also rather debatable as the provision does not seem to be aimed at overcoming evidentiary problems but rather at affirming the equal liability of the main perpetrators and accessories.

While the Tribunal repeatedly affirmed that the first and second form of JCE are embedded in Section 4(1) of the ICT Act, there is disagreement with regard to the legal basis of JCE II. In *Mujahid*, the Tribunal held that the word 'committed' in Section 4(1) encompasses participation in a JCE, 'especially the categories 1 and 3'.[1214] In *Ali*, the Tribunal found that the second part of Section 4(2) of the ICT Act ('is connected with any plans and activities') corresponds to JCE II,[1215] whereas in *Jabbar Engineer*, Tribunal 1 defined the three forms of JCE and reinforced that they are incorporated in

---

1211 SC (AD), *Kamaruzzaman v. The Chief Prosecutor*, Appeal Judgment, 3 November 2014, p. 169.
1212 SC (AD), *Kamaruzzaman v. The Chief Prosecutor*, Appeal Judgment, 3 November 2014, p. 170.
1213 SC (AD), *Kamaruzzaman v. The Chief Prosecutor*, Appeal Judgment, 3 November 2014, p. 171.
1214 ICT 2, *The Chief Prosecutor v. Mujahid*, case no. 04/2012, Judgment, 17 July 2013, para. 444.
1215 ICT 2, *The Chief Prosecutor v. Ali*, case no. 03/2013, Judgment, 2 November 2014, para. 659.

3 The modes of liability of the ICT Act

the ICT Act through Section 4(1)[1216]. The latter finding is, however, more convincing because Section 4(2) refers to commanders and superior officers.

The concept of JCE first emerged in the ICT's jurisprudence in the case of *Mujahid*. The Tribunal determined that the following criteria must be examined: (1) whether the accused took consenting part in the commission of the crime; (2) whether he or she was connected with the plans or with the enterprise; and (3) whether the accused belonged to the perpetrator organisation or group.[1217] The Tribunal held that, if these criteria were fulfilled, the accused was 'concerned in [sic] the commission'[1218] and clarified that concerned with the commission of a crime refers to indirect participation.[1219] These criteria evince imprecision as they merely require a 'connection with the plans or with the enterprise' instead of a common plan and participation. Nevertheless, the Tribunal then also invoked the requirements of JCE as established in international jurisprudence: (1) plurality of persons; (2) existence of a common plan, design or purpose; and (3) participation of the accused in the common design.[1220] The Tribunal clarified that participation in the JCE does not need to consist of a physical act and, relying on *Stakić*,[1221] it held that participation may take the form of assistance in or contribution to the execution of the common purpose.[1222] The Tribunal failed to establish the mental requirements. Instead, Tribunal 1 reframed these criteria, adding the mental requirement that 'the accused intended the aim of the common plan'.[1223] However, this definition of the mens rea is rather vague.

In *Mujahid*, the Tribunal also failed to specify the form of JCE it found applicable. The charges are already imprecise in this regard as they describe that the accused used

---

1216 ICT 1, *The Chief Prosecutor v. Jabbar Engineer*, case no. 01/2014, Judgment, 24 February 2015, para. 146.
1217 ICT 2, *The Chief Prosecutor v. Mujahid*, case no. 04/2012, Judgment, 17 July 2013, para. 445.
1218 ICT 2, *The Chief Prosecutor v. Mujahid*, case no. 04/2012, Judgment, 17 July 2013, para. 446.
1219 ICT 2, *The Chief Prosecutor v. Mujahid*, case no. 04/2012, Judgment, 17 July 2013, para. 446.
1220 ICT 2, *The Chief Prosecutor v. Mujahid*, case no. 04/2012, Judgment, 17 July 2013, para. 449. See also ICT 2, *The Chief Prosecutor v. Qaiser*, case no. 04/2013, Judgment, 23 December 2014, para. 919.
1221 ICTY (AC), *Prosecutor v. Stakić*, Appeal Judgment, 22 March 2006, para. 64.
1222 ICT 2, *The Chief Prosecutor v. Mujahid*, case no. 04/2012, Judgment, 17 July 2013, paras. 449, 450.
1223 ICT 1, *The Chief Prosecutor v. Chowdhury*, case no. 02/2011, Judgment, 1 October 2013, para. 156. The same criteria were applied in ICT 1, *The Chief Prosecutor v. Nizami*, case no. 03/2011, Judgment, 29 October 2014, para. 417; ICT 1, *The Chief Prosecutor v. Jabbar Engineer*, case no. 01/2014, Judgment, 24 February 2015, para. 277.

Part IV: Compliance of the ICT Act, the Rules of Procedure and the ICT's jurisprudence

to visit a torture camp regularly with his co-leaders 'with intent to annihilate the Bangalee population' and that he conspired with the senior officers of the camp.[1224] The charges allege that, as a consequence of the 'conspiracy and planning', the killing of intellectuals was initiated.[1225] Although the charges seem to indicate a case of JCE II, with the torture camp being the institution in which the system of ill-treatment was implemented, the adjudication of the charges suggests that the Tribunal considered JCE I as no link to a system of ill-treatment was established. It is also not clear whether the charges refer to intellectuals who were actually killed at the specific torture camp or more generally to the intellectual killings during the last days of the Liberation War.

Also, the application of the requirements for JCE to this case is unclear. The Tribunal found that the common plan of the criminal enterprise was to kill intellectuals 'with intent to cripple the Bengali nation'[1226] and held that the common plan may be inferred from the circumstances[1227]. It invoked the superior position of the accused in Islami Chhatra Sangha (ICS) to argue that he was part of the common plan of Al-Badr because he knew the organisation's aim.[1228] The Tribunal held that Al-Badr was formed exclusively of members of ICS.[1229] Yet, this finding is controversial because, even if the members of Al-Badr were mainly recruited from ICS, this does not mean that every ICS member was simultaneously a member of Al-Badr and that this can be assumed without proof.[1230] Since the accused was the leader of ICS, the Tribunal concluded that he must have been a member of Al-Badr, which it found to be a criminal organisation with a common plan.[1231]

The Tribunal found that the accused contributed to the execution of the common purpose through advice he provided to Al-Badr leaders, his visits to the army camp, through speeches in which he encouraged the annihilation of the 'Indian agents' and

---

1224 ICT 2, *The Chief Prosecutor v. Mujahid*, case no. 04/2012, Charge Framing Order, 21 June 2012, p. 13.
1225 ICT 2, *The Chief Prosecutor v. Mujahid*, case no. 04/2012, Charge Framing Order, 21 June 2012, p. 13.
1226 ICT 2, *The Chief Prosecutor v. Mujahid*, case no. 04/2012, Judgment, 17 July 2013, para. 434.
1227 ICT 2, *The Chief Prosecutor v. Mujahid*, case no. 04/2012, Judgment, 17 July 2013, para. 432.
1228 ICT 2, *The Chief Prosecutor v. Mujahid*, case no. 04/2012, Judgment, 17 July 2013, paras. 265, 469. The same approach was taken in: ICT 2, *The Chief Prosecutor v. Uddin et al.*, case no. 01/2013, Judgment, 3 November 2013, para. 243.
1229 ICT 2, *The Chief Prosecutor v. Mujahid*, case no. 04/2012, Judgment, 17 July 2013, para. 457.
1230 ICT 2, *The Chief Prosecutor v. Mujahid*, case no. 04/2012, Judgment, 17 July 2013, para. 172.
1231 ICT 2, *The Chief Prosecutor v. Mujahid*, case no. 04/2012, Judgment, 17 July 2013, para. 451.

'miscreants' and through a published article in which he criticised pro-liberation views.[1232]

The Tribunal failed to identify the accused's significant contribution to the common purpose of killing intellectuals, for which he was ultimately held accountable, but instead assumed that the contribution to the Al-Badr organisation in general by dint of the accused's office was sufficient for JCE liability[1233]. The Tribunal's findings show similarities with the crime of membership in a criminal organisation under Articles 9 to 11 of the IMT Charter. Yet, for liability under JCE, mere membership of the criminal enterprise is not sufficient.[1234] Rather, the accused has to participate in the commission of a crime committed by the JCE.[1235] Beyond that, as outlined above, the Act does not establish criminal liability based on membership of a criminal organisation. The Tribunal concluded that:

> The accused Mujahid's act of conscious encouragement provided substantial support constituting "abetment" to the AB [Al-Badr] members to cripple the Bengalis in the area of education and culture. Making frequent visit [sic] to "torture camp" (Mohammadpur AB HQ training centre) accompanied by other senior leaders of JEC and ICS lends unerring assurance that the accused had sufficient reason of being aware of activities and plan[s] of carrying out criminal acts by the AB men, by virtue of his superior position. And thereby he (accused) participated to [sic] the commission of organized crimes and failed to prevent crimes, despite his superior position on the AB force.[1236]

This finding shows the vague application of legal concepts as it suddenly relies on omission and determines that the accused abetted even though his participation in a JCE had been proved.

In *Ali*, the Tribunal established that the following elements need to be fulfilled for JCE II: (1) existence of an organised system to ill-treat the detainees and commission of various crimes alleged; (2) knowledge and awareness of the nature of such system; and (3) the accused's intention to further the system or to participate in enforcing it.[1237] With regard to the mens rea, it argued that, in this specific case, the intent to contribute to the system of ill-treatment could be inferred from the fact that the ac-

---

1232 ICT 2, *The Chief Prosecutor v. Mujahid*, case no. 04/2012, Judgment, 17 July 2013, para. 451.
1233 ICT 2, *The Chief Prosecutor v. Mujahid*, case no. 04/2012, Judgment, 17 July 2013, para. 460.
1234 *Cassese*, International Criminal Law, 3. edn, p. 163.
1235 ICTY (AC), *Prosecutor v. Milutinović et al.*, Decision on Ojdanić's Motion Challenging Jurisdiction – Joint Criminal Enterprise, 21 May 2003, para. 25.
1236 ICT 2, *The Chief Prosecutor v. Mujahid*, case no. 04/2012, Judgment, 17 July 2013, para. 481.
1237 ICT 2, *The Chief Prosecutor v. Ali*, case no. 03/2013, Judgment, 2 November 2014, para. 651.

cused was aware of the system of ill-treatment and had agreed to it.[1238] The Tribunal held that the accused's knowledge of the nature of the system could be inferred from his position of authority[1239] and found that he gave orders at a torture camp[1240]. However, the Tribunal discussed the accused's liability for participation in a JCE at the end of the judgment after it had found the accused guilty of the respective charges under different modes of liability, such as abetment and instigation.

In *Jabbar Engineer*, the Tribunal invoked ICTR jurisprudence which establishes the difference between aiding and abetting and JCE.[1241] Nevertheless, the Tribunal failed to apply the criteria to the case and held the accused liable for aiding and abetting and participation in JCE I simultaneously and without further clarifications.[1242]

Razzaq argues that the Tribunal relied on JCE III in *Kamaruzzaman*.[1243] In this case, the Tribunal held that the members of the group of Al-Badr led by the accused were 'aware of [the] predictable consequence of their criminal acts that eventually resulted in [the] killing of the victim and thus none of the group including the accused can evade the responsibility of [the] murder of Badiuzzaman'.[1244] The accused participated in the abduction of the victim who was taken to an army camp where he was tortured and afterwards killed but the accused's direct participation in the acts of torture and killing could not be proved. The Tribunal invoked jurisprudence that dealt with JCE II, JCE III and aiding and abetting.[1245] Also, the common purpose of the enterprise was not determined and the accused was ultimately found guilty of complicity.[1246] Although the Tribunal partly invoked the concept of JCE III, the combination of jurisprudence impeded the identification of the specific standards the Tribunal ultimately applied.

1238 ICT 2, *The Chief Prosecutor v. Ali*, case no. 03/2013, Judgment, 2 November 2014, para. 654.
1239 ICT 2, *The Chief Prosecutor v. Ali*, case no. 03/2013, Judgment, 2 November 2014, para. 656.
1240 ICT 2, *The Chief Prosecutor v. Ali*, case no. 03/2013, Judgment, 2 November 2014, para. 508.
1241 ICTR (TC), *Prosecutor v. Mpambara*, Judgment, 11 September 2006, paras. 17, 37; cited in ICT 1, *The Chief Prosecutor v. Jabbar Engineer*, case no. 01/2014, Judgment, 24 February 2015, para. 154.
1242 ICT 1, *The Chief Prosecutor v. Jabbar Engineer*, case no. 01/2014, Judgment, 24 February 2015, para. 155.
1243 *Razzaq*, in: *Sellars* (ed.), Trials for International Crimes in Asia, p. 341, at 349.
1244 ICT 2, *The Chief Prosecutor v. Kamaruzzaman*, case no. 03/2012, Judgment, 9 May 2013, para. 240.
1245 ICT 2, *The Chief Prosecutor v. Kamaruzzaman*, case no. 03/2012, Judgment, 9 May 2013, paras. 240, 246.
1246 ICT 2, *The Chief Prosecutor v. Kamaruzzaman*, case no. 03/2012, Judgment, 9 May 2013, para. 252.

3 The modes of liability of the ICT Act

3.2.4 Superior liability

Section 4(2) of the ICT Act refers to liability of superiors. As outlined above, this provision does not incorporate the concept of superior responsibility as recognised in international criminal law. Nevertheless, it was invoked by the Tribunal in this context. However, how this conforms to the wording of Section 4(2) was not discussed. The first part of the provision lists ordering, permitting and participating of a commander or superior officer and, therefore, determines the responsibility for positive acts of the superior. On the other hand, the last part of Section 4(2) establishes criminal liability of a commander or superior officer 'who fails or omits to discharge his duty to maintain discipline, or to control or supervise the actions of the persons under his command or his subordinates, whereby such persons or subordinates or any of them commit any such crimes, or who fails to take necessary measures to prevent the commission of such crimes'.

The Penal Code does not contain a similar provision so that the Tribunal mainly had to rely on international jurisprudence for the definition of command responsibility. Problems arise with regard to the restriction of Section 4(2) to superior officers and commanders and the absence of a knowledge requirement.

The elements of superior responsibility as established in international jurisprudence[1247] are as follows: (1) there must be a superior-subordinate relationship between the accused as the superior and the perpetrator of the crime as his subordinate; (2) the superior knew or had reasons to know that the crime was about to be or had been committed; (3) the superior failed to take the necessary and reasonable measures to prevent the criminal acts or punish the perpetrators thereof. The key factor for the determination of the superior-subordinate relations is the criterion of 'effective control' of the superior over his subordinates.[1248]

The Tribunal acknowledged that the doctrine of command responsibility was accepted as customary international law in 1977 when it was codified in the Additional Protocol I to the Geneva Conventions.[1249] Since it rejected the requirement that the application of the ICT Act should be in accordance with the customary international law of 1971 in order to comply with the principle of legality, it did not relate this finding to the applicability of superior responsibility in the present case. Therefore, in

---

1247 For instance: ICTY (TC), *Prosecutor v. Delalić et al.*, Judgment, 16 November 1998, para. 346; ICTY (AC), *Prosecutor v. Kordić et al.*, Appeal Judgment, 17 December 2004, paras. 827, 839.
1248 ICTY (AC), *Prosecutor v. Delalić et al.*, Appeal Judgment, 20 February 2001, paras. 197–198.
1249 ICT 1, *The Chief Prosecutor v. Azam*, case no. 06/2011, Judgment, 15 July 2013, para. 311.

addition, it did not discuss when the doctrine of civilian superior responsibility emerged but merely stated that it now forms part of customary international law.[1250]

Command responsibility was examined for the first time in *Azam*. The Tribunal introduced this issue in a celebratory manner, stating that the whole nation and also the international community had been eagerly awaiting the decision on how command responsibility finds application in this case.[1251] For the determination of the elements of command responsibility, Tribunal 1 referred to the jurisprudence of the ICTY[1252] and established the following elements: (1) an international crime was committed by someone other than the accused; (2) a superior-subordinate relationship existed between the accused and the perpetrator; (3) the accused as a superior knew or had reason to know that the subordinate was about to commit or had committed the crime; and (4) the accused as a superior failed to take necessary and reasonable measures to prevent the crime or punish the perpetrator.[1253]

While these elements correspond to the internationally recognised requirements of superior responsibility, in other cases the Tribunal departed from these criteria. In *Mujahid* and *Kamaruzzaman*, Tribunal 2 held that superior responsibility has the following requirements: (1) a crime was perpetrated by someone other than the accused; (2) the accused had material ability or influence or authority over the activities of the perpetrators; and (3) the accused failed to prevent the perpetrators from committing the crime.[1254] The superior-subordinate relationship was thus broadened and, as will be discussed below, the knowledge requirement was renounced.

In *Azam*, the Tribunal dealt with the question of whether Section 4(2) encompasses also civilian superior responsibility. Since the provision refers to superior officers and commanders, it held that the interpretation of the term 'officer' is crucial for the determination of the scope of this provision.[1255] The Tribunal held that the interpretation of a legal framework has to occur in consideration of the context of the respective provision and, to this end, other provisions of the framework, the prior state of law, provisions of other statutes on the same matter and the effect of the provision have to be

---

1250 ICT 1, *The Chief Prosecutor v. Azam*, case no. 06/2011, Judgment, 15 July 2013, para. 345.
1251 ICT 1, *The Chief Prosecutor vs. Azam*, case no. 06/2011, Judgment, 15 July 2013, para. 308.
1252 ICTY (TC), *Prosecutor v. Orić*, Trial Judgment, 30 June 2006, para. 294.
1253 ICT 1, *The Chief Prosecutor v. Azam*, case no. 06/2011, Judgment, 15 July 2013, para. 312. The same requirements were also considered in ICT 1, *The Chief Prosecutor v. Nizami*, case no. 03/2011, Judgment, 29 October 2014, para. 370; ICT 1, *The Chief Prosecutor v. Islam*, case no. 05/2013, Judgment, 30 December 2014, para. 286.
1254 ICT 2, *The Chief Prosecutor v. Kamaruzzaman*, case no. 03/2012, Judgment, 9 May 2013, para. 620; ICT 2, *The Chief Prosecutor v. Mujahid*, case no. 04/2012, Judgment, 17 July 2013, para. 178.
1255 ICT 1, *The Chief Prosecutor v. Azam*, case no. 06/2011, Judgment, 15 July 2013, para. 347.

3 The modes of liability of the ICT Act

considered.[1256] It emphasised that an interpretation should not render any provision of the same act superfluous.[1257]

The defence rightly argued that the legislators could have amended Section 4(2) to include civilian superiors in the course of the revision of the ICT Act, if the trial of civilian superiors was intended.[1258] The Tribunal instead relied on Section 5(2) of the ICT Act for the determination of the scope of the word officer. Section 5(2) clarifies that acting pursuant to domestic law or to an order of the government or of a superior does not exclude an accused's responsibility but can be considered to mitigate the punishment. Given that Section 5(2) refers to 'superiors' but does not limit the scope of application to superior officers, the Tribunal found that the use of the word 'officer' in Section 4(2) is merely incidental because, otherwise, it would have been used in Section 5(2) as well.[1259] This line of reasoning does not have much persuasive power. Instead, the comparison to Section 5(2) indicates that the drafters of the Act intended to restrict the scope of Section 4(2) to superior officers because, otherwise, they would have employed the same wording as in Section 5(2). Section 4(2) was also drafted in accordance with the personal jurisdiction of the Tribunal which, at the time of drafting, was restricted to members of armed, defence or auxiliary forces, and the intention behind the ICT Act was to bring the high-level perpetrators of the Pakistani army to trial.

Based on the personal jurisdiction of the ICT, the Tribunal argued that the drafters intended to refer also to civilian officers under Section 4(2).[1260] This, however, does not take into account that the intention to prosecute civilians arose only in 2009 when the Act was amended for the first time. Also, the ICT's personal jurisdiction over civilians does not necessarily mean that the legislators intended their superior liability as they may also have intended to criminalise acts of civilians only, if they directly participated in the commission of the crimes. The fact that the legislators failed to amend this provision in 2009 or later confirms this.

Based on the intention of the drafters as assumed by the Tribunal, it concluded that the word 'officer' was not meant to refer only to army officers.[1261] Beyond that, it argued that also persons who hold an office in organisations can be called 'officer' and,

---

1256 ICT 1, *The Chief Prosecutor v. Azam*, case no. 06/2011, Judgment, 15 July 2013, para. 348, quoting *World Tel Bangladesh Ltd v. Bangladesh* 58 DLR (2006), pp. 14 ff. and *Janab Ali v. State*, 12 DLR (1960), pp. 808 ff.
1257 ICT 1, *The Chief Prosecutor v. Azam*, case no. 06/2011, Judgment, 15 July 2013, para. 348.
1258 ICT 1, *The Chief Prosecutor v. Azam*, case no. 06/2011, Judgment, 15 July 2013, para. 351.
1259 ICT 1, *The Chief Prosecutor v. Azam*, case no. 06/2011, Judgment, 15 July 2013, para. 349.
1260 ICT 1, *The Chief Prosecutor v. Azam*, case no. 06/2011, Judgment, 15 July 2013, para. 352; ICT 1, *The Chief Prosecutor v. Nizami*, case no. 03/2011, Judgment, 29 October 2014, paras. 382–383; ICT 2, *The Chief Prosecutor v. Ali*, case no. 03/2013, Judgment, 2 November 2014, para. 641.
1261 ICT 1, *The Chief Prosecutor v. Azam*, case no. 06/2011, Judgment, 15 July 2013, para. 352.

for that reason, even the head of a political party is encompassed by the term 'superior officer'.[1262] It concluded that an interpretation that complies with customary international law and, in this case, in favour of civilian superior responsibility must be given precedence.[1263]

According to the Tribunal, the superior-subordinate relationship can be established either de jure, if the commander has structural authority over the subordinate, or de facto, if the superior has no formal authority but actual command and influence over the subordinates.[1264] No formal document of appointment as a superior is required.[1265] It further acknowledged that criminal liability could even arise when the perpetrators are not directly subordinated in the chain of command.[1266] The superior must, however, have effective control over the perpetrators to the effect that he or she has the material ability to prevent and punish the commission of offences.[1267] It was further clarified by the Tribunal that the effective control requirement is a question of fact and that the degree of effective control is decisive.[1268]

The 'effective control' criterion was, however, not applied to the case. The Tribunal found that the accused was liable as a civilian superior based on his function as Ameer of Jamaat-e-Islami from 1969 to 1971 and based on his membership of the Central Peace Committee and of the executive committee of the Central Peace Committee.[1269] It observed that the accused in his function as Ameer exercised his superior power in forming Peace Committees, Razakars, Al-Badr and Al-Shams.[1270] The Tribunal invoked the accused's membership of the Central Peace Committee to argue that he was an 'indispensable person as well as de facto administrator to run the civil administration of the then East Pakistan'.[1271] It also stressed that the accused, as 'a religious leader', had command and control over the auxiliary forces[1272] and con-

---

1262 ICT 1, *The Chief Prosecutor v. Azam*, case no. 06/2011, Judgment, 15 July 2013, para. 353.
1263 ICT 1, *The Chief Prosecutor v. Azam*, case no. 06/2011, Judgment, 15 July 2013, para. 352.
1264 ICT 1, *The Chief Prosecutor v. Azam*, case no. 06/2011, Judgment, 15 July 2013, para. 313; ICT 2, *The Chief Prosecutor v. Kamaruzzaman*, case no. 03/2012, Judgment, 9 May 2013, para. 612.
1265 ICT 2, *The Chief Prosecutor v. Kamaruzzaman*, case no. 03/2012, Judgment, 9 May 2013, para. 613.
1266 ICT 1, *The Chief Prosecutor v. Azam*, case no. 06/2011, Judgment, 15 July 2013, para. 319.
1267 ICT 2, *The Chief Prosecutor v. Kamaruzzaman*, case no. 03/2012, Judgment, 9 May 2013, para. 611; ICT 2, *The Chief Prosecutor v. Mujahid*, case no. 04/2012, Judgment, 17 July 2013, para. 195.
1268 ICT 2, *The Chief Prosecutor v. Mujahid*, case no. 04/2012, Judgment, 17 July 2013, para. 203.
1269 ICT 1, *The Chief Prosecutor v. Azam*, case no. 06/2011, Judgment, 15 July 2013, para. 376.
1270 ICT 1, *The Chief Prosecutor v. Azam*, case no. 06/2011, Judgment, 15 July 2013, para. 376.
1271 ICT 1, *The Chief Prosecutor v. Azam*, case no. 06/2011, Judgment, 15 July 2013, para. 356.
1272 ICT 1, *The Chief Prosecutor v. Azam*, case no. 06/2011, Judgment, 15 July 2013, para. 370.

cluded that, as a civilian superior, he 'masterminded all the atrocities committed on the soil of Bangladesh through his subordinates in 1971'[1273]. The Tribunal noted that the defence failed to produce any document that showed that the accused as a leader of a political party 'ever asked his subordinates not to kill any unarmed civilian' or that he took disciplinary measures against the perpetrators.[1274] On the contrary, the Tribunal did not discuss whether the accused actually had the authority to prevent and punish the crimes committed by the army and the Razakars.[1275] The argument of the Tribunal, in this case, shows that it relies exclusively on the function of the accused in the respective organisations instead of applying the criterion of effective control.

In *Sobhan*, the Tribunal held that the accused was the Ameer of Jamaat-e-Islami of Pabna District but that there was no superior-subordinate relationship between the accused and the main perpetrators who, in this case, were Biharis who did not belong to any specific auxiliary force.[1276] The Tribunal observed that the substantial influence the accused might have had on them does not prove that he had effective control over them.[1277]

In *Alim*, the Tribunal cumulatively applied the requirements for civilian superior responsibility and for the mode of liability of ordering. As a consequence, the Tribunal first established the requirement of 'effective control' but then merely examined the 'position of authority' of the accused.[1278] The latter was defined as being in control, being able to make others listen and 'the right to command, suggest or pursue a situation by act or conduct'.[1279] The position of authority was established in this case based on the accused's function as chairman of the Joypurhat Peace Committee.[1280] While in the Statutes of the international criminal tribunals, 'ordering' is a distinct mode of liability, Section 4(2) of the ICT Act refers to ordering only in the context of superiors. It therefore remains unclear whether the Tribunal considers 'ordering' a mode of liability for which it applies the term 'civilian superior responsibility' or whether it considers ordering a mode of liability for which only superiors that meet the 'effective

---

1273 ICT 1, *The Chief Prosecutor v. Azam*, case no. 06/2011, Judgment, 15 July 2013, para. 382.
1274 ICT 1, *The Chief Prosecutor v. Azam*, case no. 06/2011, Judgment, 15 July 2013, para. 370.
1275 *Razzaq*, in: *Sellars* (ed.), Trials for International Crimes in Asia, p. 341, at 349.
1276 ICT 2, *The Chief Prosecutor v. Sobhan*, case no. 01/2014, Judgment, 18 February 2015, para. 543.
1277 ICT 2, *The Chief Prosecutor v. Sobhan*, case no. 01/2014, Judgment, 18 February 2015, para. 548.
1278 ICT 2, *The Chief Prosecutor v. Alim*, case no. 01/2012, Judgment, 9 October 2012, paras. 624, 628.
1279 ICT 2, *The Chief Prosecutor v. Alim*, case no. 01/2012, Judgment, 9 October 2012, para. 628.
1280 ICT 2, *The Chief Prosecutor v. Alim*, case no. 01/2012, Judgment, 9 October 2012, para. 630.

control' prerequisite can be held accountable. The Tribunal also determined that knowledge of the committed crimes is not a requirement for superior responsibility under the ICT Act.[1281]

In *Ali*, the accused was found liable as a civilian superior as well as for participation in JCE II.[1282] As the criterion for the determination of the superior position, the Tribunal relied on the 'degree of control' the superior had over the perpetrators. It held that the 'power of influence' is a key indicator for superior responsibility.[1283] In this specific case, it found that the accused had a position of authority based on his leading position in ICS and it adhered to its finding in *Azam* that Al-Badr was formed of ICS members.[1284] It held that the accused, in exercise of his superior position, induced Al-Badr members to commit the crimes.[1285] Since the accused was present when crimes were committed at the torture camp and he also ordered Al-Badr members to beat up detainees, the Tribunal came to the conclusion that he had knowledge of the crimes committed.[1286] It determined that superior responsibility does not require 'explicit legal capacity' to prevent the crimes but rather 'material ability to act'.[1287] The accused's material ability to control Al-Badr subordinates was based on his de facto superior position within the Al-Badr torture camp.[1288] Despite the accused's direct involvement in the crimes, the Tribunal relied on the accused's omission to prevent the crimes.

Likewise, in *Qaiser*, the Tribunal examined the accused's superior responsibility after it had found him guilty under different modes of liability. Superior responsibility was, however, rejected because there was no superior-subordinate relationship between the accused and the members of the Pakistani army who committed the crimes.[1289] The accused did not have effective control over the Pakistani army – a

---

1281 ICT 2, *The Chief Prosecutor v. Alim*, case no. 01/2012, Judgment, 9 October 2012, para. 629.
1282 ICT 2, *The Chief Prosecutor v. Ali*, case no. 03/2013, Judgment, 2 November 2014, para. 659.
1283 ICT 2, *The Chief Prosecutor v. Ali*, case no. 03/2013, Judgment, 2 November 2014, para. 645.
1284 ICT 2, *The Chief Prosecutor v. Ali*, case no. 03/2013, Judgment, 2 November 2014, para. 643.
1285 ICT 2, *The Chief Prosecutor v. Ali*, case no. 03/2013, Judgment, 2 November 2014, para. 643.
1286 ICT 2, *The Chief Prosecutor v. Ali*, case no. 03/2013, Judgment, 2 November 2014, para. 664.
1287 ICT 2, *The Chief Prosecutor v. Ali*, case no. 03/2013, Ali, Judgment, 2 November 2014, para. 642.
1288 ICT 2, *The Chief Prosecutor v. Ali*, case no. 03/2013, Judgment, 2 November 2014, para. 642.
1289 ICT 2, *The Chief Prosecutor v. Qaiser*, case no. 04/2013, Judgment, 23 December 2014, para. 910.

3 The modes of liability of the ICT Act

requirement the Tribunal found applicable for both civilian and military superiors.[1290] The Tribunal based its findings on the absence of proof that the accused had effective control over the Pakistani army.[1291]

With regard to the mental elements of superior responsibility, the ICT came to very contradictory findings. In *Azam*, Tribunal 1 clarified that the different knowledge requirements for civilian and military superiors established in the Rome Statute do not reflect customary international law and rejected their application.[1292] With regard to the ICT Act, it held that 'it would be highly repugnant to common sense and natural justice to hold someone responsible for the crimes committed by his subordinates which was [sic] unbeknown to him'.[1293] The Tribunal determined that it was authorised to add the knowledge requirement, although not expressly established in Section 4(2), because 'not doing so would frustrate the ends of justice and doing so would be conforming to natural justice and customary international laws [sic]'.[1294]

According to the Tribunal, the knowledge of the superior has to be inferred from the facts, circumstances and the context of the case, especially when examining whether the accused had reason to know.[1295] Considering that the knowledge requirement is not explicitly mentioned in the ICT Act, the Tribunal found that the burden lies on the Tribunal rather than on the prosecution to produce respective evidence.[1296]

An entirely different interpretation of Section 4(2) was adopted in *Mujahid* and *Kamaruzzaman*, in which the Tribunal, without any further reasoning, stated that superior responsibility under the ICT Act does not establish a knowledge requirement.[1297] In both cases, it was affirmed that, although knowledge is not required under the ICT Act, the superior position of the accused is a significant indicator that he actu-

---

1290 ICT 2, *The Chief Prosecutor v. Qaiser*, case no. 04/2013, Judgment, 23 December 2014, para. 911.
1291 ICT 2, *The Chief Prosecutor v. Qaiser*, case no. 04/2013, Judgment, 23 December 2014, para. 912.
1292 ICT 1, *The Chief Prosecutor v. Azam*, case no. 06/2011, Judgment, 15 July 2013, paras. 334, 335.
1293 ICT 1, *The Chief Prosecutor v. Azam*, case no. 06/2011, Judgment, 15 July 2013, para. 336.
1294 ICT 1, *The Chief Prosecutor v. Azam*, case no. 06/2011, Judgment, 15 July 2013, para. 338. The same approach was followed in ICT 1, *The Chief Prosecutor v. Nizami*, case no. 03/2011, Judgment, 29 October 2014, para. 379.
1295 ICT 1, *The Chief Prosecutor v. Azam*, case no. 06/2011, Judgment, 15 July 2013, para. 339.
1296 ICT 1, *The Chief Prosecutor v. Azam*, case no. 06/2011, Judgment, 15 July 2013, para. 339.
1297 ICT 2, *The Chief Prosecutor v. Mujahid*, case no. 04/2012, Judgment, 17 July 2013, para. 454.

Part IV: Compliance of the ICT Act, the Rules of Procedure and the ICT's jurisprudence

ally had knowledge of the commission of crimes.[1298] It appears that the Tribunal considers the knowledge requirement always fulfilled based on the superior position of the accused. Nevertheless, it is evident that an obligation to prevent crimes can only exist if the superior knew about the crimes or at least had reason to know about the specific crimes.

The Appellate Division dealt with the specific requirements of superior responsibility in *Kamaruzzaman* and, contrary to the Tribunal's findings, rejected the accused's superior liability.[1299] The Tribunal had found Kamaruzzaman liable as a civilian superior based on his effective control over the Al-Badr members who committed the crimes.[1300]

In its findings, the Appellate Division reproduced almost an entire academic article[1301] on civilian superior responsibility.[1302] It then scrutinised whether the accused had de jure authority based on his function as an Al-Badr leader in larger Mymensingh.[1303] The Division invoked Sections 8(2), 8(3) and 8(4) of the Razakars Ordinance in order to determine who had superior powers within the Razakars' force.

Section 8 of the East Pakistan Razakars Ordinance, 1971
(1) There shall be a Director of Razakars who shall be appointed by the Provincial Government on such terms and conditions as may be prescribed.
(2) The administration of the Razakars shall, under the general control and direction of the provincial Government, be vested in the Director.
(3) To assist the Director in the performance of his functions, the Provincial Government may appoint such officers and staff as it may deem fit on such terms and conditions as may be prescribed.
(4) The Director and other officers appointed under this section shall exercise such powers and perform such duties as may be prescribed or as may be directed by the provincial Government.

1298 ICT 2, *The Chief Prosecutor v. Kamaruzzaman*, case no. 03/2012, Judgment, 9 May 2013, para. 624; ICT 2, *The Chief Prosecutor v. Mujahid*, case no. 04/2012, Judgment, 17 July 2013, para. 211. Later also adopted in ICT 2, *The Chief Prosecutor v. Alim*, case no. 01/2012, Judgment, 9 October 2012, para. 629.
1299 SC (AD), *Kamaruzzaman v. The Chief Prosecutor*, Appeal Judgment, 3 November 2014, pp. 115–172.
1300 ICT 2, *The Chief Prosecutor v. Kamaruzzaman*, case no. 03/2012, Judgment, 9 May 2013, para. 631.
1301 *Ronen*, VJTL, 2010, 43(2), pp. 313–356. The Tribunal copied large parts of the article and deleted the footnotes.
1302 SC (AD), *Kamaruzzaman v. The Chief Prosecutor*, Appeal Judgment, 3 November 2014, pp. 116–153.
1303 SC (AD), *Kamaruzzaman v. The Chief Prosecutor*, Appeal Judgment, 3 November 2014, p. 153.

3 The modes of liability of the ICT Act

The Division held that the Ordinance was later also invoked for the formation and administration of Al-Badr and Al-Shams[1304] and concluded that the accused as an Al-Badr leader performed his responsibilities as an officer under the Razakars Ordinance, whereas the director was the chief executive officer[1305].

The Razakars Ordinance was replaced in the course of the Liberation War. A Government Notification dated 7 September 1971 amended the Army Act and declared all the provisions of the Army Act applicable to Razakars and, at the same time, suspended the Razakars Ordinance.[1306] The Notification placed the Razakars under the command of the Pakistani army[1307] and, according to the Appellate Division, the Pakistani army, therefore, had command responsibility[1308]. Since the accused was not an officer within the meaning of the Army Act but rather an officer under the Razakars Ordinance, the Division concluded that he had no superior responsibility based on his office.[1309]

The quintessence of the Division's finding is thus that only the superior who is on top of the chain of command can incur superior responsibility based on de jure authority. Justice Choudhury in his dissenting opinion criticised the majority judgment arguing that although the Razakars Ordinance created only one post of a director, there were evidently sub-superiors.[1310] The Ordinance established posts of officers who de jure or at least de facto acted as regional superiors.[1311] He held that the legislators, by employing the term 'superior officer' in Section 4(2) of the ICT Act, must have intended all officers who were superiors because the Razakars Ordinance created posts of officers only.[1312] He also emphasised that the mere fact that the accused himself

---

1304 SC (AD), *Kamaruzzaman v. The Chief Prosecutor*, Appeal Judgment, 3 November 2014, p. 156.
1305 SC (AD), *Kamaruzzaman v. The Chief Prosecutor*, Appeal Judgment, 3 November 2014, p. 157.
1306 SC (AD), *Kamaruzzaman v. The Chief Prosecutor*, Appeal Judgment, 3 November 2014, pp. 157, 158.
1307 For the relevant provision of the Government's Notification, see SC (AD), *Kamaruzzaman v. The Chief Prosecutor*, Appeal Judgment, 3 November 2014, p. 158.
1308 SC (AD), *Kamaruzzaman v. The Chief Prosecutor*, Appeal Judgment, 3 November 2014, p. 159.
1309 SC (AD), *Kamaruzzaman v. The Chief Prosecutor*, Appeal Judgment, 3 November 2014, pp. 159–160.
1310 SC (AD), *Kamaruzzaman v. The Chief Prosecutor*, Dissenting Opinion of Justice Choudhury, Appeal Judgment, 3 November 2014, p. 557.
1311 SC (AD), *Kamaruzzaman v. The Chief Prosecutor*, Dissenting Opinion of Justice Choudhury, Appeal Judgment, 3 November 2014, p. 557.
1312 SC (AD), *Kamaruzzaman v. The Chief Prosecutor*, Dissenting Opinion of Justice Choudhury, Appeal Judgment, 3 November 2014, p. 559.

was under the command of an army officer does not exclude his command over his subordinates.[1313]

The Division's conclusion that the accused did not incur superior responsibility by dint of his office is followed by an ambiguous finding on the scope of superior responsibility. With regard to civilian superior responsibility, the Division held that the 'application of the doctrine to civilian settings is fraught with challenges'.[1314] It emphasised that civilians have only rarely been convicted under the doctrine.[1315] However, the question of whether the Division considers superior responsibility, in general, to be applicable to civilians has not been clearly answered. The Division merely concluded that it would be difficult to apply the doctrine to the present case[1316] because the accused as an Al-Badr leader was not a civilian who holds a high civilian position with command responsibility.[1317] The Division found that 'civilian superiors were members of top political echelons and in charge of both military and para-military forces'.[1318]

Since the majority judgment rejected the existence of a superior-subordinate relationship, the knowledge requirement was not further discussed. However, Justice Choudhury in his dissenting opinion rightly emphasised that it would be unreasonable to impose upon a superior a duty to prevent the commission of crimes if he was unaware of their commission.[1319] He also expressed his dissenting opinion with regard to the non-applicability of the concept of superior responsibility to civilian settings[1320] and argued that there are many instances of convictions of civilians under superior responsibility.[1321] Choudhury rightly pointed out that the fact that, in many cases of international criminal law, civilians have been acquitted does not have any influence on the applicability of the doctrine to civilians because the grounds for acquittal were

---

1313 SC (AD), *Kamaruzzaman v. The Chief Prosecutor*, Dissenting Opinion of Justice Choudhury, Appeal Judgment, 3 November 2014, pp. 564–565.
1314 SC (AD), *Kamaruzzaman v. The Chief Prosecutor*, Appeal Judgment, 3 November 2014, p. 152.
1315 SC (AD), *Kamaruzzaman v. The Chief Prosecutor*, Appeal Judgment, 3 November 2014, p. 127.
1316 SC (AD), *Kamaruzzaman v. The Chief Prosecutor*, Appeal Judgment, 3 November 2014, p. 166.
1317 SC (AD), *Kamaruzzaman v. The Chief Prosecutor*, Appeal Judgment, 3 November 2014, p. 159.
1318 SC (AD), *Kamaruzzaman v. The Chief Prosecutor*, Appeal Judgment, 3 November 2014, p. 159.
1319 SC (AD), *Kamaruzzaman v. The Chief Prosecutor*, Dissenting Opinion of Justice Choudhury, Appeal Judgment, 3 November 2014, p. 524.
1320 SC (AD), *Kamaruzzaman v. The Chief Prosecutor*, Dissenting Opinion of Justice Choudhury, Appeal Judgment, 3 November 2014, pp. 535–536.
1321 SC (AD), *Kamaruzzaman v. The Chief Prosecutor*, Dissenting Opinion of Justice Choudhury, Appeal Judgment, 3 November 2014, p. 548.

mainly of an evidentiary nature.[1322] With regard to Section 4(2), he held that the wording of the provisions does not restrict superior command responsibility to military superiors[1323] and that the legislators had no intention to restrict superior command responsibility to army personnel.[1324]

3.2.5 The modes of liability and sentence

Although international customary law does not establish a mandatory lower sentence for aiding and abetting,[1325] in practice, a lower punishment has been imposed[1326]. The ICT Act is silent on sentencing criteria in general. In the sentencing practice of the Tribunal, the different modes of liability have not had a major impact, except in the case of superior responsibility.

The Tribunal's approach conforms to the Penal Code. With regard to the penalty of abetment, Section 109 of the Penal Code generally imposes the same penalty upon an abettor as upon the main perpetrator, unless a differing provision is expressly made in the Penal Code. However, this does not apply, for instance, if the perpetrator acts with a different intention to that of the abettor (Section 110). In this case, the abettor shall be punished in accordance with the offence that would have been committed if the crime had been committed with the intention or knowledge of the abettor. Different penalties apply also if the offence is not committed as a consequence of the abetment (Sections 115, 116). The latter provision takes into account the Penal Code's wide notion of abetment that includes conspiracy or instigation and thus does not always require that the act be committed.

The jurisprudence of the Appellate Division also shows, although not explicitly, that the mode of liability is not considered relevant for the sentencing. In *Molla*, the Division found that the accused committed the crimes as principal offender rather than as abettor, as found by the Tribunal.[1327] Even though the Division clarified that the imposed penalty did not reflect the gravity of the crimes in this case, this finding

---

1322 SC (AD), *Kamaruzzaman v. The Chief Prosecutor*, Dissenting Opinion of Justice Choudhury, Appeal Judgment, 3 November 2014, p. 551.
1323 SC (AD), *Kamaruzzaman v. The Chief Prosecutor*, Dissenting opinion of Justice Choudhury, Appeal Judgment, 3 November 2014, p. 552.
1324 SC (AD), *Kamaruzzaman v. The Chief Prosecutor*, Dissenting Opinion of Justice Choudhury to the Appeal Judgment, 3 November 2014, p. 552.
1325 *Cassese*, International Criminal Law, 3. edn, p. 195.
1326 For example, ICTY (AC), *Prosecutor v. Krstić*, Appeal Judgment, 19 April 2004, para. 275; ICTY (AC), *Prosecutor v. Vasiljević*, Appeal Judgment, para. 182.
1327 SC (AD), *Molla v. The Chief Prosecutor*, Appeal Judgment, 17 September 2013, pp. 238–239.

does not make reference to the wrongly applied mode of liability.[1328] The Division merely remarked that it found some 'inconsistencies' in the findings of the Tribunal and thereby referred to the modes of liability as well.[1329]

The Tribunal considered superior responsibility to be an aggravating factor in several judgments in which the accused was held liable simultaneously as superior and under a different mode of liability. In *Azam*, the ICT suggested that superior responsibility shall be taken into account as an aggravating factor and that civilian and military commanders shall be awarded heavier sentences.[1330] Likewise, in *Kamaruzzaman*, the Tribunal considered the accused's superior responsibility merely as an aggravating factor but not one that established criminal liability.[1331] In this context, it clarified that, since the liability of the accused was already based on Section 4(1), he should not be convicted under Section 4(2) simultaneously.[1332] Likewise, in *Ali*, the Tribunal emphasised that active abuse of authority aggravates the liability of the accused.[1333]

In *Chowdhury*, on the other hand, active participation and the presence of the accused during the commission of the crimes were considered aggravating factors.[1334] However, since 'active participation' and 'presence' do not shed light on the mode of liability of the accused, this aggravating factor does not seem to relate to the legal classification of the mode of liability as such but rather to the concrete way in which the accused contributed to the crime. It is further to be noted that, in other judgments, presence and direct participation have not been considered as aggravating factors.

The Appellate Division overruled the admissibility of command responsibility as an aggravating factor and concluded that this was a misconception of law.[1335] For this finding, it relied on the wording of Section 4(2) which refers to liability and not to sentencing[1336] and further clarified that direct participation prevails over superior re-

---

1328 For the line of reasoning on the penalty, see SC (AD), *Molla v. The Chief Prosecutor*, Appeal Judgment, 17 September 2013, pp. 247–252.
1329 SC (AD), *Molla v. The Chief Prosecutor*, Appeal Judgment, 17 September 2013, p. 238.
1330 ICT 1, *The Chief Prosecutor v. Azam*, case no. 06/2011, Judgment, 15 July 2013, paras. 343, 390.
1331 ICT 2, *The Chief Prosecutor v. Kamaruzzaman*, case no. 03/2012, Judgment, 9 May 2013, paras. 499, 632.
1332 ICT 2, *The Chief Prosecutor v. Kamaruzzaman*, case no. 03/2012, Judgment, 9 May 2013, para. 632.
1333 ICT 2, *The Chief Prosecutor v. Ali*, case no. 03/2013, Judgment, 2 November 2014, para. 731.
1334 ICT 1, *The Chief Prosecutor v. Chowdhury*, case no. 02/2011, Judgment, 1 October 2013, para. 294.
1335 SC (AD), *Kamaruzzaman v. The Chief Prosecutor*, Appeal Judgment, 3 November 2014, p. 167.
1336 SC (AD), *Kamaruzzaman v. The Chief Prosecutor*, Appeal Judgment, 3 November 2014, p. 167.

sponsibility[1337]. Contrary to the Tribunal's findings, it stipulated that direct participation in the commission of crimes is an aggravating factor.[1338]

3.3 Interim findings

The application of the modes of liability in the jurisprudence of the ICT shows unacceptable inconsistencies. Several criteria are blurred and criminal liability is extended beyond the scope of the ICT Act.

However, the problem derives from the legal framework because the modes of liability embedded in the ICT Act are highly problematic. The Act establishes a liability system that is alien to the domestic criminal law of Bangladesh. At the same time, it does not incorporate the system of the modes of liability as established under international criminal law. A revision of the ICT Act would have been necessary and desirable before the commencement of the trials.

Severe problems arise through the refusal of the Tribunal to consistently apply international criminal law jurisprudence despite the obvious impossibility to invoke domestic law as an interpretation tool. Although the Tribunal generally applies international criminal law jurisprudence in the context of the modes of liability, it departs from it in several crucial aspects.

The interpretation of the modes of liability shows a clear tendency to establish liability based on membership and thus exceeds the wording of the ICT Act. Some interpretative approaches of the Tribunal conflict with the general understanding of criminal law. This holds true, for instance, with regard to the waiver of the knowledge requirement in the context of superior responsibility as applied in some judgments. Also, the Tribunal's reliance on mere membership in determined organisations to establish criminal liability is not covered by the provisions of the ICT Act. The flawed application of the modes of liability raises severe concerns as to the Tribunal's ability to credibly establish individual guilt or innocence.

4 Procedural rights

Given that the ICT Act explicitly precludes the application of the Code of Criminal Procedure and the Evidence Act, the ICT Act and the RoP are the only sources of procedural law applicable to the ICT. While the Constitution of Bangladesh contains some fundamental procedural guarantees, it also many of them inapplicable to those

---

1337 SC (AD), *Kamaruzzaman v. The Chief Prosecutor*, Appeal Judgment, 3 November 2014, p. 167.
1338 SC (AD), *Kamaruzzaman v. The Chief Prosecutor*, Appeal Judgment, 3 November 2014, pp. 167, 182.

accused under the ICT. Although the establishment of special or military tribunals is not per se impeded by the ICCPR, the Human Rights Committee has warned that the formation of special courts shall only take place in exceptional situations and that, in any event, the rights enshrined in Article 14 must be guaranteed.[1339]

The Tribunal stated in a rather formulaic manner that the ICT Act and the RoP incorporate all procedural rights of the ICCPR.[1340] In particular, it found that the following provisions implement international fair trial standards: (1) Right to a fair and impartial trial, Section 6(2A) of the ICT Act; (2) Right to a public trial, Section 10(4) of the ICT Act; (3) Right of the accused to know the charges brought against him and the relevant evidence, Rules 9(3) and 18(4) of the RoP and Sections 9(3) and 16(2) of the ICT Act; (4) Presumption of innocence, Rule 43(2) of the RoP; (5) Adequate time for preparation of defence, Section 9(3) of the ICT Act and Rule 38(2) of the RoP; (6) Right to a defence counsel and an interpreter, Sections 10(3) and 17(2) of the ICT Act; (7) Right to call witnesses and to produce evidence, Section 10(1)(f) and Section 17(3) of the ICT Act; (8) Right to cross-examine witnesses, Section 10(1)(f) of the ICT Act; (9) Right to be tried without undue delay, Section 11(3) of the ICT Act; (10) *Nemo tenetur se ipsum acusare*, Rule 43(7) of the RoP; and (11) Right to appeal, Section 21(1) of the ICT Act.[1341]

It is striking that several of these fundamental rights are only contained in the RoP even though fundamental rights should not be regulated by judges but rather be protected through an Act of Parliament. For instance, this holds true for the presumption of innocence as well as for the *nemo tenetur* principle.

Several of these fundamental rights have been introduced only in the course of the amendments of the Act. Nevertheless, it is quite evident that the 66 rules of the RoP and the few provisions in the ICT Act related to procedural law are not at all sufficient to regulate procedural law in a satisfactory manner and to replace an entire Code of Criminal Procedure. Significant gaps can be anticipated.

Rule 46A allows the Tribunal to make such orders as may be necessary to meet the ends of justice or to prevent abuse of the process. The Tribunal claimed that, based on this Rule, it has adopted several practices with the aim of strengthening the accused's

---

1339 Human Rights Committee, General Comment No. 32, Article 14, 23 August 2007, para. 22 (UN Doc. CCPR/C/GC/32).
1340 ICT 2, *The Chief Prosecutor v. Molla*, case no. 02/2012, Judgment, 5 February 2013, para. 40; ICT 2, *The Chief Prosecutor v. Kamaruzzaman*, case no. 03/2012, Judgment, 9 May 2013, para. 62.
1341 This finding is reiterated in several judgments. See, for instance, ICT 2, *The Chief Prosecutor v. Molla*, case no. 02/2012, Judgment, 5 February 2013, para. 41; ICT 2, *The Chief Prosecutor v. Kamaruzzaman*, case no. 03/2012, Judgment, 9 May 2013, para. 63.

rights.[1342] While such practice is certainly positive, the protection of fundamental rights should not have to depend on initiatives of the Tribunal but rather be guaranteed sufficiently through the law.

The IMT Charter barely defined the rights of suspects in the investigation phase.[1343] The only provisions geared to this end were Article 16(b) which guaranteed the right to give any explanation relevant to the charges and Article 16(c) which contained the right to be examined in a language the suspect understands and the right to translation. It appears that this approach was adopted in the ICT Act because the Act is mostly silent on the rights of the accused during the pre-indictment phase. Considering the vulnerability of an accused under arrest during the pre-trial phase, this is highly problematic. Beyond that, neither the ICT Act nor the RoP contain general obligations to inform the accused of his rights.

4.1 Right to legal assistance and to an interpreter

Article 14(3)(f) of the ICCPR stipulates the right of an accused to the assistance of an interpreter, whereas Article 14(3)(d) enshrines the right of the accused to legal assistance. Under the ICT Act, the right to legal assistance and the right to an interpreter are dealt with in Sections 10, 17 and 12.

The accused has the right to an interpreter under Section 10(3) of the ICT Act if he is unable to express himself in English or if he does not understand English. This provision formed part of the ICT Act from the beginning and was probably based on the fact that the trial was originally intended to be entirely in English. However, since Bengali has now been added as a court language (Section 10(2)), and the accused are Bangladeshi nationals, the importance of interpreters has diminished. This right is provided only during trial because Section 10 explicitly refers to the procedure of trial. Yet, in practice, the restriction to the trial phase is not likely to lead to disadvantages because the entire investigation and the procedure of charging are conducted in Bengali. Also, the trials as such are held mostly in Bengali. Certainly, more problematic is the fact that the orders (including the charge framing orders) and the judgments of the Tribunal are in English and there is no provision that establishes the right to obtain a translated version in Bengali, if required.

Legal assistance is dealt with in Sections 17(2) and 12 but these Sections do not grant the right to legal assistance during investigation. Section 12 allows the Tribunal to appoint a defence counsel at the expense of the government at any stage of the case if the accused is not legally represented. Although this Section also applies to the in-

---

1342 ICT 2, *The Chief Prosecutor v. Molla*, case no. 02/2012, Judgment, 5 January 2013, para. 33.
1343 *Zappalà*, Human Rights in International Criminal Proceedings, p. 45.

vestigation stage, the wording establishes the appointment of a defence counsel as a discretionary power of the Tribunal[1344] because the Tribunal <u>may</u> appoint a defence counsel. Therefore, the power to decide on the point of time of appointment is also upon the Tribunal.

Section 17(2) determines that an accused has the right to conduct his own defence or to have a defence counsel during trial. Likewise, Rule 43(1) of the RoP determines that the Tribunal shall appoint a defence counsel at the expense of the government if the accused is not represented during trial.

Given that the right to legal assistance is not guaranteed for the pre-trial phase, this right is only insufficiently protected under the ICT Act. Beyond that, the discretionary power of the Tribunal to decide at which stage it appoints a counsel curtails the rights of the accused in this regard.

Also, external factors have become relevant and have hampered proper legal assistance. The defence of the accused under the ICT Act has proven extremely challenging and is connected to severe security threats. Some ICT defence lawyers have been intimidated through office searches or even been arbitrarily arrested.[1345] Human Rights Watch has strongly recommended the establishment of a Defence Office for better protection of the defence lawyers[1346] but, to date, no steps to prevent future harassment have been taken.

4.2 Right not to be subjected to arbitrary arrest or detention and to be informed of the reasons for arrest

The ICCPR establishes several rights of persons under arrest. Article 9(1) of the ICCPR prohibits, in general, arbitrary arrest and detention, whereas Article 9(2) establishes a right to be informed about the reasons for arrest and to be promptly informed of the charges. Pursuant to Article 9(3), anyone under arrest shall also be brought promptly before a judge.

The right not to be subjected to arbitrary arrest or detention is enshrined in the Constitution of Bangladesh. Article 31 determines that 'no action detrimental to the life, liberty, body, reputation or property of any person shall be taken except in accordance with law'. Yet, Article 47A of the Constitution bars the application of this fundamental principle to the accused under the ICT Act. Nevertheless, Article 32 of the

---

1344 *Linton*, CLF, 2010, 21(2), p. 191, at 297.
1345 *Human Rights Watch*, Bangladesh: End Harassment of War Crimes Defence Counsel, 17 October 2012; *Human Rights Watch*, Bangladesh: Charge or Release Detained Counsel, 26 October 2015.
1346 *Human Rights Watch*, Bangladesh: End Harassment of War Crimes Defence Counsel, 17 October 2012.

Constitution remains applicable and also determines that no person shall be deprived of liberty save in accordance with the law.

Article 33 of the Constitution defines further rules with regard to detention and establishes the right to be informed about the reasons for arrest 'as soon as may be' and the right to consult a lawyer and to be defended by a lawyer. While the right to be informed of the reasons for arrest is contained in the RoP, there is no provision that relates to the right to consult a defence counsel at the time of arrest or, in general, during detention. Article 33(2) of the Constitution contains the right to be produced before the nearest magistrate within 24 hours (excluding the time of the journey) and a prohibition to detain a person beyond this time without the authority of a magistrate.

The only provision in the ICT Act that deals with arrest is Section 11(5). It gives any Tribunal member the power 'to direct, or issue a warrant for, the arrest of, and to commit to custody, and to authorise the continued detention in custody of, any person charged with any crime specified in Section 3'.

Rule 9 of the RoP regulates some aspects of arrest: sub-rule (1) clarifies that the Investigation Officer may obtain a warrant of arrest from the Tribunal at any stage of the investigation, 'if he can satisfy the Tribunal that such arrest is necessary for effective and proper investigation'; sub-rule (3) establishes the obligation to furnish a copy of allegations to the arrested person at the time of arrest 'or later'; and sub-rule (5) limits the period of investigation to one year after the arrest of the accused. In the case of failure to comply with this period, the accused may be released on bail. However, in exceptional circumstances, the period of one year may be extended for a further six months.

Rule 9(6) determines that the Investigation Officer shall submit a progress report of the investigation through the Prosecutor every three months during the detention of the accused. Based on this report, the Tribunal may review the order on the detention of the accused. Pursuant to Rule 34, an arrested accused must be produced before the Tribunal within 24 hours (excluding the time required for the journey).

However, some fundamental issues are not addressed at all. For instance, there is no provision that states that only reasonable grounds to believe that the person actually committed the crime allow for arrest. On the contrary, Rule 9(1) determines that arrest merely has to be necessary for effective and proper investigation. This provision is highly problematic as it significantly extends the possibility to impose pre-trial detention. Section 16 of the ICT Act stipulates the content of the charges but charging takes place after completion of the investigation. Further, the ICT Act is silent on the minimum requirements for a warrant of arrest and an obligation to inform the accused under arrest of his rights.[1347]

1347 See also *Linton*, CLF, 2010, 21(2), p. 191, at 292.

Part IV: Compliance of the ICT Act, the Rules of Procedure and the ICT's jurisprudence

The absence of reasonable grounds to believe that the person committed the crimes has been criticised by the defence in the cases of *Nizami, Molla, Kamaruzzaman* and *Mujahid*. It was contended that the accused were in custody for almost nine months based on vague allegations and that no Investigation Report had been submitted.[1348] The Tribunal rejected the application for release of the accused but ordered the prosecution to submit the Investigation Report or at least a progress report.[1349] Nevertheless, no specifications were made for the grounds that allow for detention and whether they were given in these cases.

The Tribunal found that Rules 9(3) and 18(4) of the RoP correspond to Article 9(3) of the ICCPR.[1350] Pursuant to these rules, the accused shall be handed a copy of the allegations and shall be provided with copies of the formal charges and other documents in support of the charges. However, Rule 9(3) lacks specificity because it reads 'at the time of executing the warrant of arrest [...] or later on'. There is thus no obligation to hand a copy of the allegations to the accused at the time of the arrest, and which time span amounts to 'later on' remains questionable.

Further problems arise with regard to the accused's right to be informed of the charges. This right is essential for the accused to prepare their defence[1351] and is thus a key element of a fair trial[1352]. Section 16(1) of the ICT Act determines the elements that must be contained in the charges: the name and particulars of the accused person, the crime of which the accused is charged, and such particulars of the alleged crime as are reasonably sufficient to give the accused person notice of the matter with which he is charged. As outlined above, the Tribunal found that the determination of the mode of liability does not have to be specified in the charge framing order.[1353]

The general imprecision of the charge framing orders of the Tribunal violate the accused's right to be informed of the charges. In *Azam*, the defence raised the issue of imprecise charge framing orders because the order referred only to crimes under Section 3(2) of the ICT Act but did not further specify the crimes that were allegedly committed.[1354] The Tribunal found that the charges were sufficiently clear and precise

---

1348 ICT, *The Chief Prosecutor v. Kamaruzzaman, Mujahid, Molla & Nizami*, misc. case no. 01/2010 (pre-trial), Order no. 13, 21 April 2011, pp. 1–2.
1349 ICT, *The Chief Prosecutor v. Kamaruzzaman, Mujahid, Molla & Nizami*, misc. case no. 01/2010 (pre-trial), Order no. 13, 21 April 2011, p. 3.
1350 ICT 2, *The Chief Prosecutor v. Molla*, case no. 02/2012, Judgment, 5 January 2013, para. 36.
1351 Zappalà, Human Rights in International Criminal Proceedings, p. 119.
1352 ECHR, *Bendenoun v. France*, Judgment, 24 February 1994, para. 53.
1353 ICT 2, *The Chief Prosecutor v. Kamaruzzaman*, case no. 03/2012, Judgment, 9 May 2013, para. 498.
1354 ICT 1, *The Chief Prosecutor v. Azam*, case no. 06/2011, Order no. 34, 18 June 2012, para. 7.

considering the stage of the trial.[1355] With regard to the charge of conspiracy to commit crimes under Section 3(2) of the ICT Act, the Tribunal argued that it considered it a fact of common knowledge that crimes under Section 3(2) were committed during the Liberation War and that, therefore, no precision of the crimes was required.[1356] If there is no right to be informed of the specific crime which the accused allegedly conspired to commit and also no right to be informed of the mode of liability, the core of the right to be informed of the charges is in fact dissolved. Although many charge framing orders contain the mode of liability and also specify the crimes that were committed, the jurisprudence of the Tribunal clearly shows that the accused has no right to be informed of these aspects.

Article 9(3) of the ICCPR expressly states that pre-trial detention shall not be the rule. While the ICT Act itself does not contain any provision dealing with bail, Rule 21 clarifies that the offences under Section 3(2) of the Act shall be non-bailable. At the same time, Rule 34(3) of the RoP allows the Tribunal to release an accused on bail subject to the fulfilment of some conditions, and, in the interest of justice, it may modify any of these conditions on its own motion or at the request of either party. In the case of violation of any such conditions, the accused's bail may be cancelled. Neither the RoP nor the ICT Act contain criteria for the denial or granting of bail, and it is left entirely for the Tribunal to decide what it considers a case for bail and also to lay down the conditions of bail.

Bail has been applied for in various cases but it has been granted only once. In *Sayeedi*, the defence based the application for bail on the fragile health of the accused and his advanced age (70 years). The application was rejected but the Tribunal allowed for hospital treatment and a special diet in accordance with the needs of the accused as a diabetic.[1357] This also occurred in the case of *Azam* in which the defence applied for bail based on the age of the accused (89 years) and his ill-health.[1358] The accused was advised by the doctor to take complete bed rest and he had to use walking sticks and a corset.[1359] The Tribunal rejected the application and held that 'mere old age cannot give protection to people who committed very serious crimes'.[1360] This statement is problematic in the context of the presumption of innocence. However, at the same time, the Tribunal emphasised that the accused's guilt would only be deter-

---

1355 ICT 1, *The Chief Prosecutor v. Azam*, case no. 06/2011, Order no. 34, 18 June 2012, para. 27.
1356 ICT 1, *The Chief Prosecutor v. Azam*, case no. 06/2011, Order no. 34, 18 June 2012, para. 28.
1357 ICT 1, *The Chief Prosecutor v. Sayeedi*, case no. 01/2011, Order no. 20, 20 April 2011, pp. 2–3.
1358 ICT 1, *The Chief Prosecutor v. Azam*, case no. 06/2011, Order no. 5, 11 January 2012, p. 2.
1359 ICT 1, *The Chief Prosecutor v. Azam*, case no. 06/2011, Order no. 5, 11 January 2012, p. 2.
1360 ICT 1, *The Chief Prosecutor v. Azam*, case no. 06/2011, Order no. 5, 11 January 2012, p. 3.

mined after trial and relied on the nature of the crimes to justify the rejection of the application for bail.[1361] The defence's renewed application for bail at a later stage was likewise rejected.[1362] The Tribunal conceded that the gravity of the offence alone is not sufficient reason to deny bail but still found that there were reasonable grounds to believe that the accused was actually guilty of the respective crimes.[1363] In the same case, another application for temporary bail was filed for the month of Ramadan to enable the accused to spend the festive season with his family.[1364] The application was rejected based on the obvious reason that Ramadan is not a ground for bail.[1365] Likewise, in Chowdhury, an application for bail in order for the accused to attend a session of Parliament was dismissed.[1366]

In none of the cases did the Tribunal apply universally recognised criteria for pre-trial detention, such as risk of flight, risk of threats or harm to witnesses or risk of tampering with evidence. On the contrary, no criteria for bail were determined in the Tribunal's decisions. The reasoning of the Tribunal in fact shows that it applies denial of bail as a general rule and that it is for the defence to show exceptional circumstances that would allow the accused to be released on bail.

Only in the case of *Alim* was conditional bail granted during the pre-trial phase as well as during trial.[1367] A condition for the release on bail was that the accused would submit his passport and that he would stay at the address provided in the bail application.[1368] He was also impeded from making any public statements to the media.[1369] The Tribunal based its decision on the ill-health of the accused and the fact that he was not able to move without a wheelchair.[1370] The conditional bail was revoked shortly before the delivery of the judgment due to safety reasons[1371] because of the frequent

---

1361 ICT 1, *The Chief Prosecutor v. Azam*, case no. 06/2011, Order no. 5, 11 January 2012, p. 4.
1362 ICT 1, *The Chief Prosecutor v. Azam*, case no. 06/2011, Order no. 13, 23 February 2012.
1363 ICT 1, *The Chief Prosecutor v. Azam*, case no. 06/2011, Order no. 13, 23 February 2012, p. 10.
1364 ICT 1, *The Chief Prosecutor v. Azam*, case no. 06/2011, Order no. 42, 18 July 2012, p. 1.
1365 ICT 1, *The Chief Prosecutor v. Azam*, case no. 06/2011, Order no. 42, 18 July 2012, p. 3.
1366 ICT 1, *The Chief Prosecutor v. Chowdhury*, case no. 02/2011, Order no. 125, 30 January 2013, pp. 1–2.
1367 ICT 2, *The Chief Prosecutor v. Alim*, case no. 01/2012, Judgment, 9 October 2013, para. 15. For the pre-trial phase, see ICT, *The Chief Prosecutor v. Alim*, misc. case no. 01/2011, Order no. 4, 31 March 2011, p. 2.
1368 ICT 2, *The Chief Prosecutor v. Alim*, case no. 01/2012, Order no. 7, 3 May 2012, p. 2.
1369 ICT 2, *The Chief Prosecutor v. Alim*, case no. 01/2012, Order no. 7, 3 May 2012, p. 3.
1370 ICT 2, *The Chief Prosecutor v. Alim*, case no. 01/2012, Order no. 7, 3 May 2012, p. 2.
1371 ICT 2, *The Chief Prosecutor v. Alim*, case no. 01/2012, Order no. 166, 22 September 2013, para. 8.

violent riots that take place on the occasion of judgments which would impede the accused from appearing in court.[1372]

Immediately after the decision to set up the ICT, several suspects were arrested. The United Nations Working Group on Arbitrary Detention found that Islam, Azam and Ali were detained arbitrarily and in violation of their rights under Section 9(3) of the ICCPR.[1373] However, the government of Bangladesh did not respond to these allegations.[1374] The Working Group found that the denial of bail in these three cases was mainly based on the gravity of the crimes and, with reference to the findings of the European Court of Human Rights (ECHR), it held that the seriousness of the offences could be relevant and sufficient only provided that there were facts that showed that a release would prejudice public order.[1375] The Working Group further found that, in the relevant cases, the burden of proof that normally lies with the prosecution was shifted to the accused to show exceptional circumstances that would justify the conditional release.[1376] As a consequence, pre-trial detention was treated as a rule and not, as determined under Article 9(3) of the ICCPR, an exception.[1377] This is also reflected in the above-cited jurisprudence of the Tribunal. The Working Group determined that an appropriate remedy would be the reconsideration of the bail applications in accordance with international human rights law.[1378] However, neither the RoP nor the ICT Act have been revised accordingly.

The ICT Act and the RoP do not recognise a right to compensation in the case of unlawful arrest and detention as stipulated by Article 9(5) of the ICCPR. As outlined above, Bangladesh acceded to the ICCPR with a reservation on Article 9(5) because the domestic law, in general, does not recognise a right to compensation. Therefore, the shortcomings of the ICT Act in this regard reflect general domestic law.

Section 25 of the ICT Act determines that no suit, prosecution or other legal proceeding shall lie against the government or any person for anything, in good faith,

---

1372 ICT 2, *The Chief Prosecutor v. Alim*, case no. 01/2012, Order no. 166, 22 September 2013, paras. 6, 7.
1373 General Assembly, Opinions Adopted by the Working Group on Arbitrary Detention at its Sixty-Fifth Session, 16 January 2013 (UN Doc. A/HRC/WGAD/2012/66).
1374 General Assembly, Opinions Adopted by the Working Group on Arbitrary Detention at its Sixty-Fifth Session, 16 January 2013, para. 43 (UN Doc. A/HRC/WGAD/2012/66).
1375 General Assembly, Opinions Adopted by the Working Group on Arbitrary Detention at its Sixty-Fifth Session, 16 January 2013, para. 48 (UN Doc. A/HRC/WGAD/2012/66).
1376 General Assembly, Opinions Adopted by the Working Group on Arbitrary Detention at its Sixty-Fifth Session, 16 January 2013, para. 51 (UN Doc. A/HRC/WGAD/2012/66).
1377 General Assembly, Opinions Adopted by the Working Group on Arbitrary Detention at its Sixty-Fifth Session, 16 January 2013, paras. 51, 52 (UN Doc. A/HRC/WGAD/2012/66).
1378 General Assembly, Opinions Adopted by the Working Group on Arbitrary Detention at its Sixty-Fifth Session, 16 January 2013, para. 59 (UN Doc. A/HRC/WGAD/2012/66).

done or purporting to have been done under this Act and excludes, inter alia, the possibility to challenge the lawfulness of arrest or detention as established in Article 9(4) of the ICCPR.[1379] While Rule 26(3) of the RoP allows the Tribunal, on its own motion or on the application of either party, to review its orders and thus also its orders related to detention, this provision does not establish a right but rather a discretionary power of the Tribunal because the provision reads 'may[1380] review'. Beyond that, it is for the Tribunal itself to reconsider its orders and there is no right to review by a higher court.

The ICT Act and the RoP also do not establish any rules on the detention itself. To that effect, the Appellate Division ruled that the Jail Code is applicable inasmuch as the ICT Act is silent about the confinement and treatment of prisoners.[1381]

4.3 Right not to be compelled to incriminate oneself or to confess guilt and to remain silent

The right not to be compelled to testify against oneself or to confess guilt is enshrined in Article 14(3)(g) of the ICCPR. This provision prohibits direct or indirect physical or undue psychological pressure from the investigating authorities on the accused, aimed at obtaining a confession of guilt.[1382]

Article 35(4) of the Constitution of Bangladesh also determines that no person shall be compelled to be a witness against himself. According to Islam, Article 35(4) comprises also the right to remain silent, which applies from the moment a person is considered accused and is not restricted to court proceedings.[1383] Article 35(5) of the Constitution stipulates that no person shall be subjected to torture or to cruel, inhuman or degrading punishment or treatment.

A provision that prohibits torture is contained only in Rule 16(2) which clarifies that 'no person during investigation under the Act shall be subjected to any form of coercion, duress or threat of any kind'. Given that the prohibition of torture is not a matter to be regulated by the Tribunal, this provision should be part of the ICT Act. Torture is widespread in Bangladesh and, despite the enactment of the Torture and Custodial Death (Prevention) Act, prosecution of torture remains the exception.

The right to remain silent applies when there are grounds for believing that the person has committed a crime within the jurisdiction of the court, whereas, at an earlier stage of the investigation, there is a general right not to be compelled to incrimi-

---

1379 *Linton*, CLF, 2010, 21(2), p. 191, at 306.
1380 My emphasis.
1381 SC (AD), *Molla v. The Chief Prosecutor*, Review Judgment, 12 December 2013, p. 52.
1382 Human Rights Committee, General Comment No. 32, Article 14, 23 August 2007, para. 41 (UN Doc. CCPR/C/GC/32).
1383 *Islam*, Constitutional Law, 3. edn, p. 304.

nate oneself.[1384] The Statutes of the international criminal tribunals as well as the Rome Statute recognise such a right. The Rome Statute explicitly distinguishes in Article 55 between those rights that apply to any person during investigation and those that apply when there are grounds to believe that the person actually committed the crimes. In the latter case, the person has a right to remain silent without such silence being a consideration in the determination of guilt or innocence (Article 55(2)(c)). A major problem with the ICT Act is that it is does not establish a point of time when a person is considered as accused and thus has a right to remain silent. The ICT Act in fact does not establish a right to remain silent at all.

Pursuant to Rule 43(7) of the RoP, 'no accused shall be compelled to testify against his will or to confess his guilt'. Although Rule 43 determines several rights of the accused, most of them refer to the trial stage and it is ultimately unclear whether Rule 43(7) refers to the investigation stage as well. As outlined above, the Tribunal found that this provision incorporates the *nemo tenetur* principle.

The practice, however, suggests that during the investigation phase there is an obligation to testify, even for the accused. Rule 16(1) allows the Investigation Officer to 'apply through the Prosecutor to the Tribunal to commit the arrested person(s) in his custody for the purpose of interrogation' for up to three days. This does not require the consent of the accused and, even if he decides to remain silent, he can be subjected to a three-day interrogation. Although Rule 16(2) determines that no person during investigation shall be subjected to any coercion, duress or threat, the absence of an explicit right to silence jeopardises the accused.

Interrogations under Rule 16(1) have been granted by the Tribunal on a regular basis. During these interrogations, the defence counsel is not allowed to be present but has to remain in an adjacent room and can be consulted by the accused only during breaks and after the interrogation.[1385] In the cases of *Molla* and *Kamaruzzaman*, the Investigation Agency made use of this right to apply for interrogation arguing that, unless the accused was interrogated, the entire investigation would be incomplete and defective.[1386] At this stage, the accused were already in pre-trial detention and thus clearly had to be considered as accused. The Tribunal granted the interrogation under some conditions and ordered the defence counsel to be informed at least 48 hours prior to the interrogations and to be allowed to be present in the adjacent room along-

---

1384 *Zappalà*, Human Rights in International Criminal Proceedings, p. 77.
1385 ICT 1, *The Chief Prosecutor v. Nizami*, case no. 03/2011, Judgment, 29 October 2014, para 49.
1386 ICT, *The Chief Prosecutor v. Kamaruzzaman & Molla*, misc. case no. 01/2010 (pre-trial), Order no. 23, 1 June 2011, p. 2. See also: ICT, *The Chief Prosecutor v. Nizami & Mujahid*, misc. case no. 01/2010 (pre-trial), Order no. 9, 5 April 2011.

side a doctor.[1387] It also held that the Investigation Officer 'shall not put any pressure or threat upon the accused at the time of interrogation'[1388] and emphasised that the Investigation Agency was clearly bound by Rule 16 of the RoP.[1389] The interrogation was allowed for an entire day from 10am to 5pm with a one-hour break in between.[1390] If an accused wants to make use of his right to remain silent, he nevertheless has to undergo interrogation for the determined period of time and without the right for his lawyer to be present. There are neither further rules on the conduct of these interrogations nor a provision that obligates the Investigation Officer to record them. On the contrary, Section 8(6) of the ICT Act determines that the Investigation Officer may record in writing any statement made to him during investigation but there is no obligation to record statements. As a result, there is no requirement of verification of the statement either by the accused or his counsel,[1391] and these long interrogations remain entirely undocumented.

In addition, a right to silence during the pre-trial phase is not enshrined in the ICT Act. Section 8(4) allows the Investigation Officer to examine orally any person 'acquainted with the facts and circumstances of the case', whereas sub-section (5) imposes a general duty upon such person to answer all questions, even if the answer incriminates the person, but no such answer shall subject the person to arrest or detention and it shall not be used against the person in trial. The provision fails to differentiate between witnesses and persons against whom there are sufficient grounds to believe that they have actually committed the crime.

Further problems arise with regard to confessions of the accused. Section 14(1) allows any magistrate of the first class to record a confession of an accused person at any time during investigation or before the commencement of the trial. Pursuant to Section 14(2), the magistrate has to inform the person beforehand that he is not compelled to make a confession and that, if he makes one, it can be used as evidence against him. This provision is the only one that establishes a duty to inform the accused about his rights, but this duty clearly has to exist independently of the express wish to make a confession. The magistrate shall only record the confession if, upon questioning the accused, he has reason to believe that it was not made voluntarily. Yet, there is no provision that the magistrate shall investigate if he considers the confession

---

1387 ICT, *The Chief Prosecutor v. Kamaruzzaman & Molla*, misc. case no. 01/2010 (pre-trial), Order no. 23, 1 June 2011, p. 3.
1388 ICT, *The Chief Prosecutor v. Kamaruzzaman & Molla*, misc. case no. 01/2010 (pre-trial), Order no. 23, 1 June 2011, p. 3.
1389 ICT, *The Chief Prosecutor v. Kamaruzzaman & Molla*, misc. case no. 01/2010 (pre-trial), Order no. 23, 1 June 2011, p. 3.
1390 ICT, *The Chief Prosecutor v. Kamaruzzaman & Molla*, misc. case no. 01/2010 (pre-trial), Order no. 23, 1 June 2011, p. 3.
1391 *Linton*, CLF, 2010, 21(2), p. 191, at 298.

coerced.[1392] Beyond that, it is only in the RoP that a right to have a defence counsel present is provided for (Rule 24(1A)).

The right to remain silent during trial is significantly curtailed in the ICT Act. Section 11(2) determines that the Tribunal may, 'at any stage of the trial without previously warning the accused person, put such questions to him as the Tribunal considers necessary'. Although the provision clarifies that the accused 'shall not render himself liable to punishment by refusing to answer such questions or by giving false answers to them', the Tribunal may explicitly 'draw such inference from such refusal or answers as it thinks just'. This provision clearly abrogates the right to remain silent and endangers the presumption of innocence. Linton correctly holds that this provision 'must not be allowed to stand'.[1393] However, this provision stems from ordinary domestic criminal law. Likewise, Section 342 of the Code of Criminal Procedure allows unscheduled interrogations of the accused during criminal trials, whereas sub-section (2) clarifies that the accused shall not be punished if he refuses to answer the question or if he gives false answers, but that the court may draw inference from the refusal or the answers. The problem is thus not merely related to the ICT Act but rather to the domestic law of Bangladesh in general. Section 11(2) is also in conflict with Rule 43(7) of the RoP which determines that 'no accused shall be compelled to testify against his will or to confess his guilt'. Yet, since the ICT Act has prevalence over the RoP, Rule 43(7) does not have a binding effect.

4.4 Presumption of innocence

The presumption of innocence of the accused is a fundamental procedural guarantee established in Article 14(2) of the ICCPR. This guarantee imposes the burden of proving the charge on the prosecution, establishes the requirement of charges being proven beyond reasonable doubt in order to determine guilt and the right of the accused to be treated in accordance with this principle.[1394]

The ICT Act does not enshrine the presumption of innocence. This is clearly due to the absence of an express presumption of innocence in the IMT Charter. Nevertheless, also, in the course of the amendments, this deficit has not been redressed, but the presumption of innocence was merely inserted in Rule 43(2) of the RoP.

Rule 50 determines that the burden of proof shall lie upon the prosecution beyond reasonable doubt. Several other rules, however, diverge from this general principle. Problems arise with regard to Rule 51(1) which determines that the onus of proof of

---

1392 *Linton*, CLF, 2010, 21(2), p. 191, at 295.
1393 *Linton*, CLF, 2010, 21(2), p. 191, at 301.
1394 Human Rights Committee, General Comment No. 32, Article 14, 23 August 2007, para. 30 (UN Doc. CCPR/C/GC/32).

an alibi plea is upon the defence, whereas Rule 51(3) clarifies that the failure to prove the alibi plea shall not render the accused guilty. This reversal of the burden of proof is problematic and runs counter to international as well as common law.[1395] Nevertheless, it has been applied by the Tribunal in all cases in which the plea of alibi has been raised.[1396] Yet, also, this provision of the RoP incorporates domestic law as enshrined in the Evidence Act, 1872.[1397]

> *Section 103 of the Evidence Act, 1872: Burden of proof as to a particular fact*
> The burden of proof as to any particular fact lies on that person who wishes the Court to believe in its existence, unless it is provided by any law that the proof of that fact shall lie on any particular person.
> *Illustration*
> (a) A prosecutes B for theft, and wishes the Court to believe that B admitted to the theft to C. A must prove the admission.
> B wishes the Court to believe that, at the time in question, he was elsewhere. He must prove it.

Another problem lies in the standard of proof applied to the plea of alibi. The Tribunal affirmed in several judgments that the plea of alibi has to be proved by the defence 'with absolute certainty',[1398] which requires even more than beyond reasonable doubt. The ICTR clarified that the accused does not have to prove the alibi beyond reasonable doubt but that he must merely present evidence 'tending to show that he was not present at the time of the alleged crime'[1399] or that is 'likely to raise a reasonable doubt in the prosecution case'[1400]. The alibi has to be accepted if it is 'reasonably possibly true',[1401] whereas the prosecution has to prove beyond reasonable doubt that the alleged facts are true despite the alibi.[1402]

1395 *Robertson*, Report on the ICT Bangladesh, p. 111.
1396 See, for instance, ICT 2, *The Chief Prosecutor v. Molla*, case no. 02/2012, Judgment, 5 February 2013, para. 408; ICT 1, *The Chief Prosecutor v. Chowdhury*, case no. 02/2011, Judgment, 1 October 2013, para. 247. This has been confirmed by the Appellate Division in: SC (AD), *Molla v. The Chief Prosecutor*, Appeal Judgment, 17 September 2013, p. 234.
1397 Act no. I of 1872.
1398 ICT 2, *The Chief Prosecutor v. Ali*, case no. 03/2013, Judgment, 2 November 2014, para. 698. ICT 2, *The Chief Prosecutor v. Molla*, case no. 02/2012, Judgment, 5 February 2013, para. 408.
1399 ICTR (AC), *Prosecutor v. Musema*, Appeal Judgment, 16 November 2001, para. 202.
1400 ICTR (AC), *Prosecutor v. Karera*, Appeal Judgment, 02 February 2009, para. 330; ICTR (AC), *Prosecutor v. Simba*, Appeal Judgment, 27 November 2007, para. 184.
1401 ICTR (AC), *Prosecutor v. Nahimana et al.*, Appeal Judgment, 28 November 2007, para. 414; ICTR (AC), *Prosecutor v. Kamuhanda*, Appeal Judgment, 19 September 2005, para. 38.
1402 ICTR (AC), *Prosecutor v. Zigiranyirazo*, Appeal Judgment, 16 November 2009, para. 18; ICTR (AC), *Prosecutor v. Karera*, Appeal Judgment, 2 February 2009, para. 330; ICTR (AC), *Prosecutor v. Nahimana et al.*, Appeal Judgment, 16 May 2008, para. 414.

The burden of proof of the prosecution has also been weakened through excessive use of judicial notice. Section 19(4) of the ICT Act determines that the Tribunal does not need to prove facts of common knowledge but it shall take judicial notice thereof. In practice, Section 19(4) of the ICT Act has been applied extensively. In several cases, the Tribunal took judicial notice of the historical background outlined in the judgments and considered it a fact of common knowledge that genocide and crimes against humanity were committed during the Liberation War.[1403] It also considered it a fact of common knowledge that the Liberation War was an attack, that there was a policy and plan to commit genocide and that the Razakars and Al-Badr were formed by the Pakistani army in order to commit atrocities in furtherance of the Pakistani army's plans and policy.[1404] With regard to all of these 'facts of common knowledge', the prosecution was exempted from its burden of proof, and beyond that, the defence was impeded from challenging it. As Robertson rightly points out, all of these facts have to be proved during a criminal trial.[1405]

The presumption of innocence is also affected by the guilty plea procedure. Section 10(1)(c) of the ICT Act determines that, in the case of a guilty plea, the Tribunal may, at its discretion, convict the accused. Considering that the ICT Act establishes the death penalty as the normal punishment for crimes under Section 3(2), the guilty plea procedure is highly problematic. Although the Tribunal is not compelled to convict the accused, the law does not establish criteria that must be fulfilled for the Tribunal to follow the guilty plea procedure.

The Rome Statute determines three requirements in the case of admissions of guilt: the accused must understand the nature and consequences of the admission of guilt; the admission of guilt must be made voluntarily after sufficient consultation with the defence counsel; the admission of guilt is supported by the facts of the case.[1406] The ICT Act and the RoP are silent on this issue but these criteria should definitely be applied by the Tribunal as well. However, none of the accused has pleaded guilty before the Tribunal.

1403 See, for instance, ICT 1, *The Chief Prosecutor v. Azam*, case no. 06/2011, Judgment, 15 July 2013, para. 91; ICT 1, *The Chief Prosecutor v. Chowdhury*, case no. 02/2011, Judgment, 1 October 2013, para. 46.
1404 See, for instance, ICT 1, *The Chief Prosecutor v. Azam*, case no. 06/2011, Judgment, 15 July 2013, para. 43; ICT 1, *The Chief Prosecutor v. Chowdhury*, case no. 02/2011, Judgment, 1 October 2013, para. 46; ICT 2, *The Chief Prosecutor v. Ali*, case no. 03/2013, Judgment, 2 November 2014, paras. 10, 567.
1405 *Robertson*, Report on the ICT Bangladesh, 2015, p. 113.
1406 Article 65(1) of the Rome Statute.

Part IV: Compliance of the ICT Act, the Rules of Procedure and the ICT's jurisprudence

The presumption of innocence also becomes relevant for the media, which should avoid coverage that undermines the presumption of innocence.[1407] With regard to the international criminal tribunals, Zappalà argues that they mainly circulate documents of the prosecution and thereby contribute to a one-sided portrayal.[1408] In the context of the ICT, this becomes highly relevant because the Tribunal itself has exerted direct influence on the media through contempt proceedings and thereby impeded a critical portrayal of the trials. This has led to one-sided media coverage of the proceedings in favour of the prosecution and critical views on the proceedings that would, at the same time, represent the interests of the accused being banned.

Section 11(4) of the ICT Act gives the Tribunal the power to punish a person 'who obstructs or abuses its process or disobeys any of its orders or directions, or does anything which tends to prejudice the case of a party before it, or tends to bring it or any of its members into hatred or contempt, or does anything which constitutes contempt of the Tribunal' with imprisonment of up to one year or with a fine. Rule 45 of the RoP repeats the wording of this Section but adds that the Tribunal may initiate proceedings against such person. Rule 46(1) allows the Tribunal to convict and punish the person after hearing the person and considering the explanation. In the case of *Bergman*, the proceedings were initiated through an application filed by a third party and the Tribunal argued that it is not only the prosecution, the defence and the Investigation Agency that have the right to bring contemptuous behaviour to the Tribunal's notice but also any third party because neither the ICT Act nor the RoP explicitly prohibit this.[1409]

The ICT has made excessive use of contempt proceedings. To date, in none of the cases has a higher punishment than three months of imprisonment been imposed.[1410] Nevertheless, the possibility to impose a year of imprisonment is clearly problematic if one considers the absence of a right to appeal against contempt orders under the ICT Act.[1411] There are also no provisions that further determine the proceedings and Section 11(4) gives the Tribunal the power to decide on the case merely after an explanation from the contemnor.

Contempt proceedings also exist before international criminal tribunals. Nevertheless, the situations leading to contempt are clearly defined and have no similarities with the cases that were considered contempt before the ICT. For instance, Rule 77 of

---

1407 *Human Rights Committee*, General Comment No. 32, Article 14, 23 August 2007, para. 30 (UN Doc CCPR/C/GC/32).
1408 *Zappalà*, Human Rights in International Criminal Proceedings, p. 85, fn. 13.
1409 ICT 2, *Azad v. Bergman*, misc. case no. 01/2014, Order, 2 December 2014, para 30.
1410 In ICT 2, *The Chief Prosecutor v. Selim Uddin et al.*, misc. case no. 04/2013, Order, 9 June 2013, p. 18, three months of imprisonment were imposed. However, this case was not related to media coverage.
1411 As will be outlined below, the High Court Division ruled that a right to appeal against contempt orders must be granted under the ICT Act.

the Rules of Procedure and Evidence of the ICTY defines contempt as wilful interference with the administration of justice and contains a list of acts that amount to contempt of the Tribunal.

The ICT Act and the RoP, on the other hand, leave it entirely up to the Tribunal to define contempt. The Tribunal relied on domestic jurisprudence for the interpretation of 'contempt'.[1412] According to the Appellate Division of the Supreme Court, contempt can consist of 'any conduct that brings [the] authority of the court into disrespect or disregard or undermines its dignity and prestige'.[1413] The Tribunal affirmed in several of its contempt orders that 'fair criticism of the conduct of a Judge may not amount to contempt, if it is made in good faith and in public interest'.[1414] That is, in order to amount to contempt, a statement has to be made with the intention to 'bring down the prestige and authority of Courts'.[1415] At the same time, it was held that the constitutional right to freedom of speech and expression are to be considered.[1416] Apologies from the contemnors in cases in which the contempt is not 'of a very gross nature' have been considered.[1417]

The above-illustrated case against Bergman was probably the most prominent case of contempt proceedings before the ICT. Yet, against several other individuals and organisations contempt proceedings were initiated.

A contempt case was filed against Channel 24 and seven other parties based on comments made by a participant in the talk show 'Muktobaag' broadcast on the channel on 18 September 2013.[1418] In this live talk show, some participants commented on the ongoing trial against Chowdhury.[1419] The criticism was that the accused was deprived of his right to defence because the Tribunal took exception to a witness named

---

1412 ICT 1, *The Chief Prosecutor v. Hossain*, misc. case no. 04/2013, Order, 22 June 2014, p. 8; ICT 1, *The Chief Prosecutor v. Channel 24 et al.*, misc. case no. 02/2013, Order, 4 September 2014, p. 15.
1413 *Moazzem Hossain v. State*, 35 DLR (AD) (1983), pp. 290 ff., at 309.
1414 ICT 1, *The Chief Prosecutor v. Hossain*, misc. case no. 04/2013, Order, 22 June 2014, p. 11. See also: ICT 1, *The Chief Prosecutor v. Channel 24 et al.*, misc. case no. 02/2013, Order, 4 September 2014, p. 40.
1415 ICT 1, *The Chief Prosecutor v. Hossain*, misc. case no. 04/2013, Order, 22 June 2014, p. 20.
1416 ICT 1, *The Chief Prosecutor v. Hossain*, misc. case no. 04/2013, Order, 22 June 2014, p. 16; ICT 1, *The Chief Prosecutor v Human Rights Watch et al.*, misc. case no. 02/2013, Order, 4 September 2014, p. 22.
1417 ICT 1, *The Chief Prosecutor v. Channel 24 et al.*, misc. case no. 03/2013, Order, 12 June 2014, p. 15; ICT 1, *The Chief Prosecutor v. Human Rights Watch et al.*, misc. case no. 02/2013, Order, 4 September 2014, p. 37.
1418 ICT 1, *The Chief Prosecutor v. Channel 24 et al.*, misc. case no. 03/2013, Order, 12 June 2014.
1419 ICT 1, *The Chief Prosecutor v. Chowdhury*, case no. 01/2011, Judgment, 1 October 2013.

by the defence.[1420] The Tribunal ruled that the contemnors deliberately criticised the trials with the intention of undermining people's confidence in the Tribunal and that they tried to tarnish its image by making these statements and by broadcasting them.[1421] The Tribunal accepted the apologies, ordered the contemnors to be more cautious in the future and directed Channel 24 to no longer broadcast the talk show.[1422]

An order of contempt was also passed against the organisation Human Rights Watch and two others[1423] based on a press release entitled 'Bangladesh: Azam Conviction Based on Flawed Proceedings' published on 16 August 2013, a month after the verdict against Azam. The concerns expressed by the organisation encompassed bias among judges and prosecutors, insufficient protection of defence witnesses, lack of evidence to establish guilt beyond reasonable doubt, and changes in the court panel and investigations conducted by judges.[1424] The Tribunal stated that it welcomes constructive criticism from people who have knowledge on the issue as long as the judiciary or authority of the court is not 'disregarded, dishonoured or undermined with its dignity and prestige in any way under criticism in the name of freedom of speech and expression'.[1425] It disposed of the petition with a note in which it expressed its desire that, in future, the contemnor shall be more careful and respectful in commenting on the judicial proceedings before the ICT.[1426]

Although the imposed penalties have been low, the contempt proceedings have sent very clear signals and have contributed to a one-sided portrayal of the trials and silenced the media. The Tribunal's power in this context is highly problematic. Freedom of speech should be restricted within the limits of criminal law and it should not be for the Tribunal itself to decide when it considers its authority questioned.

1420 ICT 1, *The Chief Prosecutor v. Channel 24 et al.*, misc. case no. 03/2013, Order, 26 September 2013, p. 2.
1421 ICT 1, *The Chief Prosecutor v. Channel 24 et al.*, misc. case no. 03/2013, Order, 26 September 2013, p. 3.
1422 ICT 1, *The Chief Prosecutor v. Channel 24 et al.*, misc. case no. 03/2013, Order, 12 June 2014, p. 15.
1423 ICT 1, *The Chief Prosecutor v. Human Rights Watch et al.*, misc. case no. 02/2013, Order, 4 September 2014.
1424 *Human Rights Watch*, Bangladesh: Azam Conviction Based on Flawed Proceedings, 16 August 2013.
1425 ICT 1, *The Chief Prosecutor v. Human Rights Watch et al.*, misc. case no. 02/2013, Order, 4 September 2014, p. 40.
1426 ICT 1, *The Chief Prosecutor v. Human Rights Watch et al.*, misc. case no. 02/2013, Order, 4 September 2014 p. 43.

4.5 Right to be tried by an independent and impartial tribunal

The right to be tried by an independent and impartial tribunal is enshrined in Article 14 of the ICCPR. The concept of independence and impartiality applies to the organisation and structure of a court as well as to the judges in the context of individual cases.[1427] The notion of independence refers to a judge's ability to adjudicate a case without improper influence of the legislature, the executive, the parties or others with interest in the outcome of the process,[1428] whereas impartiality obligates judges to act in an unprejudiced manner.[1429]

The right to be tried by an independent and impartial tribunal is enshrined in Article 35(3) of the Constitution but because of Article 47A this right does not apply to those accused under the ICT Act. Section 6(2A) of the ICT Act merely determines that the Tribunal shall be independent and ensure a fair trial but does not refer to impartiality. Yet, the practical relevance of this provision is doubtful because it evidently runs counter to the Constitution. This raises the question of what the drafters intended to achieve when they inserted Section 6(2A) through the amendment in 2009. Without a parallel constitutional amendment, the provision is pointless. That impartiality is not guaranteed under the ICT Act also becomes clear through Section 6(8) which affirms that neither the constitution of the Tribunal nor the appointment of its chairman or members can be challenged by the accused or the prosecution.

The independence of the judges is at risk of being undermined through the appointment procedure. The judges are appointed by the government. Section 6(2) of the ICT Act determines that any person who is qualified to be a judge or has been a judge of the Supreme Court can be appointed to the ICT. Yet, the Act is silent on the selection procedure and selection criteria. This bears the risk of politically motivated decisions instead of selection based on qualifications. This is particularly problematic if one considers that the ICT is an extremely politically charged issue. On the other hand, the requirement of a qualification as a Supreme Court judge establishes some kind of bar to political arbitrariness. Nevertheless, also, the appointment of judges to the Supreme Court is conducted by the executive and the risk of political influence exists even under ordinary law. The Constitution determines the appointment procedure for Supreme Court judges in Article 95. The president appoints the chief justice on his own and the other judges after consultation with the chief justice. Article 48(3) stipulates that the president shall act on the advice of the prime minister in appointing the judges, with the exception of the chief justice. The office requires a minimum of 10 years practice as an advocate of the Supreme Court or in a judicial office in Bang-

---

1427 *Zappalà*, Human Rights in International Criminal Proceedings, p. 100.
1428 *Linton*, JICJ, 2006, 4(2), p. 327, at 328.
1429 *Linton*, JICJ, 2006, 4(2), p. 327, at 328.

ladesh. However, political considerations are frequent in the appointment of judges of the Supreme Court.[1430] Beyond that, the law does not establish any specific selection criteria for Supreme Court judges and there is no judicial commission for their appointment.[1431]

The immense political and social pressure the office of the judges at the ICT is exposed to hampers independent and impartial work. The Shahbag protests have unmistakably shown the expectations of large parts of society. Whether the fact that the Appellate Division commuted Molla's life sentence to a death sentence was a reaction to the demands of the Shahbag movement or to pressure from the government cannot be stated with certainty, but it also cannot be excluded that, in imposing the death penalty, the judges yielded to these pressures.

Several cases indeed raise serious doubts about the impartiality of the Tribunal. This issue has been discussed at length in the case of *Sayeedi* with respect to Judge Nizamul Huq, former chairman of Tribunal 1. As outlined above, Huq was a member of the Secretariat of the People's Inquiry Commission in 1994, which had issued an investigative report about the accused's role during the Liberation War. The defence argued that Huq's involvement in the investigation rendered him biased.[1432]

In the absence of a specific provision that allows for a bias petition, the defence filed a petition for his recusal based on bias under Rule 46A of the RoP. This provision allows the Tribunal to make such orders that it considers necessary to meet the ends of justice. The defence based its arguments inter alia on Article 14 of the ICCPR.[1433] The application was rejected because the law related to the ICT does not contain a provision for recusal.[1434] The Tribunal further held that there were no grounds for bias. It stated that Huq was merely a member of the Secretariat of the Commission but that he was not involved in the drafting of the report.[1435]

The Tribunal also discussed the case of Judge Winter of the SCSL in this context.[1436] Winter directly reviewed and approved a UNICEF report on international

---

1430 *Hoque*, in: *Yeh* (ed.), Asian Courts, p. 447, at 464–465.
1431 *Hoque*, in: *Yeh* (ed.), Asian Courts, p. 447, at 466.
1432 ICT 1, *The Chief Prosecutor v. Sayeedi*, case no. 01/2011, Order no. 36, 28 November 2011, para. 4.
1433 ICT 1, *The Chief Prosecutor v. Sayeedi*, case no. 01/2011, Order no. 36, 28 November 2011, para. 10.
1434 ICT 1, *The Chief Prosecutor v. Sayeedi*, case no. 01/2011, Order no. 36, 28 November 2011, para. 10.
1435 ICT 1, *The Chief Prosecutor v. Sayeedi*, case no. 01/2011, Order no. 36, 28 November 2011, para. 63. The same reasons were reiterated in ICT 1, *The Chief Prosecutor v. Azam*, case no. 06/2011, Order no. 33, 18 June 2012.
1436 ICT 1, *The Chief Prosecutor v. Sayeedi*, case no. 01/2011, Order no. 36, 28 November 2011, paras. 55–60.

criminal justice and children but she was not found to be biased in the context of a motion on child soldiers.[1437] The Tribunal held that Judge Huq's involvement in the report of the Commission was to a lesser extent than in the case of Winter.[1438] Yet, this finding of the Tribunal overlooked a significant difference between the case of Huq and that of Winter which was that Huq's investigation was directly related to the accused and not merely to the Liberation War. While mere activities related to the subject matter of a case are not sufficient grounds for bias, the involvement in activities related to the person of the accused certainly are.[1439]

Impartiality and independence have also been challenged based on the Skype conversations between Huq and the Belgium-based Bangladeshi lawyer Ahmed Ziauddin. The defence applied for retrial in the cases of *Sayeedi*, *Nizami* and *Azam*.[1440] Huq, in the meantime, had withdrawn from his post and been replaced by a member of Tribunal 2, but the proceedings were taken up at the same stage. The defence argued that the Skype conversations revealed that the charge framing order was drafted by Ziauddin and that Huq was extensively advised by him even in the final decision.[1441] The Tribunal countered that the evidence on which the defence based its allegations of collusion between judges, prosecution and activists were obtained illegally and were therefore inadmissible.[1442] It further argued that these allegations concerned only one judge but that there were three judges involved in the proceedings and the decisions were taken by the majority.[1443] The latter argument is clearly untenable because every judge has to be impartial and independent, not only the majority of a tri-

---

1437 SCSL (AC), *Prosecutor v. Norman*, Decision on the Motion to Recuse Judge Winter from the Deliberation in the Preliminary Motion on the Recruitment of Child Soldiers, 28 May 2004.
1438 ICT 1, *The Chief Prosecutor v. Sayeedi*, case no. 01/2011, Order no. 36, 28 November 2011, para. 63.
1439 *Sluiter et al.*, International Criminal Procedure, pp. 782–783.
1440 ICT 1, *The Chief Prosecutor v. Sayeedi*, case no. 01/2011, Order no. 230, 1 January 2013; ICT 1, *The Chief Prosecutor v. Nizami*, case no. 03/2011, Order no. 65, 3 January 2013; ICT 1, *The Chief Prosecutor v. Azam*, case no. 06/2011, Order no. 123, 3 January 2013.
1441 ICT 1, *The Chief Prosecutor v. Sayeedi*, case no. 01/2011, Order no. 230, 1 January 2013, p. 2; ICT 1, *The Chief Prosecutor v. Azam*, case no. 06/2011, Order no. 123, 3 January 2013, p. 2; ICT 1, *The Chief Prosecutor v. Nizami*, case no. 03/2011, Order no. 65, 3 January 2013, p. 2.
1442 ICT 1, *The Chief Prosecutor v. Sayeedi*, case no. 01/2011, Order no. 230, 1 January 2013, p. 4; ICT 1, *The Chief Prosecutor v. Azam*, case no. 06/2011, Order no. 123, 3 January 2013, p. 4; ICT 1, *The Chief Prosecutor v. Nizami*, case no. 03/2011, Order no. 65, 3 January 2013, p. 4.
1443 ICT 1, *The Chief Prosecutor v. Sayeedi*, case no. 01/2011, Order no. 230, 1 January 2013, p. 5; ICT 1, *The Chief Prosecutor v. Azam*, case no. 06/2011, Order no. 123, 3 January 2013, p. 5.

bunal. The application for retrial was finally also rejected because the ICT Act does not establish retrial as a remedy.[1444] The Tribunal invoked Section 6(6) of the ICT Act to argue that, in case of any change in membership, the Tribunal can proceed from the same stage of the case.[1445]

Another application was filed to exclude prosecutor Zead-Al-Malum from the prosecution based on bias.[1446] Al-Malum was also involved in the Skype conversations with Huq and the defence argued that the decisions made by Huq were, to a great extent, influenced by the prosecution and lacked impartiality.[1447] The Tribunal rejected the application, arguing that the power to appoint prosecutors lies exclusively with the government.[1448]

The question of impartiality also arises with regard to the personal experiences of the judges and their families during the Liberation War. Judicial independence requires judges to set aside their personal memories and their personal perceptions of the war throughout the entire process. This is a difficult task if one considers the strong patriotism and the emotional historical narrative prevailing in Bangladesh. The entire issue of the Liberation War is charged with emotion. The fact that the Awami League is, at present, the ruling party and that the prime minister is the daughter of Sheikh Mujibur Rahman contribute to the emotional, uncritical and heroic portrayal of the Liberation War. The fact that the *Sayeedi* judgment was delivered on 16 December 2012, Victory Day, indicates the determination of the government to put convictions on show[1449] and further contributes to the emotional perception of the trials in society.

The emotional involvement of the judges is apparent in several judgments. In some judgments, the drafters employ emotionally loaded language that gives the impression that they themselves or their families were direct victims of the respective crimes. In *Uddin et al.*, the Tribunal commented on the committed crimes as follows:

1444 ICT 1, *The Chief Prosecutor v. Sayeedi*, case no. 01/2011, Order no. 230, 1 January 2013, p. 5; ICT 1, *The Chief Prosecutor v. Azam*, case no. 06/2011, Order no. 123, 3 January 2013, p. 5; ICT 1, *The Chief Prosecutor v. Nizami*, case no. 03/2011, Order no. 65, 3 January 2013, p. 5.
1445 ICT 1, *The Chief Prosecutor v. Sayeedi*, case no. 01/2011, Order no. 230, 1 January 2013, p. 5; ICT 1, *The Chief Prosecutor v. Azam*, case no. 06/2011, Order no. 123, 3 January 2013, p. 5; ICT 1, *The Chief Prosecutor v. Nizami*, case no. 03/2011, Order no. 65, 3 January 2013, p. 5.
1446 ICT 1, *The Chief Prosecutor v. Azam*, case no. 06/2011, Order no. 133, 20 January 2013, p. 1.
1447 ICT 1, *The Chief Prosecutor v. Azam*, case no. 06/2011, Order no. 133, 20 January 2013, p. 2.
1448 ICT 1, *The Chief Prosecutor v. Azam*, case no. 06/2011, Order no. 133, 20 January 2013, pp. 4–5.
1449 *Robertson*, Report on the ICT Bangladesh, p. 63.

> What an impious butchery! What a sacrilegious butchery! What a shame for human civilization! Selina Parveen was a mother. The appalling attack was done not only to Selina Parveen but to the mother's line. The killing was rather a "matricide". This indescribable brutality shocks the human conscience indeed.[1450]

In the same judgment, the Tribunal noted that one of the accused fled abroad and commented in the following way: 'What a shame! What a shame! This fact indubitably shakes and debases the nation.'[1451]

The Tribunal also frequently refers to the feelings of the nation in its reasoning:

> We believe too that the nation feels ashamed as it could not bring the notorious perpetrators to book during [the] last four decades for healing the relentless wound it sustained caused by the beastly act of [the] systematic liquidation of eminent sons and daughters of the soil. The event of calculated killing of intellectuals in 1971 will ever torment the Bengali nation.[1452]

While these cited passages from the judgments already show the emotional approach of the judges, in some judgments the impartiality of the judges really has to be questioned. The emotional comments reach the extent of directly insulting the accused. In *Qaiser*, the Tribunal called the accused a 'perverted man'[1453] in the context of examining a charge of rape. The Tribunal continued by stating that 'it is hard to believe that the accused was a Bengali Muslim'.[1454] Later on, it again held that it failed to understand 'how the accused Qaiser being a Bengali Muslim actively aided, abetted and facilitated the commission of such beastly physical invasion upon the women which was worse than murder'.[1455] In *Sobhan*, the Tribunal commented on the crimes committed by the accused as follows: 'What a brutality! It is hard to believe indeed that the accused was a man of slightest humanity and kindness.'[1456]

Insulting passages can also be found in the judgments of the Appellate Division. In *Kamaruzzaman*, the Appellate Division held that it found no difference between the conduct of a man and a beast considering the perpetration of the crimes and thus indi-

---

1450 ICT 2, *The Chief Prosecutor v. Uddin et al.*, case no. 01/2013, Judgment, 3 November 2013, para. 316.
1451 ICT 2, *The Chief Prosecutor v. Uddin et al.*, case no. 01/2013, Judgment, 3 November 2013, para. 418.
1452 ICT 2, *The Chief Prosecutor v. Uddin et al.*, case no. 01/2013, Judgment, 3 November 2013, para. 446.
1453 ICT 2, *The Chief Prosecutor v. Qaiser*, case no. 04/2013, Judgment, 23 December 2014, para. 473.
1454 ICT 2, *The Chief Prosecutor v. Qaiser*, case no. 04/2013, Judgment, 23 December 2014, para. 473.
1455 ICT 2, *The Chief Prosecutor v. Qaiser*, case no. 04/2013, Judgment, 23 December 2014, para. 996.
1456 ICT 2, *The Chief Prosecutor v. Sobhan*, case no. 01/2014, Judgment, 18 February 2015, para. 584.

Part IV: Compliance of the ICT Act, the Rules of Procedure and the ICT's jurisprudence

rectly termed the accused a beast.[1457] Justice Choudhury, in his dissenting opinion, referred to the accused as a 'human monster'.[1458] These examples raise severe doubts about the ability of the judges to act impartially and to set their emotions aside during the proceedings before the Tribunal.

4.6 Right to be tried without undue delay

Article 14(3)(c) of the ICCPR establishes the right to be tried without undue delay. The ICT Act also refers to expeditious proceedings in several provisions. Section 11(3)(a) determines that the Tribunal shall confine the trial to an expeditious hearing of the issues raised by the charges, and Section 11(3)(b) allows the Tribunal to take measures to ensure an expeditious trial and to rule out irrelevant issues and statements. Section 19(1) of the ICT Act clarifies that the principle of an expeditious trial shall also govern the rules of evidence. Rule 43(5) affirms that the accused shall be tried without undue delay, whereas Rule 53(3) allows the Tribunal to regulate the time management for ensuring effective and expeditious trials.

In practice, the Tribunal has proven itself extremely quick in conducting the proceedings as well in the delivery of the judgments. The reasons for this are partly of an external nature. The uncertainty of the Tribunal's future in case the Awami League does not remain in power as well as the pressure arising from society's demand to promptly put an end to impunity have certainly been crucial in this. Nevertheless, the proceedings have taken more time in the Appellate Division. Although there are no general rules regarding the proper length of an international criminal trial,[1459] it is certain that some trials before the ICT have been so fast that they provoke severe concerns about the standards adhered to. For instance, in the case of *Azad* who was tried in absentia, the trial took less than three months, from the charge framing order on 4 November 2012 until the delivery of the judgment on 21 January 2013. In cases in which the accused were present, the trials instead took around one year from the charge framing order until the delivery of the judgments. Considering the complexity of the cases, this is still extremely fast.

The guarantee of an expeditious trial encompasses the right of an accused to be tried without undue delay but also imposes a duty upon courts to ensure expeditious trials.[1460] Zappalà points out that the duty to conduct speedy trials can under no cir-

---

1457 SC (AD), *Kamaruzzaman v. The Chief Prosecutor*, Appeal Judgment, 3 November 2014, p. 184.
1458 SC (AD), *Kamaruzzaman v. The Chief Prosecutor*, Dissenting Opinion of Justice Choudhury, Appeal Judgment, 3 November 2014, p. 576.
1459 *Cassese*, International Criminal Law, 3. edn, p. 355.
1460 *Zappalà*, Human Rights in International Criminal Proceedings, p. 124.

4 Procedural rights

cumstances justify the curtailing of the rights of the accused.[1461] For her part, Hoven convincingly argues that this approach is too broad and that the right to a trial without undue delay must be balanced against other procedural guarantees.[1462]

In the jurisprudence of the ICT, the right to an expeditious trial has been mainly regarded as a duty of the Tribunal to accelerate the proceedings and it has been invoked in several cases to justify restrictions to the rights of the accused. In *Kamaruzzaman*, the Tribunal held that the right to be tried without undue delay forms part of the right to a fair trial and that it impedes the Tribunal from granting adjournments.[1463] While it is clear that adjournments must be based on reasonable grounds, the very limited time for preparing the defence in practice forces the defence to rely on adjournments for an adequate preparation. The Tribunal also invoked the right of the accused to an expeditious trial to justify the restriction of the number of defence witnesses.[1464] In *Kamaruzzaman*, as well as in several other cases, the defence submitted a list of more than 900 defence witnesses.[1465] The Tribunal argued that the submission of a list with more than one thousand witnesses demonstrates an intention to cause a delay in the trial, which must be prevented.[1466] It is obvious that this is a delaying tactic and the Tribunal was right to intervene.[1467] Nevertheless, drastic restrictions to the number of defence witnesses as practised by the Tribunal cannot be regarded as a measure to ensure a fair trial or as something to be required in the name of an expeditious trial. The Tribunal's practice was carried to extremes in *Nizami* in which the accused was only allowed to produce four witnesses for a case of 16 charges.[1468] Likewise, in *Molla*, the defence was restricted to examining six witnesses, whereas the prosecution examined 12;[1469] in Chowdhury, the

---

1461 *Zappalà*, Human Rights in International Criminal Proceedings, p. 28.
1462 *Hoven*, Rechtsstaatliche Anforderungen, p. 387.
1463 ICT 2, *The Chief Prosecutor v. Kamaruzzaman*, case no. 03/2012, Judgment, 9 May 2013, para. 59.
1464 ICT 2, *The Chief Prosecutor v. Kamaruzzaman*, case no. 03/2012, Judgment, 9 May 2013, para. 59.
1465 ICT 2, *The Chief Prosecutor v. Kamaruzzaman*, case no. 03/2012, Judgment, 9 May 2013, para. 61. See also 2939 witnesses in ICT 1, *The Chief Prosecutor v. Azam*, case no. 06/2011, Judgment, 15 July 2013, para. 35 and 965 witnesses in ICT 2, *The Chief Prosecutor v. Molla*, case no. 02/2012, Judgment, 5 February 2013, paras. 26–27.
1466 ICT 2, *The Chief Prosecutor v. Kamaruzzaman*, case no. 03/2012, Order no. 114, 20 February 2013, para. 11
1467 *Robertson*, Report on the ICT Bangladesh, p. 118.
1468 ICT 1, *The Chief Prosecutor v. Nizami*, case no. 03/2011, Order no. 141, 6 October 2013.
1469 ICT 2, *The Chief Prosecutor v. Molla*, case no. 02/2012, Judgment, 5 February 2013, paras. 26–27.

accused was even impeded from adducing more than five witnesses even though the prosecution examined 41[1470].

However, the reasoning for the restrictions of the number of defence witnesses was not based merely on the right to be tried without delay. In *Kamaruzzaman*, the Tribunal also relied on its right to regulate its own procedure enshrined in Section 22 of the ICT Act.[1471] It further justified this practice with the fact that the defence is not obligated to disprove the prosecution case by adducing evidence[1472] and held that the alibi plea by the defence was not a different one for each charge but rather the same and, for that reason, there was no need to examine seven witnesses.[1473] According to the Tribunal, equality of arms does not mean that the defence is permitted to examine the same number of witnesses as the prosecution.[1474] In *Alim*, it justified the restriction of witnesses by invoking its right to regulate the matter of time management for ensuring effective and expeditious trials in Rule 53(3) of the RoP.[1475] It also relied on Rule 46A which empowers the Tribunal to make orders that are necessary to meet the ends of justice and to prevent abuse of process.[1476]

The right to be tried without undue delay was also invoked by the Tribunal to limit the time for cross-examination. In *Azam*, based on Section 11(3)(b) and under the guise of an expeditious trial, the Tribunal held that the time for cross-examination of a witness should be restricted.[1477]

4.7 Right to a fair and public hearing

The right to a fair and public hearing is enshrined in Article 14(1) of the ICCPR. Under domestic law, Article 35(3) of the Constitution guarantees that every accused person has the right to a public trial by an independent and impartial court or tribunal established by law but, again, Article 47A of the Constitution bars the application of

---

1470 ICT 1, *The Chief Prosecutor v. Chowdhury*, case no. 02/2011, Judgment, 21 October 2013, para. 41.
1471 ICT 2, *The Chief Prosecutor v. Kamaruzzaman*, case no. 03/2012, Judgment, 9 May 2013, para. 37.
1472 ICT 2, *The Chief Prosecutor v. Kamaruzzaman*, case no. 03/2012, Order no. 124, 3 March 2013, p. 1.
1473 ICT 2, *The Chief Prosecutor v. Kamaruzzaman*, case no. 03/2012, Order no. 124, 3 March 2013, p. 1.
1474 ICT 2, *The Chief Prosecutor v. Kamaruzzaman*, case no. 03/2012, Order no. 124, 3 March 2013, p. 1.
1475 ICT 2, *The Chief Prosecutor v. Alim*, case no. 01/2012, Judgment, 9 October 2013, para. 26.
1476 ICT 2, *The Chief Prosecutor v. Alim*, case no. 01/2012, Judgment, 9 October 2013, para. 26.
1477 ICT 1, *The Chief Prosecutor v. Azam*, case no 06/2011, Order no. 40, 5 July 2012.

this fundamental right. Nevertheless, the ICT Act establishes in Section 10(4) that the trials shall be public.

Section 10(4) of the ICT Act allows the Tribunal to take proceedings in camera if it considers it necessary. Unfortunately, the provision does not stipulate conditions for in camera proceedings but rather grants the Tribunal broad discretion. Also, Rule 43(4) provides for a right to a public hearing. Rule 58A(3) of the RoP, which regulates the protection of witnesses and victims, also refers to proceedings in camera under Section 10(4) of the ICT Act and determines that the parties shall not reveal any information arising from such proceedings. The possibility to examine witnesses in camera has been made use of on only a few occasions and mainly in the context of sexual violence. In *Kamaruzzaman*, three rape victims were examined in camera.[1478] Nevertheless, as will be outlined below, other witnesses and victims were exposed to threats and put at risk through the disclosure of their identities. Although not provided for in the RoP and the ICT Act, the entire proceedings before the ICT are recorded on video but the video material has not been made public.

Problems arise also with regard to the accessibility of the Tribunal. Pursuant to Rule 62(1), the Registrar may control the entry of people to the Tribunal to maintain discipline and order. Every person needs an entry pass, which is issued by the Registrar. The defence raised concerns on the restricted access to the Tribunal in several cases.[1479] Also the Ambassador-at-Large for War Crimes Issues Rapp has criticised the difficulties in accessing the Tribunal for members of the public and recommended measures to make the trials accessible to all.[1480]

The ICT Act determines in Section 6(2A) that the Tribunal shall ensure fair trials, and Rule 43(4) of the RoP entitles the accused to a fair hearing. However, the fairness of the hearings is severely hampered by Sections 6(5) and 11A(2) of the ICT Act and Rule 26(1). Section 6(5) and Rule 26(1) stipulate that the presence of all Tribunal members in all sittings is not compulsory, and, in the case of the transfer of a case to another Tribunal, Section 11A(2) of the ICT Act allows the Tribunal to proceed from the same stage. Beyond that, pursuant to Section 6(6) of the ICT Act, the Tribunal is not bound to recall any witnesses in the case of absence of a member or the transfer of a case. As a consequence, judges who might not have heard the entire evidence still decide on the case. These provisions are unacceptable. The case of *Azam* is an example in which such practice led to a situation in which none of the judges had heard the entire evidence.[1481]

1478 ICT 2, *The Chief Prosecutor v. Kamaruzzaman*, case no. 03/2012, Judgment, 9 May 2013, para. 53.
1479 *Taylor*, Issue No. 3 – Weekly Digest, p. 4.
1480 *Rapp*, ICT Remarks, 28 November 2011.
1481 *Human Rights Watch*, Bangladesh: Azam Trial Concerns, 16 August 2013.

4.8 Right to adequate time and facilities for preparation

The right to adequate time and facilities for the preparation of the defence and to communicate with the counsel of choice is enshrined in Article 14(3)(b) of the ICCPR. As mentioned above, the Tribunal found that Section 9(3) of the ICT Act and Rule 18(4) of the RoP incorporate the right to adequate time and facilities for the preparation of the defence.

However, Rule 18(4) merely determines that the prosecutor shall supply to the accused additional copies of the formal charge and the documents on which it intends to rely. While Section 16(2) of the ICT Act determines that the accused shall be furnished with a copy of the formal charges and the relevant documents 'at a reasonable time before the trial', in the context of Section 9(3) of the ICT Act it becomes clear that 'reasonable time' means three weeks. Section 9(3) of the ICT Act compels the chief prosecutor to submit a list of witnesses and recorded statements as well as other documents that the prosecution will rely on at least three weeks before the commencement of the trial. Also, Rule 38(2) of the RoP affirms that an accused pleading non-guilty shall have at least three weeks to prepare his defence.

Considering the complexity of the cases, three weeks are obviously insufficient for an adequate preparation of a defence.[1482] In practice, the Tribunal has granted adjournments to the proceedings under different circumstances.

The fact that the legally established timeframe is too short obligates the defence as a general rule to pray for adjournment but the power to grant adjournments lies with the Tribunal. As a consequence, the right to adequate time to prepare the defence is undermined. In *Azam*, the Tribunal found an application for adjournment insufficient but still allowed the adjournment and compelled the defence to pay 1,000 taka.[1483] The RoP do not contain a rule according to which the Tribunal is allowed to adjourn proceedings against payment. Nevertheless, Rule 46A certainly allows the Tribunal to pass such orders. There also seems to be no rule with regard to the amount of money that the Tribunal can request for adjournment. Following another application for adjournment, it requested the defence to pay 5,000 taka for two days of adjournment.[1484] In Chowdhury, payment of 5,000 taka was imposed for the non-appearance of the defence counsel.[1485]

1482 *Linton*, CLF, 2010, 21(2), p. 191, at 300.
1483 ICT 1, *The Chief Prosecutor v. Azam*, case no. 06/2011, Order no. 161, 12 March 2013.
1484 ICT 1, *The Chief Prosecutor v. Azam*, case no. 06/2011, Order no. 164, 18 March 2013, p. 1.
1485 ICT 1, *The Chief Prosecutor v. Chowdhury*, case no. 02/2011, Order no. 144, 27 March 2013.

4 Procedural rights

The right to adequate facilities includes access to documents and other evidence.[1486] In the context of the ICT, this right is frequently restricted through the denial of access to investigation documents. As has been confirmed in several cases, the defence has no right to access the Investigation Report.[1487] In *Sayeedi*, the Tribunal held that the reason for this was the requirement to protect the witnesses whose addresses are mentioned in the Report[1488] and their disclosure would endanger them[1489]. It also held that the Investigation Report is not admissible as evidence.[1490] Based on the latter argument, the Tribunal also rejected the defence's motion to view the Investigation Report without the respective particulars of the witnesses.[1491] The absence of disclosure rules in the ICT Act and the RoP significantly curtail the rights of the defence. Without information on the investigation, the accused's ability to adequately prepare their defence is limited. Beyond that, equal access to evidence also constitutes a basic requirement for equality of arms.[1492] Unlike the Statutes of the international criminal tribunals, which guarantee a general duty to disclosure of the prosecution, the practice of the Tribunal shows a general denial of access to important investigative documents such as the Investigation Report by the defence.

Adequate facilities to prepare the defence require the accused to have sufficient possibilities to communicate with his lawyer. The right of pre-trial detainees to communicate with their lawyers after permission of the competent jail authority is enshrined in Section 683 of the Jail Code. The Tribunal found this provision applicable in the context of the accused under the ICT Act.[1493]

1486 Human Rights Committee, General Comment No. 33, 23 August 2007, para 33 (UN Doc. CCPR/C/GC/32).
1487 ICT 2, *The Chief Prosecutor v. Molla*, case no. 02/2012, Order no. 5, 22 January 2012, p. 3; ICT 2, *The Chief Prosecutor v. Molla*, case no. 02/2012, Judgment, 5 February 2013, para. 36; ICT 2, *The Chief Prosecutor v. Kamaruzzaman*, case no. 03/2012, Order no. 107, 13 February 2013; ICT 1, *The Chief Prosecutor v. Nizami*, case no. 03/2011, Order no. 11, 7 March 2012.
1488 ICT 2, *The Chief Prosecutor v. Sayeedi*, case no. 01/2011, Order no. 66, 22 January 2012, pp. 3–4. See also: ICT 1, *The Chief Prosecutor v. Nizami*, case no. 03/2011, Order no. 11, 7 March 2012, pp. 5–6.
1489 ICT 2, *The Chief Prosecutor v. Sayeedi*, case no. 01/2011, Order no. 66, 22 January 2012, p. 4. See also: ICT 1, *The Chief Prosecutor v. Nizami*, case no. 03/2011, Order no. 11, 7 March 2012, pp. 5–6.
1490 ICT 2, *The Chief Prosecutor v. Sayeedi*, case no. 01/2011, Order no. 66, 22 January 2012, p. 4. See also: ICT 1, *The Chief Prosecutor v. Nizami*, case no. 03/2011, Order no. 11, 7 March 2012, p. 6.
1491 ICT 2, *The Chief Prosecutor v. Sayeedi*, case no. 01/2011, Order no. 84, 27 March 2012.
1492 *Hoven*, Rechtsstaatliche Anforderungen, p. 461.
1493 ICT 2, *The Chief Prosecutor v. Sayeedi*, case no. 01/2011, Order (not numbered), 18 August 2011, pp. 4–5.

Part IV: Compliance of the ICT Act, the Rules of Procedure and the ICT's jurisprudence

The right to privileged communication with the counsel is not regulated in the ICT Act or the RoP. In fact, this right must be applied for to the Tribunal but has often been restricted. In *Kamaruzzaman*, the right to privileged communication with the accused was allowed only three times: at the pre-trial stage, at the trial stage and at the stage of summing up the case.[1494] The Tribunal considered this sufficient and for this reason allowed the counsel to meet and discuss with the accused only on the dates fixed for proceedings at the Tribunal's custody whenever applied for orally.[1495] An application for privileged communication was also rejected in the case of *Sayeedi* in which the Tribunal argued that sufficient occasion for privileged communication had been given throughout the trial and that, at the final stage, the defence could consult with the accused during court hours.[1496] Sufficient communication between the accused and his counsel is essential for the preparation of the defence and this right should not be placed at the Tribunal's disposal.

4.9 The right to be present and trials in absentia

The right of an accused to be present during his trial is enshrined in Article 14(3)(d) of the ICCPR. Bangladesh acceded to the ICCPR with a reservation on this Article based on the fact that its domestic law allows for trials in absentia under certain circumstances, and the provision is thus not binding upon Bangladesh.

Trials in absentia are admissible under Section 10A of the ICT Act. This Section was inserted by an amendment in 2012 and allows a trial to be held without the presence of the accused if the tribunal has 'reason to believe that the accused person has absconded or concealed himself so that he cannot be produced for trial'.[1497] The RoP further specify in Rules 31 and 32 that an order to appear within a specific date has to be published in two daily newspapers, one in English and one in Bengali, and only if the accused fails to appear after that can the trial be held in absentia. The provisions of the ICT and the RoP resemble those of ordinary domestic law. Section 339B of the Code of Criminal Procedure permits trials in absentia under the same conditions.

Several accused have been tried in absentia before the ICT. With regard to the admissibility of trials in absentia, the Tribunal stated that jurisprudence on the ICCPR and of the ECHR confirmed that the accused's right to be present during trial is not

---

1494 ICT 2, *The Chief Prosecutor v. Kamaruzzaman*, case no. 03/2012, Judgment, 9 May 2013, para. 58.
1495 ICT 2, *The Chief Prosecutor v. Kamaruzzaman*, case no. 03/2012, Judgment, 9 May 2013, para. 58.
1496 ICT 2, *The Chief Prosecutor v. Sayeedi*, case no. 01/2011, Order no. 94, 22 October 2012, p. 3.
1497 Section 10A(1) of the ICT Act.

violated by in absentia trials if the accused expressly declined to exercise this right.[1498] The Tribunal also invoked the Statute of the Special Tribunal for the Lebanon (STL) to argue that trials in absentia are generally permissible.[1499] However, the admissibility of trials in absentia under the STL Statute is subject to several requirements. Article 22 of the STL Statute allows for trials in absentia provided that the accused has expressly waived his right to be present, has not been handed over by the state authorities concerned or has absconded or otherwise cannot be found provided that all reasonable steps have been taken to secure his appearance to inform him of the charges. Beyond that, the STL Statute allows for a retrial in presence if the convicted person had not been represented by a defence counsel of his choice during trial and does not accept the judgment.[1500]

In international criminal law, trials in absentia do not per se infringe the rights of the accused.[1501] The United Nations Human Rights Committee (UNHRC) determined that trials in absentia can be permissible in the interests of the proper administration of justice if the accused declines his right to be present after having been informed in advance of the proceedings.[1502] However, such trials are only in accordance with Article 14(3)(d) of the ICCPR if necessary steps have been taken to summon the accused and to request his attendance in a timely manner.[1503]

With regard to the accused tried in absentia before the ICT, it is highly questionable whether they actually met the requirements as stipulated under the ICT Act. In *Azad*, the Tribunal held that, if the warrant of arrest could have been executed, the accused would have had the opportunity to be informed of the proceedings.[1504] It found that by leaving the country and continuing to abscond he declined his right to be present during trial.[1505] The Tribunal had followed the procedure under the ICT Act

---

[1498] ICT 2, *The Chief Prosecutor v. Azad*, case no. 05/2012, Judgment, 21 January 2013, para. 53; ICT 1, *The Chief Prosecutor v. Khokon*, case no. 04/2013, Judgment, 13 November 2014, para. 47.
[1499] ICT 2, *The Chief Prosecutor v. Azad*, case no. 05/2012, Judgment, 21 January 2013, para. 50.
[1500] Article 23(3) of the STL Statute.
[1501] Zappalà, Human Rights in International Proceedings, p. 126.
[1502] Human Rights Committee, General Comment No. 32, 23 August 2007, para 36 (UN Doc. CCPR/C/GC/32).
[1503] Human Rights Committee, General Comment No. 32, 23 August 2007, para 36 (UN Doc. CCPR/C/GC/32).
[1504] ICT 2, *The Chief Prosecutor v. Azad*, case no. 05/2012, Judgment, 21 January 2013, para. 52.
[1505] ICT 2, *The Chief Prosecutor v. Azad*, case no. 05/2012, Judgment, 21 January 2013, para. 52.

and published an order in two newspapers.[1506] However, it did not explain how it arrived at the conclusion that the accused had absconded; it appears that it merely assumed it based on the fact that he could not be found. In *Khokon*, the Tribunal concluded from the circumstances, time and way the accused allegedly disappeared while he held the post of mayor in Nagarkanda Pourashava that he willingly declined his right to be present.[1507] In *Uddin et al.*, both of the accused left the country immediately after the Liberation War and it is officially known that they have resided abroad since then. The Tribunal therefore assumed that they had absconded.[1508] These cases show that the requirements the Tribunal sets for the assumption that an accused has declined his right to be present are extremely low and do not reflect the standards established in international law. Two notices published in newspapers are also not at all sufficient to conclude that the accused has absconded or declined his right to be present.[1509]

Beyond that, the Tribunal combines two different situations under which a trial can be held in absentia: waiver of the accused and abscondence of the accused.[1510] Yet, under the ICT Act, only the latter is a reason to justify trials in absentia. It cannot be concluded from the mere absence of the accused that he expressly declined his right to be present during the trial.[1511] A waiver of the right to be present rather has to be made expressly, but in none of the cases before the ICT was an express statement given by any of the accused. Beyond that, the requirements for considering the accused absconded were not met in these cases. The Tribunal would have to demonstrate that the accused are absconding; the mere fact that they cannot be located does not suffice to this end. The assumption that the accused has absconded requires also that he has been informed and the publishing of an order in two newspapers does not suffice to this end.[1512]

The trials in absentia before the ICT are also problematic because the Tribunal assumes culpability from the accused's absence. In *Azad*, it argued that, if the accused was not guilty, he would have faced trial.[1513] The Tribunal then stated that the accused

---

1506 ICT 2, *The Chief Prosecutor v. Azad*, case no. 05/2012, Judgment, 21 January 2013, para. 53.
1507 ICT 2, *The Chief Prosecutor v. Khokon*, case no. 04/2013, Judgment, 13 November 2014, para. 47.
1508 ICT 2, *The Chief Prosecutor v. Uddin et al.*, case no. 01/2013, Judgment, 3 November 2013, para. 21.
1509 *Herath*, Harvard ILJ Online, Features, 2014, 55, p. 1, at 10.
1510 *Herath*, Harvard ILJ Online, Features, 2014, 55, p. 1, at 11.
1511 *Herath*, Harvard ILJ Online, Features, 2014, 55, p. 1, at 11.
1512 *Herath*, Harvard ILJ Online, Features, 2014, 55, p. 1, at 10.
1513 ICT 2, *The Chief Prosecutor v. Azad*, case no. 05/2012, Judgment, 21 January 2013, para. 330.

waived his right to be present and that this adds further to his culpability and considered this fact as a material incriminating circumstance to reinforce the evidence and circumstances available in the case.[1514] Also, in *Uddin et al.*, it argued that 'fleeing instantly after the independence is a fair indicative of their guilty mind'.[1515] This greatly infringes the presumption of innocence.

However, the absent accused have the right to a defence counsel pursuant to Section 10A(2) of the ICT Act. The expenses of the defence are determined and borne by the government. Yet, adequate defence is impossible without communication with the accused. Beyond that, the defence in these cases is often taken up by state defence counsels and, given the political problems connected with the defence of those accused under the ICT Act, their mandate is very challenging. In *Uddin et al.*, the defence counsel produced very few arguments for the defence of the accused. In *Azad*, the counsel was not able to examine any witnesses because he did not receive any information on the relatives of the accused.[1516] Robertson rightly points out that the state counsels in absentia cases should have rejected their mandates for ethical reasons.[1517]

The right to be present is also affected in the context of situations in which the accused was not produced in court. Rule 43A of the RoP allows the Tribunal to continue the trial if the accused on bail refuses to appear or if the accused in custody refuses to come to the Tribunal for any reason or if he could not be produced in court due to long-standing ill-health. The Tribunal held that the rationale behind this provision is to expedite proceedings.[1518] A similar provision does not exist under ordinary domestic criminal law. In *Sayeedi*, the Tribunal allowed the trial to continue despite the fact that the accused was in hospital for heart treatment[1519] and refused to adjourn the proceedings for more than three days. This Rule abrogates the right to be present during trial as under no circumstance can long-standing ill-health be interpreted as a waiver by the accused of his right to be present. In *Azam*, the trial was allowed to continue despite the absence of the accused because of sickness but the defence had

---

1514 ICT 2, *The Chief Prosecutor v. Azad*, case no. 05/2012, Judgment, 21 January 2013, para. 330.
1515 ICT 2, *The Chief Prosecutor v. Uddin et al.*, case no. 01/2013, Judgment, 3 November 2013, para. 187.
1516 ICT 2, *The Chief Prosecutor v. Azad*, case no. 05/2012, Judgment, 21 January 2013, para. 28.
1517 *Robertson*, Report on the ICT Bangladesh, pp. 117–118.
1518 ICT 1, *The Chief Prosecutor v. Sayeedi*, case no. 01/2011, Order no. 125, 20 June 2012, p. 3.
1519 ICT 1, *The Chief Prosecutor v. Sayeedi*, case no. 01/2011, Order no. 125, 20 June 2012, pp. 2–3.

argued that his presence was not required until the recording of the witnesses.[1520] In this case, the accused thus seems to have waived his right to be present through the counsel. In *Chowdhury*, an order was passed upon application of the accused even though the accused was not produced in court on that day.[1521] The reasons for his absence are not disclosed in the Order. However, Judge Ahmed rightly opposed the majority view and held that orders shall, as a general rule, be passed in the presence of the accused.[1522] The Tribunal held that the presence of the accused was at least always required during the delivery of the judgment in order to ensure the fairness of the proceedings.[1523]

The eagerness of the prosecution to achieve convictions exceeded a threshold of rationality in the case of *Yusuf* in which the prosecution applied for a verdict after the accused died in custody, arguing that the trial does not terminate with the death of the accused.[1524] A verdict against a deceased accused is evidently against the basic principles of criminal law and was rightly rejected by the Tribunal[1525].

4.10 Legal remedies

The right of a convict to have the judgment reviewed by a higher court is a fundamental right enshrined in Article 14(5) of the ICCPR. In accordance with the ICCPR, Section 21(1) of the ICT Act gives a convict the right to appeal to the Appellate Division of the Supreme Court of Bangladesh. This right has been made use of in all cases in which the accused were tried in their presence.

Nevertheless, in *Molla*, the repeal of the sentence of life imprisonment and the sentencing to the death penalty by the Appellate Division deprived the accused of a legal remedy against the death sentence. Although the accused has a right to file a review petition, these petitions are not decided upon by a higher court and, as will be outlined below, have a limited effect. Increasing the sentence after appeal or entering a conviction after appeal is, in general, admissible under international criminal law. Nevertheless, Judge Pocar has systematically opposed this practice, arguing that it violates the fundamental right to have a conviction and sentence reviewed by a higher

---

1520 ICT 1, *The Chief Prosecutor v. Azam*, case no. 06/2011, Order no. 31, 10 June 2012, p. 1.
1521 ICT 1, *The Chief Prosecutor v. Chowdhury*, case no. 02/2011, Order no. 17, 13 March 2012, p. 1.
1522 ICT 1, *The Chief Prosecutor v. Chowdhury*, case no. 02/2011, Order no. 17, 13 March 2012, p. 14.
1523 ICT 1, *The Chief Prosecutor v. Nizami*, case no. 03/2011, Order no. 178, 24 June 2014.
1524 ICT 2, *The Chief Prosecutor v. Yusuf*, case no. 02/2013, Order no. 76, 12 February 2014, para. 4.
1525 ICT 2, *The Chief Prosecutor v. Yusuf*, case no. 02/2013, Order no. 76, 12 February 2014, para 7.

court.[1526] When the death penalty comes into play, the absence of a possibility to have the sentence reviewed by a higher court is inacceptable. Molla filed a review petition, which was rejected, and he was hanged in December 2013. Molla did not make use of the possibility to file a mercy petition.

The right to file a review petition against an appeal judgment is not enshrined in the ICT Act but has been granted in all cases. The prosecution invoked Article 47A(2) of the Constitution to argue that the right to review was excluded because an accused under the ICT Act has no right to appeal to the Supreme Court for any of the remedies under the Constitution and also the ICT Act does not contain the right to file a review petition.[1527] On the other hand, the Tribunal stated that Article 47A(2) neither expressly nor implicitly establishes a prohibition to file a review petition and that the power of the Appellate Division to review its judgments has not been excluded.[1528] The Division argued that, with the appeal, it also has the right to review the entire material on record, which amounts to an inherent power to review its orders or judgments, if a part is affected by it, even though specific provisions are absent.[1529] It derived this power from its primary function 'to do justice', which comprises the power to review its judgments in case of errors.[1530] This inherent power of a court can be utilised by it to fill a lacuna in the law or where an unforeseeable case arises and no specific provision exists.[1531]

In the absence of further provisions, the Division also had to determine the time limit to file a review petition. While under the general rules of the Appellate Division review petitions must be filed within 30 days, the Tribunal found this provision inapplicable because it is contrary to the provisions of the ICT Act.[1532] The Division considered fifteen days a reasonable time to secure the ends of justice.[1533] Again, the requirement of a speedy trial has been invoked as an argument to curtail the rights of the accused.

The practice of the Appellate Division to generally accept review petitions is welcome and strengthens the rights of the accused. Nevertheless, the scope of review petitions is limited. Grounds for a review can only be an error that is so obvious and

---

1526 See, for instance, ICTY (AC), *Prosecutor v. Mrkšić et al.*, Appeal Judgment, 5 May 2009, Partially Dissenting Opinion of Judge Pocar, para. 3; ICTY (AC), *Prosecutor v. Galić*, Appeal Judgment, 30 November 2006, Partially Dissenting Opinion of Judge Pocar, para. 2.
1527 SC (AD), *Molla v. The Chief Prosecutor*, Review Judgment, 12 December 2013, p. 5.
1528 SC (AD), *Molla v. The Chief Prosecutor*, Review Judgment, 12 December 2013, pp. 7–8.
1529 SC (AD), *Molla v. The Chief Prosecutor*, Review Judgment, 12 December 2013, p. 10.
1530 SC (AD), *Molla v. The Chief Prosecutor*, Review Judgment, 12 December 2013, p. 11.
1531 SC (AD), *Molla v. The Chief Prosecutor*, Review Judgment, 12 December 2013, pp. 11, 18.
1532 SC (AD), *Molla v. The Chief Prosecutor*, Review Judgment, 12 December 2013, p. 20.
1533 SC (AD), *Molla v. The Chief Prosecutor*, Review Judgment, 12 December 2013, p. 21.

Part IV: Compliance of the ICT Act, the Rules of Procedure and the ICT's jurisprudence

leads to a legal wrong if kept on record.[1534] The error must be of material importance for the case.[1535] That is, with a review petition, the petitioner cannot seek a new decision for the case and he cannot raise objections that were already brought forward and have been dealt with in the appeal judgment.[1536] The petitioner, therefore, has to show that the Division 'resorted to a fundamental error of law, which remains apparent on the face of the judgment'.[1537]

After the review judgment, there is the possibility to file a mercy petition to the president pursuant to Article 49 of the Constitution. According to the Appellate Division, such a petition is not subject to any constitutional or judicial restraints.[1538] The president decides on the consideration of such a petition and the convict has no right to insist on an oral hearing on the petition.[1539] The convicts in the considered cases have not made use of this possibility. The right to seek pardon corresponds to Article 6(4) of the ICCPR, which determines that such a possibility must be granted in the case of death sentences.

No right to appeal against decisions other than judgments is established under the ICT Act. In fact, Section 24 precludes the appeal against any order, judgment or sentence of the Tribunal except against the final judgment. As a consequence, there is also no right to appeal against interim orders and contempt orders. Considering that the Tribunal can impose up to one year of imprisonment for contempt, the absence of a right to appeal is unacceptable and violates fundamental rights. This shortcoming of the ICT Act was at least recognised by the High Court Division of the Supreme Court in 2015. The Division affirmed that a contemnor has a right to appeal against a contempt order under Article 104, which empowers the Appellate Division to issue orders as necessary for imparting 'complete justice'.[1540] Nevertheless, this right would have to be included in the ICT Act.

Although there is no right to a review of orders, they can be reviewed under Rule 26(3) of the RoP, which determines that the Tribunal 'may review' its orders on application or on its own motion. However, the scope of such legal remedy is limited because it is the Tribunal itself that reviews the orders and not a higher court.

1534 SC (AD), *Molla v. The Chief Prosecutor*, Review Judgment, 12 December 2013, p. 45; SC (AD), *Chowdhury v. The Chief Prosecutor*, Review Judgment, 18 November 2015, p. 12.
1535 SC (AD), *Molla v. The Chief Prosecutor*, Review Judgment, 12 December 2013, p. 46.
1536 SC (AD), *Molla v. The Chief Prosecutor*, Review Judgment, 12 December 2013, pp. 45.46; SC (AD), *Kamaruzzaman v. The Chief Prosecutor*, Review Judgment, 5 April 2015, pp. 12, 34.
1537 SC (AD), *Kamaruzzaman v. The Chief Prosecutor*, Review Judgment, 5 April 2015, p. 12.
1538 SC (AD), *Molla v. The Chief Prosecutor*, Review Judgment, 12 December 2013, p. 48.
1539 SC (AD), *Molla v. The Chief Prosecutor*, Review Judgment, 12 December 2013, p. 48.
1540 *The Daily Star*, Contemnor Has the Right to Appeal, 30 April 2015.

Section 25 of the ICT Act impedes remedies for miscarriages of justice if done in good faith and for that reason runs counter to Bangladesh's obligations assumed under Article 14(6) of the ICCPR. Yet, this shortcoming concerns domestic law in general and, in its reservation on Article 14 of the ICCPR, Bangladesh has expressed its willingness to comply with this obligation in the near future.

4.11 Penalties

Article 32 of the Constitution determines that nobody shall be deprived of life or liberty except in accordance with the law. This constitutional provision requires a punishment to be reasonable and non-arbitrary.[1541]

Section 20(2) of the ICT Act establishes that the death penalty or any other penalty proportionate to the gravity of the crime that appears just and proper to the Tribunal shall be imposed. The ICT Act is silent on sentencing criteria and establishes the principle of proportionality only partly because it determines that the death penalty shall be imposed as a general rule. From Section 20, it follows that the drafters of the Act considered the death penalty the regular penalty but left the Tribunal with the option to deviate from this general rule.

This interpretation was adopted by the Appellate Division which argued that any punishment other than the death penalty would be the exception.[1542] The Division held that, even in the light of Article 6(5) of the ICCPR, only the death penalty would be appropriate in this case because of the specific seriousness of the crimes committed during the Liberation War.[1543]

Although the death penalty is not prohibited internationally, there are efforts towards its abolishment as reflected in the Second Additional Protocol to the ICCPR. Nevertheless, the possibility to impose the death penalty corresponds with ordinary domestic law in Bangladesh. Contrary to the ICT Act, Section 374 of the Code of Criminal Procedure allows the execution of death penalties only if confirmed by the High Court Division. No such rule was included in the ICT Act. Although all the convicts appealed against their judgments, this does not hold true for those tried in absentia. The possibility that these death sentences will ever be executed is certainly low but, technically, their execution would be admissible without confirmation by the High Court Division. Likewise, in the case of *Molla* in which the death sentence was imposed by the Appellate Division, no further remedy was given to the accused.

1541 *Islam*, Constitutional Law, 3. edn, p. 306.
1542 SC (AD), *Molla v. The Chief Prosecutor*, Appeal Judgment, 17 September 2013, p. 247.
1543 SC (AD), *Kamaruzzaman v. The Chief Prosecutor*, Review Judgment, 5 April 2015, p. 34.

Part IV: Compliance of the ICT Act, the Rules of Procedure and the ICT's jurisprudence

The Appellate Division held that, unlike Indian law, Bangladeshi law does not require special reasons to be given in order to impose the death penalty.[1544] Section 354(3) of the Indian Code of Criminal Procedure determines that the death penalty shall be an exceptional penalty, whereas Section 357(5) of the Bangladesh Code of Criminal Procedure merely determines that the court shall state the reasons for the sentence awarded. With regard to the ICT Act, the Division held that reasons have to be given only if the Tribunal imposes a lesser sentence.[1545] Individual sentencing is thus restricted because these findings in practice require the Tribunal to disprove the assumption that the convict deserves the death penalty.

On the other hand, a mandatory death penalty has been abolished in Bangladesh. The High Court Division declared laws imposing the death penalty as a mandatory penalty to be ultra vires of the Constitution because they curtail the court's discretion to adjudicate on the imposition of the penalty.[1546] However, this does not concern the ICT Act because it does not establish a mandatory death penalty.

The practical implementation of the executions in Bangladesh is problematic. The death penalty is executed through hanging, which is carried out by other prisoners who are offered incentives in the form of remission of their sentence.[1547] There is no public statistic on the number of death sentences and only cases with a certain public interest are publicly reported.[1548] Most convicts under the ICT Act have been awarded death sentences and have been executed with surprising speed immediately after the review judgments of the Appellate Division. Cases under the ICT Act have been adjudicated with priority,[1549] whereas approximately 1,200 prisoners convicted under ordinary law are on death row awaiting their appeal judgments[1550].

Further problems arise from Section 20(2) of the ICT Act as it does not specify the penalties that can be imposed. Although, as outlined above, the Tribunal has invoked the penalties from the Penal Code, the provision in theory empowers the Tribunal to even impose penalties that do not exist under ordinary criminal law.

The jurisprudence of the ICT has not been consistent in the application of sentencing criteria. Although in several judgments the Tribunal determined three factors that must be considered: (1) the position of the accused: leadership, level of influence and

---

1544 SC (AD), *Molla v. The Chief Prosecutor*, Review Judgment, 12 December 2013, p. 58.
1545 SC (AD), *Molla v. The Chief Prosecutor*, Review Judgment, 12 December 2013, p. 58.
1546 *Blast and another v. Bangladesh*, 30 BLD (2010) (HCD), pp. 194 ff. See also *Islam*, Constitutional Law, 3. edn, pp. 306–307. The decision was confirmed by the Appellate Division on 5 May 2015.
1547 *FIDH/Odhikar*, Capital Punishment Report, p. 26.
1548 *FIDH/Odhikar*, Capital Punishment Report, p. 13.
1549 *International Crisis Group*, Political Conflict, p. 18.
1550 *Moneruzzaman*, Nearly 1,200 Condemned Prisoners Await SC Verdict, 19 December 2015.

control; (2) the role of the accused in the commission of the crime and his participation as a superior in criminal acts of his subordinates; and (3) the nature of the crimes and the vulnerability of the victims,[1551] in several cases these criteria were actually not applied.

In *Uddin et al.*, the Tribunal made very emotionally charged statements in the context of sentencing and mainly invoked the 'pain of the nation' to justify the death penalty. The Tribunal found that 'letters of law cannot remain non[-]reactive to the enormous colossal and unspeakable pains being carried for decades together by the relatives of martyred intellectuals and the nation too'.[1552] It concluded that 'only the capital punishment can reinforce the expectations of the nation and the relatives of murdered intellectuals'.[1553] The Tribunal reinforced that it was imperative to impose the death penalty because 'no punishment other than death will be equal to the horrendous crimes for which the accused persons have been found guilty and accountable'.[1554] These findings on the sentencing lack objectivity and specific criteria. In *Khokon* and *Hossain*, the Tribunal did not establish any sentencing criteria but merely found that it had weighed up the gravity of the offences.[1555]

The age of the accused was taken into account when sentencing in several cases and led the Tribunal to abstain from imposing the death penalty. In *Azam*, the Tribunal found the death penalty to be the appropriate punishment but considered the age of the accused (91 years) and his fragile health condition as mitigating circumstances[1556] and, therefore, imposed imprisonment for 90 years. The same approach was taken in the case of *Alim* in which the Tribunal considered his health problems and age of 91 years mitigating factors.[1557] The Tribunal underlined that a mitigating circumstance

---

1551 ICT 2, *The Chief Prosecutor v. Kamaruzzaman*, case no. 03/2012, Judgment, 9 May 2013, para. 643; ICT 2, *The Chief Prosecutor v. Mujahid*, case no. 04/2012, Judgment, 17 July 2013, para. 635; ICT 1, *The Chief Prosecutor v. Nizami*, case no. 03/2011, Judgment, 29 October 2014, para. 422.
1552 ICT 2, *The Chief Prosecutor v. Uddin et al.*, case no. 01/2013, Judgment, 3 November 2013, para. 449.
1553 ICT 2, *The Chief Prosecutor v. Uddin et al.*, case no. 01/2013, Judgment, 3 November 2013, para. 450.
1554 ICT 2, *The Chief Prosecutor v. Uddin et al.*, case no. 01/2013, Judgment, 3 November 2013, para. 450.
1555 ICT 1, *The Chief Prosecutor v. Khokon*, case no. 04/2013, Judgment, 13 November 2014, p. 106; ICT 1, *The Chief Prosecutor v. Hossain*, case no. 01/2013, Judgment, 24 November 2014, para. 174.
1556 ICT 1, *The Chief Prosecutor v. Azam*, case no. 06/2011, Judgment, 15 July 2013, para. 393.
1557 ICT 2, *The Chief Prosecutor v. Alim*, case no. 01/2012, Judgment, 9 October 2012, para. 684.

merely relates to the sentence but does not diminish the gravity of the crime.[1558] In *Sobhan*, the Tribunal instead found that advanced age does not necessarily lead to lower sentences but rather carries very little weight as a mitigating circumstance and concluded that, under consideration of the accused's mode of participation, his age should not be taken into account.[1559]

The Appellate Division established specific sentencing criteria and stated that the following circumstances 'amongst many other factors' must be considered: (1) the nature of the offence; (2) the culpability of the offender; (3) the circumstances of its commission; (4) the age and character of the offender; (5) the injuries caused to individuals or to society; and (5) the effect of the punishment on the offender.[1560] Although these criteria were already established in the appeal judgment of *Molla*, they have not found their way to the judgments of the ICT delivered after the Appellate Division's decision.

4.12 Witnesses and victims

The lack of the protection of rights in the ICT Act is not limited to the accused but also extends to witnesses and victims. The ICT Act does not regulate this important aspect at all but only contains a provision that allows for proceedings in camera in Section 10(4). Only Rule 58A of the RoP determines some basic rules on witness and victim protection.

The absence of adequate witness and victim protection mechanisms is also a reality under ordinary domestic law because the Code of Criminal Procedure does not contain any provisions in this regard.[1561] Rules on victim protection are contained in the Legal Aid Act (2000), the Prevention of Oppression Against Women and Children Act (2000), the Act for Control of Acid (2002), the Acid Offences Act (2000) and the Prevention of Human Trafficking Act (2012).[1562] The regulations of these acts apply to specific victims and so do not provide a generally applicable scheme.

The silence of the ICT Act on the question of witness and victim protection is highly problematic. Rule 58A(1) of the RoP merely determines that the Tribunal 'on its own initiative, or on application of either party, may pass necessary order directing the concerned authorities of the government to ensure protection, privacy and well-being of the witnesses and victims'. This rule lacks precision and does not establish

---

1558 ICT 2, *The Chief Prosecutor v. Alim*, case no. 01/2012, Judgment, 9 October 2012, para. 684.
1559 ICT 2, *The Chief Prosecutor v. Sobhan*, case no. 01/2014, Judgment, 18 February 2015, para. 589.
1560 SC (AD), *Molla v. The Chief Prosecutor*, Review Judgment, 12 December 2013, p. 59.
1561 *Al Faruque/Rahaman*, BD JL, 2013, 13(1/2), p. 33, at 37.
1562 *Al Faruque/Rahaman*, BD JL, 2013, 13(1/2), p. 33, at 37–41.

effective protection measures. Beyond that, the decision on the scope of the protection of witnesses and victims is left entirely with the Tribunal.

Rule 58A(2) determines that the government shall arrange accommodation for witnesses and victims if applied for, that it shall ensure security and surveillance during the stay of the witnesses and victims, and that it shall take necessary measures to escort the witnesses and victims to the Tribunal. The Tribunal through its RoP establishes a duty upon the government to arrange for accommodation and to ensure security, but the binding effect of the RoP on the government seems doubtful. On the other hand, effective protection of the rights of victims and witnesses requires a parliamentary act. Accommodation and security of witnesses and victims have in fact proven difficult in practice and the lack of resources has led to untenable deficits.

Rule 58A(3) determines that, when proceedings are held in camera, the prosecution and the defence counsel shall not reveal any information, including the identity of the witness, and that the violations of this rule shall be prosecuted under Section 11(4) of the ICT Act.

It is striking that the victims, whose interests have always been highlighted during the entire procedure of establishing the Tribunal as well as in the judgments, have been entirely ignored in the legal framework. Given the sensitivity of testimonies related to the Liberation War, it is evident that witnesses find themselves in a conflict of interest. While, on the one hand, there is certainly an interest in bringing the perpetrators to trial and in testifying, on the other hand, there are severe security concerns. After the testimony, the witnesses have to continue living in their communities. In rural structures, this is particularly difficult and, considering the politically tense environment, testifying in the Tribunal easily becomes a risk to life.

In fact, there have been numerous scandals that raise serious doubts about the Tribunal's ability to protect witnesses. In 2013, the defence witness Shukhoranjan Bali in the trial of Sayeedi is said to have been abducted by the Bangladesh police in front of the ICT and to have been brought to the Indian border where he claims to have been tortured by the Border Security Force.[1563] Bali was originally a prosecution witness but then agreed to testify for the defence. In the same case, one prosecution witness was attacked and killed at his home.[1564] Beyond that, there are allegations that prosecution witnesses have been coerced to testify.[1565] These incidents obviously intimidate witnesses, nourish fear and thus decrease the willingness of witnesses to testify. Coercion of witnesses can also lead to false statements.

1563 *Human Rights Watch*, Bangladesh: Find Abducted Victims, 16 January 2013; *Taylor*, Special Issue No. 1 – Sayeedi Verdict, p. 3.
1564 *Human Rights Watch*, Bangladesh: Investigate Killing of Witness, 23 December 2013.
1565 *Human Rights Watch*, Bangladesh: Stop Harassment of Defence at War Tribunal, 2 November 2011.

Part IV: Compliance of the ICT Act, the Rules of Procedure and the ICT's jurisprudence

Neither the ICT Act nor the RoP establish a duty to record witness statements during the investigation procedure. Under general criminal law, Sections 161 and 162 of the Criminal Procedure Code as well as Rule 265 of the Bangladesh Police Regulations contain provisions on the recording of statements of witnesses made during the investigation procedure. Section 145 of the Evidence Act allows the cross-examination of a witness as to previous statements made by him in writing or recorded in writing. From the fact that neither the ICT Act nor the RoP contain any provisions in this regard, the Appellate Division concluded that the examination of witnesses by the Investigation Officer could either be done in writing or orally.[1566] The Division held that, in the absence of any rules on the examination of witnesses in the RoP, the Investigation Officer is not obligated to record the statements.[1567] Only Justice Miah came to a different finding in his dissenting opinion. He argued that a combined reading of Sections 8(4), 8(6) and 9 of the ICT Act as well as Rules 8 and 11 of the RoP shows that the Investigation Officer is obligated to record the statements of the witnesses.[1568] Rule 8(1) establishes a duty to maintain a case diary for each case, which has to mention the progress on a daily basis. Sub-rule (2) allows the Investigation Officer to use the case diary to refresh his memory before his deposition in court, and sub-rule (4) allows the Tribunal to peruse the case diary for clarification. Rule 11 of the RoP obligates the Investigation Officer to submit an Investigation Report. Finally, pursuant to Section 9(3) of the ICT Act, the Chief Prosecutor has an obligation to submit a list of witnesses along with the recorded statements of the witnesses. Justice Miah held that from the latter follows the duty of the Investigation Officer to record the statements of the witnesses during the investigation procedure.[1569] He further argued that Rule 53(2), which permits the examination of a witness in terms of his or her credibility, also allows the defence to cross-examine a witness regarding the omissions made by him to the Investigation Officer in order to question his or her credibility.[1570]

The Appellate Division itself also affirmed that there are serious flaws in the investigation procedure. The Division held that the Investigation Officers are often not able to assess properly what is important in terms of the evidence and thus record whatever seems essential to them.[1571] It clarified that the witnesses' statements are recorded in a hurry because of frequent interruptions and they are not read over or signed by the

---

1566 SC (AD), *Molla v. The Chief Prosecutor*, Appeal Judgment, 17 September 2013, p. 196.
1567 SC (AD), *Molla v. Prosecutor*, Appeal Judgment, 17 September 2013, p. 198.
1568 SC (AD), *Kamaruzzaman v. The Chief Prosecutor*, Dissenting Opinion of Justice Miah, Appeal Judgment, 3 November 2014, p. 432.
1569 SC (AD), *Kamaruzzaman v. The Chief Prosecutor*, Dissenting Opinion of Justice Miah, Appeal Judgment, 3 November 2014, p. 433.
1570 SC (AD), *Kamaruzzaman v. The Chief Prosecutor*, Dissenting Opinion of Justice Miah, Appeal Judgment, 3 November 2014, p. 434.
1571 SC (AD), *Molla v. The Chief Prosecutor*, Review Judgment, 12 December 2013, p. 33.

witnesses.[1572] For this reason, they can exceed a witness's statement or lack some details.[1573]

This finding is worrying and raises serious doubts about the investigation procedure. Proper documentation is essential for the protection of the witnesses because it offers transparency to the interrogation. In the absence of a right to legal aid for witnesses and victims, the investigation procedure appears even more problematic. There is also no obvious reason why the ICT Act and the RoP should diverge from ordinary criminal law in this regard.

The protection of witnesses is further impaired through Sections 8(5) and 18 of the ICT Act. These provisions impose upon witnesses a duty to testify and to answer any question even if the answer amounts to self-incrimination. The witness is only protected through the prohibition to utilise the statement. This provision diverges from domestic criminal law to the detriment of witnesses. Section 161(2) of the Code of Criminal Procedure imposes upon witnesses a duty to answer all questions but excludes those questions to which the answer would have a tendency to expose him to a criminal charge or to a penalty or forfeiture.

The ICT Act does not establish a right of victims to compensation. In *Qaiser*, the prosecution held that the accused should be sentenced to payment of compensation or reparation to the rape victim.[1574] It argued that the phrase 'or such other punishment proportionate to the gravity of the crimes' in Section 20(2) would allow the Tribunal to impose the payment of compensation.[1575] In fact, Rule 46(3) of the RoP establishes that the Tribunal may also impose a fine or pass a reparation order against the accused. The Tribunal, however, concluded that the RoP cannot override the provisions of the ICT Act and, since the ICT Act does not contain any provisions that allow the Tribunal to pass an order for reparation or compensation, such an order would not be in accordance with the law.[1576] Likewise, in *Islam*, the Tribunal rejected the possibility of imposing a duty to pay compensation and confirmed that it is bound by the penalties listed in Section 53 of the Penal Code.[1577]

1572 SC (AD), *Molla v. The Chief Prosecutor*, Review Judgment, 12 December 2013, p. 33.
1573 SC (AD), *Molla v. The Chief Prosecutor*, Review Judgment, 12 December 2013, p. 33.
1574 ICT 2, *The Chief Prosecutor v. Qaiser*, case no. 04/2013, Judgment, 23 December 2014, para. 970.
1575 ICT 2, *The Chief Prosecutor v. Qaiser*, case no. 04/2013, Judgment, 23 December 2014, para. 970.
1576 ICT 2, *The Chief Prosecutor v. Qaiser*, case no. 04/2013, Judgment, 23 December 2014, paras. 981, 982.
1577 ICT 1, *The Chief Prosecutor v. Islam*, case no. 05/2013, Judgment, 30 December 2014, para. 331.

Part IV: Compliance of the ICT Act, the Rules of Procedure and the ICT's jurisprudence

At the same time, the Tribunal emphasised that the government should take the initiative to form a reparation or compensation scheme for rape victims.[1578] It further stressed that thousands of rape victims have not been compensated and that they should be recognised as war heroines and honoured as freedom fighters.[1579] The Tribunal also addressed the Ministry of Liberation War Affairs and the Ministry of Social Welfare as well as non-governmental organisations and expressed its expectation that necessary steps would be taken to identify rape victims and war babies, to formulate an effective programme to honour them and to provide assistance to them as well as a monthly payment.[1580] The inconsistency between the ICT Act and the RoP reveal the necessity for Parliament to act and to amend the ICT Act accordingly. As mentioned above, also with regard to several aspects related to the rights of the accused, the RoP determine areas of law that require protection through a parliamentary act. Nevertheless, the drafters of the RoP have apparently gone beyond their remit in determining a power to impose the payment of compensation.

As outlined above, several rape victims were officially recognised and granted freedom fighter pensions by the government. However, considering the estimated number of actual victims, the action taken in this regard is insufficient for comprehensive rehabilitation.

As mentioned previously, the case of *Jabbar Engineer* was the first time the Tribunal imposed the payment of a fine and, based on Section 20(2) of the Penal Code, it held that a fine is an admissible penalty under the ICT Act.[1581] Section 545(1)(b) of the Code of Criminal Procedure allows courts when imposing a fine to order that the fine or parts of it shall be paid as compensation to persons who have suffered any loss or injury through the offence. However, no such provision exists under the ICT Act or the RoP and, as a consequence, this possibility has not been considered by the Tribunal.

As Linton rightly points out, investigation officers need to be trained in gender sensitivity, and psycho-social support for victims has to be provided.[1582] In particular, victims of sexual violence might also need protection when they go back to their communities after they have testified before the ICT.[1583] Victims of severe human rights

---

1578 ICT 2, *The Chief Prosecutor v. Qaiser*, case no. 04/2013, Judgment, 23 December 2014, para. 984.
1579 ICT 2, *The Chief Prosecutor v. Qaiser*, case no. 04/2013, Judgment, 23 December 2014, paras. 986, 988; ICT 1, *The Chief Prosecutor v. Islam*, case no. 05/2013, Judgment, 30 December 2014, para. 331.
1580 ICT 2, *The Chief Prosecutor v. Qaiser*, case no. 04/2013, Judgment, 23 December 2014, para. 991.
1581 ICT 1, *The Chief Prosecutor v. Jabbar Engineer*, case no. 01/2014, Judgment, 24 February 2015, para. 316.
1582 *Linton*, CLF, 2010, 21(2), p. 191, at 304.
1583 *Linton*, CLF, 2010, 21(2), p. 191, at 304–305.

violations who are subjected to cross-examination during criminal trials have to recall extremely painful events and there is a high risk of re-traumatisation.[1584] The pace with which the Investigation Agency as well as the Tribunal have been set up shows that there has been little preparation and training of the participating stakeholders to deal with such sensitive issues. The lack of resources also impedes the introduction of further measures in this regard.

4.13 Interim findings

The scrutiny of the legal framework and its application in the context of fundamental procedural rights has shown that there are severe shortcomings that impede a fair trial. Other than with regard to material law, the problem lies mainly in flawed legal provisions as well as gaps in the legal framework.

In some cases, the provisions of the ICT Act and the RoP merely reproduce domestic law and reveal that these shortcomings in the protection of the accused and of victims and witnesses are a problem of general domestic law and not inherent in the ICT Act. Nevertheless, in the majority of instances, the provisions and practices adopted by the Tribunal clearly diverge from domestic standards to the detriment of the accused. The constitutional restrictions and also the right to an expeditious trial are usually invoked to justify the curtailing of rights. Several procedural rights are also not regulated as a duty the Tribunal has to respect but rather provide the Tribunal with a discretionary power to decide whether it wants to grant the right. In practice, in all these instances, the Tribunal has decided to the detriment of the accused.

The concerns that the RoP, with only 66 rules, cannot substitute the entire Code of Criminal Procedure and that the legal framework therefore lacks precision have proven true. The absence of clear guidelines that determine the issues the Tribunal can actually regulate through its own procedural rules and those that require regulation through a parliamentary act further contribute to the insufficient protection of the rights of the accused.

1584 *Hazan*, IRCR, 2006, 88(861), p. 19, at 40.

Part V: The ICT in the context of transitional justice in Bangladesh

In Bangladesh, the process of dealing with the past started extremely late if one discounts the short-lived initiatives immediately after the Liberation War. The adoption of the ICT Act as well as the Collaborators Order can undoubtedly be considered a progressive approach in 1972 to combat impunity. In practice, however, both legal frameworks failed. The ICT Act was never implemented due to the amnesty granted to the Pakistani suspects, and the Collaborators Order was highly problematic because of the broad notion of collaboration. Nevertheless, the trials under the Collaborators Order were very quickly given up through a general amnesty. The culture of impunity was already starting to flourish, therefore, immediately after the war.

Setting up the ICT was a major step in ending the culture of impunity which has dominated over the past several decades in Bangladesh. Criminal trials play an important role in a society's process of transitional justice. Nevertheless, their successful contribution to transitional justice depends, to a large extent, on the method of implementation but also on the political and social environment that surrounds them.

This part outlines the different aspects and aims of transitional justice with a focus on criminal trials. It determines factors that influence the transitional justice process in Bangladesh and shows the extent to which the ICT has been able to contribute to this process, taking into account the findings of the scrutiny in Part IV.

1 The role of criminal trials in the process of transitional justice

Criminal trials are an important mechanism for the process of transitional justice. However, there are a variety of other measures that are often implemented simultaneously. The choice between different transitional justice measures depends not only on the willingness of the respective government but also, to a great extent, on the nature of the conflict and the specific circumstances in the post-conflict society.

1.1 Measures and aims of transitional justice

There is no universal definition of transitional justice in the scholarly work that clearly delineates the notion. The United Nations has defined transitional justice as 'the full range of processes and mechanisms associated with a society's attempts to come to terms with a legacy of large-scale past abuses, in order to ensure accountability, serve justice and achieve reconciliation'.[1585] Transitional justice thus comprises a multitude

---

1585 Report of the Secretary-General, The Rule of Law and Transitional Justice in Conflict and Post-Conflict Societies, 23 August 2004, para. 8 (UN Doc. S/2004/616).

of measures. It is usually claimed that transitional justice mechanisms are aimed at truth, justice and reconciliation; over the longer term these factors are expected to contribute to peace and democracy.

The concept of transitional justice comprises retributive as well as restorative justice. Retributive justice is mainly achieved through criminal trials but other measures can be employed to impose non-criminal sanctions as well. For instance, truth commissions can have a punitive effect because they publicly mention the perpetrators and thus expose them to social exclusion,[1586] and lustrations are a form of administrative sanction[1587]. Retributive justice is aimed at establishing individual accountability, ending impunity and punishing the guilty. On the other hand, restorative justice views crime as a conflict between victims, perpetrators and the affected society and strives for reconciliation and conflict resolution.[1588] Victims and their suffering are at the centre of restorative justice[1589] and the punishment is aimed at making reparations to the victims[1590].

Measures of transitional justice are manifold and their application, combination and effectiveness depend on the specific circumstances of the case. Considering the diverse range of types of conflict, it is evident that an individual approach must be taken in each situation. In the determination of specific measures that could be implemented, several factors must be considered. Economic, political, social, cultural and religious factors are decisive in establishing the goals as well as the feasibility of different transitional justice mechanisms.[1591] The principal mechanisms include judicial proceedings, amnesties, truth and reconciliation commissions, reparation programmes, lustrations, security sector reforms, memorialisation efforts and public apologies. Beyond that, traditional reconciliation mechanisms that may exist in a specific region can be employed. However, the measures have different objectives and complement each other. Whereas truth commissions, reparations and traditional mechanisms mainly work restoratively, criminal trials and lustrations have a primarily retributive effect.[1592] The different transitional justice measures can be employed selectively, simultaneously but also successively depending on the specific situation.[1593]

1586 *Aukerman*, Harvard HRJ, 2002, 39(15), p. 39, at 57.
1587 *Kritz*, Law & Contemp. Probs., 1996, 59(4), p. 127, at 139.
1588 *Aukerman*, Harvard HRJ, 2002, 39(15), p. 39, at 77.
1589 *Hazan*, IRCR, 2006, 88(861), p. 19, at 26.
1590 *Aukerman*, Harvard HRJ, 2002, 39(15), p. 39, at 77.
1591 *Aukerman*, Harvard HRJ, 2002, 39(15), p. 39, at 92.
1592 *Schilling*, Vergessen, p. 165.
1593 *Hazan*, IRCR, 2006, 88(861), p. 19, at 23.

1.2 Objectives and limitations of criminal trials in transitional justice processes

Criminal trials, whether at the domestic or international level, are a frequently employed transitional justice mechanism and have gained in importance with the establishment of the ad hoc international tribunals and the International Criminal Court. While the need for criminal trials for transitional justice is generally undisputed, it is also clear that trials in isolation are not able to achieve the aims of transitional justice. The objectives of criminal trials in the context of transitional justice differ from trials in ordinary criminal law because they deal with crimes that affect broader society and do not only concern the relationship between victims and perpetrators.

Criminal trials establish individual accountability and thereby impede assignation of collective guilt to an entire community.[1594] Individual accountability also shows that the crimes were not carried out by abstract entities.[1595] Nevertheless, the scope of trials in this context is limited inasmuch as trials are always selective and it will never be possible to call all perpetrators to account.[1596]

Beyond that, criminal prosecutions set an end to the culture of impunity. In fact, deterrence is often brought up as an aim of international criminal justice. The ICTY Trial Chamber defined retribution as well as general and individual deterrence as the main purposes for imposing sentences.[1597] At the same time, ending impunity helps to avoid acts of revenge on the private level.[1598]

An important effect of criminal trials is that they satisfy the victims' need for retribution as they see that the perpetrators pay for their crimes,[1599] and thereby contribute to reconciliation[1600]. Nevertheless, it must also be mentioned that true retribution for crimes of such a nature cannot be achieved.[1601]

Criminal trials serve also to recognise facts and thereby contribute to the establishment of truth. Court verdicts that confirm that certain crimes were committed are an effective measure to counter the frequent practice of denial and they prevent historical revisionism.[1602] Nevertheless, the historical record a court creates is limited by several factors such as the jurisdiction of a tribunal.[1603] In contrast, truth commissions are certainly far more effective for establishing an overall national narrative of the his-

---

1594 *Kritz*, Law & Contemp. Probs., 1996, 59(4), p. 127, at 128.
1595 *Werle/Jessberger*, International Criminal Law, 3. edn, marginal no. 112.
1596 *Aukerman*, Harvard HRJ, 2002, 39(15), p. 39, at 61.
1597 ICTY (TC), *Prosecutor v. Kupreškić et al.*, Judgment, 14 January 2000, paras. 848, 849.
1598 *Huyse*, in: *Bloomfeld/Barnes/Huyse* (eds), Reconciliation after Conflict, p. 89, at 98.
1599 *Cassese*, MLR, 1998, 61(1), p. 1, at 6.
1600 *Cassese*, MLR, 1998, 61(1), p. 1, at 6.
1601 *Aukerman*, Harvard HRJ, 2002, 39(15), p. 39, at 57.
1602 *Werle/Jessberger*, International Criminal Law, 3. edn, marginal no. 111.
1603 *Gaynor*, JICJ, 2012, 10(5), p. 1257, at 1263–1271.

torical events.[1604] In fact, the ICTY Trial Chamber affirmed that the ICTY was not established 'to create a historical record'.[1605] However, Gaynor rightly argues that a trial of political leaders that involves numerous documents and witness testimonies necessarily creates a historical record, regardless of the intention framed.[1606] The right to know the truth is also a right of the victims, and trials contribute to the satisfaction of this right.[1607]

Furthermore, criminal trials can officially recognise victims. This not only recognises the suffering of the victims and thereby contributes to their rehabilitation but can also identify those who are entitled to reparations.[1608] If the legal framework allows for it, courts can even directly impose the payment of reparations as a fine through the verdict and thereby directly satisfy the victims' right to compensation. Nevertheless, the fact that compensation is imposed through a verdict does not mean that the payment actually takes place as it depends on the liquidity of the convict.[1609] Beyond that, the fact that trials are selective results in an inability to recognise all victims and leaves out those who are not victims of the particular perpetrators who are prosecuted.

Criminal trials are further said to strengthen the rule of law and to reinforce moral norms.[1610] Trials on the domestic level can help to rebuild or strengthen the domestic judiciary and to reinforce its credibility.[1611] Beyond that, a criminal trial reinforces moral norms because it determines what is wrong[1612] and positively defines and strengthens norms.[1613] Nevertheless, the reinforcement of moral norms can only take place if the trials find acceptance. Trials that are perceived as victor's justice will certainly not incentivise society to accept the moral values reinforced through them.[1614]

While criminal justice can certainly have a variety of positive effects in the process of transitional justice, it is also clear that the method of implementation is crucial for success in achieving these aims. Criminal trials are unable to contribute to reconciliation or to a sense of justice if they do not comply with fair trial standards because they

---

1604 *Minow* in: *Buchanan/Zumbansen* (eds), Law in Transition, p. 203, at 211.
1605 ICTY (TC), *Prosecutor v. Stanišić et al.*, Decision Pursuant to Rule 73bis(D), 4 February 2008, para. 21.
1606 *Gaynor*, JICJ, 2012, 10(5), p. 1257, at 1262.
1607 *Werle/Jessberger*, International Criminal Law, 3. edn, marginal no. 112.
1608 *Schilling*, Vergessen, p. 137.
1609 *Schilling*, Vergessen, p. 137.
1610 *Aukerman*, Harvard HRJ, 2002, 39(15), p. 39, at 72–73.
1611 *Kritz*, Law & Contemp. Probs., 1996, 59(4), p. 127, at 133.
1612 *Aukerman*, Harvard HRJ, 2002, 39(15), p. 39, at 74.
1613 *Aukerman*, Harvard HRJ, 2002, 39(15), p. 39, at 75.
1614 *Aukerman*, Harvard HRJ, 2002, 39(15), p. 39, at 90.

will create a feeling of victor's justice.[1615] In this case, trials can have a rather negative effect and can nourish new violence instead of contributing to ending the conflict.[1616]

Impunity also adversely affects the rights of victims of gross human rights violations. The relation between the rights of victims and impunity was determined in a UN study on impunity in 1997. In this study, Joinet identified three major rights of victims: the right to know, the right to justice and the right to reparation, and established principles on measures to be taken to implement these rights.[1617] The study was continued in 2004 by independent expert Diane Orentlicher who updated the set of principles to combat impunity.[1618]

The right to justice encompasses the right of a victim to have a fair and effective remedy. This means that victims have a right to see the oppressor stand trial as well as a right to reparations.[1619] The right to know encompasses the right of an individual victim and his or her relatives to know what happened but also a collective right of society to know with the intention of preserving history and preventing its reoccurrence.[1620] The right to reparations embraces the right of individual victims and relatives to compensation, rehabilitation and restitution and a right to non-recurrence.[1621] While not all of these rights are sufficiently satisfied through criminal trials, ending impunity is essential for their enforcement.

2 The ICT's contribution to the process of transitional justice

The case of Bangladesh is marked by the absence of a transitional justice process and impunity over many years. Reinitiating a process of transitional justice after 40 years is a particular task and overcoming more than 40 years of impunity and denial of

---

1615 *Kritz*, Law & Contemp. Probs., 1996, 59(4), p. 127, at 137.
1616 *Aukerman*, Harvard HRJ, 2002, 39(15), p. 39, at 60.
1617 Economic and Social Council, Commission on Human Rights, Sub-Commission on Prevention of Discrimination and Protection of Minorities, 26 June 1997 (UN Doc. E/CN.4/Sub.2/1997/20).
1618 Report of the Independent Expert to Update the Set of Principles to Combat Impunity, Diane Orentlicher, 8 February 2005 (UN Doc. E/CN.4/2005/102/Add.1).
1619 Economic and Social Council, Commission on Human Rights, Sub-Commission on Prevention of Discrimination and Protection of Minorities, 26 June 1997, para. 26 (UN Doc. E/CN.4/Sub.2/1997/20).
1620 Economic and Social Council, Commission on Human Rights, Sub-Commission on Prevention of Discrimination and Protection of Minorities, 26 June 1997, para. 17 (UN Doc. E/CN.4/Sub.2/1997/20).
1621 Economic and Social Council, Commission on Human Rights, Sub-Commission on Prevention of Discrimination and Protection of Minorities, 26 June 1997, paras. 41–43 (UN Doc. E/CN.4/Sub.2/1997/20).

compensation and rehabilitation for victims is challenging. While some perpetrators have lived as a part of society and some have even held important political offices in the country, the main perpetrators evaded prosecution. Breaking with this culture encounters resistance and runs the risk of polarising society and generating new conflicts.

2.1 Factors that determine and limit transitional justice in Bangladesh

The process of transitional justice in Bangladesh is influenced by several factors such as the nature of the conflict, the long lapse of time since the commission of the crimes, cultural aspects, financial resources and the political environment in the country.

The nature of the conflict in Bangladesh has had a substantial influence on the culture of impunity. Since the crimes were committed in the course of the Liberation War, the main perpetrators of the Pakistani army were not nationals of the seceded state of Bangladesh. The Pakistani army officers were granted amnesties and evaded not only criminal responsibility but also moral responsibility because Pakistan never officially assumed responsibility for the crimes and never publicly apologised. Pakistani women's rights associations have issued apologies to Bengali victims of sexual violence but this is a symbolic gesture that clearly cannot replace an apology from the government.[1622]

The refusal of Pakistan to deal with the events of 1971 and to prosecute the main perpetrators will always obstruct the process of ending impunity. In fact, the Pakistani national narrative differs greatly from that of Bangladesh. Apart from the denial of the army's involvement in the crimes, the Bengalis are blamed for their 'betrayal' based on their alliance with India.[1623] The fact that the Pakistani perpetrators will probably never stand trial not only hampers the recognition of the suffering of the victims but also creates severe problems in terms of justice. Those who collaborated with the main perpetrators incur liability and are executed, whereas the main perpetrators remain unidentified and unpunished.

Of great influence on the transitional process in Bangladesh is also the political instability in the country. The strong rivalries between the leading political parties do not favour the process of coming to terms with the past. The role of today's political parties during the Liberation War significantly contributes to a tense environment. While the Awami League led the country during the struggle for liberation, Jamaat-e-Islami strongly opposed it and supported the Pakistani army. Perceptions of the Liberation War differ greatly in Bangladesh. In addition, the fact that today's prime minister is the daughter of Sheikh Mujibur Rahman means that there is a risk that the

---

1622 *D'Costa*, Nationbuilding, p. 158.
1623 *Saikia*, JGR, 2011, 13(4), p. 475, at 481.

transitional justice process is motivated by personal retaliation rather than by society's needs and interests.

The prevailing historical narrative in Bangladesh and its legal reinforcement prevent a nuanced approach towards the historical events and impose a one-sided narrative that works only with the categories of heroes and enemies. Differing perspectives are suppressed, as is criticism of the national narrative. The ICT has been employed as one of the mechanisms to silence criticism. Even more worrying in this context is the Bangladesh Liberation War (Denial, Distortion, Opposition) Crime Law which criminalises diversions from the official narrative of the Liberation War[1624]. Among other things, the Law criminalises giving a malicious statement in the media that undermines the Liberation War, the misinterpretation or devaluation of any government publication on the history of the Liberation War, and the trivialising of any information related to the martyrs, female war heroines, killing of civilians, arson, rape and looting. The Law not only curtails freedom of speech but also impedes historical research on the Liberation War.[1625] Beyond that, it establishes an extremely broad notion of participation. Section 4(2) and Section 6(1) criminalise 'any supporting activities' and assistance and conspiracy to commit any of the crimes. Between three months and five years of imprisonment can be imposed as well as a fine of up to one crore (10 million) taka. Moreover, Section 5(2) determines that, if a person repeats the crime for which he has been convicted, the penalty imposed for the first crime will be doubled. While the aim of transitional justice is to develop a shared perspective of history, in Bangladesh this process is hampered through the forceful imposition of a narrative.

This official historical narrative also influences the perception of the role of women during the Liberation War. Although women contributed to the Liberation War by taking care of families, providing support for freedom fighters or even directly as freedom fighters,[1626] in the official narrative they appear predominantly as victims[1627]. Women's memories of the Liberation War have mainly been excluded from the national narrative.[1628] In fact, most rape victims in Bangladesh feel that they cannot 'control their own narratives' and that they suffer from the labels imposed upon them by others.[1629] It will be difficult to break victimisation and to empower women to shape their own narrative.

1624 *Riaz*, Bangladesh – Islamist Militancy, Democracy Deficit and Where to Next?, Al Jazeera, 28 June 2016. For an unofficial translation of the Law, see http://bangladeshpolitico.blogspot.de/2016/04/crime-of-distortion-of-history-of.html, accessed 17 December 2017.
1625 *Bergman*, The Politics of Bangladesh's Genocide Debate, New York Times, 5 April 2016.
1626 *D'Costa*, Nationbuilding, p. 140.
1627 *Alam*, Women and Transitional Justice, p. 57.
1628 *D'Costa*, Nationbuilding, p. 143.
1629 *Herman, Elizabeth* quoted in: *Alam*, Women and Transitional Justice, p. 57.

Part V: The ICT in the context of transitional justice in Bangladesh

Due to the long lapse of time since the Liberation War, many victims as well as perpetrators have passed away. Those victims' accounts will remain untold, and the perpetrators will remain unpunished and unidentified. While this certainly leads to severe evidence problems in the context of criminal accountability, it also leads to a fragmentary construction of the historical events.

At the same time, the fact that many victims have lived with their traumatic and often untold experiences for decades may complicate the process of breaking the silence and lead to re-traumatisation; for victims of sexual violence, in particular, this could lead to stigmatisation and expulsion from their community.

Religious factors also shape the process of transitional justice. In particular, the process of dealing with sexual violence might be different from the approach taken in western societies where the focus is on victims speaking up about their experiences.[1630]

The process of transitional justice and the measures, as well as their quality, depend, to a large extent, on financial resources. Without contributions from the international community, financial resources are tight and limit the possibility of employing different measures, and their quality. In the context of the ICT, this leads to limitations in the capacities. The lack of financial resources also constitutes a barrier to the implementation of further non-judicial mechanisms in Bangladesh which would allow a more comprehensive approach.

2.2 The ICT as a transitional justice mechanism

After the first endeavours of prosecuting war criminals in the aftermath of the Liberation War, the ICT was the first official step towards ending impunity. It quickly satisfied society's demands for heavy punishment and fulfilled the need to see that justice is done. Nevertheless, its ability to contribute to a transitional justice process aimed at reconciliation is questionable.

2.2.1 Contribution to justice

The ICT has contributed to a process of justice inasmuch as it ended impunity and started to bring alleged perpetrators to trial. In Bangladesh, impunity is not a problem that is merely related to the Liberation War but rather a phenomenon that governs the entire legal system. Impunity is a frequent practice in cases of torture, arbitrary arrests and enforced disappearances.[1631] The ICT has thus been an important step and a positive signal for the victims and society. Beyond that, setting up the Tribunal was ex-

---

1630 *Linton*, CLF, 2010, 21(2), p. 191, at 304.
1631 *Human Rights Watch*, World Report 2016, p. 106.

tremely fast and the delivery of judgments followed instantly. Also, executions were carried out without a time lag. The fact that the Tribunal was established as a domestic accountability mechanism contributed to the pace with which the process to end impunity was initiated. It would have taken significantly more time to set up an internationalised tribunal. Nevertheless, the scrutiny in Part IV has shown that this has led to compromises with regard to the quality of the jurisprudence and legal framework.

Because of practical problems, the Tribunal has not been able to fill the impunity gap caused by the amnesties granted to the Pakistani perpetrators. The fact that the main perpetrators will never be tried means that impunity will continue to prevail for them. Although this problem is not directly caused by the ICT, it raises the question of whether impunity can really end if those most responsible are spared. The trial of the Pakistani perpetrators could only be addressed at the international level. Although the Tribunal has personal jurisdiction over foreign nationals also, no attempts to try Pakistani nationals in absentia have been made. In fact, this would lead to an escalation of the already tense relations between Pakistan and Bangladesh. Due to the flawed proceedings and the imposition of the death penalty, the Tribunal has not received support from the international community and there will be no international support for the trial of Pakistani nationals before the ICT.

However, even with regard to Bangladeshi nationals, it will not be possible to hold every perpetrator accountable. Criminal trials in the context of gross human rights violations are always selective. In the context of the ICT, there is no formulated strategy on this issue. While the Investigation Agency says that investigations are ongoing in at least 3,000 further cases,[1632] it is quite clear that the Tribunal with its current capacity will not be able to try all of these cases. In fact, the recent merger of both Tribunals indicates that the trial of only a limited number of perpetrators is intended. Nevertheless, this issue has not been officially raised and no policy on how to deal with this form of impunity has been formulated.

Although the ICT has ended impunity, it is debatable whether the Tribunal has actually established individual accountability. The Tribunal has tried individuals, found them guilty and convicted them. However, the flawed application of the modes of liability and the elements of crimes raises severe concerns as to whether the Tribunal has really established individual accountability. As scrutinised above, the Tribunal has in several judgments assumed accountability based on membership. Beyond that, the excessive use of judicial notice has allowed the Tribunal to dispense with evidence that would have been required to establish individual accountability. In Bangladesh, it is often argued that everyone knows who the perpetrators were in order to justify the shortcomings of the Tribunal. As the Tribunal has pointed out frequently, a lot of evi-

---

1632 *Adhikary*, Government Plan Not Welcome, The Daily Star, 17 August 2015.

dence was destroyed after the war[1633] and is therefore no longer available. However, this argument can under no circumstances be applied in a court as it violates the presumption of innocence and the requirement that charges have to be proven beyond reasonable doubt.

Problems in this context arise also with regard to the lack of impartiality and independence of the Tribunal, which influences its ability to establish individual accountability based on the law. The tense environment that surrounds the ICT raises doubts as to whether an acquittal, if justified, would be an option at all for the Tribunal. The Shahbag movement has also shown that large parts of society demand the death penalty and it is clear that an acquittal would not find acceptance in society very easily.

The assessment of the Tribunal's contribution to justice must be viewed also in the context of its obligation to the victims. As outlined above, criminal trials fulfil a moral duty to the victims and contribute to their official recognition as victims. It seems doubtful whether the Tribunal has been able to comply with these aims.

Although the needs of the victims are always highlighted in the debate about the Tribunal and to justify the trials in front of the international community, their rights and needs have not been at the centre of the ICT. On the contrary, in the framing of the ICT Act as well as in the amendments the rights of victims were entirely left out. The Tribunal has partly tried to fill this gap with the RoP but, as scrutinised above, the scope of these provisions is limited. Trials in cases of mass human rights abuses are particularly important for victims and it is therefore necessary to take into account their interests during trial. The ICT is entirely perpetrator-orientated and victims have no right of participation except in their function as witnesses. Although victims who testify before the Tribunal are officially recognised as victims, the benefit for them is limited if one considers the absence of sufficient protection mechanisms. The several instances of harassment of witnesses have shown that testifying before the Tribunal is risky. Without a functioning victim protection mechanism and a strong focus on victims, the Tribunal will not be able to fulfil its moral duty and contribute to justice for the victims.

This problem becomes even more relevant in the context of female victims. Insufficient participation of women in the trials has led to a disregard for their interests. It is men who deal with the issue of sexual violence and decide on the approach that shall be taken. The absence of a participatory approach reproduces gender inequality and injustice.[1634] In this context, the judgments reveal that the judges have adopted

---

1633 See, for instance, ICT 1, *The Chief Prosecutor v. Azam*, case no. 05/2013, Judgment, 30 December 2014, para. 41; ICT 1, *The Chief Prosecutor v. Nizami*, case no. 03/2011, Judgment, 29 October 2014, para. 385; ICT 1, *The Chief Prosecutor v. Islam*, case no. 05/2013, Judgment, 30 September 2014, para. 41.
1634 *Alam*, Women and Transitional Justice, p. 71.

2 The ICT's contribution to the process of transitional justice

patriarchal views of rape that further reemphasise the perception of rape as a loss of dignity. This approach has not helped to overcome victimisation.

It is recognised that justice must also be seen to be done. Yet, the visibility of the ICT's justice is hampered by a lack of outreach and accessibility of the Tribunal. A fundamental principle of transitional justice is to address society as a whole and not merely some individuals.[1635] With regard to the ICT, it is necessary to create greater transparency of the entire proceedings and not merely of the outcomes.[1636] Access must be granted to all parts of society. The restrictions and difficulties with regard to the physical accessibility of the Tribunal have been outlined above.

Several factors further limit the Tribunal's outreach. The judgments are written in English, which makes them inaccessible for large parts of society. Translations into Bengali are not provided which means that not even the witnesses who testify for the Tribunal and who often come from rural areas and only speak Bengali are able to access the results of the proceedings contained in the judgments. Besides the language barrier, illiteracy also hampers the outreach. The literacy rate in Bangladesh among adults is 61 %.[1637] The average Bangladeshi also has no access to the internet, which is currently used by the Tribunal to distribute the judgments and the charge framing orders. The trials are all recorded on video but there is no information on what these tapes are or will be used for. They have not been made public.

Although criminal trials in the context of transitional justice can strengthen the rule of law, improve the effectiveness of criminal justice and promote trust in the judiciary, the ICT has not been able to contribute significantly to these purposes. As the scrutiny in Part IV has shown, the ICT's jurisprudence and procedure are marked by major flaws in the application of the law as well as procedure, which significantly violates the rights of the accused.

Yet, for the analysis of the Tribunal's contribution to the strengthening of the rule of law in Bangladesh, the domestic standards must be the point of reference. Nevertheless, as the scrutiny in Part IV has shown, the procedural standards applied to the ICT lag behind the domestic standards in ordinary criminal trials on several counts. The constitutional restrictions are one of the major causes of this practice. Under these circumstances, the ICT is a step backward and rather drives Bangladesh's legal system away from the basic rule of law standards. This can even have a negative impact on standards applied to ordinary criminal trials as the ICT Act can serve as a justification for curtailing the rights of the accused under other laws as well and can promote the practice of special tribunals that deprive the accused of fundamental procedural rights.

1635 *Alam*, Women and Transitional Justice, p. 72.
1636 *Alam*, Women and Transitional Justice, p. 72.
1637 *The World Bank*, data from 2015, http://data.worldbank.org/indicator/SE.ADT.LITR.ZS/countries, accessed 18 December 2016.

On the other hand, with regard to the organisational structure, the ICT could serve as a role model of effective criminal justice for the domestic judiciary. The ICT's method of functioning is outstanding in many ways against the background of ordinary criminal trials in the Bangladeshi judicial system. The ICT was extremely fast in its establishment and in the delivery of judgments. The entire process is highly organised, time schedules are usually complied with and judgments are delivered promptly. This is definitely an improvement in comparison to the domestic legal system which is characterised by chronic overloading with cases pending for years.

The impact of the Tribunal on strengthening the trust in the judiciary is likewise limited. As mentioned above, opinion polls have shown that the majority of society considers the trials before the ICT to be unfair but still want them to continue. This clearly reveals that society has, in fact, no trust in the judiciary and that unfair trials are considered the norm. Although the Tribunal is a strong signal against impunity, building trust in the judiciary requires strict compliance with the rule of law.

2.2.2 Contribution to establishment of truth

Whether the ICT has made a contribution to the establishment of truth must be viewed in the context of specific cases as well as in the context of a general historical narrative.

Although the effect of criminal trials in establishing a historical narrative is limited, the jurisprudence of the Tribunal suggests that this was one of the main objectives of the ICT. All of the judgments contain a historical background which repeats the heroic national narrative of the Liberation War and, at the same time, is considered a fact of common knowledge and invoked for the adjudication of the charges. This narrative also contains legal classifications of the crimes that were committed by the Pakistani army. In this context, the trials were instrumentalised as an authorised body to award official validity to the historical narrative framed by the Awami League. The Liberation War Denial Law is a further and worrying step in this direction. It is evident that a national narrative cannot be imposed but rather requires a societal discourse. Trials can initiate a societal discourse because they bring the issue into the public spotlight. Yet, the ICT has had the opposite effect.

Also, the ICT's contribution to the establishment of truth through evidence and in the context of specific cases must be viewed critically. The flawed application of the modes of liability impedes the determination of the actual roles of the accused during the war. Beyond that, the excessive use of judicial notice leads to formulaic confirmation of a 'truth' that has been established prior to the trial.

The numerous scandals of influenced witnesses as well as the disappearances of witnesses also raise serious doubts as to whether the truth can be established at all without sufficient witness protection. The risk of false testimonies is high if witnesses are threatened and coerced.

However, the trials have contributed to establishing the truth inasmuch as they have ended the denial that serious crimes were committed during the Liberation War and certainly have a positive impact on the victims in this regard. Although the Pakistan government continues to deny its responsibility in the commission of the crimes, the suffering of the victims found at least approval through national recognition confirmed by the ICT. After decades of silence, this is undoubtedly an important step.

2.2.3 Contribution to reparations

The Tribunal's impact on the victims' right to reparations has been low. This shortcoming has its origins in the absence of a legal framework that empowers the Tribunal to take measures in this regard. Although the Tribunal has introduced the possibility to pass a compensation order into the RoP, this provision has, as the Tribunal found, no practical impact because the RoP cannot overrule an act of Parliament. There is also no possibility of an adhesion procedure under the ICT Act that enables victims to enforce their claims for compensation against the perpetrators.

Independently from the trials, reparations have been provided in the form of pensions for freedom fighters through the Freedom Fighters Welfare Trust Order, 1972. Freedom fighters and their families further benefit from a quota in government jobs. As outlined above, in this context, the recent development of the recognition of rape victims as freedom fighters to entitle them to pensions is remarkable. Nevertheless, the number of victims that have benefited from this action is low compared to the total number of victims and, to date, many have not received any compensation at all. In particular, many rape victims have led their lives in poverty since the war.

Other forms of reparation such as medical and psychological support are also not provided for in the ICT Act, and the Tribunal, in fact, lacks the respective facilities to this end.

2.3 Interim findings

The ICT has not made major contributions either to justice or to the establishment of the truth or to reparations. Its function as a transitional justice mechanism, therefore, must be questioned. The most important contribution was probably the symbolic effect the Tribunal had. Nevertheless, against the background of the severe flaws in the proceedings, it is difficult to consider this a contribution to justice.

Also, the assumption that the implementation of justice through new injustice creates new conflicts and leads to new violence has proven true in the case of Bangladesh. With the trials, a new degree of hostility and political divide has arisen in the country, and countrywide *hartals* have become a routine answer to the ICT's verdicts.

Part VI: Conclusion and outlook

The scrutiny under Part IV has revealed the severe shortcomings of the legal sources and their interpretation in jurisprudence. These shortcomings are partly based on the imprecise and incomplete legal sources but also, to a large extent, on their restrictive interpretation by the Tribunal.

With regard to the material law, the problem lies mainly in the flawed application of the elements of crime to the specific cases rather than in the legal framework. Although the definitions under the ICT Act differ from the internationally established definitions, these discrepancies could easily have been overcome through interpretation and the consequent application of international jurisprudence.

On the other hand, in the context of the modes of liability, the causes for the extension of criminal liability lie partly in the confusing system of criminal liability established in the ICT Act. The Act adopts neither the domestic nor the international modes of liability and thus domestic law can hardly be invoked for the interpretation. Nevertheless, with regard to the modes of liability, the application of international jurisprudence to the cases is flawed and the Tribunal frequently relies on the concept of membership of a criminal organisation, although this was not implemented in the ICT Act and does not exist under current international criminal law.

On the contrary, with regard to procedural law, the scrutiny has shown that the legal framework is the main reason for the lack of fair trial standards. The ICT Act and the RoP are incomplete with regard to procedural law and have several gaps. Beyond that, the way in which both legal sources implement the rights of the accused is highly problematic because the application of several rights is at the discretion of the Tribunal. Yet, the major problem lies with the constitutional restrictions which significantly curtail the fundamental rights of the accused. Although not all of these constitutional restrictions were implemented in the ICT Act and the RoP, the effect of legal provisions that exceed these restrictions is doubtful. With regard to several procedural rights, the ICT Act also clearly lags behind ordinary domestic criminal law.

Overall, the application and interpretation of the law by the ICT is characterised by the absence of a systematic approach, the establishment of imprecise definitions or even the renunciation of definitions, as well as the flawed application of definitions to the cases.

These severe shortcomings hamper the ICT's contribution to the process of transitional justice in Bangladesh. While the Tribunal was able to satisfy the demands of large parts of society for fast and capital punishment, it did not take into account the interests of the victims and, overall, the trials failed to contribute to the establishment of justice, truth and reparations and to initiate a process of reconciliation.

In the light of the foregoing, the ICT in Bangladesh cannot be deemed a role model for the domestic implementation of international criminal justice. On the contrary, the

Part VI: Conclusion and outlook

flawed application of international criminal law reveals the unfamiliarity of the judges with the subject matter as well as the lack of proper training and preparation of the judges and the prosecution. For this reason, the ICT has not contributed to jurisprudence in international criminal law and it is clear that its jurisprudence will have no significance beyond state borders.

While the ICC lacks temporal jurisdiction over crimes committed during the Liberation War, and the admissibility of cases based on the inability of Bangladesh genuinely to prosecute is out of question in this context, the issue of admissibility could become relevant in relation to future trials. That is, despite prosecutions on the domestic level, cases that fall into the ICC's temporal jurisdiction could be admissible before the ICC if Bangladesh is considered unable genuinely to prosecute. As outlined in Part I, the drafters of the informal expert paper on the principle of complementarity determined that proceedings need to be conducted with 'a basic level of objective quality'.[1638] Whether this threshold would indeed be exceeded if trials were conducted with the standards applied by the ICT is questionable. Nevertheless, there are strong indications that the ICT lacks a basic level of objective quality and that the ability to prosecute genuinely would at least have to be questioned earnestly.

The future of the ICT and international criminal law in Bangladesh is uncertain. This is due to practical reasons because, if the opposition comes to power, it is clear that the removal of the ICT will be one of their first actions. Beyond that, no strategies have been formulated with regard to the number of cases that will be prosecuted and possible restrictions with regard to the levels of the perpetrators. There is no official completion strategy and no timeline has been officially announced.

It is also unclear whether the ICT and its legal framework are aimed at the creation of a permanent domestic accountability mechanism for the trial of perpetrators of international crimes or whether the Tribunal will deal only with cases related to 1971. However, considering that Bangladesh is a state party to the Rome Statute, it would clearly be desirable for there to be a permanent law that implements international criminal law.

With regard to the prosecution of crimes committed during the Liberation War, the standards are set and there are no indications that the participating stakeholders have any intention of changing the course. Pressure and criticism from the international community and international human rights organisations have fallen on deaf ears. This shows that there continues to be no interest in setting up an internationalised tribunal. Nevertheless, even amendments to the domestic law could contribute significantly to improvements in the trials. Although this would not help to overcome the flawed application of the law, it would be an important step to create legal certainty. A

1638 *Office of the Prosecutor*, Informal Expert Paper, para. 23.

comprehensive revision of the Act is also indispensable to comply with international law and to fill the gaps if the ICT Act remains a permanent law to implement international criminal law at the domestic level.

References

Adhikary, Tuhin Shubhra, Government Plan Not Welcome, The Daily Star, 17 August 2015, http://www.thedailystar.net/backpage/govt-plan-not-welcome-128119, accessed 11 December 2016 (cited: Adhikary, Government Plan Not Welcome, The Daily Star, 17 August 2015)

Ahmed, Imtiaz, Historicizing 1971 Genocide: State versus Person, Dhaka, 2009 (cited: Ahmed, Historicizing Genocide)

Ahmad, Jamil-ud-Din (ed.), Speeches and Writings of Mr. Jinnah, Vol. 2, Lahore, 1947, reprinted 1964 (cited: Ahmad, Speeches and Writings of Jinnah, Vol. 2)

Ahmed, Kawser / Sunga, Lyal S., A Critical Appraisal of Laws Relating to Sexual Offences in Bangladesh – A Study Commissioned by the National Human Rights Commission Bangladesh, 2015, http://nhrc.portal.gov.bd/sites/default/files/files/nhrc.portal.gov.bd/page/348ec5eb_22f8_4754_bb62_6a0d15ba1513/Study%20Report%20on%20Sexual%20Offences_Final.pdf, accessed 11 December 2016 (cited: Ahmed/Sunga, Critical Appraisal of Laws Relating to Sexual Offences in Bangladesh)

Akmam, Wardatul, Atrocities against Humanity during the Liberation War in Bangladesh: A Case of Genocide, in: Journal of Genocide Research (JGR), 2002, 4(4), pp. 543–559 (cited: Wardatul, JGR, 2002, 4(4))

Alam, Mayesha, Women and Transitional Justice: Progress and Persistent Challenges in Retributive and Restorative Processes, Basingstoke (Hampshire) et al., 2014 (cited: Alam, Women and Transitional Justice)

Alam, M. Shah, Enforcement of International Human Rights Law by Domestic Courts, Dhaka, 2007 (cited: Alam, Enforcement of International Human Rights Law)

Al Faruque, Abdullah / Rahaman, Sazzatur, Victim Protection in Bangladesh – A Critical Appraisal of Legal and Institutional Framework, in: Bangladesh Journal of Law (BD JL), 2013, 13(1/2), pp. 33–48 (cited: Al Faruque/Rahaman, BD JL, 2013, 13(1/2))

Ali, Syed Mahmud, Understanding Bangladesh, London, 2010 (cited: Ali, Understanding Bangladesh)

Al-Masum, Abdullah, Muslim Reaction to the Annulment of the Partition of Bengal and Establishment of Dhaka University, in: Journal of the Pakistan Historical Society (JPHS), 2003, LI(4), pp. 95–119 (cited: Al-Masum, JPHS 2003, LI(4))

Ambos, Kai, Nulla Poena Sine Lege in International Criminal Law, in: Haveman, Roelof / Olusanya, Olaoluwa (eds), Sentencing and Sanctioning in Supranational

References

Criminal Law, Antwerp et al., 2006, pp. 17–35 (cited: Ambos, in: Haveman/Olusanya (eds), Sentencing and Sanctioning in Supranational Criminal Law)

– The Legal Framework of Transitional Justice: A Systematic Study with a Special Focus on the Role of the ICC, in: Ambos, Kai / Large, Judith / Wierda, Marieke (eds), Building a Future on Peace and Justice, Berlin et al., 2009, pp. 19–103 (cited: Ambos, in: Ambos, Kai / Large, Judith / Wierda, Marieke (eds), Building a Future)

– What does 'Intent to Destroy' in Genocide Mean?, in: International Review of the Red Cross (IRRC), 2009, 91(876), pp. 833–858 (cited: Ambos, IRRC, 2009, 91(876))

Amnesty International, Letter to the Chairman of the International Crimes Tribunal, 21 June 2011, http://ictbd-defenceteam.org/wp-content/uploads/2014/08/Amnesty_Letter_Tribunals.pdf, accessed 27 July 2016 (cited: Amnesty International, Letter to the Chairman of the ICT, 21 June 2011)

Askin, Kelly D., Prosecuting Wartime Rape and Other Gender Related Crimes under International Law: Extraordinary Advances, Enduring Obstacles, in: Berkeley Journal of International law (Berkeley JIL), 2003, 21, pp. 288–349 (cited: Askin, Berkeley JIL, 2003, 21)

Aukerman, Miriam J., Extraordinary Evil, Ordinary Crime: A Framework for Understanding Transitional Justice, in: Harvard Human Rights Journal (Harvard HRJ), 2002, 39(15), pp. 39–97 (cited: Aukerman, Harvard HRJ, 2002, 39(15))

Ayub Khan, Mohammad, Friends Not Masters: A Political Autobiography, Karachi et al., 1976 (cited: Ayub Khan, Friends not masters)

Basher Anik, Syed Samiul, Birangonas Get Freedom Fighter Status, Dhaka Tribune, 13 October 2015, http://www.dhakatribune.com/bangladesh/2015/oct/13/41-birangonas-get-freedom-fighter-status, accessed 11 December 2016 (cited: Basher Anik, Birangonas Get Freedom Fighter Status, Dhaka Tribune, 13 October 2015)

Bassiouni, M. Cherif, Crimes against Humanity – Historical Evolution and Contemporary Application, Cambridge et al., 2011 (cited: Bassiouni, Crimes against humanity)

Baxter, Craig, Bangladesh: From a Nation to a State, Boulder (Colorado), 1998 (cited: Baxter, Bangladesh)

Bdnews24, Bangladesh Keeps One 1971 War Crimes Tribunal in Operation, 15 September 2015, http://bdnews24.com/bangladesh/2015/09/15/bangladesh-keeps-one-1971-war-crimes-tribunal-in-operation, accessed 11 December 2011 (cited: Bdnews24, Bangladesh Keeps one 1971 War Crimes Tribunal in Operation, 15 September 2015)

Beachler, Donald, The Politics of Genocide Scholarship: The Case of Bangladesh, in: Patterns of Prejudice (PP), 2007, 41(5) (cited: Beachler, PP, 2007, 41(5))

Beloff, Michael J., Bangladesh – International Crimes (Tribunals) Act 1973 – Advice, 2009, http://ictbd-defenceteam.org/wp-content/uploads/2014/08/Beloff-QC_2009-Act.pdf, accessed 28 July 2016 (cited: Beloff, International Crimes (Tribunals) Act, 1973)

Bergman, David, Sayeedi Indictment – 1971 Deaths, 11 November 2011, http://bangladeshwarcrimes.blogspot.de/2011/11/sayedee-indictment-analysis-1971-death.html, accessed 11 December 2016 (cited: Bergman, Sayeedi indictment – 1971 deaths)

– Nielsen/Democracy International Polls, 19 September 2013, http://bangladesh politico.blogspot.de/2013/09/nielsendemocracy-international-polls-on.html, accessed 11 December 2016 (Bergman, Nielsen/Democracy International Polls, 19 September 2013)

– Bangladesh War Trials: Justice or Politics?, Al Jazeera, 23 December 2014, http://www.aljazeera.com/humanrights/2014/11/bangladesh-war-trials-justice-politics-2014112575656287496.html, accessed 11 December 2016 (cited: Bergman, Bangladesh War Trials: Justice or Politics?, Al Jazeera, 23 December 2014)

– The Politics of Bangladesh's Genocide Debate, The New York Times, 05 April 2016, http://www.nytimes.com/2016/04/06/opinion/the-politics-of-bangladeshs-genocide-debate.html?_r=0, accessed 11 December 2016 (cited: Bergman, The Politics of Bangladesh's Genocide Debate, The New York Times, 05 April 2016)

Bergsmo, Morten/Novic, Elisa, Justice after Decades in Bangladesh: National Trials for International Crimes, in: Journal of Genocide Research (JGR), 2011, 13(4), pp. 503–511 (cited: Bergsmo/Novic, JGR, 2011, 13(4))

Blast (Bangladesh Legal Aid and Services Trust), Review of the Torture and Custodial Death (Prevention) Act, 2013, http://www.blast.org.bd/content/publications/Review%20of%20The%20Torture%20&%20Custodial%20Death(Prevention)%20Act,%202013.pdf, accessed 11 December 2016 (cited: Blast, Review of the Torture and Custodial Death (Prevention) Act)

Blaustein, Albert/Paust, Jordan J., War Crimes Jurisdiction and Due Process: The Bangladesh Experience, Vanderbilt Journal of Transnational Law (Vanderbilt JTL), 1978, 11 (1), pp. 1–38 (cited: Blaustein/Paust, Vanderbilt JTL, 1978, 11 (1))

– Efforts after the Independence of Bangladesh, in: Paust, Jordan J. (ed.), International Criminal Law: Cases and Materials, pp. 510–517, 4. edn, Durham, 2013 (cited: Blaustein/Paust, in: Paust (ed.), International Criminal Law, 4. edn)

References

Boas, Gideon/Bischoff, James L./Reid, Natalie L., Forms of Responsibility in International Criminal Law, International Criminal Practitioner Library Series, Vol. 1, Cambridge et al., 2007 (cited: Gideon/Bischoff/Boas, Forms of Responsibility)

Boed, Roman, Individual Criminal Responsibility for Violations of Article 3 Common to the Geneva Conventions of 1949 and of Additional Protocol II Thereto in the Case Law of the International Criminal Tribunal for Rwanda, in: Criminal Law Forum (CLF), 2002, 13(3), pp. 293–322 (cited: Boed, CLF, 2002, 13(3))

Bose, Sarmila, Dead Reckoning: Memories of the 1971 Bangladesh War, London, 2011 (cited: Bose, Dead Reckoning)

– The Question of Genocide and the Quest for Justice in the 1971 War, in: Journal of Genocide Research (JGR), 2011, 13(4), pp. 393–419 (cited: Bose, JGR, 2011, 13(4))

Brownmiller, Susan, Against our Will: men, women and rape, London, 1975 (cited: Brownmiller, Against our Will)

Burke, S. M., The Postwar Diplomacy of the Indo-Pakistani War of 1971, in: Asian Survey (AS), November 1973, 13(11), pp. 1036–1049 (cited: Burke, AS, 1973, 13(11))

Cadman, Toby, Communication to the ICC Prosecutor Pursuant to Article 15 of the Rome Statute of the International Criminal Court to Open Preliminary Inquiry into the Situation of Bangladesh, 31 January 2014, http://9bri.com/wp-content/uploads/2014/02/ICC-Bangladesh-Submission-Summary.pdf, accessed 11 December 2016 (cited: Cadman, Communication, 31 January 2014)

Carnero Rojo, Enrique, The Role of Fair Trial Considerations in the Complementarity Regime of the International Criminal Court: From 'No Peace without Justice' to 'No Peace with Victor's Justice'?, in: Leiden Journal of International Law (LJIL), 2005, 18(4), pp. 829–869 (cited: Carnero Rojo, LJIL, 2005, 18(4))

Cassese, Antonio, Reflections on International Criminal Justice, in: Modern Law Review (MLR), 1998, 61(1), pp. 1–10 (cited: Cassese, MLR, 1998, 61(1))

– Balancing the Prosecution of Crimes against Humanity and Non-Retroactivity of Criminal Law, in: Journal of International Criminal Justice (JICJ), 2006, 4(2), pp. 410–418 (cited: Cassese, JICJ, 2006, 4(2))

– Cassese's International Criminal Law, 3. edn, Oxford, 2013 (cited: Cassese, International Criminal Law, 3. edn)

Cassese, Antonio/Gaeta, Paola/Jones, John R. W. D. (eds), The Rome Statute of the International Criminal Court: A Commentary, Volume 1 & 2, Oxford et al., 2002 (cited: Cassese/Gaeta/Jones/Contributor, Rome Statute Commentary, Vol. 1/ Vol. 2)

References

Charlesworth, Hilary/Chinkin, Christine, The Boundaries of International Law – A Feminist Analysis, Manchester, 2000 (cited: Charlesworth/Chinkin, Boundaries of International Law)

Chatterji, Joya, The Making of a Borderline: The Radcliffe Award for Bengal, in: Talbot, Ian/Singh, Gurharpal (eds), Region and Partition: Bengal, Punjab and the Partition of the Subcontinent, pp. 168–202, Oxford et al., 1999 (cited: Chatterji, in: Talbot/Singh (eds), Region and Partition)

Chaudhuri, Kalyan, Genocide in Bangladesh, Bombay et al., 1972 (cited: Chaudhuri, Genocide in Bangladesh)

Chowdhury, Abdul Mu'min, Behind the Myth of Three Million, London, 1996, (cited: Chowdhury, Myth of Three Million)

Corten, Olivier/Klein, Pierre, The Vienna Conventions on the Law of Treaties – A Commentary, Volume 2, Oxford et al., 2011 (cited: Corten/Klein/Contributor, Commentary Vienna Conventions on the Law of Treaties, Vol. 2)

Cryer, Robert/Friman, Håkan/Robinson, Darryl, Wilmshurst, Elizabeth, An Introduction to International Criminal Law and Procedure, 3. edn, Cambridge, 2014 (cited: Cryer et al., International Criminal Law, 3. edn)

Daily Star, The, Stop War Crimes Trial, 4 December 2011, http://archive.thedailystar.net/newDesign/news-details.php?nid=212824, accessed 11 December 2016 (cited: The Daily Star, Amend War Crimes Act to Try Jamaat, 16 November 2014)

– Blogger Brutally Killed, 16 February 2013, http://archive.thedailystar.net/newDesign/news-details.php?nid=269336, accessed 11 December 2016 (cited: The Daily Star, Blogger brutally killed, 16 February 2013)

– Amend War Crimes Act to Try Jamaat, 16 November 2014, http://www.thedailystar.net/amend-war-crimes-act-to-try-jamaat-50567, accessed 11 December 2016 (cited: The Daily Star, Amend War Crimes Act to Try Jamaat, 16 November 2014)

– Contemnor Has the Right to Appeal, 30 April 2015, http://www.thedailystar.net/frontpage/contemnor-has-right-appeal-79852, accessed 11 December 2016 (cited: The Daily Star, Contemnor Has the Right to Appeal, 30 April 2015)

– Trial Begins with Father's Deposition, 29 May 2015, http://www.thedailystar.net/city/trial-begins-fathers-deposition-88606, accessed 11 December 2016 (cited: The Daily Star, Trial Begins with Father's Deposition, 29 May 2015)

– Khaleda Draws Flak for Martyrs Remark, 23 December 2015, http://www.thedailystar.net/frontpage/khaleda-remark-draws-flak-191164, accessed 11 December 2016 (cited: The Daily Star, Khaleda Draws Flak for Martyrs Remark, 23 December 2015)

References

- Int'l Court in Hague Rejects Allegations, 26 May 2016, http://www.thedailystar.net/frontpage/intl-court-hague-rejects-allegations-1229575, accessed 11 December 2016 (cited: The Daily Star, Int'l Court in Hague Rejects Allegations, 26 May 2016)

D'Costa, Bina, Nationbuilding, Gender and War Crimes in South Asia, London et al., 2011 (cited: D'Costa, Nationbuilding)

D'Costa, Bina/Hossain, Sara, Redress for Sexual Violence before the International Crimes Tribunal in Bangladesh: Lessons from History, and Hopes for the Future, in: Criminal Law Forum (CLF), 2010, 21(2), pp. 331–359 (cited: D'Costa/Hossain, CLF, 2010, 21(2))

Dickinson, Laura A., The Promise of Hybrid Courts, in: American Journal of International Law (AJIL), 2003, 97(2), pp. 295–310 (cited: Dickinson, AJIL, 2003, 97(2))

Dil, Anwar/Dil, Afia, Bengali Language Movement and Creation of Bangladesh, Contributions to Bangladesh Studies, Volume 8, 2. edn, Dhaka, 2011 (cited: Dil/Dil, Bengali Language Movement)

Economist, The, The Trial of the Birth of a Nation, 15 December 2012, http://www.economist.com/news/briefing/21568349-week-chairman-bangladeshs-international-crimes-tribunal-resigned-we-explain, accessed 11 December 2016 (cited: The Economist, The Trial of the Birth of a Nation, 15 December 2012)

- Final Sentence, 17 September 2013, http://www.economist.com/blogs/banyan/2013/09/bangladesh-s-war-crimes-trials, accessed 11 December 2016 (cited: The Economist, Final Sentence, 17 September 2013)

Ellis, Mark S., The International Criminal Court and its Implication for Domestic Law and National Capacity Building, in: Florida Journal of International Law (Fla. JIL), 2002, 15(2), pp. 215–242 (cited: Ellis, Fla. JIL, 2002, 15(2))

FIDH (International Federation for Human Rights)/Odhikar, Bangladesh: Criminal Justice through the Prism of Capital Punishment and the Fight against Terrorism, 2010, https://www.fidh.org/IMG/pdf/Report_eng.pdf, accessed 11 December 2016 (cited: FIDH/Odhikar, Capital Punishment Report)

Forstein, Carolyn, The International Crimes Tribunal Observer, Special Issue No. 4 – Legal Conclusions from Chief Prosecutor vs. Kamaruzzaman, 15 August 2013, https://bangladeshtrialobserver.files.wordpress.com/2013/08/special-issue-4-kamaruzzaman-legal-conclusions-final.pdf, accessed 11 December 2016 (cited: Forstein, Special Issue No. 4 – Legal Conclusions Kamaruzzaman)

Fry, Elinor, Between Show Trials and Sham Prosecutions: The Rome Statute's Potential Effect on Domestic Due Process Protections, in: Criminal Law Forum (CLF), 2012, 23(1), pp. 35–62 (cited: Fry, CLF, 2012, 23(1))

Gaynor, Fergal, Uneasy Partners – Evidence, Truth and History in International Trials, in: Journal of International Criminal Justice (JICJ), 2012, 10(5), pp. 1257–1275 (cited: Gaynor, JICJ, 2012, 10(5))

Gallant, Kenneth S., The Principle of Legality in International and Comparative Criminal Law, Cambridge et al., 2009 (cited: Gallant, Principle of Legality)

Gerlach, Christian, Extremely Violent Societies: Mass Violence in the Twentieth Century World, Cambridge et al., 2010 (cited: Gerlach, Societies)

Gropengießer, Helmut / Meißner, Jörg, Amnesties and the Rome Statute of the International Criminal Court, in: International Criminal Law Review (ICLR), 2005, 5(2), pp. 267–300 (cited: Gropengießner/Meißner, ICLR, 2005, 5 (2))

Halim, Md. Abdul, The Legal System of Bangladesh: A Comparative Study of Problems and Procedure in Legal Institutions, Dhaka, 2004 (cited: Halim, Legal system of Bangladesh)

Hamoodur Rahman Commission, Hamoodur Rahman Commission Report, 1972 (cited: Hamoodur Rahman Commission, Report)

Hazan, Pierre, Measuring the Impact of Punishment and Forgiveness: A Framework for Evaluating Transitional Justice, International Review of the Red Cross (IRRC), 2006, 88(861), pp. 19–47 (cited: Hazan, IRRC, 2006, 88(861))

Haqqani, Husain, Pakistan: Between Mosque and Military, Washington, D.C., 2005 (cited: Haqqani, Pakistan)

Heller, Kevin Jon, The Shadow Side of Complementarity: The Effect of Article 17 of the Rome Statute on National Due Process, Criminal Law Forum (CLF), 2006, 17(3), pp. 255–280 (cited: Heller, CLF, 2006, 17(3))

Herath, Elizabeth, Trials in Absentia: Jurisprudence and Commentary on the Judgment in Chief Prosecutor v. Abul Kalam Azad in the Bangladesh International Crimes Tribunal, in: Harvard International Law Journal Online (Harvard IJC Online), 2014, 55, pp. 1–12 (cited: Harvard IJC Online, 2014, 55)

Hoque, Ridwanul / Naser, Mostafa Mahmud, The Judicial Invocation of International Human Rights Law in Bangladesh: Questing a Better Approach, in: Indian Journal of International Law (Indian JIL), 2006, 46(2), pp. 151–186 (cited: Ridwanul/Naser, Indian JIL, 2006, 46(2))

Hoque, Riwanul, Courts and the Adjudication System in Bangladesh – In Quest of Viable Reforms, in: Yeh, Jiunn-rong (ed.), Asian Courts in Context, Cambridge, 2015, pp. 447–486 (cited: Hoque, in: Yeh, Asian courts)

Hossain, Rubaiyat, Trauma of Women, Trauma of the Nation – A Feminist Discourse on Izzat, in: Hoque, Mofidul (ed.), Bangladesh Genocide 1971 and the Quest for Justice: Papers Presented in the Second International Conference on Genocide,

References

Truth and Justice on 30–31 July 2009, Dhaka, 2009, pp. 98–112 (cited: *Hossain*, in: Hoque (ed.), Genocide Conference Papers, 2009)

Hossain, Sara, A Long and Winding Road – Justice and Accountability for War Crimes in 1971, in: Liberation War Museum (ed.), International Conference on Genocide, Truth and Justice, 1–2 March 2008, Dhaka, 2008, pp. 51–54 (cited: Hossain, in: Liberation War Museum (ed.), Genocide Conference Papers, 2008)

Hoven, Elisa, Rechtsstaatliche Anforderungen an völkerstrafrechtliche Verfahren, Berlin, 2012 (cited: Hove, Rechtsstaatliche Anforderungen)

Human Rights Watch, Bangladesh: Stop Harassment of Defence at War Tribunal, 02 November 2011, https://www.hrw.org/news/2011/11/02/bangladesh-stop-harassment-defense-war-tribunal, accessed 11 December 2016 (cited: Human Rights Watch, Bangladesh: Stop Harassment of Defence at War Tribunal, 02 November 2011)

– Bangladesh: Halt Execution of War Crimes Accused, 09 November 2011, https://www.hrw.org/news/2014/11/09/bangladesh-halt-execution-war-crimes-accused, accessed 11 December 2016 (cited: Human Rights Watch, Bangladesh: Halt Execution of War Crimes Accused, 09 November 2011)

– Bangladesh: End Harassment of War Crimes Defence Counsel, 17 October 2012, https://www.hrw.org/news/2012/10/17/bangladesh-end-harassment-war-crimes-defense-counsel, accessed 11 December 2016 (cited: Human Rights Watch, Bangladesh: End Harassment of War Crimes Defence Counsel, 17 October 2012)

– Blood on the Street: The Use of Excessive Force during Bangladesh Protests, 2013, https://www.hrw.org/sites/default/files/reports/bangladesh0813_ForUp load_1.pdf, accessed 11 December 2016 (cited: Human Rights Watch, Blood on the Street)

– Bangladesh: Find Abducted Victims, 16 January 2013, https://www.hrw.org/news/2013/01/16/bangladesh-find-abducted-witness, accessed 11 December 2016 (cited: Human Rights Watch, Bangladesh: Find Abducted Victims, 16 January 2013)

– Bangladesh: Azam Conviction Based on Flawed Proceedings, 16 August 2013 http://www.hrw.org/news/2013/08/16/bangladesh-azam-conviction-based-flawed-proceedings, accessed 11 December 2016 (cited: Human Rights Watch, Bangladesh: Azam Conviction Based on Flawed Proceedings, 16 August 2013)

– Bangladesh: Azam Trial Concerns, 16 August 2013, https://www.hrw.org/news/2013/08/16/bangladesh-azam-trial-concerns, accessed 11 December 2016 (cited: Human Rights Watch, Bangladesh: Azam Trial Concerns, 16 August 2013)

– Bangladesh: Investigate Killing of Witness, 23 December 2013, https://www.hrw.org/news/2013/12/23/bangladesh-investigate-killing-witness, accessed 11 December

2016 (cited: Human Rights Watch, Bangladesh: Investigate Killing of Witness, 23 December 2013)

– Letter to Bangladesh's Prime Minister Sheikh Hasina Wajed Re: Bangladesh Rapid Action Battalion, 18 July 2014, http://www.hrw.org/news/2014/07/18/letter-prime-minister-sheikh-hasina-re-bangladesh-rapid-action-battalion, accessed 11 December 2016 (cited: Human Rights Watch, Letter to Bangladesh's Prime Minister Sheikh Hasina Wajed, Re: Bangladesh Rapid Action Battalion, 18 July 2014)

– Bangladesh: Charge or Release Detained Counsel, 26 October 2015, https://www.hrw.org/news/2015/10/26/bangladesh-charge-or-release-detained-counsel, accessed 11 December 2016 (cited: Human Rights Watch, Bangladesh: Charge or Release Detained Counsel, 26 October 2012)

– World Report 2016, https://www.hrw.org/sites/default/files/world_report_download/wr2016_web.pdf, accessed 11 December 2016 (cited: Human Rights Watch, World Report 2016)

Husain, Syed Anwar, Genocide in Bangladesh, 1971: Fixing Responsibility, in: Hoque, Mofidul (ed.), Bangladesh Genocide 1971 and the Quest for Justice: Papers Presented in the Second International Conference on Genocide, Truth and Justice on 30–31 July 2009, Dhaka, 2009, pp. 43–48 (cited: Husain, in: Hoque, Genocide Conference Papers, 2009)

Huyse, Luc, Justice, in: Bloomfield, David / Barnes, Teresa / Huyse, Luc, Reconciliation after Violent Conflict: A Handbook, pp. 97–115, reprint, Stockholm, 2005 (cited: Huyse, in: Bloomfeld/Barnes/Huyse (eds), Reconciliation after Conflict)

International Commission of Jurists, The Events in East Pakistan, 1971: A Legal Study by the Secretariat of the International Commission of Jurists, Geneva, 1971 (cited: International Commission of Jurists, Events in East Pakistan)

– The Review, December 1972, 9, pp. 8–10 (cited: International Commission of Jurists, The Review, 1972, 9)

– The Review, December 1973, 11, pp. 9–10 (cited: International Commission of Jurists, The Review, 1973, 11)

International Crisis Group, Political Conflict, Extremism and Criminal Justice in Bangladesh, 11 April 2016, https://d2071andvip0wj.cloudfront.net/277-political-conflict-extremism-and-criminal-justice-in-bangladesh.pdf, accessed 07 August 2016 (cited: International Crisis Group, Political Conflict)

Iqbal, Muhammed Zafar, History of the Liberation War, Dhaka, 2008, English version, http://bangla2000.com/blog/sample-page/brief-history/#surrender, accessed 13 March 2016 (cited: Iqbal, History of the Liberation War)

References

Islam, M. Amir-Ul, Bringing Perpetrators of Genocide to Justice, in: Hoque, Mofidul (ed.), Bangladesh genocide 1971 and the Quest for Justice: Papers Presented in the Second International Conference on Genocide, Truth and Justice on 30–31 July, 2009, pp. 125–135, Dhaka 2009 (cited: Islam in: Hoque (ed.), Genocide Conference Papers, 2009)

Islam, Mahmudul, Constitutional Law of Bangladesh, 3. edn, Dhaka, 2002 (cited: Islam, Constitutional Law, 3. edn)

Islam, M. Rafiqul, National Trial of International Crimes in Bangladesh: Its Significance in International Criminal Law, in: Hoque, Mofidul/Wara, Umme (eds), Genocide and Justice in Bangladesh: National and Global Perspectives, 1st Winter School Journal, pp. 51–70, Dhaka, 2014 (cited: Islam, in: Hoque/Wara (eds), Journal of the 1st Winter School)

– Trials for International Crimes in Bangladesh – Prosecutorial Strategies, Defence Arguments and Judgments, in: Sellars, Kirsten (ed.), Trials for International Crimes in Asia, pp. 301–317, Cambridge, 2016 (cited: Islam, in: Sellars (ed.), Trials for International Crimes in Asia)

Jahan, Rounaq, Pakistan: Failure in National Integration, New York et al., 1972 (cited: Jahan, Pakistan)

– Genocide in Bangladesh, in: Totten, Samuel/Parsons, William S./Charny, Israel W. (eds), Century of Genocide – Eyewitness Accounts and Critical Views, New York et al., 1997, pp. 291–316 (cited: Jahan, in: Totten/Parsons/Charny, Century of Genocide, 1997)

– Genocide in Bangladesh: in: Jones, Adam (ed.), Genocide, Volume 2: Genocide in History, Los Angeles, 2008, pp. 282–295 (cited: Jahan, in: Jones (ed.), Genocide, Vol. 2)

– Genocide in Bangladesh, in: Totten, Samuel/Parsons, William S. (eds), Centuries of Genocide – Essays and Eyewitness Accounts, 4. edn, New York et al., 2013, pp. 249–276 (cited: Jahan in: Totten/Parsons, Centuries of Genocide, 4. edn)

– Political Parties in Bangladesh – Challenges of Democratization, Dhaka, 2015 (cited: Jahan, Political Parties)

Jamaat-e-Islami, Allegations of War Crimes against the Leaders of Jamaat, undated, http://www.jamaat-e-islami.org/en/articlepdf/105_Allegations%20of%20War%20Crimes%20against%20the%20leaders%20of%20Jamaat.pdf, accessed 11 December 201t (cited: Jamaat-e-Islami, Allegations of War Crimes against the Leaders of Jamaat)

– War Crimes Law and the Constitution, undated, http://www.jamaat-e-islami.org/en/articlepdf/113_War%20Crimes%20Law%20and%20the%20Constitution.pdf, accessed 18 March 2016 (cited: Jamaat-e-Islami, War Crimes Law and the Constitution)

Karim, Bianca / Theunissen, Tirza, Bangladesh, in: Shelton, Dinah (ed.), International Law and Domestic Legal Systems – Incorporation, Transformation and Persuasion, Oxford et al., 2011, p. 98–115 (cited: Karim/Theunissen, in: Shelton (ed.), International law and Domestic Legal Systems)

Karim, Sayyid A., Sheikh Mujib: Triumph and Tragedy, reprinted, Dhaka, 2005 (cited: Karim, Sheikh Mujib)

Kaczorowska, Alina, Public International Law, 4. edn, London et al., 2010 (cited: Kaczorowska, Public International Law, 4. edn)

Khalidi, Toufique Imrose, Behind the Rise of Bangladesh's Hifazat, Al Jazeera, 09 May 2013, http://www.aljazeera.com/indepth/features/2013/05/201356134629980318. html, accessed 11 December 2016 (cited: Khalidi, Behind the Rise of Bangladesh's Hifazat, Al Jazeera, 9 May 2013)

Kleffner, Jann K., The Impact of Complementarity on National Implementation of Substantive International Criminal Law, in: Journal of International Criminal Justice (JICJ), 2003, 1(1), pp. 86–113 (cited: Kleffner, JICL, 2003, 1(1))

Kreß, Claus, Nulla Nullum Crimen Sine Lege, in: Wolfrum, Rüdiger (ed.), The Max Planck Encyclopedia of Public International Law, Volume 7, Oxford et al., 2012, pp. 889–899 (cited: Kreß, in: Wolfrum (ed.), Max Planck Encyclopedia, Vol. 7)

Kritz, Neil J., Transitional Justice – How emerging Democracies Reckon with Former Regimes, Volume 3: Laws, Rulings, and Reports, Washington D.C., 1995 (cited: Neil, Transitional Justice, Vol. 3)

– Coming to Terms with Atrocities – A Review of Accountability Mechanisms for Mass Violations of Human Rights, in: Law & Contemporary Problems (Law & Contemp. Probs.), 1996, 59(4), pp. 127–152 (cited: Kritz, Law & Contemp. Probs., 59(4))

La Haye, Eva, War Crimes in Internal Armed Conflicts, Cambridge et al., 2008 (cited: La Haye, War Crimes in Internal Armed Conflicts)

Levie, Howard S., Legal Aspects of the Continued Detention of the Pakistani Prisoners of War by India, in: American Journal of International Law (AJIL), 1973, 67(3), pp. 512–516 (cited: Levie, AJIL, 1973, 67(3))

Linton, Suzannah, Cambodia, East Timor and Sierra Leone: Experiments in Internatinal Justice, in: Criminal Law Forum (CLF), 2001, 12(2), pp. 185–246 (cited: Linton, CLF, 2001, 12(2))

References

- Safeguarding the Independence and Impartiality of the CEC, in: Journal of International Criminal Justice (JICJ), 2006, 4(2), pp. 327–341 (cited: Linton, JICJ, 2006, 4(2))
- Dealing with the Legacies of the Past, in: Hoque, Mofidul (ed.), Bangladesh Genocide 1971 and the Quest for Justice: Papers Presented in the Second International Conference on Genocide, Truth and Justice on 30–31 July 2009, Dhaka 2009, pp. 155–162 (cited: Linton, in: Hoque (ed.), Genocide Conference Papers, 2009)
- Completing the Circle: Accountability for the Crimes of the 1971 Bangladesh War of Liberation, in: Criminal Law Forum (CLF), 2010, 21(2), pp. 191–311 (cited: Linton, CLF, 2010, 21(2))

MacDermot, Niall, Crimes against Humanity in Bangladesh, in: International Lawyer (IL), 1973, 7(2), pp. 476–484 (cited: MacDermot, IL, 1973, 7(2))

Mascarenhas, Anthony, Bangladesh – A Legacy of Blood, London et al., 1986 (cited: Mascarenhas, Legacy of Blood)

Matas, David, International Tribunals – Lessons Learned, in: Hoque, Mofidul (ed.), Bangladesh Genocide 1971 and the Quest for Justice: Papers Presented in the Second International Conference on Genocide, Truth and Justice on 30–31 July 2009, Dhaka, 2009, pp. 39–42 (cited: Matas, in: Hoque (ed.), Genocide Conference Papers, 2009)

Mclane, John R., Partition of Bengal 1905 – A Political Analysis, in: Islam, Sirajul (ed.), History of Bangladesh 1904–1971, Volume 1, Political History, Dhaka, 1992, pp. 126–158 (cited: Mclane, in: Islam (ed.), History of Bangladesh, Vol. 1)

Mégret, Frédéric, Too Much of a Good Thing? Implementation and the Uses of Complementarity, in: Stahn, Carsten/El Zeidy, Mohamed (eds), The International Criminal Court and Complementarity – From Theory to Practice, Volume 1, Cambridge et al., 2011, pp. 361–390 (cited: Mégret in: Stahn/El Zeidy (eds), ICC and Complementarity, Vol. 1)

Mégret, Frédéric/Samson, Marika Giles, Holding the Line on Complementarity in Libya: The Case for Tolerating Flawed Domestic Trials, in: Journal of International Criminal Justice (JICJ), 2013, 11(3), pp. 571–589 (cited: Mégret/Samson, JICJ, 2013, 11(3))

Minow, Martha, Making History or Making Peace – When Prosecutions Should Give Way to Truth Commissions and Peace Negotiations, in: Buchanan, Ruth/Zumbansen, Peer (eds), Law in Transition – Human Rights, Development and Transitional Justice, Oxford et al., 2014 (cited: Minow in: Buchanan/Zumbansen (eds), Law in Transition)

Moneruzzaman, M., New Age, Nearly 1,200 Condemned Prisoners Await SC Verdict, New Age, 19 December 2015, http://newagebd.net/185676/nearly-1200-condemned-prisoners-await-sc-verdict/, accessed 11 December 2016 (cited: Moneruzzaman, Nearly 1,200 Condemned Prisoners Await SC Verdict, New Age, 19 December 2015)

Moses, Dirk, Introduction, in: Journal of Genocide Research (JGR), 2011, 13(4), pp. 391–392 (cited: Moses, JGR, 2011, 13(4))

Murshid, Tazeen M., The Sacred and the Secular – Bengal Muslim Discourses 1871–1977, Calcutta et al., 1995 (cited: Murshid, Sacred and Secular)

Nair, M. B., Politics in Bangladesh – A Study of Awami League 1949–58, New Delhi, 1990 (cited: Nair, Politics)

National Coordinating Committee for the Realisation of Bangladesh Liberation War Ideals and Trials of Bangladesh War Criminals of 1971, Report on the Findings of the People's Inquiry Commission on the Activities of War Criminals and the Collaborators – Summary of Investigation into Activities of Eight War Criminals and Collaborators of Pakistan Military Junta during the Bangladesh Liberation War of 1971, Dhaka, 1994 (cited: National Coordinating Committee for the Realisation of Bangladesh Liberation War Ideals and Trials of Bangladesh War Criminals of 1971, Report)

Nersessian, David L., Genocide and Political Groups, Oxford et al., 2010 (cited: Nersessian, Genocide and Political Groups)

Niazi, Amir Abdullah Khan, The Betrayal of East Pakistan, Karachi, 1998 (cited: Niazi, East Pakistan)

Oette, Lutz/Ferstman, Carla, Torture in Bangladesh 1971–2004 – Making International Commitments a Reality and Providing Justice and Reparations to Victims, 2004, <www.redress.org/downloads/publications/bangladesh.pdf, accessed 11 December 2016 (cited: Oette/Ferstman, Torture in Bangladesh)

Office of the Prosecutor, Informal Expert Paper – The Principle of Complementarity in Practice, 2003, http://www.icc-cpi.int/iccdocs/doc/doc654724.PDF, accessed 27 September 2015 (cited: Office of the Prosecutor, Informal Expert Paper)

O'Keefe, Roger, International Criminal Law, Oxford et al., 2015 (cited: O'Keefe, International criminal law)

Pandey, Gyanendra, Remembering Partition – Violence, Nationalism and History in India, Cambridge, 2001 (cited: Pandey, Remembering Partition)

Paulsen, Eric, The Citizenship of the Urdu-speakers/Biharis in Bangladesh, in: Refugee Survey Quarterly (RSQ), 2006, 25(3), pp. 54–69 (cited: Paulsen, RSQ, 2006, 25(3))

References

Rahman, Mizanur/Billah, S. M. Masum, War Crimes and Genocide 1971 – Bringing the Perpetrators to Justice, in: Hoque, Mofidul (ed.) Bangladesh Genocide 1971 and the Quest for Justice: Papers Presented in the Second International Conference on Genocide, Truth and Justice on 30–31 July 2009, Dhaka 2009, pp. 82–97 (cited: Rahman/Billah, in: Hoque (ed.), Genocide Conference Papers, 2009)

Rahman, Mizanur, International Crimes Tribunal, Bangladesh & Trial of Crimes against Humanity, Frequently Asked Questions (FAQs), National Human Rights Commission, 2012 (cited: Rahman, FAQs)

Rahman, Sheikh Mujibur, Bangladesh, My Bangladesh, edited with notes by Majumdar, Ramendu (ed.), reprinted, New Delhi, 1972 (cited: Rahman, My Bangladesh)

Rahman Karzon, Sheikh Hafizur/Al-Faruque, Abdullah, Status of International Law under the Constitution of Bangladesh – An Appraisal, in: Bangladesh Journal of Law (BD JL), 1999, 3(1), pp. 23–47 (zitiert: Rahman Karzon/Al-Faruque, BD JL, 1999, 3(1))

Rahman, Wali-ur, A Brief History of the Framing of the International Crimes (Tribunals) Act, 1973, incorporated in the Constitution as Genocide Act, Dhaka, undated (cited: Rahman, Brief History)

Rapp, Stephen J., Bangladesh International Crimes Tribunal – Remarks, 28 November 2011, http://www.state.gov/j/gcj/us_releases/remarks/2011/177811.htm, accessed 7 August 2016 (cited: Rapp, ICT Remarks, 28 November 2011)

Ratner, Steben R./Abrams, Jason S./Bischoff, James L., Accountability for Human Rights Atrocities in International Law – Beyond the Nuremberg Legacy, 3. edn, Oxford et al., 2009 (cited: Ratner/Abrams/Bischoff, Accountability for Human Rights Atrocities, 3. edn)

Razzaq, Abdur, The Tribunals in Bangladesh: Falling Short of International Standards, in: Sellars, Kirsten (ed.), Trials for International Crimes in Asia, Cambridge 2016, pp. 341–359 (cited: Razzaq, in: Sellars (ed.), Trials for International Crimes in Asia)

Reza, Humayun, War Crimes & Genocide in 1971: The Reality of the Trial, in: Liberation War Museum (ed.), International Conference on Genocide, Truth and Justice, 1–2 March 2008, Dhaka, 2008, pp. 55–58 (cited: Reza, in: Liberation War Museum (ed.), Genocide Conference Papers, 2008)

Reiger, Caitlin, Fighting Past Impunity in Bangladesh – A National Tribunal for the Crimes of 1971, International Center for Transitional Justice, Briefing paper, 2010, https://www.ictj.org/sites/default/files/ICTJ-BGD-NationalTribunal-Briefing-2010-English.pdf, (cited: Reiger, ICTJ Briefing Paper)

Riaz, Ali, Bangladesh – Islamist Militancy, Democracy Deficit and Where to Next?, Al Jazeera, 28 June 2016, http://studies.aljazeera.net/en/reports/2016/06/bangladesh-islamist-militancy-democracy-deficit-160628100147561.html, accessed 17 July 2016 (cited: Riaz, Bangladesh – Islamist Militancy, Democracy Deficit and Where to Next?, Al Jazeera, 28 June 2016)

Rikhof, Joseph, Fewer Places to Hide? The Impact of Domestic War Crimes Prosecutions on International Impunity, in: Criminal Law Forum (CLF), 2009, 20(1), pp. 1–51 (cited: Rikhof, Criminal Law Forum, 2009, 20(1))

Robertson, Geoffrey, Report on the International Crimes Tribunal of Bangladesh, 2015, https://www.barhumanrights.org.uk/sites/default/files/documents/news/grqc_bangladesh_final.pdf, accessed 27 September 2015 (cited: Robertson, Report on the ICT Bangladesh)

Robinson, Darryl, Serving the Interests of Justice – Amnesties, Truth Commissions and the International Criminal Court, in: European Journal of International Law (EJIL), 2003, 14(3), p. 481–505 (cited: Robinson, EJIL, 2003, 14(3))

Ronen, Yaël, Superior Responsibility of Civilians for International Crimes Committed in Civilian Settings, in: Vanderbilt Journal of Transnational Law (VJTL), 2010, 43(2), pp. 313–356 (cited: Ronen, VJTL, 2010, 43(2))

Rummel, Rudolph J., Statistics of Democide – Genocide and Mass Murder since 1900, Münster, 1998 (cited: Rummel, Democide)

Ryngaert, Cedric, Horizontal Complementarity, in: in: Stahn, Carsten / El Zeidy, Mohamed M. (eds), The International Criminal Court and Complementarity – From Theory to Practice, Volume 2, Cambridge et al., 2011, pp. 855–887 (cited: Ryngaert, in: Stahn/El Zeidy, The ICC and Complementarity, Vol. 2)

Saikia, Yasmin, Women, War, and the Making of Bangladesh – Remembering 1971, London, 2011 (cited: Saikia, Making of Bangladesh)

– Insāniyat for Peace – Survivors' Narrative of the 1971 War of Bangladesh, in: Journal of Genocide Research (JGR), 2011, 13(4), pp. 475–501 (cited: Saikia, JGR, 2011, 13(4))

Schabas, William A., Follow up to Rome – Preparing for Entry into Force of the International Criminal Court Statute, in: Human Rights Law Journal (HRLJ), 1999, 20(4–6) (cited: Schabas, HRLJ, 1999, 20(4–6))

– Genocide in International Law – The Crime of Crimes, Cambridge et al., 2. edn, 2009 (cited: Schabas, Genocide in International Law, 2. edn)

– Introduction to the International Criminal Court, 4. edn, Cambridge et al., 2011 (cited: Schabas, International Criminal Court, 4. edn)

Schilling, Sandrine, Gegen das Vergessen: Justiz, Wahrheitsfindung und Versöhnung nach dem Genozid in Rwanda durch Mechanismen transitionaler Justiz: Gacaca Gerichte, Bern et al., 2005 (cited: Schilling, Vergessen)

Simma, Bruno/Khan, Daniel-Erasmus/Nolte, Georg/Paulus, Andreas (eds), The Charter of the United Nations – A Commentary, Volume 2, 3. edn, Oxford et al., 2012 (cited: Simma/Khan/Nolte/Paulus/Contributor, UN Charter Commentary, Vol. 2, 3. edn)

Sisson, Richard/Rose, Leo E., War and Secession – Pakistan, India and the Creation of Bangladesh, Berkeley et al., 1990 (cited: Sisson/Rose, War and Secession)

Sluiter, Göran/Friman, Håkan/Linton, Suzannah/Vasiliev, Sergey/Zappalà, Salvatore (eds), International Criminal Procedure – Principles and Rules, Oxford, 2013 (cited: Sluiter et al., International Criminal Procedure)

Stahn, Carsten, Complementarity, Amnesties and Alternative Forms of Justice, in: Journal of International Criminal Justice (JICJ), 2005, 13(3), p. 695–720 (cited: Stahn, JICJ, 2005, 13(3))

– Complementarity – A Tale of Two Notions, in: Criminal Law Forum (CLF), 2008, 19(1), pp. 87–113 (cited: Stahn, CLF, 2008 19(1))

Stigen, Jo, The Relationship between the International Criminal Court and National Jurisdictions, Leiden et al., 2008 (cited: Stigen, ICC and National Jurisdictions)

Talbot, Ian/Singh, Guharpal, The Partition of India, Cambridge et al., 2009 (cited: Talbot/Singh, Partition of India)

Taylor, Cole, Issue No. 3 – Weekly Digest, 3–7 February 2013, https://bangladesh trialobserver.files.wordpress.com/2013/02/weekly-digest-issue-3-feb-3-7.pdf, accessed 11 December 2016 (cited: Taylor, Issue No. 3 – Weekly Digest)

– Special Issue No. 1 – The Sayeedi Verdict, 28 February 2013, https://bangla deshtrial-observer.files.wordpress.com/2013/03/special-issue-no-1-sayedee-verdict.pdf, accessed 11 December 2016 (cited: Taylor, Special Issue No. 1 – Sayeedi Verdict)

– The International Crimes Tribunal Observer, Special Issue No. 5 – Legal Conclusions Chief Prosecutor vs. Gholam Azam, 08 October 2013, https://bangla desh-trialobserver.files.wordpress.com/2013/10/special-issue-no-5-gholam-azam-case-verdict-final.pdf, accessed 11 December 2016 (cited: Taylor, Special Issue No. 5 – Legal Conclusions Azam)

Tomuschat, Christian, The Duty to Prosecute International Crimes Committed by Individuals, in: Cremer, Hans-Joachim/Giegerich, Thomas/Richter, Dagmar/Zimmermann, Andreas (eds), Festschrift für Helmut Steinberger, Berlin et al., 2002, pp. 315–349 (cited: Tomuschat, in: Cremer/Giegerich/Richter/Zimmermann (eds), FS Steinberger)

Triffterer, Otto (ed.), Commentary on the Rome Statute of the International Criminal Court: Observers' Notes – Article by Article, 2. edn, München et al., 2008 (cited: Triffterer/Contributor, Commentary Rome Statute, 2. edn)

– Bangladesh's Attempts to Achieve Post-War (or Transitional?) Justice in Accordance with International Legal Standards, in: *Bergsmo, Morten/Wui Ling, Cheah* (eds), Old Evidence and Core International Crimes, Beijing, 2012, pp. 257–300 (cited: Triffterer, in: Bergsmo, Morten/Wui Ling, Cheah (eds), Old Evidence)

Uddin, Sufia M., Constructing Bangladesh – Religion, Ethnicity, and Language in an Islamic Nation, Chapel Hill (N.C.), 2006 (cited: Uddin, Constructing Bangladesh)

Ullah, Ansar Ahmed, Building an International Network – Campaign to seek Justice & the Efforts in the UK, in: Hoque, Mofidul (ed.), Bangladesh Genocide 1971 and the Quest for Justice: Papers Presented in the Second International Conference on Genocide, Truth and Justice on 30–31 July 2009, Dhaka 2009, pp. 139–146 (cited: Ullah, in: Hoque (ed.), Genocide Conference Papers, 2009)

Umar, Badruddin, The Emergence of Bangladesh, Volume 2: Rise of Bengali Nationalism (1958–1971), Oxford, 2006 (cited: Umar, Emergence of Bangladesh)

Van Schendel, Willem, A History of Bangladesh, Cambridge et al., 2009, reprinted 2013 (cited: Van Schendel, History of Bangladesh)

War Crimes Committee of the International Bar Association, Consistency of Bangladesh's International Crimes (Tribunals) Act 1973 with International Standards, 2009, http://ictbd-defenceteam.org/wp-content/uploads/2014/08/IBAOpinion.pdf, accessed 28 July 2016 (cited: War Crimes Committee of the International Bar Association, Consistency of the ICT Act 1973 with International Standards)

Werle, Gerhard/Jessberger, Florian, Principles of International Criminal Law, 3. edn, The Hague, 2014 (cited: Werle/Jessberger, International Criminal Law, 3. edn)

Williams, Sarah, Hybrid and Internationalised Criminal Tribunals – Selected Jurisdictional Issues, Oxford et al., 2012 (cited: Williams, Criminal Tribunals)

Zappalà, Salvatore, Human Rights in International Criminal Proceedings, Oxford et al., 2003 (cited: Zappalà, Human Rights in International Criminal Proceedings)

Ziauddin, Ahmed, The Case of Bangladesh – Bringing to Trial the Perpetrators of the 1971 Genocide, in: Jongman, Albert J. (ed.), Contemporary Genocides – Causes, Cases, Consequences, Leiden, 1996, pp. 95–115, (cited: Ziauddin, in: Jongman (ed.), Contemporary Genocides)

Appendix

The International Crimes Tribunals Act

The International Crimes (Tribunals) Act, 1973
Act No. XIX of 1973

[20th July, 1973]

An Act to provide for the detention, prosecution and punishment of persons for genocide, crimes against humanity, war crimes and other crimes under international law.

Whereas it is expedient to provide for the detention, prosecution and punishment of persons for genocide, crimes against humanity, war crimes and other crimes under international law, and for matters connected therewith;

It is hereby enacted as follows :–

1. **Short title, extent and commencement**
   (1) This Act may be called the International Crimes (Tribunals) Act, 1973.
   (2) It extends to the whole of Bangladesh.
   (3) It shall come into force at once.

2. **Definitions**
   In this Act, unless there is anything repugnant in the subject or context, –
   (a) "auxiliary force" includes forces placed under the control of the Armed Forces for operational administrative, static and other purposes;
   [(aa) "armed forces" means the forces raised and maintained under the Army Act, 1952 (XXXIX of 1952), the Air Force Act, 1953 (VI of 1953), or the Navy Ordinance, 1961 (XXXV of 1961);][1]
   (b) "Government" means Government of the People's Republic of Bangladesh
   (c) "Republic" means the People's Republic of Bangladesh
   [(d)][2]
   (d) "territory of Bangladesh" means the territory of the Republic as defined in article 2 of the Constitution of the People's Republic of Bangladesh;
   (e) "Tribunal" means a Tribunal set up under this Act.

---

1 Clause (aa) was inserted by Section 2(a) of the International (Crimes) Tribunals (Amendment) Act, 2009 (Act no. LV of 2009).
2 Clause (d) was omitted by section 2 (b) of the International (Crimes) Tribunals (Amendment) Act, 2009 (Act no. LV of 2009). It read: "service law" means the Army Act, 1952 (XXXIX of 1952), the Air Force Act, 1953 (VI of 1953), or the Navy Ordinance, 1961 (XXXV of 1961), and includes the rules and regulations made under any of them.

Appendix

3. Jurisdiction of Tribunal and crimes

(1) [A Tribunal shall have the power to try and punish any individual or group of individuals [or organisation,][3] or any member of any armed, defence or auxiliary forces, irrespective of his nationality, who commits or has committed in the territory of Bangladesh, whether before or after the commencement of this Act, any of the crimes mentioned in sub-section (2).][4]

(2) The following acts or any of them are crimes within the jurisdiction of a Tribunal for which there shall be individual responsibility, namely: –

   (a) Crimes against Humanity: namely, murder, extermination, enslavement, deportation, imprisonment, abduction, confinement, torture, rape or other inhumane acts committed against any civilian population or persecutions on political grounds, whether or not in violation of the domestic law of the country where perpetrated;

   (b) Crimes against Peace: namely, planning, preparation, initiation or waging of a war of aggression or a war in violation of international treaties, agreements or assurances;

   (c) Genocide: meaning and including any of the following acts committed with intent to destroy, in whole or in part, a national, ethnic, racial, religious or political group, such as:
   (i) killing members of the group;
   (ii) causing serious bodily or mental harm to members of the group;
   (iii) deliberately inflicting on the group conditions of life calculated to bring about its physical destruction in whole or in part;
   (iv) imposing measures intended to prevent births within the group;
   (v) forcibly transferring children of the group to another group;

   (d) War Crimes: namely, violation of laws or customs of war which include but are not limited to murder, ill-treatment or deportation to slave labour or for any other purpose of civilian population in the territory of Bangladesh; murder or ill-treatment of prisoners of war or persons on the seas, killing of hostages and detenues, plunder of public or private property,

---

3   Sub-section 1 was substituted by Section 3 (1) of the International Crimes (Tribunals) (Amendment) Act 2009 (Act no. LV of 2009). The original section read: A Tribunal shall have the power to try and punish any person irrespective of his nationality who, being a member of any armed, defence or auxiliary forces commits or has committed, in the territory of Bangladesh, whether before or after the commencement of this Act, any of the following crimes.

4   The words and comma 'or organisation,' were inserted after the word and comma 'individuals' by section 2 of the International Crimes (Tribunals) (Amendment) Act, 2013 (Act No. III of 2013) (with effect from 14th July 2009).

The International Crimes Tribunals Act

wanton destruction of cities, towns or villages, or devastation not justified by military necessity;
(e) violation of any humanitarian rules applicable in armed conflicts laid down in the Geneva Conventions of 1949;
(f) any other crimes under international law;
(g) attempt, abetment or conspiracy to commit any such crimes;
(h) complicity in or failure to prevent commission of any such crimes.

4. **Liability for crimes**
   (1) When any crime as specified in section 3 is committed by several persons, each of such persons is liable for that crime in the same manner as if it were done by him alone.
   (2) Any commander or superior officer who orders, permits, acquiesces or participates in the commission of any of the crimes specified in section 3 or is connected with any plans and activities involving the commission of such crimes or who fails or omits to discharge his duty to maintain discipline, or to control or supervise the actions of the persons under his command or his subordinates, whereby such persons or subordinates or any of them commit any such crimes, or who fails to take necessary measures to prevent the commission of such crimes, is guilty of such crimes.

5. **Official position, etc. not to free an accused from responsibility for any crime**
   (1) The official position, at any time, of any accused shall not be considered freeing hi from responsibility or mitigating punishment.
   (2) The fact that the accused acted pursuant to his domestic law or to order of his Government or of a superior shall not free him from responsibility, but may be considered in mitigation of punishment if the Tribunal deems that justice so requires.

6. **Tribunal**
   (1) For the purpose of section 3, the Government may, by notification in the *official Gazette*, set up one or more Tribunals, each consisting of a Chairman and not less than two and not more than four other members.
   [(2) Any person who is a Judge, or is qualified to be a Judge, or has been a Judge, of the Supreme Court of Bangladesh, may be appointed as a Chairman or member of the Tribunal.][5]

---

5   Sub-section (2) was substituted by section 4 (a) of the International Crimes (Tribunals) (Amendment) Act 2009 (Act no. LV of 2009). The initial version read: Any person who is qualified to be a Judge of the Supreme Court of Bangladesh or has been a Judge of any High Court or Supreme Court which at any time was in existence in the territory of Bang-

Appendix

[(2A) The Tribunal shall be independent in the exercise of its judicial functions and shall ensure fair trials.][6]

(3) The permanent seat of a Tribunal shall be in [Dhaka][7]:

Provided that a Tribunal may hold its sittings at such other place or places as it deems fit.

(4) If any member of a Tribunal dies or is, due to illness or any other reason, unable to continue or perform his functions, the Government may, by notification in the *official Gazette*, declare the office of such member to be vacant and appoint thereto another person qualified to hold the office.

(5) If, in the course of a trial, any one of the members of a Tribunal is, for any reason, unable to attend any sitting thereof, the trial may continue before the other members.

(6) A Tribunal shall not, merely by reason of any change in its membership or the absence of any member thereof from any sitting, be bound to recall and re-hear any witness who has already given any evidence and may act on the evidence already given or produced before it.

(7) If, upon any matter requiring the decision of a Tribunal, there is a difference of opinion among its members, the opinion of the majority shall prevail and the decision of the Tribunal shall be expressed in terms of the views of the majority.

(8) Neither the constitution of a Tribunal nor the appointment of its Chairman or members shall be challenged by the prosecution or by the accused or their counsel.

7. Prosecutors

(1) The Government may appoint one or more persons to conduct the prosecution before a Tribunal on such terms and conditions as may be determined by the Government; and every such person shall be deemed to be a Prosecutor for the purposes of this Act.

(2) The Government may designate one of such persons as the Chief Prosecutor.

8. Investigation

(1) The Government may establish an Agency for the purposes of investigation into crimes specified in section 3; and any officer belonging to the Agency shall have the right to assist the prosecution during the trial.

---

ladesh or who is qualified to be a member of General Court Martial under any service law of Bangladesh may be appointed as a Chairman or member of a Tribunal.

6 Sub-section (2A) was inserted by sub-section 4(b) of the of the International Crimes (Tribunals) (Amendment) Act 2009 (Act no. LV of 2009).

7 The word 'Dacca' was replaced by the word 'Dhaka' through Section 4(c) of the International Crimes (Tribunals) (Amendment) Act 2009 (Act no. LV of 2009).

(2) Any person appointed as a Prosecutor is competent to act as an Investigation Officer and the provisions relating to investigation shall apply to such Prosecutor.
(3) Any Investigation Officer making an investigation under this Act may, by order in writing, require the attendance before himself of any person who appears to be acquainted with the circumstances of the case; and such person shall attend as so required.
(4) Any Investigation Officer making an investigation under this Act may examine orally any person who appears to be acquainted with the facts and circumstances of the case.
(5) Such person shall be bound to answer all questions put to him by an Investigation Officer and shall not be excused from answering any question on the ground that the answer to such question will criminate, or may tend directly or indirectly to criminate, such person:
Provided that no such answer, which a person shall be compelled to give, shall subject him to any arrest or prosecution, or to be proved against him in any criminal proceeding.
(6) The Investigation Officer may reduce into writing any statement made to him in the course of examination under this section.
(7) Any person who fails to appear before an Investigation Officer for the purpose of examination or refuses to answer the questions put to him by such Investigation Officer shall be punished with simple imprisonment which may extend to six months, or with fine which may extend to Taka two thousand, or with both.
(8) Any Magistrate of the first class may take cognizance of an offence punishable under sub-section (7) upon a complaint in writing by an Investigation Officer.
(9) Any investigation done into the crimes specified in section 3 shall be deemed to have been done under the provisions of this Act.

9. **Commencement of the Proceedings**
    (1) The proceedings before a Tribunal shall commence upon the submission by the Chief Prosecutor, or a Prosecutor authorised by the Chief Prosecutor in this behalf, of formal charges of crimes alleged to have been committed by each of the accused persons.
    (2) The Tribunal shall thereafter fix a date for the trial of such accused person.
    (3) The Chief Prosecutor shall, at least three weeks before the commencement of the trial, furnish to the Tribunal a list of witnesses intended to be produced along with the recorded statement of such witnesses or copies thereof and copies of documents which the prosecution intends to rely upon in support of such charges.

Appendix

(4) The submission of a list of witnesses and documents under sub-section (3) shall not preclude the prosecution from calling, with the permission of the Tribunal, additional witnesses or tendering any further evidence at any stage of the trial:

Provided that notice shall be given to the defence of the additional witnesses intended to be called or additional evidence sought to be tendered by the prosecution.

(5) A list of witnesses for the defence, if any, along with the documents or copies thereof, which the defence intends to rely upon, shall be furnished to the Tribunal and the prosecution at the time of the commencement of the trial.

10. Procedure of trial

(1) The following procedure shall be followed at a trial before a Tribunal, namely: –

   (a) the charge shall be read out;
   (b) the Tribunal shall ask each accused person whether he pleads guilty or not-guilty;
   (c) if the accused person pleads guilty, the Tribunal shall record the plea, and may, in its discretion, convict him, thereon;
   (d) the prosecution shall make an opening statement;
   (e) the witnesses for the prosecution shall be examined, the defence may cross-examine such witnesses and the prosecution may re-examine them;
   (f) the witnesses for the defence, if any, shall be examined, the prosecution may cross-examine such witnesses and the defence may re-examine them;
   (g) the Tribunal may, in its discretion, permit the party which calls a witness to put any question to him which might be put in cross-examination by the adverse party;
   (h) the Tribunal may, in order to discover or obtain proof of relevant facts, ask any witness any question it pleases, in any form and at any time about any fact; and may order production of any document or thing or summon any witness, and neither the prosecution nor the defence shall be entitled either to make any objection to any such question or order or, without the leave of the Tribunal, to cross-examine any witness upon my answer given in reply to any such question;
   (i) the prosecution shall first sum up its case; and thereafter the defence shall sum up its case:

   Provided that if any witness is examined by the defence, the prosecution shall have the right to sum up its case after the defence has done so;
   (j) the Tribunal shall deliver its judgment and pronounce its verdict.

The International Crimes Tribunals Act

(2) All proceedings before the Tribunal shall be in [Bangla or][8] English.
(3) Any accused person or witness who is unable to express himself in, or does not understand, English may be provided the assistance of an interpreter.
(4) The proceedings of the Tribunal shall be in public:
Provided that the Tribunal may, if it thinks fit, take proceedings in camera.
(5) No oath shall be administered to any accused person.

10A. [Trial in absentia
(1) Where a proceeding is commenced under sub-section (1) of sub-section 9, the tribunal, before fixing the date for the trial under sub-section (2) of the said section, has reason to believe that the accused person has absconded or concealed himself so that he cannot be produced for trial, may hold the trial in his absence following the procedure as laid down in the Rules of Procedure made under section 22 for such trial.
(2) Where the accused person is tried under sub-section (1), the Tribunal may direct that a Counsel shall be engaged at the expense of the Government to defend the accused person and may also determine the fees to be paid to such Counsel.][9]

11. Powers of Tribunal
(1) A Tribunal shall have power –
   (a) to summon witnesses to the trial and to require their attendance and testimony and to put questions to them;
   (b) to administer oaths to witnesses;
   (c) to require the production of document and other evidentiary material;
   (d) to appoint persons for carrying out any task designated by the Tribunal.
(2) For the purpose of enabling any accused person to explain any circumstances appearing in the evidence against him, a Tribunal may, at any stage of the trial without previously warning the accused person, put such questions to him as the Tribunal considers necessary:
Provided that the accused person shall not render himself liable to punishment by refusing to answer such questions or by giving false answers to them; but the Tribunal may draw such inference from refusal or answers as it thinks just;

---

[8] The words 'Bangla or' were inserted before the word 'English' by section 5 of the International Crimes (Tribunals) (Amendment) Act 2009 (Act no. LV of 2009).
[9] Section 10A was inserted by section 2 of the International Crimes (Tribunals) (Amendment) Act, 2012 (Act No. XLIII).

Appendix

(3) A Tribunal shall –
  (a) confine the trial to an expeditious hearing of the issues raised by the charges;
  (b) take measures to prevent any action which may cause unreasonable delay, and rule out irrelevant issues and statements.
(4) A Tribunal may punish any person, who obstructs or abuses its process or disobeys any of its orders or directions, or does anything which tends to prejudice the case of a party before it, or tends to bring it or any of its members into hatred or contempt, or does anything which constitutes contempt of the Tribunal, with simple imprisonment which may extend to one year, or with fine which may extend to Taka five thousand or with both.
(5) Any member of a Tribunal shall have power to direct, or issue a warrant for, the arrest of, and to commit to custody, and to authorise the continued detention in custody of, any person charged with any crime specified in section 3.
(6) The Chairman of a Tribunal may make such administrative arrangements as he considers necessary for the performance of the functions of the Tribunal under this Act.

[11A. **Power to transfer cases**
  (1) At any stage of a case, a Tribunal may, on its own motion or on the application of the Chief Prosecutor, by an order in writing, transfer the case to another Tribunal, whenever it considers such transfer to be just, expedient and convenient for the proper dispensation of justice and expeditious disposal of such cases.
  (2) Where a case has been transferred under sub-section (1), the Tribunal which thereafter tries such case shall, subject to the provisions of this Act, proceed from the stage at which it was so transferred.][10]

12. **Provision for defence counsel**
Where an accused person is not represented by counsel, the Tribunal may, at any stage of the case, direct that a counsel shall be engaged at the expense of the Government to defend the accused person and may also determine the fees to be paid to such counsel.

13. **Restriction of adjournment**
No trial before a Tribunal shall be adjourned for any purpose unless the Tribunal is of the opinion that the adjournment is in the interest of justice.

---

10 Section 11A was inserted by section 2 of the International Crimes (Tribunals) (Amendment) Act, 2012 (Act No. XLIII).

14. Statement or confession of accused person

(1) Any Magistrate of the first class may record any statement or confession made to him by an accused person at any time in the course of investigation or at any time before the commencement of the trial.

(2) The Magistrate shall, before recording any such confession, explain to the accused person making it that he is not bound to make a confession and that if he does so it may be used as evidence against him and no Magistrate shall record any such confession unless, upon questioning the accused making it, he has reason to believe that it was made voluntarily.

15. Pardon of an approver

(1) At any stage of the trial, a Tribunal may with a view to obtaining the evidence of any person supposed to have been directly or indirectly concerned in, or privy to, any of the crimes specified in section 3, tender a pardon to such person on condition of his making a full and true disclosure of the whole of the circumstances within his knowledge relative to the crime and to every other person concerned, whether as principal or abettor, in the commission thereof.

(2) Every person accepting the tender under this section shall be examined as a witness in the trial.

(3) Such person shall be detained in custody until the termination of the trial.

16. Charge, etc.

(1) Every charge against an accused person shall state –
  (a) the name and particulars of the accused person;
  (b) the crime of which the accused person is charged;
  (c) such particulars of the alleged crime as are reasonably sufficient to give the accused person notice of the matter with which he is charged.

(2) A copy of the formal charge and a copy of each of the documents lodged with the formal charge shall be furnished to the accused person at a reasonable time before the trial; and in case of any difficulty in furnishing copies of the documents, reasonable opportunity for inspection shall be given to the accused person in such manner as the Tribunal may decide.

17. Right of accused person during trial

(1) During trial of an accused person he shall have the right to give any explanation relevant to the charge made against him.

(2) An accused person shall have the right to conduct his own defence before the Tribunal or to have the assistance of counsel.

(3) An accused person shall have the right to present evidence at all trial in support of his defence, and to cross-examine any witness called by the prosecution.

18. No excuse from answering any question

A witness shall not be excused from answering any question put to him on the ground that the answer to such question will criminate or may tend directly or indirectly to criminate such witness, or that it will expose or tend directly or indirectly to expose such witness to a penalty or forfeiture of any kind:

Provided that no such answer which a witness shall be compelled to give shall subject him to any arrest or prosecution or be proved against him in any criminal proceeding, except a prosecution for giving false evidence.

19. Rules of evidence

(1) A Tribunal shall not be bound by technical rules of evidence; and it shall adopt and apply to the greatest possible extent expeditious and non-technical procedure, and may admit any evidence, including reports and photographs published in newspapers, periodicals and magazines, films and tape-recordings and other materials as may be tendered before it, which it deems to have probative value.

(2) A Tribunal may receive in evidence any statement recorded by a Magistrate or an Investigation Officer being a statement made by any person who, at the time of the trial, is dead or whose attendance cannot be procured without an amount of delay or expense which the Tribunal considers unreasonable.

(3) A Tribunal shall not require proof of facts of common knowledge but shall take judicial notice thereof.

(4) A Tribunal shall take judicial notice of official governmental documents and reports of the United Nations and its subsidiary agencies or other international bodies including non-governmental organisations.

20. Judgment and sentence

(1) The Judgment of a Tribunal as to the guilt or the innocence of any accused person shall give the reasons on which it is based:

Provided that each member of the Tribunal shall be competent to deliver a judgment of his own.

(2) Upon conviction of an accused person, the Tribunal shall award sentence of death or such other punishment proportionate to the gravity of the crime as appears to the Tribunal just and proper.

[(2A) A copy of judgment under the seal and signature of the Registrar of a Tribunal shall be provided, free of cost, to the prosecution and the accused person on the date of delivery of the Judgment.

(2B) Notwithstanding anything contained in any other law, rule or legal instrument for the time being in force, when a copy of judgment is provided under sub-section (2A), it shall be used as certified copy of the judgment of the Tribunal for the purpose of preferring an appeal under section 21.][11]

(3) The sentence awarded under this Act shall be carried out in accordance with the orders of the Government.

21. [Right of appeal

(1) A person convicted of any crime specified in section 3 and sentenced by a Tribunal may appeal, as of right, to the Appellate Division of the Supreme Court of Bangladesh against such conviction and sentence.

(2) The Government or the complainant or the informant, as the case may be, may appeal, as of right, to the Appellate Division of the Supreme Court of Bangladesh against the order of acquittal or an order of sentence.

(3) An appeal under sub-section (1) and (2) shall be preferred within 30 (thirty) days from the date of conviction and sentence, or acquittal or any sentence, and no appeal shall lie after the expiry of the aforesaid period.

(4) The appeal shall be disposed of within 60 (sixty) days from the date of its filing.

(5) At the time of filing the appeal, the appellant shall submit all documents as may be relied upon by him.][12]

22. Rules of procedure

Subject to the provision of this Act, a Tribunal may regulate its own procedure.

---

11   Sub-sections (2A) and (2B were inserted by section 3 of the International Crimes (Tribunals) (Amendment) Act, 2012 (Act No. XLIII).

12   Section 21 was substituted by Section 3 of the International Crimes (Tribunals) (Amendment) Act, 2013 (Act No. III of 2013) (with effect from 14th July, 2009). The initial version from 1973 reads:
A person convicted of any crime specified in section 3 and sentenced by a Tribunal shall have the right of appeal to the Appellate Division of the Supreme Court of Bangladesh against such conviction and sentence;
Provided that such appeal may be preferred with in sixty days of the date of order of conviction and sentence.
Section 21 was revised for the first time through the International Crimes (Tribunals) (Amendment) Act, 2009 (Act no. LV of 2009). The 2009 version reads: (1) A person convicted of any crime specified in section 3 and sentenced by a Tribunal shall have the right of appeal to the Appellate Division of the Supreme Court of Bangladesh against such conviction and sentence. (2) The Government shall have the right of appeal to the Appellate Division of the Supreme Court of Bangladesh against an order of acquittal. (3) An appeal under sub-section (1) or (2) shall be preferred within 60 days of the date of order of conviction and sentence or acquittal.
With the International Crimes (Tribunals) (Amendment) Act, 2012 (Act No. XLIII) the words '60 (sixty)' in sub-section (3) were substituted by the words '30 (thirty)'.

Appendix

23. Certain laws not to apply
The provisions of the Criminal Procedure Code, 1898 (V of 1898), and the Evidence Act, 1872 (I of 1872), shall not apply in any proceedings under this Act.

24. Bar of Jurisdiction
No order, judgment or sentence of a Tribunal shall be called in question in any manner whatsoever in or before any Court or other authority in any legal proceedings whatsoever except in the manner provided in section 21.

25. Indemnity
No suit, prosecution or other legal proceeding shall lie against the Government or any person for anything, in good faith, done or purporting to have been done under this Act.

26. Provisions of the Act overriding all other laws
The provisions of this Act shall have effect notwithstanding anything inconsistent therewith contained in any other law for the time being in force.

The Rules of Procedure of Tribunal 2

International Crimes (Tribunal-2) Rules of Procedure, 2012
Old High Court Building
Dhaka, Bangladesh
NOTIFICATION
28 March 2012

No. Anto: Apto: Tri-2:/06/Bidhi/12 – In exercise of powers given under section 22 of the International Crimes (Tribunals) Act, 1973 (Act XIX of 1973), this Tribunal created newly under section 6 of the International Crimes (Tribunals) Act, 1973 (Act No. XIX of 1973) which is named as 'International Crimes Tribunal-2' with a view to keeping pace with the trial procedure hereby promulgates the following Rules of Procedure for investigation, prosecution, trial of the offences as are described and enumerated in the Act by way of adopting the procedures including all of its amendments thereto embodied in the International Crimes Tribunals Rules of Procedure 2010 formulated by the first Tribunal in 2010 and also by incorporating some additions and changes in Rule 18 (4), Rule 26, Rule 29 (1), Rule 43, Rule 53, Rule 54 (1) and Rule 55 for smooth functioning of the Tribunal:

Chapter I
General Provisions

1. **Short title and commencement**
   (1) These Rules may be called the International Crimes (Tribunal-2) Rules of Procedure, 2012.
   (2) It shall be deemed to have come into force on and from 22nd March of 2012.

2. **Definitions**
   In these Rules, unless there is anything repugnant in the subject or context,
   (1) "accused" means the person against whom an investigation of an offence under the Act has been started;
   (2) "Act" refers to the International Crimes (Tribunals) Act, 1973 (Act XIX of 1973)
   (3) "bail" refers to setting an accused at large on furnishing bond before the Tribunal;
   (4) "Chairman" refers to the Chairman of the Tribunal;
   (5) "charge" refers to the accusation of crimes against an accused framed by the Tribunal;
   (6) "complaint" means any information oral or in writing obtained by the Investigation Agency including its own knowledge relating to the commission of a crime under section 3 (2) of the Act;

Appendix

(7) "counsel" refers to a person who is enrolled as an advocate in the Bangladesh Bar Council;
(8) "Deputy Registrar" refers to the Deputy Registrar of the Tribunal;
(9) "evidence" means all statements which the Tribunal permits or requires to be made before it by witnesses, and it includes all other materials, collected during investigation, placed before the Tribunal in relation to matters of fact;
(10) "Form" refers to Forms as are contained in the Schedule;
(11) "formal charge" means accusation of crimes against the accused in the form of a petition lodged by the Prosecutor with the Tribunal on receipt of the Investigation Report;
(12) "International Crimes Tribunal-2" refers to the Tribunal constituted under section 6 of the Act;
(13) "Investigation Agency" refers to the Agency established under section 8 of the Act;
(14) "Investigation Officer" refers to any member of the Investigation Agency;
(15) "Investigation Report" refers to the report submitted by the Investigation Agency after completion of investigation in a case under the Act;
(16) "law enforcing agency" refers to any member of the Bangladesh Police under the Police Act, 1861 (Act V of 1861), or the Armed Police Battalions or the Rapid Action Battalions (RAB) under the Armed Police Battalions Ordinance, 1979 (Ord. XXV of 1979), or the Bangladesh Rifles under the Bangladesh Rifles Order, 1972 (P. O. 148 of 1972), or the Ansar Force under the Ansar Force Act, 1995 (Act 3 of 1995), or the Battalion Ansar under the Battalion Ansar Act, 1995 (Act 4 of 1995), or the Coast Guard Force under the Coast Guard Act, 1994 (Act 26 of 1894);
(17) "Member" refers to a Member of the Tribunal;
(18) "oath" refers to making such declaration on affirmation by a witness prior to testifying before the Tribunal in Form No. 12;
(19) "offence" means any of the crimes described in section 3 (2) of the Act;
(20) "Prosecutor" refers to a Prosecutor appointed under section 7 of the Act;
(21) "Registrar" refers to the Registrar of the Tribunal;
(22) "Rules" refers to these Rules of Procedure;
(23) "Schedule" refers to the Schedule appended at the end of these Rules;
(24) "seal" refers to the seal of the Tribunal;
(25) "section" refers to the section of the Act;
(26) "victim" refers to a person who has suffered harm as a result of commission of the crimes under section 3 (2) of the International Crimes (Tribunals) Act, 1973.

Chapter II
Powers and Functions of the Investigation Agency

3. (1) The Investigation Agency established by the Government shall be responsible for investigation of a case.
   (2) The Government may nominate or assign a member of the Investigation Agency as Coordinator to –
   (a) supervise overall functions of the Agency;
   (b) control and monitor the speedy progress of any investigation; and
   (c) perform any other function for efficient running of the Agency.
4. An Investigation Officer shall act and work in accordance with the provisions of sections 8(1), 8(3), 8(4), 8(5), 8(6) and 8(7) of the Act while investigating a case.
5. The Investigation Agency shall maintain a Complaint Register with necessary particulars on putting date and serial numbers of the complaints meant for initiating investigation under the Act.
6. If the Investigation Officer has reason to believe that any offence has been committed, he shall proceed in person to the spot, investigate the facts and circumstances of the case and if necessary, take steps for the discovery and arrest of the accused.
7. If the Investigation Officer finds and is satisfied that there is no sufficient ground for investigation, he may stop investigation with the concurrence of the Chief Prosecutor.
8. (1) The Investigation Officer shall maintain a Case Diary for each case in connection with the investigation mentioning its day to day progress until completion of such investigation.
   (2) The Investigation Officer may use the Case Diary at the time of deposition before the Tribunal to refresh his memory or to explain any fact entered therein.
   (3) The defence shall have no right to examine or use the Case Diary in defence of a case.
   (4) The Tribunal may peruse the Case Diary for clarification or understanding of any fact transpired at the time of investigation.
   (5) The Tribunal, if it considers expedient, may direct the prosecutors to present the progress report of investigation for its perusal.
9. (1) The Investigation Officer, through the Prosecutor, may obtain a warrant of arrest from the Tribunal for arrest of a person at any stage of the investigation, if he can satisfy the Tribunal that such arrest is necessary for effective and proper investigation.
   (2) The law enforcing agency of the area where the person to be arrested resides shall execute the warrant of arrest issued by the Tribunal.
   (3) At the time of executing the warrant of arrest under sub-rule (2) or later on, a copy of allegations is to be served upon such person.

Appendix

(4) If a person is already in custody in connection with an offence or any case other than under the Act and the Tribunal is satisfied that a detention order is necessary for effective and proper investigation of any offence under the Act, the Tribunal may issue a production warrant and direct the person to be detained in custody.

(5) If an accused is in custody during investigation period, the investigation officer shall conclude the investigation within one year of his arrest under the Rules. In case of failure to complete the investigation as specified above, the accused may be released on bail subject to fulfilment of some conditions as imposed by the Tribunal. But, in exceptional circumstances, the Tribunal by showing reasons to be recorded in writing may extend the period of investigation and also the order detaining the accused in custody for a further period of six months.

(6) After every three months of detention of the accused in custody the investigation officer through the prosecutor shall submit a progress report of investigation before the Tribunal on perusal of which it may make a review of its order relating to the detention of the accused.

10. An Investigation Officer, if he thinks it necessary, may search and seize any documents or things under a seizure list prepared in presence of two witnesses.
11. After completion of investigation, the Investigation Officer shall submit an Investigation Report together with all the documents, papers and the evidence collected during investigation of offence(s) as specified in the Act committed by a person(s) before the Chief Prosecutor.
12. The Investigation Officer shall prepare more than one set of his Investigation Report together with all the accompanying documents for the purpose of preserving one set in the office of the Investigation Agency.
13. Each and every document, paper and evidence accompanying the Investigation Report under rules 11 and 12 shall be duly authenticated and endorsed by the Investigation Officer who investigated the case.
14. The Prosecutors and the Investigation Agency shall take necessary measures to ensure the confidentiality of any information, the protection of any witness or victim and the preservation of all the evidence collected.
15. Any Judicial Magistrate of the first class may take cognizance and hold trial of an offence under sub-section (7) of section 8 of the Act upon a complaint in writing by an Investigation Officer.
16. (1) The Investigation Officer if thinks it necessary, may apply through the Prosecutor to the Tribunal to commit the arrested person(s) in his custody for the purpose of interrogation and the Tribunal can pass order for such custody of the person(s) arrested, for a maximum period of three (3) days if it upon consideration of facts and circumstances of the case is of opinion that for proper investigation such order is indispensible.

(2) No person during investigation under the Act shall be subjected to any form of coercion, duress or threat of any kind.

Chapter III
Powers and Functions of the Prosecution

17. The Chief Prosecutor or any other Prosecutor authorized by the Chief Prosecutor shall conduct the prosecution of a case or appear before the Tribunal for any matter relating to the case.
18. (1) Upon receipt of report of investigation of offence(s), the Chief Prosecutor or any other Prosecutor authorized by him shall prepare a formal charge in the form of a petition on the basis of the papers and documents and the evidences collected and submitted by the Investigation Officer and shall submit the same before the Tribunal.
   (2) The Investigation Agency shall
      (a) work with the Prosecutors in preparing the report under rule 18 (1), and after submission of the report, shall assist the Prosecutors in the task of formulating the formal charge including arrangement of documents and materials; and
      (b) also assist the Prosecutors in tendering evidence at any stage of trial.
   (3) As and when directed by the Tribunal the Investigation Agency shall produce witness before the Tribunal as required by the Prosecutors. The law enforcing agency of the concerned area shall provide all necessary assistance to the Investigation Agency in executing the process issued for securing attendance of witness.
   (4) The Chief Prosecutor shall file extra copies of formal charge and copies of other documents for supplying the same to the accused(s) which the Prosecution intends to relay upon in support of such charges so that the accused can prepare his defence. Provided that for ensuring protection of witness and victim only the name of witnesses and victims without disclosing their full particulars, along with documents, shall be supplied to the defence.
   (5) The Chief Prosecutor shall also file three sets of formal charge and other documents intended to be relied upon before the Tribunal in compact disk (CD) or digital versatile disk (DVD) while submitting the formal charge under sub-rule (1).
   (6) The defence shall also require to submit three sets of list of witnesses along with the documents which the defence intends to rely upon before the Tribunal in compact disk (CD) or digital versatile disk (DVD) while furnishing the same under section 9 (5) of the Act.
19. If any Investigation Report does not disclose a prima facie case against an accused the Chief Prosecutor may initiate further investigation or stop the said investigation.

Appendix

20. (1) At the time of submitting a formal charge in the form of a petition, it must contain the name and address of the accused person, witness, and the date, time and place of the occurrence.
(2) The Chief Prosecutor, or any other Prosecutor authorized by him in this regard, shall file necessary papers, documents and materials in support of such case for a process to be issued by the Tribunal for appearance of the accused before the Tribunal if the accused is not already arrested.

Chapter IV
Procedure

21. All the offences as are described in section 3 (2) shall be cognizable, non-compoundable and non-bailable.

22. After taking cognizance of an offence the Tribunal shall fix a date for appearance if he is not already in custody of the accused and issue summons or warrant for appearance as it thinks proper.

23. If the Tribunal does not take cognizance of an offence, the case shall be dismissed.

24. (1) Where the Tribunal makes an order for recording of confession, a Judicial Magistrate of the first class directed by the Tribunal shall record the confession of an accused pursuant to that order.
(1A) At the time of recording confession under rule 24(1) the Judicial Magistrate shall allow the engaged counsel for the accused to be present there, provided that the counsel shall not be allowed to interfere or speak in course of recording such confession.
(2) If any member of the Investigation Agency makes a petition to any Judicial Magistrate of the first class for recording any statement of witness, that Magistrates shall record such statement.

25. (1) The Judicial Magistrate shall record the confession of an accused or the statement of a witness in plain white papers.
(2) The Judicial Magistrate shall then make a memorandum or endorsement indicating whether the confession so recorded is voluntary, and while recording confession, shall also comply with the requirements of section 14(2) of the Act.

26. (1) Presence of all the Members in all sittings of the Tribunal is not compulsory, but at the time of taking cognizance of an offence and delivery of the judgment the presence of all the Members of the Tribunal is compulsory.
(2) All other orders may be passed even by one Member in sitting and shall be deemed to have been passed by the Tribunal.
(3) The Tribunal, on its own motion or on the application of either party, may review any of its order including the order of framing charge(s) in the interest of justice.

(4) If an application is filed, the chairman or any member nominated by him shall peruse the same and if he finds that there are materials for considering the application only then the application shall be referred to the Tribunal for hearing before it otherwise the same shall stand dismissed.

(5) An application seeking review of an order may be filed only for once, and any such application together with the copy of the order shall have to be filed within 7 (seven) days of the order under review.

(6) All applications shall be filed to the Registrar by 03:00 pm of working days.

Chapter V
Powers and Functions of the Tribunal

27. After recording of the testimony, the witness shall put his signature or thumb impression on each page of the deposition sheet.
28. (1) Bench Officers and Assistant Bench Officers shall be individually and collectively responsible for preservation of the documents, materials and evidence produced before the Tribunal along with the records of the respective cases pending before the Tribunal.

    (2) Record of disposed of cases shall be preserved and archived forever by the Tribunal at the place and in the manner as arranged by the Government.
29. The Tribunal shall take cognizance of offence against any accused upon examination of the formal charge, the Investigation Report, the papers, documents and the evidence submitted by a Prosecutor in support thereof, if they disclose a prima facie case.
30. After cognizance of an offence is taken, the Tribunal shall issue processor warrant, as it thinks fit and proper, in accordance with rule 22.
31. If the process issued under rule 22 is returned unserved, the Tribunal shall make an order to publish a notice in two daily newspapers, one in English and another in Bangla asking the accused to appear before the Tribunal on the date fixed therein.
32. If the accused, despite publication of notice in daily newspapers, fails to appear before the Tribunal on the date and time so specified therein, and the Tribunal has reason to believe that the accused has absconded or concealing himself so that he cannot be arrested and produced for trial and there is no immediate prospect for arresting him, the trial of such accused shall commence and be held in absentia.
33. In pursuance of any summons, when an accused appears before the Tribunal, he shall be sent to the prison if he is not enlarged on bail by the Tribunal.
34. (1) The Police shall produce the arrested accused direct before the Tribunal within 24 (twenty-four) hours of arrest excluding the time needed for the journey.

    (2) When the accused is produced before the Tribunal under sub-rule (1), he shall be sent to the prison if he is not enlarged on bail by the Tribunal.

Appendix

(3) At any stage of the proceedings, the Tribunal may release an accused on bail subject to fulfilment of some conditions as imposed by it, and in the interest of justice, may modify any of such conditions on its own motion or on the prayer of either party. In case of violation of any of such conditions the accused may be taken into custody cancelling his bail.

35. When the case is ready for trial, the Tribunal shall proceed to hear the case in accordance with the procedure of trial under section 10 of the Act on the basis of a charge to be framed considering the formal charge, Investigation Report together with the documents and materials produced and submitted in support of such report.

36. Persons accused of the same offence committed in the course of the same transaction, or persons accused of abatement or attempt to commit such offence, or persons accused of conspiracy or planning or design in the commission of an offence or more than one offence, or persons accused of more than one offence may be charged with, and tried at one trial for, every such offence.

37. When the accused appears or is brought before the Tribunal, and if the Tribunal, upon consideration of record of the case and documents submitted therewith and after giving the prosecution and the accused an opportunity of being heard, finds that there is no sufficient ground to presume that the accused has committed an offence, it shall discharge the accused and record its reasons for so doing.

38. (1) If, after consideration and hearing under rule 37, the Tribunal is of opinion that there is sufficient ground to presume that the accused has committed an offence, the Tribunal shall frame one or more charges for the offences of which he is accused and he shall be asked whether he admits that he has committed the offence with which he is charged.

(2) An accused pleading not guilty will get at least three weeks in time for preparing his defence.

39. If the accused admits that he has committed the offence charged with, his admission shall be recorded in his own words, and upon such admission the Tribunal may convict him accordingly or may keep such admission with the record for consideration usually at the time of trial and pronouncement of judgment.

40. Whenever the Tribunal considers that the production of any document or other thing is necessary or desirable for the purpose of investigation or trial or other proceedings under the Act, the Tribunal may issue a summons, or an order to the person in whose possession or power such document or thing is believed to be, requiring him to attend and produce it at the time, place and date stated in the summons or order.

41. The Tribunal may, for ensuring fair justice, appoint one or more amicus curie to assist the Tribunal in a particular case.

42. The Tribunal may allow appearance of any foreign counsel for either party provided that the Bangladesh Bar Council permits such counsel to appear.
43. (1) Where an accused is not represented by any counsel in the trial of a case, the Tribunal shall appoint a counsel to defend such an accused at the expense of the Government.
(2) A person charged with crimes as described under section 3 (2) of the Act shall be presumed innocent until he is found guilty.
(3) No person shall be tried twice for the same offence described under section 3 (2) of the Act.
(4) The accused shall be entitled to a fair and public hearing to engage his counsel at his choice who is legally authorised to appear before this tribunal.
(5) The accused shall be tried without delay.
(6) No accused shall be punished without giving him an opportunity of being heard.
(7) No accused shall be compelled to testify against his will or to confess his guilt.
43A. If the accused on bail fails to appear and or the accused being in custody refuses to come to the Tribunal for any reason and or he could not be brought before the Tribunal due to his long ailment, the Tribunal shall have authority to proceed with the proceedings in presence of his counsel or pass any order which it thinks fit an proper.
44. The Tribunal shall be at liberty to admit any evidence oral or documentary, print or electronic including books, reports and photographs published in newspapers, periodicals, and magazines, films and tape recording and other materials as may be tendered before it and it may exclude any evidence which does not inspire any confidence in it, and admission or non-admission of evidence by the Tribunal is final and cannot be challenged.
45. In pursuance of section 11 (4) of the Act, the Tribunal may draw a proceeding against any person who obstructs or abuses the process of the Tribunal or disobeys any order or direction of the Tribunal, or who does anything which tends to prejudice the case of a party before the Tribunal, or tends to bring the Tribunal or any of its Members into hatred or contempt, or does anything which constitutes contempt of the Tribunal.
46. (1) Upon hearing the person and consideration of the explanation submitted, if any, to a notice to show cause issued, if the Tribunal is of opinion that such person is guilty of an offence under section 11(4), it may accordingly convict and punish such person.
(2) Upon conviction of an accused person under section 20(2) of the Act, the sentence of imprisonment shall commence from the date of judgment. In case of absconding convict, it shall commence from the date of his surrender before the Tribunal, or from the date of his arrest.

(3) Proportionate to the gravity of the crime, in sentencing the accused, the Tribunal may also impose fine and or pass reparation order which is deemed to be fit and proper.

(4) Clerical or numerical errors or omissions in the judgments or orders may at any time be corrected by the Tribunal either on its own motion or on the application of either party.

46A. Nothing in these Rules shall be deemed to limit or otherwise affect the inherent power of the Tribunal to make such order (s) as may be necessary to meet the ends of justice or to prevent abuse of the process.

47. Prior to testifying before the Tribunal, every witness shall swear an oath or make an affirmation in Form 12 of the Schedule

48. (1) The Tribunal may, at any stage of trial of a case, summon any person as a witness, or examine any person in attendance, though not summoned as a witness, or re-call and re-examine any person already examined.

(2) The Tribunal shall summon and examine or re-call and re-examine any such person if his evidence appears to it essential to the just decision of the case.

49. The Tribunal may take consideration of the confession of an accused or the statement of a witness recorded by the Judicial Magistrate under rule 25(1) and in the manner as stated in rule 25(2) if the confession is proved by such Judicial Magistrate or any other Judicial Magistrate who is acquainted with his signature or writing when the recording Judicial Magistrate is dead or not available.

50. The burden of proving the charge shall lie upon the prosecution beyond reasonable doubt.

51. (1) The onus of proof as to the plea of alibi or to any particular fact or information which is in the possession or knowledge of the defence shall be upon the defence.

(2) The defence shall also prove the documents and materials to be produced by them in accordance with the provisions of section 9 (5) of the Act.

(3) Mere failure to prove the plea of alibi and or the documents and materials by the defence shall not render the accused guilty.

52. Where there are several accused, the reference of the accused on behalf of whom the evidence was submitted, shall be noted.

53. (1) The testimony of the witness shall be recorded either in Bangla or in English through the process of computer typing or otherwise as the Tribunal directs.

(2) The cross-examination shall be strictly limited to the subject-matter of the examination-in-chief of a witness but the party shall be at liberty to cross-examine such witness on his credibility and to take contradiction of the evidence given by him.

(3) The Tribunal shall have jurisdiction to regulate the matter of time management as and when deems necessary, for ensuring effective and expeditious trial.

54. (1) The prosecution may prove a manuscript by the person who was the author of such manuscript or who knows the handwriting or signature of such author, and when any of such persons is dead or not available, the person from whom it was collected or who knows from whose possession it was collected.
(2) Pursuant to section 19(1) of the Act, the Tribunal may admit any document or its photocopies in evidence if such documents initially appear to have probative value.
55. Once the document is marked as exhibit, the contents of a document may be admissible.
56. (1) The Tribunal shall give due weight to the primary and secondary evidence and direct and circumstantial evidence of any fact as the peculiar facts and circumstances of the case demand having regard to the time and place of the occurrence.
(2) The Tribunal shall also accord in its discretion due consideration to both hearsay and non-hearsay evidence, and the reliability and probative value in respect of hearsay evidence shall be assessed and weighed separately at the end of trial.
(3) Any statement made to the investigation officer or to the prosecutor in course of investigation by the accused is not admissible in evidence except that part of the statement which leads to discovery of any incriminating material.
57. The Tribunal shall apply these Rules which will best favour a fair determination of the matter in issue before it and are consonant with the spirit of the Act.
58. (1) Evidence that is produced by the prosecution or the defence shall be suitably identified. Proved by the respective party and marked with consecutive numbers as exhibits.
(2) Exhibits of the prosecution shall be marked with English numerals while those of the defence with English alphabets and all exhibits shall constitute part of the record.

Chapter VIA
Witness and Victim Protection

58A. (1) The Tribunal on its own initiative, or on the application of either party, may pass necessary order directing the concerned authorities of the Government to ensure protection, privacy and well-being of the witnesses and or victims. This process will be confidential and the other side will not be notified.
(2) The Government shall –
    (a) arrange accommodation of witness (es)/victim (s), if so prayed for;
    (b) ensure security and surveillance during the stay of witnesses/victims as directed by the Tribunal; and

Appendix

    (c) take necessary measure to escort the witnesses/victmins to the courtroom by the members of the law enforcing agency.

(3) In case of holding proceedings in camera under section 10(4) of the Act, both the prosecution and the defence counsel shall provide undertakings regarding confidentiality of the proceeding, and shall not reveal any information arising out of such proceeding including identity of the witness. Violation of such undertaking shall be prosecuted under section 11(4) of the Act.

Chapter VII
Office of the Tribunal

59. (1) The Office of the Tribunal shall be composed of a Registrar, a Deputy Registrar, Assistant Registrar(s) and other personnel and employees.

(2) The Registrar shall, with approval of the Chairman, organize and direct the works of the Office.

(3) The Office shall provide necessary secretarial services to the Tribunal and perform such other duties as may be assigned by the Chairman.

(4) All communications intended to the Tribunal shall be delivered to the Registrar.

(5) The working hours of the Office shall be from 10.00 A.M. to 01:00 P.M. and 02.00 P.M. to 05.00 P.M., and the judicial work shall be held from 10.30 A.M. to 04.30 P.M. with recesses of one hour from 01.00 P.M. to 02.00 P.M.

(6) The Office shall remain closed on Friday and Saturday for weekly holidays.

(7) The Tribunal shall fix up fresh official and judicial working hours for the month of Ramadan.

(8) In case of absence or temporary indisposition of the Chairman, the Senior Member of the Tribunal shall be acting as the Chairman.

Chapter VIII
Powers and Functions of Registrar and Deputy Registrar

60. The Registrar shall –

(1) be the Chief Administrative Office of the Office of the Tribunal and receive the cases submitted by the Prosecutor for the purpose of laying them before the Tribunal.

(2) assist the Tribunal in the performance of its functions under the authority of the Chairman and shall be responsible for the administration, shall represent the Tribunal as its spokesman and service of the Tribunal and shall serve as its channel of communication;

(3) maintain a Duty Roster of other personnel and employees of the Office;

(4) maintain a Case Register of the cases in Form-15 and shall make entry of necessary particulars thereof, and such cases so registered and numbered shall be called as ICT-BD Case;
(5) be responsible for custody of the record of the cases;
(6) make correspondence with the government and other offices on behalf of the Chairman;
(7) be responsible for issuing summons or warrant of arrest under his signature for securing attendance of the accused or the witness or search warrant etc. from the Office as required by the Tribunal, bearing its seal, and be responsible also for maintaining a Process Register in this regard;
(8) be the 'Drawing and Disbursing Officer' (DDO) and be responsible for the accounts of the money sanctioned to the Tribunal, and he shall manage with the financial matters by taking initiative for placement of budget and spend the fund when needed for providing services to the Tribunal on sanction of the Chairman;
(9) keep Taka 20,000/00 as Permanent Advance in hand to meet up day to day expenses of the Tribunal either in cash or in voucher, or in both;
(10) maintain the Office Order Book and other registers including the Register of Letters Issued and the Register of Letters Received, and the Daily Attendance Register of staff of the Office shall be duly maintained and signed by him, and also maintain a Peon Book;
(11) supply or cause a certified copy of the Judgment of the Tribunal, upon an application filed by the accused or Prosecutor, prepared in offset white paper on payment of a fees of Taka 10 (ten) for each page of the copy while an absconding accused shall not get the such a copy unless he surrenders before the Tribunal or he is arrested; and
(12) be bound to do any official work meant for smooth functioning of the Tribunal as assigned by the Chairman.

61. Except clause (1), (2), (8) and (9) of rule 60, the Registrar may delegate any of his powers under these Rules to the Deputy Registrar and in such a case he shall inform the matter to the Chairman.

62. (1) For the smooth functioning of the Tribunal, the Registrar may control the entry of people including the counsels in the courtroom of the Tribunal as and when required by the Tribunal for maintaining discipline and order.
(2) For ensuring orderly and disciplined state of affairs inside the courtroom of the Tribunal, no counsel, journalist, media person or other people shall be allowed to enter the courtroom without having 'entry pass' issued by the Registrar.

63. (1) The Deputy Registrar shall assist the Registrar in his works and act as per direction of the Registrar.
(2) The Deputy Registrar shall automatically assume the powers and perform necessary functions of the Registrar under these Rules during the absence of the Registrar.

Appendix

Chapter IX
Representation and Fees etc.

64. A counsel may represent a party before the Tribunal upon filing a 'Vakalatnama' duly executed by and obtained from such party.

65. Every application to the Tribunal shall bear a court-fee of Taka 10 (ten) and the 'Vakalatnama' shall be affixed with a court-fee of Taka 50 (fifty).

Chapter X
Amendment

66. These Rules may be amended, altered, added or repealed by the Tribunal if it thinks necessary and expedient for the smooth functioning of the Tribunal.

Stefan Rinke

Schadensersatzklagen gegen Staaten wegen schwerer Menschenrechtsverletzungen im Europäischen Zivilprozessrecht

Zugleich ein Beitrag zum Verhältnis der EuGVVO zur Staatenimmunität

Das Europäische Zivilprozessrecht steht vor Herausforderungen, die seine Initiatoren nicht vorhersahen. Sein „Herzstück" ist Schauplatz für Verfahren von Opfern schwerer Menschenrechtsverletzungen geworden, die versuchen, erstrittene Entscheidungen unter Zuhilfenahme der EuGVVO durchzusetzen oder sie zur Begründung der Gerichtszuständigkeit heranzuziehen. Insbesondere handelt es sich dabei um Urteile aus Verfahren der Opfer von Kriegsverbrechen im Zweiten Weltkrieg gegen Deutschland. Ihren Höhepunkt erlebten die Verfahren vor dem Internationalen Gerichtshof, der tradierte Immunitätsvorstellungen nicht aufzulösen vermochte – ein Schlussstrich ist nicht in Sicht. Hier verspricht die Europäische Urteilsfreizügigkeit und justizielle Zusammenarbeit Grenzen zu überwinden, vor denen auch das Unrecht nicht Halt macht.

Diese Untersuchung hinterfragt die legislativen Initiativen und stellt die Judikatur sowie deren Zusammenhänge dar. Der Fokus liegt auf dem Verhältnis der EuGVVO zur Staatenimmunität, die den wichtigsten Vorwand dafür darstellt, Schadensersatzklagen gegen Staaten wegen schwerer Menschenrechtsverletzungen von ihrer Behandlung durch das Europäische Zivilprozessrecht fernzuhalten. Damit trägt diese Arbeit einen Teil zur Bewältigung schwerer Menschenrechtsverletzungen bei, die ohne eine zivilrechtliche Behandlung nicht stattfinden kann.

2016, 410 S., kart., 79,- €,
978-3-8305-3680-2

DER AUTOR

Dr. Stefan Rinke, geb. 1982, Studium der Rechtswissenschaften an der Europa-Universität Viadrina Frankfurt (Oder) mit einem Stipendium der Konrad-Adenauer-Stiftung, von 2012–2013 Referendariat in Dresden, 2015 Promotion an der Freien Universität Berlin am Institut für Internationales Privatrecht und Rechtsvergleichung mit Forschungsaufenthalt in Amsterdam.

INHALT

Die Entscheidung des IGH im Verfahren zwischen Deutschland und Italien | Konventionsvorschläge der Haager Konferenz für Internationales Privatrecht von 1999 und 2001 | Verhältnis der EuGVVO zur Staatenimmunität | Anwendbarkeit der EuGVVO | Zuständigkeitsstatute für schwere Menschenrechtsverletzungen | Korrekturmöglichkeiten der EuGVVO

Berliner Wissenschafts-Verlag | Markgrafenstr. 12–14 | 10969 Berlin
Tel. 030 84 17 70-0 | Fax 030 84 17 70-21
www.bwv-verlag.de | bwv@bwv-verlag.de

Berliner Wissenschafts-Verlag

Hans-Joachim Heintze

Territoriale Integrität der Staaten: Fortbestehende Grundlage des Völkerrechts

Untersuchung vor dem Hintergrund des Berg-Karabach-Konflikts zwischen Armenien und Aserbaidschan

Die russische Annexion der Krim im Frühjahr 2014 hat deutlich gemacht, dass eingefrorene Konflikte eine Bedrohung des Weltfriedens darstellen, da sie jederzeit aufbrechen können, d.h. ständig die Anwendung militärischer Gewalt droht. Damit sind aber Weltordnungsbelange betroffen, denn das Gewaltverbot ist eine Grundnorm des modernen Völkerrechts. Folglich müssen nicht nur die Konfliktparteien, sondern auch die Staatengemeinschaft alle Mittel der friedlichen Streitbeilegung anwenden, um solche Konflikte nachhaltig zu beenden.

In diesem Buch wird allgemein die Rolle des Staats im Völkerrecht analysiert. Es folgt eine Betrachtung des Berg-Karabach-Konflikts unter völkerrechtlichen Gesichtspunkten.

In den 90er Jahren kam es während der Wirren um die Auflösung der Sowjetunion zu einem bewaffneten Konflikt zwischen Armenien und Aserbaidschan um das innerhalb Aserbaidschans autonome Gebiet Berg-Karabach. Massive Vertreibungen waren die Folge. In Ergebnis des Konflikts erklärte Berg-Karabach seine von keinem Staat anerkannte Unabhängigkeit und große Gebiete Aserbaidschans wurden durch Armenien besetzt. Von der Staatengemeinschaft, dem Europarat und den Vereinten Nationen wurde immer wieder das aserbaidschanische Recht auf territoriale Integrität unterstützt. Nunmehr muss es um seine Durchsetzung gehen.

2016, 180 S., kart., 39,– €,
978-3-8305-3629-1

INHALT

Der Staat im Völkerrecht | Fehlende Legaldefinition, aber klare Kriterien der Staatlichkeit | Fähigkeit zum Eintritt in die internationalen Beziehungen | Grundlegende Rechte und Pflichten von Staaten | Menschenrechtsschutz als völkerrechtliche Verpflichtung | Menschenrechtsverletzungen als Friedensbedrohungen | Durchbruch Somalia 1992 | Ehemaliges Jugoslawien 1992–1995 | Kriterien für humanitäre Interventionen | Gewaltverbot und Selbstverteidigung | Souveräne Gleichheit der Staaten und territoriale Unverletzlichkeit | Der Berg-Karabach-Konflikt und seine völkerrechtlichen Dimensionen | Berg-Karabach als „eingefrorener" Konflikt | Völkerrecht und Territorium | Selbstbestimmungsrecht der Völker und der Berg-Karabach-Konflikt | Berg-Karabach und das völkerrechtliche Selbstbestimmungsrecht | Das Konzept der nationalen Minderheit

Berliner Wissenschafts-Verlag | Markgrafenstr. 12–14 | 10969 Berlin
Tel. 030 84 17 70-0 | Fax 030 84 17 70-21
www.bwv-verlag.de | bwv@bwv-verlag.de